What Are Journalists For?

Jay Rosen **What Are**

YALE UNIVERSITY PRESS / NEW HAVEN AND LONDON

Journalists For ?

Published with assistance from the Tew Memorial Fund.

Designed by Nancy Ovedovitz and set in Adobe Garamond type by Keystone Typesetting,Inc. Orwigsburg, Pennsylvania. Printed in the United States of America by Vail-Ballou Press, Binghamton, New York.

Library of Congress Cataloging-in-Publication Data
Rosen, Jay, 1956–
What are journalists for? / Jay Rosen.
    p.   cm.
Includes bibliographical references and index.

ISBN 978-0-300-08907-3

1. Journalism—Social aspects.   2. Journalism—Social aspects—United States.   3. Journalism—Objectivity.   4. Journalistic ethics.   I. Title.
PN4749.R668   2000
302.23'0973—dc21   99-29891

A catalog record for this book is available from the British Library.

The paper in this book meets the guidelines for permanence and durability of the Committee on Production Guidelines for Book Longevity of the Council on Library Resources.

To Hali

Contents

Acknowledgments

All books are the record of an author's debts. This one is even more so. My subject—in the main, public journalism—would not be a subject were it not for the people who made it their own. Once I realized I could write about these people, I understood why I was writing at all.

Most of them were journalists, and most of them editors and reporters at daily newspapers. A few were academic colleagues. I know of one professor who postponed his retirement because things he had written and cared about for years were suddenly in the air, not among other academics, who knew his work well, but in the work of journalists, who were doing something that made him feel well again, excited about learning and teaching.

Trained scholars can tell you a lot about what's wrong with the press. Some may try to suggest reforms, rouse the imagination by bringing a better journalism (and perhaps a better world) into view. Yet they cannot complete the act their thinking begins because they are not the makers of journalism. They—I mean we—operate at one remove. We cherish our distance, a gift of the university, and we suffer that distance, which can easily leave us out of touch.

But when there are people in the press who are carrying out their own reforms, loosening their imaginations, bringing a better—or at least different—journalism into print and on the air, then thinking about the press gets a new lease on life because you have more to think about. That happened to me. And the major debt I owe is to the people who were around at the time.

First among them is Davis Merritt, the longtime editor of the *Wichita Eagle,* who was around almost all the time. Without Merritt, a man I once called the original public journalist, the ideas in this book might well have remained stillborn. As my partner and friend, he kept me focused on the task at hand, and set a high example of civic professionalism for others.

Lisa Austin was the research director for the Project on Public Life and the Press. With long effort and great skill, she assembled much of the material on which the book is based, making it possible for me to document the spread of public journalism. She did this because she believed in the idea, and her commitment showed in everything she did to make the project work. She has my deepest thanks, along with the gratitude of hundreds of journalists she aided and befriended.

Susan Warmbrunn was my research assistant while I was drafting this book. She was also the first reader on many chapters, and I came to rely on her intelligence, insight, and good cheer. Her judgment was always sound, and I can only hope that the final product is equal to it.

David Mathews, president of the Kettering Foundation, has been a guiding presence in my professional life. From him I learned what it means to take democracy seriously, although I could never learn enough. Mathews and his colleagues at Kettering offered a home for public journalism before it had a name or momentum. From 1993 on, Kettering continued its support by operating the Project on Public Life and the Press, which I had the privilege to direct. With their wise counsel, Bob Daley and Ed Arnone, on staff at the foundation, aided the project at every turn. Robert Kingston of Kettering has offered support and guidance since I first met him in 1989. Mathews, Arnone, and Kingston read the manuscript and gave me pointed advice, as did Cheryl Gibbs, whose networking skills helped hold the public journalism movement together. I wish to thank all the people at Kettering for their patience and help over the years, especially an early friend of my work, Katherine Fanning of the foundation board, and Val Breidenbach, a tireless aide.

Equally critical to the emergence of public journalism was the John S. and James L. Knight Foundation, which never wavered in its support for the idea, despite the heated controversy that arose. By funding the Project on Public Life and the Press and granting me a year off from teaching to write, the Knight Foundation helped bring this book into being. Creed Black, Del Brinkman, and Jim Spaniolo, in particular, have my warmest thanks for their generosity and vision. They not only funded this work, they improved it.

As a 1994 fellow at Harvard University's Shorenstein Center on the Press, Politics, and Public Policy, I had the opportunity to write and think in the company of fertile minds. My thanks to Marvin Kalb, director of the center, for making that time so valuable. In 1990–91, I was a fellow at the Freedom Forum Media Studies Center in New York. I thought I was going to write a different book then. This one began to take shape during my year at the center, thanks to Everette Dennis and his welcoming staff. A sabbatical leave and other support from New York University's Department of Journalism was equally critical. Mitchell Stephens, my colleague at NYU, read portions of the completed work and helped me understand what was missing from them.

Ed Fouhy and Jan Schaffer of the Pew Center for Civic Journalism did as much for the idea as anyone. As the notes show, their center generated a good deal of the literature on which I have drawn. I am grateful for their collegiality and assistance. The Poynter Institute for Media Studies invited me to several seminars in St. Petersburg, Florida, where I could try to make myself understood to working journalists. It also published one of my earliest statements on public journalism. Roy Peter Clark, Edward Miller, and Deborah Potter of Poynter deserve special mention for their support. Richard Leone and the Twentieth Century Fund (now the Century Foundation) published some of the earliest versions of these thoughts and organized several roundtables where I could discuss them. The America Press Institute hosted a series of workshops on public journalism. My thanks to Bill Winter, Ed Baron, and Sarah Griffin for their able assistance.

Among the many academic colleagues who contributed to the enterprise, James Carey of Columbia University has a special place. My intellectual debt to him is recorded in these pages. But that cannot convey my gratitude for his many contributions to the movement for public journalism, including his inspiring presence at seminars and panel discussions. There is no scholar who has thought more deeply about the subjects that concern me, and none more willing to share what he knows. Lew Friedland of the University of Wisconsin did some of the earliest and best research on public journalism, and he brought a keen eye to his reading of the manuscript. My thanks to him for his many contributions. Ed Lambeth of the University of Missouri gave encouragement from the beginning and did much to advance the idea in his own work. Ted Glasser, Phil Meyer, Michael Schudson, Cliff Christians, John Pauly, Michael Delli Carpini, Esther Thorson, George Kennedy, Max McCombs, Harry Boyte, Judy Turk, Barbara Zang, Carol

Dykers, and Peter Levine lent their talents and advice over a period of several years. I thank them all, with a grateful nod to those who read the text and offered their response.

David Weaver invited me to deliver the Roy Howard lecture at Indiana University, the results of which are reflected in Chapter 2. James Fishkin helped secure my contract at Yale University Press, and he gave me much to think about with his own work on deliberative democracy. David Rubin was steadfast in his support from the earliest.

In the course of my travels around the American press, I met hundreds of journalists whose work became an inspiration, many of whom I have written about here. Many also invited me to address their colleagues and staffs, and I regularly benefited from these give-and-take sessions. Without the long hours of conversation I enjoyed with journalists, without their hard labor and self-scrutiny, I would not have had much to write about. There are too many to list all who contributed, but my biggest debts are these: to Cole Campbell, for his intellectual gift and personal courage; to Gil Thelen, for his warm friendship and passionate mind; to Dennis Hartig, for his endless curiosity and streak of daring; to Steve Smith, for his openness to just about anything; to Tom Warhover, for his level head and gentle humor; to Tony Wharton, for his fine writing, hard thinking, and thorough research; to Karen Weintraub, for her willful patience in murky waters; to Dennis Foley, for his inspired and inventive philosophy; to John Dinges, for his good sense and calm judgment; to Frank Denton, for his skill in breaching the gap between professors and journalists; to Pete Weitzel, for asking the right questions; to Mike Phillips, for taking chances and thinking large; to Jon and Myrne Roe, for their steady support; to Jeremy Iggers, for his early and unwavering interest; and to Ron Clark, Chris Peck, and Lou Ureneck, for theirs.

For their ideas, experiments and inspiration I also wish to thank a number of other journalists, including Jeanine Guttman, Glen Guzzo, Marty Steffens, Peter Bhatia, Holly Heyser, Karen Young, Nena Baker, Max Jennings, Rob Elder, Jennie Buckner, Tom Hamburger, Cheryl Carpenter, Tom Still, Dave Iverson, Randy Hammer, Sandy Rowe, Rick Thames, David Zeeck, Nancy Kruh, Lou Heldman, Wendy Lawton, Arthur Charity, Teresa Hanafin, Frank Caperton, Mike Knepler, Mac Daniel, Sheri Dill, Paula Ellis, Wayne Poston, Alex Marshall, Jim Morrill, Cy Porter, Doug Floyd, Walter Robinson, Chris Satullo, Tom Spencer, Bill Theobald, Glen Ritt, Billy Winn, Leonard Witt, Heath Meriwether, Marla Crockett, Ellen

Hume, James Fallows, and Hodding Carter III. Clark Hoyt and Marty Claus provided me with many a platform to improve my thinking. Karen Flake, Janice Lucas, Jessica Tomlinson, Kathleen Collins, Pete Churches, and Elizabeth Manus helped with the research for this book. John Covell, my editor at Yale University Press, was patient beyond duty, and kept his enthusiasm high, despite the missed deadlines. Joel Dinerstein provided moral support.

Jack Swift and James Batten I thank in memorium for all they did while they were here. Neil Postman and Christine Nystrom, my mentors and friends, have my enduring gratitude for everything they have taught and shown me for nearly twenty years.

Writing is a solitary act. But no one who writes can live a solitary life. So to Hali Weiss and Sylvie Weiss Rosen go all my thanks and all my love.

Introduction

What We're Doing Isn't Working

Visitors to the National Press Club in Washington can find there a plaque presented on the occasion of the club's fiftieth anniversary in 1958. Titled "The Journalist's Creed," it begins this way: "I believe in the profession of journalism. I believe that the public journal is a public trust; that all connected with it are, to the full measure of their responsibility, trustees for the public; that acceptance of a lesser service than public service is a betrayal of that trust."

As this language suggests, journalism done the American way is no mechanical act. At its center is a professed creed. Although it may strive for a disciplined factuality and a healthy profit, journalism is neither a science nor a business. Unlike law, medicine, or accounting, there is no licensing procedure or standardized training; nor do journalists own the newsroom. And because the First Amendment protects the charlatan and the scrupulous alike, the press has no power to expel wayward members.

But journalism is like the most honored professions in other ways. It expects the individual practitioner and the practice as a whole to serve the general welfare—not through the invisible hand of competition, but directly, through acts of journalism that amount to public service. If a professional is one who hears a calling in the opportunity for a career, then most journalists I know consider themselves professionals, serious people serving the public good.

It is fortunate for us that they hold this belief, for a sense of duty is one way a society can try to hold its press accountable. Indeed, it is one of the better ways, if we also want a free press. So we all have a stake in the journalist's creed: what it says, how it is interpreted, whether or not it is honored. When the National Press Club invites its members to "believe in the profession of journalism," it is inviting the rest of us to take this belief seriously, to treat a claim to public service as something more than hot air.

But if journalists are sincere in their devotion to a creed—and most of them are—we should not assume that they have the creed right. Like other professionals, they often misunderstand themselves and their work, and it is not necessary to accept these blind spots in order to respect the press and its commitment to doing good. On the contrary, to argue with journalists is one way of honoring their public commitments, for it assumes that they are indeed public—not the exclusive property of a profession keeping counsel with itself.[1]

If, as the plaque on the wall suggests, journalism is held in trust for the public, then it is in some way "our" possession, even if it is "their" profession. The trustee—the press—does not own journalism, and cannot dispose of it on a whim. How to square the notion of trusteeship with the First Amendment principle of an unregulated and independent press is the sort of problem for which we require professionals, with their felt duty to the general good. But it is also why professionals need critics, and citizens who care enough to engage the press in serious discussion of its aims.

I, too, believe in the profession of journalism, although I do not carry a press pass. I believe in it because this is my best hope of getting the sort of press that I and my fellow citizens require. That plaque at the National Press Club is there for me and for you, as well as the club's members. Finding a way to take its declarations seriously has become my job as a university professor.

Beginning in 1989, and accelerating around 1993, when I became director of the Project on Public Life and the Press, I cooperated with a group of journalists and others who were groping their way toward a revised understanding of what journalism is and what it is for. The result was that some in the press began to see their work in a different way: not as information gathering, or entertainment, or even telling the news, but as a craft that builds up the world while simultaneously describing it.[2]

What I mean by "builds up" requires some elaboration. When we glance at the day's headlines we enter the journalist's universe, which is drawn from ours but hardly identical to it. News is something that newspeople *make,* but this does not mean they make it up. It simply means that stories about what happened today are not "what happened today." While the fact seems too obvious to mention, journalists sometimes want us to overlook it. "Good evening," says my local anchorwoman. "Here's what is happening in the tri-state area." Strictly speaking, she doesn't mean that. Too much is happening and only a sliver of it becomes news. But the sliver stands for something, in the way that a road map stands for New Jersey when we unfold it and try to get our bearings.

With her introductory phrase, the tri-state area, my anchorwoman has already done some imaginative work. As far as I know, I do not live in the tri-state area. None of my mail comes there. I do not vote there. I cannot imagine telling someone who asks that I am from there. But news comes to me from this largely fictional locale because the station I am watching wants to place me there. Journalists do things like that. They place us amid exploding events, important people, far-off developments, creeping trends, regional markets. Wherever we go in their company, we get there along a route they have chosen, and there is no scandal in saying that the choice involves human judgment, which may be sound or dubious. What it can never be is absent.

Journalists build up the world because their reports about it contain more than "information," that superabundant commodity. Headlines and the stories that follow are guides to what's important, cues to what's current, a series of signs saying: "This way to what's going on out there." However we greet the news, we find that the news greets us. "Hello, sports fans." "Good evening, tri-state area." "Good morning, America." Or, as Edward R. Murrow began his famous radio reports during the Battle of Britain, "This is London." Each greeting places us somewhere, and the making of this somewhere is an art we entrust to journalists whenever we give them a chance to bring us the news.

How do we know when this art is serving a public purpose? "When it is accurate, fair, balanced, comprehensive, and compelling" is the sort of answer most in the press would give. It is a good answer. But it does not say much about the imaginative work that journalists do.[3] To be addressed as an inhabitant of the tri-state area is not "information," really. It is a way of conjuring with the sprawling terrain around New York City, lending it an identity it rarely has in the experience of the people who live there. Hardly sinister and barely noticed, this little exercise in geography points to something larger about the press. The news delivers us to a space that journalists have crafted; and if they are inclined to forget this, the rest of us should not, for the crafting of an inhabitable world is perhaps the highest demand we can make on the people who hold press passes.

The story I tell in this book is about some of those people, a minority in the mainstream press, who, after 1989, began to wonder how habitable their daily portrait was. Faced with a slow but discernible crisis in their craft, they began to ask some challenging questions: What should journalists bring back from a public square that seems disordered, ill functioning, too empty at times, far from what citizens require? What should the press be making with its telling, and how can it help make democracy work?

The people asking these questions were convinced that something was wrong—in journalism, in politics, and in the wider culture beyond, where a population either becomes an active public, or doesn't. Democracy and its discontents was thus a major theme in the inquiry, and many who joined in it were discontented themselves: with their work, their sinking standing among citizens, the place they had carved out for themselves as professionals. Amid a mood of anxiety and alarm, they set out to understand democracy in a different way, so they could see journalism from another angle: as democracy's cultivator, as well as its chronicler.

Who were these people? For the most part they were newspaper journalists—editors and reporters—joined by a few broadcast colleagues, interested academics, helpful foundations, and other sympathetic observers who wanted to see the groping get somewhere. Eventually it did. By the fall of 1993, these adventurers (for that is how I saw them), were clearing room in their minds for another variety of journalism, one tuned more to the needs of an ailing democracy than the rules of a hidebound profession. This other approach went by a number of names. I called it public journalism; some preferred civic journalism, or sometimes community journalism. Whatever it was called, it had one general aim: to restyle the work of the press so that it supported a healthier public climate.

How to do that—and how to think about it—was unclear at the outset, and it remained unclear through much of the adventure. The solution was to experiment with different vocabularies and the daily product. Most of this work was done in public: in the pages of daily newspapers across the United States, from Portland, Oregon, to Portland, Maine; in seminars and other settings where people could think aloud about the drift of their craft; in trade journals and professional meetings where topics like "Public Journalism:

Death or Savior for American Newspapers?" came alive; in partnerships between print and broadcast outlets trying to find a "citizen's agenda" to instruct their own priorities; in a blitz of news coverage and commentary about the experiment.

Through these events and others I will describe, public journalism became a kind of construction site within the American press, where some were busy building another house for journalism, while others looked on or raised questions. Soon there was a public journalism "movement" and also a controversy about it. Public journalism went public, reaching much of the press with word of what some were doing.[4]

Essentially, it was this: Politics and public life, journalism and its professional identity, could be renewed along civic lines, meaning the ties that held Americans together as a community of the whole—a public. If citizens joined in the action where possible, kept an ear tuned to current debate, found a place for themselves in the drama of politics, got to exercise their skills and voice their concerns, then maybe democracy didn't have to be the desultory affair it seemed to have become. And maybe journalism, by doing something to help, could improve itself and regain some of its lost authority.

Other writers will have to sketch the rise and spread of public journalism from a neutral stance. From 1989 on, I was inside the action of the idea. I contributed by doing what professors and writers typically do. We think with the best terms we can find, tell stories with ideas inside them. My sympathies were clearly on one side: with the journalists fumbling their way to another creed. I spoke, wrote and thought along with these people, trying to fashion a philosophy for their efforts and bring encouragement from beyond their regular orbit. In taking up this role, I became one of the point persons for public journalism—someone who tried to explain what the point was.[5]

This led me into daily interaction with the American press, as the institution took notice of what was happening and reacted. Some got curious; others grew deeply alarmed. A few raged at us. Invitations to explain and debate the idea began to come in, and I accepted as often as possible. By the time I finished drafting this book, I had addressed more than three thousand working journalists in one forum or another, made thirty or so visits to newsrooms, organized or participated in dozens of seminars, and took hundreds of calls from reporters writing about public journalism or just interested in it.[6]

I saw each of these occasions as a chance for the craft to be imagined again: as something further than a report on events or commentary about

them. Journalism as a willing sponsor of public talk, an invitation to participate, a convener of civic activity, a guide to problem solving, a constructive
art for a strengthened democracy—these were some of the ideas added to an
existing creed. Once floated, the notion of public, civic, or community-
connected journalism took its own course, which no one could easily predict
or direct. That was the adventure part, and the danger too. You hazard a
guess about what the press will accept and let the press do its work on your
guess. If I had any method in mind, this was it.

For me, the entire thing was public journalism: the philosophy put
forward, along with the journalists who stepped forward to become practical
philosophers themselves; the experiments in real-world settings and the way
they were received into larger settings. The varied reactions to the idea *were*
the idea, returned to us in improved, revised, or, at times, distorted form.
The results told of many things.

First, it turned out there was a constituency for public journalism. No
one had a complete count, but there were at least two hundred news organizations involved at one stage or another. The vast majority lay outside the big
media centers of New York, Washington, and Los Angeles, in scattered places
like Wichita, Norfolk, Charlotte, Colorado Springs, Dayton, San Jose.

Second, there was an audience for the idea, people willing to listen if not
join in. We found this audience not only within the press but outside it—
among groups like the League of Women Voters or the National Civic
League, in journals like *Governing*, and universities where the next generation of journalists was being trained.[7]

Third, it was possible to experiment with the daily news product and the
power of the press, turning both to more civic ends, however vaguely this
was defined. Journalists could break out of established routines, step into
another role, find a different aim for their efforts. And they could learn from
what they tried.

Fourth, there were plenty of people who objected to what we were
doing, including a good number of distinguished minds in the elite press.
These exchanges became a kind of contest between center and margin. They
showed that there were tensions in the craft between one vision of the press,
as an observer of the contemporary scene, and another: the press as a player
in politics, an influential actor that could alter its actions without abandoning its role as truth teller.

Finally, all this activity could go on in public—in conference settings, published commentary, the daily newspaper or broadcast, the peer culture where journalists argued about their work and wider arenas where the troubles in civic life, politics, and journalism were being discussed. In this way the experiment made use of public life to bring a concern for public life into closer contact with the mind of the American press.

At the center of the action stood a group of able and affable journalists who had all taken a similar turn. In one way or another, they said to themselves: what we're doing isn't working. They turned their gaze on public life and saw it in trouble. Turning back to their own workplace, they were able to say: we're part of the problem. We need to change our approach, because if we don't, we could lose our franchise. Not knowing exactly what to change, they looked around for ideas. And they began to read and think about citizenship, democracy, community life, and what made them all work. They got on airplanes to come to seminars, hoping to gain a fresh perspective.

Simultaneously, they ran experiments on themselves and their daily product, to see if public life could be approached from another place. And they picked up, or fashioned for themselves, a fresh language to help them. These journalists also said, "I live here, in this town, this country, at this time in its turbulent life. I'm a citizen, with a different role than other citizens but also a life in common with theirs." Around a renewed feeling of membership in the public, the same one they were pledged to inform, they gained a deeper identity as journalists—a civic identity to go with their professional persona.

Uncertain of what they were doing but more and more convinced it needed to be done, they saw their work and their words come back to them as a story the press was telling itself about the "trend" called public journalism. "Critics say . . . ," read a recurring line in the script, and the critics said a good deal. This is advocacy. This is getting too involved. This is a fad, a gimmick, a commercial ploy. This is what we've always done, nothing new. Or this is what we don't do and never should. You're caving in to the audience, endangering our credibility. In the name of some fuzzy if high-minded ideal, you're going against everything I believe. *You're messing the whole thing up.*

At times, the people aboard thought they might be. Confusion hung in the climate of ideas that suffused the term "public journalism." When commercial motives mingled with civic intentions the picture was rarely clear:

Were we promoting ourselves or permitting others a voice? When journalists got more proactive the doubts were hard to ignore: Were we making something happen because we decided it was good, or inviting citizens to fashion their own goods? And getting down to the nitty-gritty, did public journalism work? How would we know if it did?

In time, some answers moved into view. Try to get people engaged, then step back when they do. Start where citizens start, but don't end where citizens end. Listen to them in settings where they can think with each other and testify to what they know. But don't turn "the people" into gods or assume that their judgment is infallible. Experiment with public journalism, in whatever style succeeds for you and your community. Don't turn it into a formula, or draw false lines against tradition when traditional approaches work perfectly well. Get humble, even as you get excited by the possibilities afloat. Level with the community about your plans, and invite intelligent comment. Take your critics seriously; you are lucky to have them. And realize: this is going to take time, "generational, cultural change" as one editor put it.[8]

The book before you offers a tour through the idea of public journalism as it claimed its own, rather contentious, public life. I write with several audiences in mind: working journalists and those in training, students of the press and politics, scholars with an interest in democracy and civic life, professionals who interact with the news media on a daily basis, and, finally, general readers—citizens, that is—who sense that something has gone awry in our public culture. That a group of journalists agreed and tried to respond is, I believe, an important story.

The book is divided into four parts. Part 1, "Origins," describes how public journalism was imagined and then "taken public"—that is, brought to the attention of the press. Chapter 1 traces the roots of the idea to the years 1989 to 1992, when a number of thoughtful people in the press took note of a depressed civic climate, speculated about what it meant for the craft, and suggested possible changes. Chapter 2 finds roots of the idea in another terrain, the university, where good work had been done on democracy, the press, and the public, although few journalists knew about it. It then tells of the launch of public journalism as a coined term with a rationale and some illustrations attached.

Part 2, "Practice," is about doing public journalism. Chapter 3, the longest in the book, presents five stories from newspapers that joined in the experiment. Chapter 4 traces the idea's movement through a single organization: the *Virginian-Pilot* in Norfolk, where an unusually gifted editor and staff took the ball and ran with it. In Chapter 5 I turn to the personal tales some journalists told as they came to the conclusion that something was missing. This, too, was practice: learning to reflect on basic questions of purpose.

Part 3 is called "Reactions." It describes how the mainstream press and influential figures in New York and Washington responded to public journalism. In Chapter 6 the critics of public journalism have their say, and I reflect on what they said or overlooked. Chapter 7 tells what happened when the experiment collided with two of the most powerful institutions in the press—indeed, the country—the *New York Times* and its rival the *Washington Post*. Although there were common themes, the two papers differed in their treatment, with the *Times* speaking in one, mostly skeptical, voice, while the *Post* showed a range of views on the issues involved.

Part 4 I have labeled "Lessons"—what was learned or accomplished as public journalism developed. Chapter 8 is about the hazards of going public, and it discusses some of the dangers, missteps and regrets that collected around public journalism as it rose to visibility. Chapter 9 summarizes what public journalism was about and asks: what did it achieve? In a concluding chapter I address the question in my title, What are journalists for? Meaning: What do we need them for? And what do they stand for? For me, these are critical questions as the press meets the close of one century, uncertain about what it will become in the next.[9]

Beginning in Chapter 2, I scatter throughout the text a series of "exhibits," extended excerpts from speeches and articles about public journalism. I did this to emphasize how the idea generated its own literature, a body of commentary and criticism that represents, for me, one of the outcomes of the experiment. By presenting some of this literature, I hope to show how a variety of voices converged around the general theme of public life and the press. Readers will also notice that I have not written a strictly chronological account, or by any means a complete one. Each chapter provides its own tour through public journalism, another way to wrap your mind around a notion that may, at times, seem difficult to pin down. In fact, it was difficult because so many actors were involved. This is one actor's, one author's, sketch of it.

Here, then, is a story to begin my larger tale: In January 1996, with the presidential campaign season just under way, I found myself sitting around a seminar table with twenty-four journalists who had been on assignment for a week in Austin, Texas. Reports were filed, "news" was produced, and every-one was tired. All of us—journalists and a few scholars—had just been through an intriguing encounter with the American people. It was time to make sense of what we had seen.

The journalists present were reporters and editors at daily newspapers. Many in the room had been on a professional journey, moving away from one idea about the press in order to experiment with another—public journalism. Like me, they wanted to see what happens when journalists confront big questions about democracy, citizenship, and the larger purpose of their craft. In the seminar room at Austin, the big questions were on the table, put there by the journalists themselves and the powerful events they had witnessed.

For three days prior, a random sample of 459 Americans had descended on the city to talk politics with one another, face to face. They were utterly unlike the crisp professionals who had come to dominate the country's polit-ical drama. A good number in the 459 had never been on an airplane before, and they had no idea what to expect when they landed. They were there to serve as "delegates" to the National Issues Convention, itself an experiment in public discussion, sponsored by the University of Texas, the Public Broad-casting System, and several national foundations. After deliberating jury-style on three difficult issues, the citizens were asked to question major candi-dates for president in two televised forums. The appearance of the candidates gave the event some of the trappings of a campaign stop, and this made it news of a sort. But, to us, the citizens were the more interesting story.[10]

Asked why they had come, they would say they wanted to meet people from different backgrounds and learn how others think. Sitting in small circles of twelve to fifteen, they brought the diversity of their views and the reality of their lives to bear on questions typically the province of officials, experts, and commentators in the press. A fireman from Newton, North Carolina, a small-business owner from Richmond, Virginia, a college stu-dent from Waco, Texas—people who would otherwise never meet proved eager to engage each other about economic policy, their country's role in the world, and the troubled state of the American family. When faced with a crisis in a foreign land, should America defend its own interests, or the ideals of democracy and human rights? What is the best way to restore equality, opportunity, and a livable wage to the economy? What can be done about forces that seem to be tearing families apart?[11]

As they wrestled with these questions—and their vastly different starting points—the delegates made some important discoveries. They found that they had more in common than their political culture had led them to believe. They uncovered reserves of common sense, a desire to communicate across boundaries, and a deep core of shared beliefs that mattered as much to them as the doubts and differences that remained in their midst. In a setting where they could listen and be heard, they learned to have fun talking politics. And many found their voices as citizens, discovering what democracy at its best could be about: a deliberation on common problems, where everyone has a place at the table.[12]

What the journalists found in Austin was different, but equally valuable. As representatives of the American press, they arrived with inbred ideas about the public and its limited capacity for serious reflection. They bore a received image of politics as a contest or game, dominated by savvy professionals. They shared a common understanding of news that centered on conflict between determined rivals. They carried any number of half-conscious assumptions about democracy, citizens, and the "real world" that made their daily work go smoothly, their stories flow. Their professional lives were built on these routines, which permitted them to meet deadlines but also to know what "journalism" was, and what journalists were for.

The events in Austin threw much of this into doubt. Watching a representative group of citizens engage with each other, feeling democracy come alive with some of its original force, seemed to put whole portions of American journalism to shame. And this is what the group began to reflect upon around the seminar table.

The journalists talked of their habit of framing every political question with a convenient polarity: liberals versus conservatives, Republicans versus Democrats. It was impossible to listen to the discussions in Austin without sensing the poverty of this routine. Chuck Clark, government editor of the *Charlotte Observer,* was "struck by just how few Newt Gingrich conservatives and Teddy Kennedy liberals there are out there." From reading the Washington press corps, he said, "you'd think the world was divided into these two camps." Pat Harrison of the *Oregonian* in Portland noted that the delegates "didn't see things with just black and white frames. They saw the middle ground and they saw the gray area."[13]

Jim Morrill, a reporter for the *Charlotte Observer,* was struck by the civility of the discussions. "Especially in North Carolina, we live in a world of vicious attack ads and hot button issues and soundbites, and in Austin the rooms were just cleared of all that." He came away convinced that "people are hungry for something they're not getting from us." Clearing a calmer space for public discussion was an important task of the press, he felt. "Give people a chance to think about things," said Morrill. This won't occur if journalists are "too quick to fall for labels and issues" promoted by political operatives, who claim to have their finger on the public pulse.[14]

Daniel Weintraub, who covered California state government for the *Orange County Register*, gave the example of Olga Trinidad, a mother of three who lives in a housing project where the residents were overwhelmingly Democratic in party affiliation. In the style of analysis common in political journalism, a "Democrat" is assumed to be an eager defender of government programs for the poor. But here was a woman, near poverty herself and a registered Democrat, "who moved her group with some very detailed descriptions of the fraud and abuse in the welfare programs in the projects," Weintraub observed. She took positions "you don't normally hear from Democratic politicians." This tension—between a party's official positions and the actual views of its supporters—was rarely reflected in news accounts that focused on inter-party jousting. And so Weintraub was led to wonder: how good a job are we doing?[15]

Equally notable was the alchemy of group discussion. As the delegates listened they actually learned from each other, an outcome rare in the verbal face-offs journalists typically observe. Deeply felt views about welfare abuse would be met with powerful testimony from those who had lived the hard facts of poverty. Yes, there is abuse, they would say, but there is also the daily struggle to live on what welfare allows. "I had no idea," affluent Americans would reply as they came face to face with people who fit no image of the undeserving poor. A common demand to reduce the cost and size of government would come up against the equally common experience of a young mother who, were it not for a government program providing infant formula, could not have fed her baby.[16]

At work was the genius of sampling science. Combined with face-to-face discussion, the randomness of the delegates tended to cancel out such deep-seated social trends as the segregation of housing patterns, the atomization sustained by television, the withdrawal from elections by whole sectors of the population, the simple isolation from one another that fed mutual suspicion and the politics of fear. All these factors were momentarily overcome by the delegates and their willingness to engage one another. As Mike Flaherty, a reporter for the *Wisconsin State Journal* in Madison, noted, "A lot of people with strongly held views got to meet the accused." Eyes would widen, ears would open, as political opinion met personal fact. Several of these scenes ended in tears, as delegates came to realize who "the accused" were: real people with struggles much like their own.[17]

The reality check worked both ways, up and down the social hierarchy. Steve Berg, a political reporter for the Minneapolis *Star-Tribune*, recounted a discussion in which nearly everyone seem to agree on raising the minimum wage. A manager of a Kmart store said he was in favor of a higher wage himself, but he knew what his regional headquarters would say: cut six people from the payroll. Suddenly the issue looked different to the group, with more sides than the familiar "for" and "against." The Kmart manager wasn't a spokesman, an expert, or a talking head. Nor was he the proverbial man in the street. He was a fellow citizen with a different experience and a valuable view.[18]

Moments like this cut against the image of public dialogue as a contest of the committed, wherein one group, persuaded of the absolute rightness of its position, struggles against another taking the opposite stance. The delegates quickly dispensed with this script. Common sense, rather than political ideology, took command of the discussion. Should those trapped in poverty assume responsibility for their own lives, or should government help them out? "It's both!" the delegates repeatedly shouted to nodding heads.[19]

The professional culture in journalism tutors its members in a certain image of the average American: as ill informed and unequipped, too busy or bored to bother with politics, and therefore easily manipulated. As they reflected on their experience in Austin, journalists exchanged this jaundiced view for something more nuanced. "People may not exactly grasp the details," said Alan Houston, an editor at the *San Jose Mercury News*, "but they sure want to."[20] Ignorance might also reflect the distance Americans elect to keep from a bleak political scene that offers few natural entry points. Jon Roe, a reporter for the *Wichita Eagle*, noted that many delegates did seem uninformed. "They were not dumb," he said. "They were just disconnected."

"In the group I watched," Roe added, "there was a guy with green hair who was a deep sea diver. And that's what he did, he loved deep sea diving. And he couldn't have cared less about the political process because it had nothing to do with him and so he had disconnected from it. He didn't say a word the first session. And then he said one or two words the second session. And by the third session, he was chattering away. He had simply made the connection." As the delegates grew more comfortable talking about politics, they recognized a need to inform themselves. Roe told how several delegates in the group he followed vowed to start reading the newspaper. Impressed as he was by the connection the delegates were able to make, Roe was equally struck by "how efficiently and effectively the candidates and television came in and disconnected it all again."[21]

After two days of face-to-face discussions, the citizens were assembled on a vast stage at the University of Texas for televised question-and-answer sessions with the presidential candidates. Senator Richard Lugar of Indiana was the only Republican contender to appear in person; publisher Steve Forbes, Senator Phil Gramm of Texas, and former governor of Tennessee Lamar Alexander were beamed in by satellite. The next morning, Vice President Al Gore appeared in person to represent the Democratic Party.

This was politics as America had come to expect it, with most of the candidates offering rote responses. They seemed to be floating in from another world, where a smooth demeanor and a poll-tested "message" were the signs of a serious contender. But the delegates wanted them to be serious in a different way. Their questions arose from the experience they had in struggling with difficult choices. They were looking for the candidates to acknowledge and address that experience.

Vice President Gore seemed to grasp this. He did not necessarily have better answers, but he repeatedly asked his questioners what conclusions they had drawn from their own deliberations. "Tell me what your group came up with," Gore would say, as if to credit the citizens with equal standing in the public arena. Aside from a few moments like these, however, the candidates mostly struck an off note. The possibilities glimpsed in the discussions among citizens were barely present in the televised forums, which resembled at times an "electronic town meeting" where citizens are little more than visual props.[22]

To Dennis Foley, political editor of the *Orange County Register,* the lesson of Austin was that "a group of strangers can come together" and gain a common identity as citizens. This meant a great deal to the delegates—and to Foley himself. He told of one man who, by the end of the event, felt "he was leaving his home to go back to New Jersey, instead of having left his home to come here." Struck by these scenes, Foley came to realize how isolating were the patterns of his professional life. Most of his daily discussions were with other journalists and political professionals. Contact with citizens meant "people calling to yell at me because I'm the politics editor." Over time, this bred a "biased perspective of what the public is like." In Austin he thought: "I'm the one who's out of touch here."

Foley had observed himself observing the presidential candidates. He noticed how easily he reverted to the questioning style popular in political journalism: Did the candidate "do well" with voters? Did his carefully crafted message "sell"? When the delegates reconvened to discuss the candidates, Foley was present, and he saw first hand the poverty of this type of analysis. What looked to him like a convincing performance hadn't convinced anyone. He noted "how hard it is for me to jettison years of training," which supposedly made him a sound judge of how a candidate's image would play. In fact, his expertise was unreliable, based as it was on dubious assumptions about Americans and their political sense. Foley acknowledged that he was several times moved to tears by the "simple humanity" of the delegates claiming their place in the discussion.[23]

"I was really struck and touched by the fact that people aren't cynical," said Nena Baker, a young reporter for the *Oregonian*. "They may have come to this place frustrated or angry about something in particular. But they're hopeful. And they're yearning. They're searching." Others struck a similar note. "Cynicism is kind of a safety net for us," said Holly Heyser, then a staff writer at the *Mercury News*. It permits journalists to separate themselves from the depressing and disturbing facts they gather. Heyser said her experience in Austin "made me think in terms of 'our' country and 'our' government." She wanted her reporting to reflect this newfound identity: journalist as fellow citizen.[24]

The convention coincided with a sad moment in American politics. Barbara Jordan, the legendary congresswoman from Texas, passed away during the week. She was a hero to many, including Tony Wharton, a reporter for the *Virginian-Pilot* in Norfolk, who heard that Jordan's body was lying in state at the University of Texas. With directions to the site furnished by a colleague, he found himself entering the viewing room through an entrance reserved for the news media. There he stood with other reporters and camera crews, watching the mourners file by from a position behind the scenes.

Barbara Jordan had been a compelling figure to Wharton when he was first contemplating a career in journalism. Her speeches during the Watergate crisis helped inspire his "keen interest in the whole idea of constitutional government and what it meant today." That was part of what propelled him into political reporting. Now here he was, marking her death by hanging out with the press hands backstage. Something felt wrong. He decided to leave the press location and reapproach the room through the public entrance, filing past the body in line with hundreds of fellow mourners.

Wharton was one of those who had been moving for years toward public journalism. By rooting his work in ideals like civic participation and deliberative democracy, he hoped to deepen the sense of mission that originally drew him into the field. In a sense this meant leaving the press room and reentering through a "public" doorway, just as he did in paying his respects to Barbara Jordan. "Ten years ago I would have stayed right there and shot the breeze," he said.[25]

The journey taken by Tony Wharton was shared by hundreds of others in the years 1989 to 1997, when public journalism was imagined and introduced. This book tries to tell both stories: the efforts of a handful of reformers, who began to ask themselves what journalists are truly for, and the career of an idea, an answer to that question.

Part One / Origins

1

As Democracy Goes, So Goes the Press

The Roots of Public Journalism

I gave my first talk to journalists in 1989. The platform was the Associated Press Managing Editors convention, a yearly gathering of several hundred editors from around the country, held that year in Des Moines, Iowa. At the time I was an assistant professor of journalism with a Ph.D., but journalism as a craft was mostly foreign territory. What I knew of it came through the ideas in my dissertation, which had examined something scholars called the problem of the public. Roughly speaking, it asked whether the public of democratic theory resembled the public of actual practice, and if the answer was "no"—as many thought it was—what should be made of that fact.[1]

The question mattered because certain ideas about the press follow from the view of the public they contain. If the public is assumed to be "out there," more or less intact, then the job of the press is easy to state: to inform people about what goes on in their name and their midst. But suppose the public leads a more broken existence. At times it may be alert and engaged, but just as often it struggles against other pressures—including itself—that can win out in the end. Inattention to public matters is perhaps the simplest of these, atomization of society one of the more intricate. Money speaks louder than the public, problems overwhelm it, fatigue sets in, attention falters, cynicism swells. A public that leads this more fragile kind of existence suggests a different task for the press: not just to inform a public that may or may not emerge, but to improve the chances that it will emerge.

John Dewey, an early hero of mine, had suggested something like this in his 1927 book, *The Public and Its Problems*. I decided to try out a version of his ideas on the editors in Des Moines. The key passage read like this:

> The newspaper of the future will have to rethink its relationship to all the institutions that nourish public life, from libraries to universities to cafes. It will have to do more than "cover" these institutions when they happen to make news. It will have to do more than print their advertisements. The newspaper must see that its own health is dependent on the health of dozens of other agencies which pull people out of their private worlds. For the greater the pull of public life, the greater the need for the newspaper. *Empty streets are bad for editors,* despite the wealth of crime news they may gener-ate. The emptier the streets, the emptier the newspaper will seem to readers barricaded in their private homes. . . .
>
> Every town board session people attend, every public discussion they join, every PTA event, every local political club, every rally, every gathering of citizens for whatever cause is important to the newspaper—not only as something to cover, but as the kind of event that makes news matter to citizens.[2]

In delivering these remarks, I was "parachuting in," as journalists call it. I knew little about trends in the newspaper industry, and beyond a summer internship at the *Buffalo Courier Express* I had scant knowledge of newsroom life. So I was a bit startled when the Des Moines talk drew an enthusiastic response from some of those present. Engaging with journalists on their terms wasn't part of my rather limited repertoire. These people intimidated me, in the way that all occupational cultures intimidate the outsider. An academic on foreign turf, I thought my assignment was to be "interesting" and then depart. Which is exactly what I did.

But over the next few years I got more and more engaged with the sort of journalist I first met in Des Moines. As I came to understand, they and their co-workers were then living through what my academic colleagues and I were trying to think our way through—namely, what becomes of the press when the public's constitution alters or weakens? Some journalists were discovering what happens: a public was not always there for them to inform, a troubling development that caused them to think hard about what they were doing and why.

The more I grasped this, the more it involved me with people who were beginning to wrestle with some difficult problems: fewer readers for their best work, a rising disgust with politics and journalism, and a growing feeling that the craft was misfiring as it attempted to interest people in the news of the day. Eventually, I came to the conclusion that a better way to "do" ideas about the press was to interest the press in the germ of an idea: that journalism's purpose was to see the public into fuller existence. Informing people followed from that.

By 1993 this idea would have a name, public journalism, or equally often, civic journalism, terms that also described a small movement of people trying to discover what these names meant. Possible answers came from two directions. Beginning around 1989, a few daring editors had begun to experiment in their newspapers, while other thoughtful minds asked themselves whether serious journalism could survive without a stronger public climate around it. The other source for public journalism was a scholarly debate that reached back to the 1920s and remained alive in the 1990s. It asked about the nature of the modern public and current prospects for what professors typically called the public sphere. Academic work on these subjects was sophisticated and lively, but it rarely reached beyond the campus.[3]

Given the ferment in the press and a related debate among scholars, an opportunity presented itself: to join the two discussions, turning them into one. For as some in journalism started to think about their contribution to a healthier democracy, and as they connected these thoughts to the survival of their craft, they started to ask the question that had interested me and others in the academy: What does it take to make democracy work and what should be asked of the press?

Public journalism tried to address this question, but not in an academic way. Instead, working journalists were enlisted in the inquiry and a small reform movement grew up around their struggles and experiments. Without people who were willing to call themselves public or civic journalists, there would have been no point in developing an idea with those names. But it turned out that there were such people, and what they were trying to do could not be done well unless the principles behind it were explained to journalists' satisfaction—which meant in a language they could share. That became a worthy test for academic thought, concerned as it was about the public sphere, but confined in most of its movements to the university.

A few months after my talk in Des Moines, I was asked to join another gathering of editors, this one from the Knight-Ridder newspaper chain, which had its headquarters in Miami at the time. The background to the invitation involved the views of the company's president, James K. Batten, a former reporter and editor who had worked his way to the top of the nation's second largest newspaper chain. An unusually gifted leader, Batten was admired by most of the journalists who made Knight-Ridder their home. Like all managers of newspaper companies, he was worried about the steady erosion of readership, a lengthy trend that had begun to threaten the bottom line. Newspapers were still quite profitable by the standards of other industries, but for a publicly traded company like Knight-Ridder any downward slide was sure to be judged harshly by Wall Street analysts and the apostles of shareholder value.[4]

Of course, their opinion was not the only one that counted. Communities might judge harshly a newspaper that delivered a thinned-out product to boost profits. So too would the journalists on board, who were not businesspeople by training or temperament. Paradoxically, this is what made them valuable to the business. The pursuit of truth, fairness, accuracy, and public service helped maintain a precious asset, commonly called credibility. A business philosophy that contravened those values would risk wasting the asset while demoralizing the staff. Equally troublesome, however, was a journalism that satisfied journalists but allowed the community to drift away. As Jack Fuller, publisher of the *Chicago Tribune*, put it, "A newspaper that pleases its writers and editors but is not a vital part of the community's life will be a commercial failure because it is a rhetorical failure."[5]

This was the tricky terrain Batten entered in 1989, the year he took over as head of Knight-Ridder. In an address at Riverside, California, he argued that newspapers would have to change their ways. Consider, he said, the declining percentage of Americans who kept up with the daily newspaper. In 1967, some 73 percent of adults reported that they read the paper every day; in 1988 that figure was down to 51 percent. "When I was a young reporter on the *Charlotte Observer* in the 1950s and 1960s, it never occurred to me to feel any concern about the financial health of my newspaper—or about its acceptance in the marketplace," Batten recalled. "My newsroom friends and I knew that was all foreordained."

Financial strength translated into political confidence, Batten said. "We prided ourselves on our ability to tell the critics to go to hell. We were, after all, 'the press,' beholden to no one." Succeeding in the business was so easy that one of Batten's acquaintances got into it in middle age because he heard that you could succeed "even if you are brain-dead," as the friend put it. All this belonged to the past, said Batten. "The days when we could do newspapering our way, and tell the world to go to hell if it didn't like the results, are gone forever."[6]

Given declining readership and the heated competition for people's time, newspapers needed a more "customer-driven" approach, meaning ease of service for readers and advertisers. Batten said he wanted to see newspapers that were "warm and caring and funny and human, not just honest and professional and informative." Changes were also due in the culture of the press, so accustomed to glorifying the journalist's habit of defiance. Telling Richard Nixon to go to hell was one thing; it had led to the American press's finest hour during the Watergate crisis. Taking the same attitude toward anyone dissatisfied with the news was a dangerous habit, for there were threats to journalism's vitality that no spirit of defiance could address.

The daily press was imperiled "by the very same forces that seem to erode the civic health of our cities and our nation: an inclination to withdraw into narrow, personal concerns and behave with indifference to our neighbors today and our communities tomorrow," Batten argued. "From the days of Mr. Jefferson . . . our system has operated on the principle that the American people, given sufficient information, are capable of making wise decisions," Batten remarked. "But as public issues become more complex, as our private lives become ever busier, as our appetites for self-indulgence grow seemingly without limit, one wonders some days who is really caring about the public's business. And who is willing to read about it. And act on what they read."[7]

What does it take to make democracy work and what should be asked of the press? This was Batten's theme. His answers were speculative. Newspapers had to "earn their keep on behalf of this democratic society" by refusing to accept a depressing state of affairs. They should "tackle head-on the American disgrace of pathetically low voter turnout" and stop pretending that printing a few "dull op-ed pieces" was a serious effort to stimulate debate. By sponsoring public forums, bringing contending parties together to talk, and making politics so vivid it was "tough to ignore," journalists could start recalling the public to the "public's important business." Batten urged journalists not to "wait for important issues to struggle to the surface, often in blurry form, then fail to get the crisp debate and resolution they deserve."[8]

In a lecture he gave on a similar theme in 1990, Batten advanced the belief—confirmed, he said, by the company's research—that those "who feel a real sense of connection to the places they live" are more likely to become newspaper readers. But "millions of our fellow citizens" have come to "feel little interest in—or responsibility for—their communities" and are choosing to avoid, not only the newspaper, but the whole sphere of politics and civic life.[9]

Batten had set himself a difficult task, for journalists were trained to regard any intrusion of business matters as illegitimate on its face. News could only be compromised by fads like "customer obsession," which were sure to mean less attention to serious stories of public import and more attempts to brighten the atmosphere with some of the happy talk and visual flair that marked the aesthetic of television news. The Gannett Company's colorful *USA Today* had gone this route; and for a time it stood as an icon of dread in every newsroom where management began talking about lost readers.[10]

But Batten said there was another loss to be reckoned with. Even if it were true that declining readership was someone else's concern—a risky attitude, but common enough—what about the problem of a disappearing *public*? Or people's disinclination to think of themselves as citizens, with a stake in the community's affairs? Could journalists honestly say they had no stake in that? This is the rhetorical space that opened up when Batten moved from customer talk to his observations about citizens and communities. Here he was asking journalists to concern themselves, not with the share price of the company, but with the share of the citizenry that felt engaged in public life. "Newspapers grew up on the premise that people were connected to their communities and wanted to know what was going on, wanted to be involved, in many cases wanted to make a contribution," Batten wrote. "Somehow that seems less true in the 1990s."[11]

Several years later the scholar Robert Putnam would bring forward an intriguing body of work that supported much of Batten's argument. In a widely discussed essay called "Bowling Alone: America's Declining Social Capital," Putnam began to document a long-term drop in civic participation. The title of the article originated in his whimsical finding that Americans were bowling more than ever, but they were doing it alone or with their families, not in leagues that involved them in a wider social circle. In itself the fact meant nothing, but Putnam saw it as part of a larger pattern of withdrawal from what he described as "norms and networks of civic engagement," the array of clubs, associations and informal meeting grounds that had always been a distinctive feature of the American scene.[12]

In Putnam's view a rich civic life produced such assets as social trust, reciprocal respect, mutual engagement, and political participation. These he called social capital, analogous to the human capital represented by an educated workforce. Among his bits of evidence for social capital's decline: from 1973 to 1993, the number of Americans who said they had "attended a public meeting on town or school affairs" in the past year dropped from 22 percent to 13 percent. From 1964 to 1982 the number involved in parent-teacher associations (PTAs) dropped from 12 million to barely 5 million, recovering to 7 million in the 1990s. The League of Women Voters, the Boy Scouts, the Red Cross all reported big declines. Certainly there were contrary trends, but overall the picture was a disturbing one, Putnam said. "High on America's agenda should be the question of how to reverse these adverse trends in social connectedness, thus restoring civic engagement and trust."[13]

Putnam's work drew critics, who disputed the evidence of a decline in civic involvement.[14] But if he and Batten were even partly right, then journalists had reason to think, for a key premise of their work was in doubt: that people were naturally connected to the polity, whose affairs they would naturally regard as their own. If Americans saw their business in increasingly private terms, if they came to the conclusion that politics was the property of a remote class, if participating as a citizen was less and less important (or simply impractical), then the press had a problem: how to puzzle through the evidence of civic withdrawal and its many implications for their work.

This was not something journalists could easily address from within. They were accustomed to covering the news, not rebuilding the logic on which the news was based. Here, then, was the reason for my invitation from Knight-Ridder in early 1990. My remarks in Des Moines struck the same note Batten was hitting in his own speeches, and he wanted minds other than his at work on the issues involved. Still a novice in speaking to journalists, I said little at that first meeting. But I was impressed by the spirited tone of the discussion, the editors' willingness to engage one another in argument, and the sense of purpose they showed in tackling the often fuzzy topic of "community."

As a scholar of the media, I was also aware that this discussion was not supposed to be happening at all. Academics who grouped themselves on the political left (and this meant most of them) tended to view media corporations in one way: as maximizers of their profits, monopolizers of their markets, and threats to all forms of craft and culture that came under their relentlessly expanding domains. The notion that corporations themselves had cultures, some portion of which might be "public"—that is, devoted to a vital civic purpose—would have struck most of my academic colleagues as spectacularly naive. The corporation was evil, or, if this was too strong, it was plainly one-dimensional: a profit machine that would tolerate within its borders only those activities that extended its reach or enriched its share-holders. A media company was to be regarded with suspicion, broken only by occasional awe at the havoc it could wreak. Assuming that there was a genuine culture of debate within the corporation, or any deep commitment to public service, marked you as a knave or, worse, an apologist for "late capitalist" society.[15]

Well, I was not a learned student of capitalism, early or late. But as I sat in Miami listening to these editors struggle with the decay of community life, I began to get interested in their experience, which seemed to me reasonably complicated. On one hand, they were employees of a profit-maximizing company worried about its future revenues; Batten left no doubt about that. On the other hand, they were professionals concerned about the survival of something they loved. While they often called journal-ism a business (as in "I got into the business when you didn't need a college degree"), what they loved about it wasn't the money you could make, or the stock options you could earn, but the chance to tell stories, fight for justice, and feel close to the action when important events unfolded.

They had a public identity that they took seriously, no less seriously because it was assumed under the heading of a private company. In fact, they were proud of that company, if wary of its ability to turn against their values, which were in the main public values, expressed through their membership in the fraternity of journalists. Knight-Ridder, in the degree that it gave its newsrooms space to operate, was a public company in a different sense than Wall Street understood. It employed the practitioners of a public art, pro-vided the plant and equipment they needed, and allowed the pursuit of a high calling: telling the truth about the events of our time.

"Within limits," academics on the left would be quick to say, with a knowing grin. "Only the truths that don't offend the powerful interests." Denizens of the political right spoke with similar confidence about the "bias" of reporters and editors, gatekeepers who let only liberal assumptions through. Both critiques had much to recommend them. There were limits on what the mainstream press took seriously, and it was sometimes useful to see them in ideological terms. Certainly the daily news columns did not contain many critiques of late capitalism. The business pages, to take just one example, were written about and for the business classes; political news was heavily dependent on official authority. Advertising dollars, on which the enterprise depended, hardly left the press unfettered. Exposés of department stores and automobile dealers were a rare sight in daily newspapers, and everyone knew why.[16]

Meanwhile, it was hard to deny that newsrooms were citadels of secularism, and thus inclined to regard, say, religious conservatives with a mix of ignorance and contempt. There were always critiques like this to be made, but in making them consistently—at times, reflexively—critics on the left and the right seemed bent on reducing journalism to a shadow of ideology: the ideology of big business and official authority from one perspective, liberal ideology, permissive and pro-government, according to the other.

Getting simultaneously bashed from the left and the right is oddly comforting for journalists; it seems to suggest that they're steering right down the middle, which is a territory they associate with balance and truth. But the deeper defect of an ideological critique is that it fails to address the belief system of the American press as its members experience it. Journalists don't see themselves as tools of the corporation or defenders of the liberal faith. But they do regard their craft as a public service, and the way they understand this service matters. The daily rituals and peer culture of journalism advance a host of assumptions about politics, power, people, public opinion, and democracy. How could it be otherwise? Journalists need ideas and convictions to guide their search for news; these form the common sense of the profession, or, to put it another way, its soul.

But the soul of the craft can itself be crafted. This is what Batten was recognizing, in his speeches and by calling his editors to Miami. Different times call for different approaches, and different ideas to justify them. As I listened to the Knight-Ridder editors deliberate, the phrase "freedom of the press" took on fresh meaning. Perhaps the commercial press couldn't break free of the profit motive. But journalism could alter its established creed, learn again what made it valuable to democracy. It had some room to maneuver within the boundaries that made it a business and a professional code that honored neutrality over commitment.[17]

These speculations deepened when I learned that some of Batten's editors had taken him up on his ideas. Of particular interest were the efforts of the *Columbus Ledger-Enquirer*, in a sleepy Georgia town with its own charged history of race, poverty, and power. The editor in 1989–90 was Jack Swift, a Vietnam veteran and former columnist who was something of a local celebrity. Swift and some of his staff were then engaged in an unusual attempt to help bring people into politics through the agency of the newspaper.[18]

Columbus, Georgia, a small city about one hundred miles southwest of Atlanta, did not share in the economic boom that came to much of the South in the 1970s and 1980s. Its economy, long dominated by the textile industry and a nearby military base, had been slow in shifting to a new pattern. More service industries were moving to Columbus, but it was unclear whether the schools could provide the educated workforce needed for a high-wage service economy. More middle-class people were arriving, but the city lacked the amenities and civic improvements that would hold these newcomers.

Blacks were a majority in the city schools and a third of all registered voters, but the political system had been slow in adjusting to these facts. There was still time to preserve an integrated school system, but the community was missing the leadership that might gradually shift power to the black majority while also preventing white flight. New highway links were on the horizon, but the local roads that fed into these highways would have to be improved, and the tax money was unavailable. In 1982 the voters had sent a hostile message to local government. A referendum was passed placing a dollar-amount ceiling on the municipal budget. It was later thrown out by the courts, but the hostility endured. In short, a familiar picture could be seen in Columbus: deep-set problems, lack of vigorous leadership, and scant political will.

In 1987, the *Ledger-Enquirer* decided to do something. The editors planned a series of articles that would examine the future of the city and the issues it needed to confront. The paper surveyed local residents about their ties to Columbus and their vision of what they wanted it to become. A team of reporters conducted in-depth interviews with residents in their homes, while other correspondents spoke to experts and influential figures in town. The research was assembled in an eight-part series, called "Columbus: Beyond 2000," published in the spring of 1988. The report showed that most residents of Columbus liked their city and wanted to remain there. But it warned of a host of difficulties, including transportation bottlenecks, a history of low wages in the local economy, lack of nightlife in the city, a faltering school system, and the perception that a local elite dominated city politics to the exclusion of others.

If the journalists at the *Ledger-Enquirer* had stopped there, they could have congratulated themselves. They had produced a thorough portrait of the city and its problems. After the series was published, the editors waited for the responses. They got a brief period of chatter, followed by silence and inaction. It was easy to see why. The problems the newspaper had identified were serious, but they had the defect of being gradual. They could be ignored for another day, month, or year; they involved difficult choices. The *Ledger-Enquirer* tried to exert pressure through its reporting and some strongly worded editorials. But these measures emerged into a kind of vacuum. The community lacked organization, leadership, lively debate. It had a government but a weak public sphere, a politics not enough people were willing to join.

Having uncovered a need for discussion, but seeing no broad discussion at hand, the editors took a further step. They organized a public meeting where residents could discuss the future of their city. The aim was to offer a venue for what the paper suspected was a widespread sentiment: there was plenty to do in Columbus, and plenty of people who wanted to see something done. Three hundred citizens showed up for six hours of talk. They came from diverse backgrounds, and many had never participated in public life before. Journalists helped to run the meeting, but they rarely spoke. They tried to provide a forum for citizens to speak about their concerns for the future of their city and the way it was run.

Shortly after the town meeting, Jack Swift organized a barbecue at his home for seventy-five interested citizens. Out of that gathering came a new civic organization, which called itself United Beyond 2000. The group was headed by a thirteen-member steering committee, of which Swift was a leading member. In the person of the editor came a direct and visible tie between the newspaper and this new community group. As participants understood it, their goal was not to lobby for this or that policy but to encourage average citizens as well as influential people to meet and engage with some of the choices the city faced. A number of task forces sprang up to sponsor discussion on key issues. These included recreation needs, child care, race relations, and the special problems of teenagers in Columbus. All were staffed by citizen volunteers.

Among the changes Columbus needed, in the view of many, was a new climate for race relations, which were still affected by a past history of segregation and the memory of brutal violence. Swift, the white newspaper editor, had earlier made friends with a black state court judge named John Allen. The two friends decided that they could do something about the race problem in Columbus. They began to hold backyard barbecues at their homes, to which each man would invite a dozen or so friends. There was no agenda at these meetings. They simply brought together people of different races who ordinarily would not meet, in the hope that they would discover common interests or at least a mutual respect. At each barbecue, a small number of newcomers were invited so that the group would gradually expand. This "friendship network," as it was called, grew to some 250 members, from white bank executives to black barbershop owners. "Several participants said it was the first time black and white leaders had ever met in the city in a social setting," wrote one journalist who was involved in the project.[19]

The Beyond 2000 group went on to sponsor other public events, including a town meeting for teenagers that drew four hundred young people to a local mall for a discussion of their common concerns. The teenagers later organized their own mayoral forum, the first debate ever held between candidates for mayor in Columbus. Meanwhile, the newspaper continued to report the city's failure to come up with a clear agenda for the future. It explained how other cities of a similar size were trying to think about the long term. It continued to do enterprising journalism in the service of its declared aim: to keep the "Beyond 2000" discussion going.

As I learned of these events and discussed them with Jack Swift, I started thinking the thoughts of an outsider. Maybe this is what I meant in telling the editors in Des Moines that "the newspaper of the future must do everything it can to encourage a more active public life." Perhaps the Columbus case illuminated what John Dewey was talking about in *The Public and Its Problems*. In a cryptic passage that closed the book, he stressed the imperative of public talk at the local level. Publishing the news remains incomplete, the public is left "only partially informed and formed," until what is published is actually discussed by citizens. What gives reality to public opinion, Dewey wrote, is the circulation of news and other knowledge "from one to another in the communications of the local community." While an "immense intelligence" greets and surrounds us as citizens of the modern world, "that intelligence is dormant and its communications are broken, inarticulate and faint until it possesses the local community as its medium."[20]

These words seemed to apply in Columbus. Citizens followed up on the newspaper's reporting with public talk about the implications. This talk became the medium through which news was made into fully formed public opinion, with the newspaper assisting in the process. Jack Swift and his colleagues tried to redraw the journalist's position within politics. Instead of standing outside the community and reporting on its pathologies, they took up residence within its borders. Journalists often fear that leaving the sidelines will cost them their credibility. But as the *Ledger-Enquirer*'s publisher,

Billy Watson, later observed, "The biggest credibility problem we have is that we're viewed as arrogant, negative and detached from the community, as tearing the community down." The Beyond 2000 project "did more to enhance the credibility and reputation of the newspaper than anything we've done," he argued.[21]

Still, there were plenty who saw danger in the experiment. On a visit to Columbus in 1991, I interviewed some of them. I asked Jim Houston, an editor at the *Ledger-Enquirer,* if he thought the newspaper had a duty to create public discussion if serious problems were going unaddressed. He paused for a moment before saying:

> I think it has to be the exception. To do that every day would make the newspaper and its pages suspect in everyone's minds—reporters as well as people in the street. But to do it under exceptional circumstances and state what you're doing—yes, I think there's a place for it. The danger is in continuous involvement: when does motivation of a community become dictation? We brought people together at the original town meeting to tell them you don't have to do things in the traditional way—there are other ways. And it did motivate certain people, who got some things done.

The danger he cites is real. "Motivation" could indeed turn to dictating the proper course, especially for a community group so dependent on the newspaper. Was it a risk worth taking? Houston's answer came not from his profession's values but from his feel for Columbus as a longtime resident. Those at the *Ledger-Enquirer* who were new to Columbus might not see why the newspaper should take such an unorthodox step, Houston said. "You had to live in the community," as he had for some twenty years.[22]

As the Columbus experiment became known within the newspaper industry, a variety of other suspicions were raised. During a panel discussion at the American Society of Newspaper Editors conference of 1992, Howard Schneider, managing editor at *Newsday,* spoke out. "I think what Columbus did was bad," Schneider said. "I think the potential for mischief is great. I do not mean only that they had to report on what their editor was doing, but [also] buying into the idea that they are now a part of the community, and the community's agenda is the newspaper's agenda, and suddenly we have to make the community feel good. This may be a temptation to sugarcoat some of the realities of the city."[23]

This kind of criticism would flare repeatedly in the years ahead as others in the news business decided to "leap across the chasm that normally separates journalism from community," as Swift put it, while many of their colleagues learned of these leaps and drew back in disgust. "Getting involved" became one of the flashpoints for the controversy that surrounded public journalism when it surfaced as a movement after 1993.[24]

In 1990, I was more interested in the existential moment that preceded Swift's leap. When their series on the future of the city drew no visible response, the editors had to interpret this non-event. They could have felt perversely vindicated, confirmed in the dreary view that those in power merely have their eye on the next election, while the people at home are ill informed or lost in their own affairs. Or the editors might have said to themselves, "Why should Columbus jump when we say jump?" A third possibility was to see the lack of response as itself a valid response: "Look, we tried, but people don't feel this is important. So be it." All these reactions would have been supported by the common sense of the profession; none would have brought any censure or alarm.

But a fourth reaction was the one Swift and others at the newspaper chose: to be disturbed when an outstanding public challenge goes unmet. Here, they showed a certain confidence in their own reporting, and in their concern for a community that could not afford to remain complacent and inert. Behind the *Ledger-Enquirer*'s initiative was also a moral proposition: that it is wrong for communities to drift without direction when the future is closing in on them. In a democracy, the remedy for this wrong is politics, undertaken by citizens prepared to deliberate and to act. To get this kind of activity going was the cause the newspaper took up.

Taking up causes had a long and fascinating history in the American press, but it was not a history from which contemporary journalists took comfort or inspiration. To them it smacked of advocacy, an abuse of the newspaper's power for partisan purpose, which violated the professional ideal of an objective press. Journalists were constantly being accused of allowing partisan or personal bias to color the news. They were often chagrined by these complaints because they worked hard to keep the most obvious forms of bias out of their reports, harder than many of the loudest critics knew. A separation between the news pages, where facts reigned, and the editorial pages, where opinion was allowed, was widely observed in the mainstream press. Newspeople equated these efforts with the reservoir of trust that sustained them—their credibility. Objectivity, accuracy, fairness, and credibility were common watchwords for a profession that depended in unusual measure on public support.[25]

Swift's experiment fit awkwardly within this vocabulary. The leap he talked about was toward a different ethic that could only be described using different words: democracy, community, citizenship, deliberation, public life. As I conversed with Swift and studied his actions, I found myself taking on a new role: friendly interpreter of a promising venture. From 1990 to 1992 I began to speak and write about the *Ledger-Enquirer*, addressing myself to journalists and their imaginations. The aim was not to duplicate the Columbus case; it was to get journalists curious about an alternative goal: seeing the public into fuller existence.[26]

While I was testing out this approach, Swift's efforts were being promoted within Knight-Ridder. Batten named him the company's editor of the year, praising the *Ledger-Enquirer*'s determination "to build closer relations between the town's citizens, its government, and its newspaper." He then added a further point: many newspapers were unable to cultivate what he called community-connectedness because "they themselves are basically *disconnected* from their communities." Newsrooms had become "over-stocked with journalistic transients who care little about the town of the moment." With their gaze fixed on "the next (and bigger) town," these newsroom gypsies "know little about their community's past and make no effort to learn." And, Batten added, "there is always the temptation to make their byline files a little more glittering at the expense of people and institutions they will never see again."[27]

Here he hiked the stakes. In praising Swift, Batten had already sanctioned a leap into the unknown; he went on to question the mounting costs of the adversarial mentality. This is the one area where American journalism got political: its description of itself as a standing check on official authority, a kind of addition to the balance of powers laid down in the Constitution.[28] Journalists were supposed to be quasi-official doubters of what government said and did; through aggressive reporting and probing questions they would hold institutions and elected officials up to public scrutiny. Much of the glory of the profession was bound up in this view. But so were certain problems. Batten noted one of them: journalists passing through on their way to New York and Washington might overvalue the destruction of public facades and undervalue an ethic of care, in which the press tried to strengthen the community's resources for coming to grips with public problems.

The image of the press as a professional antagonist drew its considerable strength from historic events. At the national level, the litany of government lying during Vietnam, the showdown with the White House over the Pentagon Papers, and the triumph of the *Washington Post* during Watergate convinced a generation of journalists that official authority was not to be trusted. From there it was a short step to concluding that their own authority rested on rituals of mistrust. Any criticism of those rituals could be seen as a demand to "soften" the news, a deadly epithet, for to go soft was to lose your commitment to truth and thus all your credentials.[29]

This was not an irrational fear. At the local level a long history of civic boosterism, of newspapers seeing no evil in towns where the publisher was part of the power structure, gave weight to the newsroom's culture of suspicion. Here the relevant acts of heroism predated Vietnam and Watergate. They involved newspapers in the South that had defied majority opinion about civil rights during the epic struggles of the 1950s and early 1960s. In the mythology of press performance during this era, a racist community was plainly hostile to the journalist's truth-telling mission. It had been that way once and it could be that way again, many in the press felt. If truth was to be told on a daily basis, the community and its official representatives had to be resisted, their complaints put to one side. The same was true of customers— readers, viewers, or advertisers—whose demands could only lead to a softening of the news.[30]

James Squires, who later became editor of the *Chicago Tribune*, began his career at the *Nashville Tennessean* in 1962. In his memoir he describes what made journalism a heroic pursuit to his generation: "My role models were the editors and publishers who stood up to the government, who told the truth when it was not popular or profitable to do so, the people who had seen journalism as a tool with which to abolish slavery, to stand up to Fascism and racism. The greater the risks they took, the more consistent and persistent their stands, they taller they stood in my eyes."[31]

To tell the truth you needed a tough hide. Confirmation of this view came from journalists' everyday experience: the endless complaints about "negative" news when their reporting was even mildly critical, the instinct to stonewall, as Nixon had done, when legitimate questions were raised, the sheer volume of lying and calculated deceit that came their way as journalists fenced with spokespeople, tried to pin down politicians, and asked everyone in public life the rude but necessary questions in which they specialized. A kind of cult of toughness grew from these experiences. Journalists had to steel themselves for their daily battle against the truth-shaders, stonewallers, and sentimentalizers. The cult bestowed no peer penalty for excessive mistrust or outsized aggression, while it granted almost immediate censure to anyone who appeared to be going soft.[32]

Given these impressive fortifications, and the high moral ground on which it stood, adversarial journalism was exceedingly difficult to reach with any sort of intelligent critique. One of the first to try was Mike O'Neill, former editor of the New York *Daily News,* who in 1982 gave a prescient speech to the American Society of Newspaper Editors. He began by noting the astonishing growth in the power of the news media, which had come about without "any corresponding increase in responsibility." Journalism's influence had become mixed up with and multiplied by television's, to the point where the communications revolution, as O'Neill called it, had "altered the basic terms of reference between the press and American democracy."

Political parties had been weakened, direct links to the audience strengthened, and the interval between action and reaction dramatically shortened. The result was that "issues and events are often shaped as much to serve the media's demands as to promote the general welfare." Public actors turn to "creating controversy on demand, turning away from debate and petition in favor of protest and demonstration." The daily outputs of politics and journalism—what O'Neill called the raw materials of public deliberation—were now a "confusing mixture of the real and unreal, important and irrelevant."[33]

Glamorized by television and the captive attention of the press, the presidency was generating unreal expectations, "inviting the same kind of premature disappointment that destroys so many TV stars." The whole process was spinning faster, generating more conflict, more spectacle, more hype—and less attention to serious problems. The press was not a neutral bystander in these developments. "No longer are we just the messengers, observers on the sidelines, witch's mirrors faithfully telling society how it looks," O'Neill said. "Now we are deeply embedded in the democratic process itself, as principal actors rather than bit players or mere audience."[34]

O'Neill recommended a number of seismic shifts in the culture of the newsroom: an end to relentless negativity, abandonment of "the false premise that attack is the best way to flush out the truth," more tolerance of "the frailty of human institutions and their leaders," greater care in the treatment of public officials, a deeper aversion to hype, and "an openness of mind that encourages both self-criticism and outside criticism." Most of all, journalism needs "a generous spirit, infused with human warmth, as ready to see good as to suspect wrong, to find hope as well as cynicism"—a journalism finally concerned that "society has a chance to solve its problems."[35]

Although O'Neill's critique of the adversarial reflex was sure to draw the quickest objections (he even suggested that reporters should "make peace with the government," as if to invite jeers), his most challenging move was to deny his peers the comfort of the press box. By continuing to see themselves as outsiders, journalists fell victim to some dangerous illusions: that they had no investment in the health of the political system, that they could continue to watch the craziness—and feed it—without substantial cost, that their intention to be in no one's pocket meant that they were free of politics, when the reality was they were implicated in everything politics had become.

All this was sure to grate on the ears of those whose heroes "stood up to the government" and told unpopular truths, as Squires put it. Michael Gartner, a former editor at the *Wall Street Journal* (later to become president of NBC News), reacted to O'Neill's speech by denying its central claim: that journalists are actors, rather than professional onlookers, and that they rather enjoy their rising influence. To Gartner this was "hogwash." Reporting the news was quite enough excitement for him and his colleagues; they didn't need, want, or have the status O'Neill gave them. "We just happen to have jobs that are very, very nice jobs," Gartner said. To O'Neill's contention that the "good of the country" was being overlooked in the breathless pace of the adversarial climate, Gartner replied: "That's marvelous language, but what is good for the country? Who knows what's good for the country? What's good for the country is truth and openness and aggressiveness and reporting what the news is. What is bad for the country is a press that becomes a handmaiden of government. Conspiratorial secrecy is what is bad for the country."

This was the cult of toughness in action. O'Neill's point was that the press was already handmaiden to a cyclical process that was making a mockery of politics. This was bad for the nation, he reasoned. No, said Gartner, "what is bad for the country is backroom deals, papers working hand-in-hand with the government."[36] The message was clear: O'Neill is going soft, and he wants to take the rest of us down with him. Gartner's tone spoke for many in his profession, but events were slowly working in O'Neill's favor. As the pattern he described etched itself further in, thoughtful journalists found it hard to deny their role as players in the system. This perception reached a painful peak with the 1988 presidential campaign, widely considered one of the worst in modern memory.[37]

The contest pitting Michael Dukakis against George Bush came at a turning point in United States history. With the Cold War winding down, Americans were about to enter a new and far more uncertain landscape. It was reasonable to expect from the campaign some semblance of a debate about the meaning of this and other large events—such as the looming savings and loan scandal, the biggest ever involving public funds. What the nation got instead was a series of manufactured issues that flowed directly from the downward spiral O'Neill had described. The *Washington Post* was among the newspapers that declined to endorse either candidate. The race, it editorialized, "was not just a domestic disappointment but an international embarrassment . . . a screamingly tiresome, trivial, point-missing contest between two candidates who do not seem to be running for president so much as they seem to be having one of those headache-making fights that children are so good at staging in the back seat of the family car when everyone's nerves are pretty much gone anyway."[38]

Image seemed to be the entire territory on which the campaign was conducted, with flag burning, prison furloughs for rapists, and the Pledge of Allegiance as flashpoints used by Bush and his supporters to generate controversy and discredit the opposition. Struggling to respond, Dukakis came up with his own manipulative ploys, like climbing aboard an M-1 tank to demonstrate his readiness as would-be commander of the military. All this activity incorporated the news media, as a host of scholarly studies documented.[39] The candidates did what they did based in part on their knowledge of newsroom routines. They played to their constituencies and the television cameras. But they also played to the assumptions of reporters and editors about what constitutes the campaign's "story."

For much of the press, the story was interesting as a contest, an opportunity for one candidate to outmaneuver the other by demonstrating a superior grasp of the electioneering process. But the process had gained a false objectivity in the journalists' eyes. It seemed to be the way things worked, but since it was partly based on an understanding of the way journalists work, the process was often an artifact of news conventions and the ideas embedded in them.

The writer and cultural observer Joan Didion wrote of this circularity in a dispatch from the campaign trail, "Insider Baseball," in 1988. Didion pointed to the campaign's "remoteness from the actual life of the country," and found part of the explanation in the behavior of journalists who "tend to speak a language common in Washington" but foreign to the rest of us. "They talk about the 'story,' and how it will 'play.' They speak of a candidate's performance, by which they usually mean his skill at circumventing questions, not as citizens but as professional insiders, attuned to signals pitched beyond the range of normal hearing: 'I hear he did all right this afternoon,' they were saying in the press section of the Louisiana Superdome in New Orleans on the evening Dan Quayle was or was not to be nominated for the vice-presidency. 'I hear he did OK with Brinkley.'"[40]

This is how politics sounds when it is being emptied of public purpose. Journalists trying to combat the emptiness wound up adding to it, as another critic, Todd Gitlin, noted. After years of complaints about covering only the "horse race," journalists by 1988 were determined to "take the audience backstage, behind the horse race, into the paddocks, the stables, the clubhouse, and the bookie joints," Gitlin wrote. Thus, "horse-race coverage was joined by handicapping coverage—stories about campaign tactics, what the handlers were up to, how the reporters felt about being handled: in short, *How are the candidates trying to do it to us, and how are they doing at it?*"[41]

One September afternoon in 1988, Michael Dukakis took a ride on a new tank at a General Dynamics plant in Sterling, Michigan. Wearing a generously sized helmet and clutching a machine gun, he proudly toured the grounds as music from the movie *Patton* played over the sound system. "So what did you think," he shouted to reporters who were watching. "Did I look like I belonged up there?" Almost no one thought he did. Television and newspapers presented an absurd picture: the candidate as Snoopy, playing soldier. With its cartoonish imagery and hopelessly dim logic—that a tank ride could somehow establish military credentials—the episode was an immediate embarrassment, not only to the Dukakis campaign, but to the reporters in attendance who had to shape "news" from this event.[42]

What could be said about a stunt so transparent? On CBS that evening, Bruce Morton reported: "Biff, bang powee! It's not a bird, it's not a plane. It's presidential candidate Michael Dukakis in an M-1 tank as staff and reporters whoop it up." As Morton went on to explain, "Pictures are symbols that tell the voter important things about the candidate. If your candidate is seen in the polls as weak on defense, put him in a tank." In Gitlin's analysis, journalists like Morton were trying to ingratiate themselves with the audience by showing "that they were immune from the ministrations of campaign professionals." Eager to separate themselves from a degrading spectacle that was just as eager to incorporate them, they were urging citizens to become "cognoscenti of their bamboozlement," which was not the most useful task they could perform.[43]

Scholar Kathleen Hall Jamieson analyzed a similar cycle in her book *Dirty Politics,* noting how television news had by 1988 become distinctly "adlike." News reports were built around short word bursts, vivid images, and a simple story line with emotional oomph—the very features political consultants built into the television ads they regarded as the centerpiece of the campaign. Clips from the ads made their way into televised news reports. Meanwhile, other forms of campaign discourse—"candidate speeches, press conferences, one-to-one interviews, and debate answers"—were "increasingly tailored with a view toward getting adlike news coverage."

The whole cycle was reinforced when the rest of the press, not bound by the rigid formats of television news, adopted "strategy" and "process" as the themes of the most sophisticated campaign coverage. As Jamieson wrote, this way of knowing locked the entire system into place. It doubled back on journalists to debase what O'Neill had called the raw materials of public deliberation. Jamieson concluded that campaign discourse was "failing the body politic in the United States," but not because it was negative or embodied in paid ads. Rather, campaigning now relied on "genres of candidate and press discourse" that minimized any attempt at argument and encouraged the mounting of phony claims.[44]

Following the disturbing spectacle of 1988, journalists "engaged in more than the usual self-criticism," as Tom Rosenstiel, then of the *Los Angeles Times,* put it. Speaking for many of her colleagues, Gloria Borger, an editor at *U.S. News and World Report,* said, "We looked back at the last campaign and asked what prison furloughs and flags had to do with the real world." Frustrated or disgusted by the emptiness of the campaign, some of the brightest reporters quit covering politics.[45] Others began to consider how the degrading cycle could be ended.

One was the nation's most respected political reporter, David Broder of the *Washington Post,* who in early 1990 began to address his colleagues on the subject. "We cannot allow the [November] elections to be another exercise in public disillusionment and political cynicism," Broder wrote. This was a startling sentence, for it saw journalists as answerable, not only for the reports they produce, but for the realities they report. "It is time for those of us in the world's freest press to become activists, not on behalf of a particular party or politician, but on behalf of the process of self-government," he argued. The campaign must be rescued from "the electronic demagoguery favored by too many hired-gun political consultants" who merely "collect their fees and go off to another campaign in another state." Broder continued: "That means that we must be far more assertive than in the past on the public's right to hear its concerns discussed by the candidates—in ads, debates and speeches—and far more conscientious in reporting those discussions when they take place. We have to help reconnect politics and government—what happens in the campaign and what happens afterward in public policy—if we are to have accountability by our elected officials and genuine democracy in this country."[46]

A key influence on Broder's thinking was a pamphlet published in 1991 by the Kettering Foundation, a small think tank based in Dayton, Ohio. Kettering had also been involved in Jack Swift's adventure in Columbus when the newspaper had needed help in planning public forums. Part of the foundation's work sustained thousands of such forums around the country, where citizens got together on their own initiative to discuss issues in a deliberative setting, with discussion guides and trained moderators to help them get somewhere. The National Issues Forums, as they were called, were one attempt to experiment on conditions that others were simply decrying— the absence of serious reflection in politics, the country's inability to discuss issues in depth.[47]

Broder was familiar with the foundation's work, and he discovered in a report it had published in 1991, *Citizens and Politics,* a way of imagining the public that fit his own conclusions. *Citizens and Politics* was the work of Richard Harwood, a researcher Kettering had hired to conduct conversations with small groups of Americans about their views on the political system. Harwood shared with Broder a belief that citizens were worth listening to in depth, if you knew what to listen for. All wisdom did not reside in the people, but there was wisdom there that polling and election results could not convey. For years Broder had tried to tap it himself by trooping to the homes of voters for living-room discussions, the results of which worked their way into his reporting. More journalists admired this method than copied it, but every election season he and some of his colleagues at the *Post* rang doorbells in key precincts to ask people about politics.[48]

Harwood used the focus-group method: strangers around a table engaged in a discussion. There were limits to this approach, as with any attempt to map the collective mind, but among its advantages was the chance to reveal the depth of feeling beneath people's disappointment and the connections they made among issues treated as separate in the press. Americans were not apathetic or immature, Harwood said. They were angry. "They argue that politics has been taken away from them—that they have been *pushed out* of the political process." Citizens saw themselves as squeezed out by a system more responsive to lobbyists, political action committees, special interest groups, and the news media. Public officials reacted to this system, not to the public at large. Harwood said it was a "fervent belief among Americans" that the average citizen is no longer heard or even spoken to, "that many, if not most, public issues are talked about by policy and opinion leaders, the media, and others in ways that neither connect with the concerns of citizens nor make any sense to them."[49]

Beneath this sense of frustration and impotence, Harwood uncovered a foundation for a healthier democracy. It was hard to find, difficult to phrase properly, but it was there. Part of it lay in Americans' understanding that no one was able to fix politics for them, and that blaming one villain or another was too easy. Talk to them long enough and citizens "recognize that they need better to understand policy issues in order to participate in political debate; they acknowledge that public officials face political constraints and pressures that are beyond their control; and they realize they must work hard to make their voice heard." People were also willing to get involved when "there is the possibility of having a say; the possibility of creating and seeing change." Absent these conditions, his report warned, such measures as campaign finance reform, term limits, ethics codes, and voter registration drives would not address the core problem, which involved "reconnecting citizens and politics."[50]

Broder read Harwood's report with interest, and shortly afterward he gave a lecture at Riverside, California, in the same series that had earlier featured James Batten. He opened by describing a bleak political landscape in which citizens "tell us that they are disgusted by the campaigns they are offered in this country." Public confidence in politics and politicians was reaching dangerous lows. Journalists were not the cause of this development, and it was important not to overstate their role. But the widespread "disillusionment about the heart of politics—the election process—is something in which we play a part," Broder said.[51]

Along with political consultants, whose power was rising in the new system, journalists had become a "permanent part of the political establishment." Both groups characteristically denied "any responsibility for the consequences of elections." This was disingenuous at best, dishonest at worst, for the fact was that "we have colluded with the campaign consultants to produce the kind of politics which is turning off the American people." What can I do? Broder asked himself: "My answer is tentative and expressed without any great confidence. But if we are going to change the pattern, we in the press have to try deliberately to reposition ourselves in the process. We have to try to distance ourselves from the people we write about—the politicians and their political consultants—and move ourselves closer to the people that we write for—the voters and potential voters."[52]

The time had come to rethink a fundamental assumption of political journalism: "that the campaign and its contents are the property of the candidate." Journalists should treat the campaign as part of a longer drama, ("embracing both elections and government") that revolves around the American people rather than the candidates and their advisers. The campaign was the property of voters, a time when they "have a right to have their concerns addressed and their questions answered by the people who are seeking to exercise power." More time would have to be spent with citizens, uncovering the issues they wanted the candidates to address. "Let their agenda drive our agenda," as Broder put it. Why do all this? Because the situation was not beyond remedy. Like Harwood, Broder held to a belief that the American people were not apathetic or unconcerned, nor were they selfish or indifferent. They were simply tired of seeing politics treated as a "sport for a relative handful of political insiders." He closed on a personal note. "I would like to leave some better legacy than that behind when I get out of this business."[53]

Broder's argument challenged a view popular among journalists: that while many in the country might long for a more serious politics, the American people had time and again shown their culpability in current trends. They had increasingly short attention spans, a limited tolerance for complex arguments, and a weakness for the attack style of campaigning, which worked only because voters allowed it to work. A skeptical view of the average citizen—bordering on contempt—was an article of common sense for many in the press. An illustrative example is this observation from Katharine Seelye, a reporter for the *New York Times,* who noted how calls for a more serious discourse were in the air. "But for all their longing for civility," she wrote, "voters respond to negative campaigning the way children respond to Power Rangers: they love to watch politicians punch and kick and blow one another to smithereens. The voters can't help themselves. They see a negative ad, they respond."[54]

Seelye's is an ironist's perspective, an emotional style as much as an empirical conclusion. The ironist is constantly noting those surprising or depressing facts that put the lie to noble sentiments like democracy as self-government. In Seelye's treatment the American people will inevitably show their Pavlovian nature, their essential childishness. ("The voters can't help themselves.") They may say they want serious discourse but prove unequal to the task of demanding it. Observing such ironies is the journalist's route to truth, for only those unclouded by the dreamy rhetoric of democracy can see how the system really works.

Placed next to Broder's more hopeful perspective, Seelye's ironic and skeptical stance illuminated a critical choice for the press: when confronted with dismal facts about the state of democracy, do we take them in or try to take them on? In choosing the second option, Broder advanced a cogent analysis of the press as a player in the system. He declared his faith in the average citizen's capacity, and put aside irony as a preferred style of knowing—without, however, surrendering the native realism of the experienced reporter. This was an intriguing series of rhetorical moves by a man at the top of the professional pyramid. If David Broder of the *Washington Post* was thinking revolutionary thoughts ("It is time for those of us in the world's freest press to become activists"), could others be far behind?

As it happened, some in the mainstream press were already moving ahead, without waiting for a nod from the likes of Broder. Out in the plains of Kansas, Davis Merritt, editor of the *Wichita Eagle,* had begun refashioning his newspaper's approach to political coverage. Merritt, known by the nickname "Buzz," was a thirty-five-year veteran of the newspaper world. Almost all of it was with Knight-Ridder. Despite his long association with the company and his personal affection for James Batten, Merritt had grown nervous about the customer talk he was hearing. While he admired Jack Swift's courage in the Columbus experiment, Merritt felt the *Ledger-Enquirer* had gone too far: nothing but trouble could come from Swift's personal leadership in a citizens' group. To allow himself or the *Eagle* to become so involved was unimaginable to Merritt, and he had a hard time seeing the Columbus case as inspirational.[55]

But as he examined his own paper's role in politics, Merritt began to think hard about other possible reforms. Shortly after the 1988 election, he wrote a column calling for "a total rearranging of the contract between the candidates and journalists." The existing arrangement, a "mutual bond of expediency," was satisfying only to the campaign professionals who had learned how to profit from it. In the 1990 gubernatorial campaign in Kansas, the *Eagle* would try something different. Sensing a repeat of the prevailing pattern—a campaign of phony charges and countercharges with only minimal attention to important issues—Merritt announced a break with tradition in a Sunday column headlined, "Up Front, Here's Our Election Bias."

The headline was itself noteworthy: a news organization shares its plans with the public by announcing the "bias" it will bring to campaign coverage. Of course the particular slant Merritt had in mind was hardly controversial: "We believe the voters are entitled to have the candidates talk about the issues in depth." Few would dare to challenge that. But making good on this pledge involved a shift in thinking. The notion of covering the campaign was effectively replaced by a new principle: making the campaign cover what mattered to citizens. The *Eagle* vowed to give readers "the opportunity to understand in great detail the candidates' positions on every major issue Kansas faces."

Merritt's pledge meant that the point of departure for the *Eagle* would no longer be the daily events along the campaign trail or what the candidates were doing to win votes. It would be the needs of citizens who had a "right to know what the candidates intend to do once in office." Campaign coverage could then approach the candidates with this priority in mind. This was new only because it departed from what had become the norm; but it could also be seen as a return to fundamentals. Elections are self-government in action, and journalism should serve that end.[56]

If the *Eagle* was going to focus on every major issue Kansas faced, then defining those issues would have to become the newspaper's responsibility. In effect, the *Eagle* was planning to argue with the candidates over what the campaign should be about. Merritt was betting on his staff's knowledge of Kansas politics, along with their judgment about the importance of various issues. They had polling data to help them, but this data still had to be interpreted, raising the question: what were the grounds for determining the key issues in the campaign?

For a campaign adviser, the grounds are clear. A good issue solidifies a base of support, motivates new recruits, weakens an opponent's coalition, or targets an important subgroup—typically, undecided voters. A bad issue is one that angers supporters, alienates potential recruits, or exposes a weakness in the candidate's record. The image of a wedge issue—one that divides the electorate to one side's advantage—suggests the values at work when campaign professionals do the naming and framing of issues.[57]

One way a journalist can counter those values is to expose the candidate's strategy, by writing about the wedge and how it works, for example. But how does this help citizens form a sound judgment about the Kansas governor's race? Should they vote for the candidate with the better strategy? Reporters who expose the machinations of politicians and handlers feel they are striking a blow for truth. And they are, in a "buyer beware" manner typical of consumer reporting. But Merritt wanted the *Eagle*'s journalism to be more than a prophylactic, more than a series of signs reading "Beware of manipulation by candidates trying to win." Picture two ways of telling the story of the governor's race: one assumes that a campaign has its own reality, which journalists ought to decipher for us; the other assumes that the campaign becomes decipherable *by* us when it addresses the realities facing the electorate. The *Eagle* chose the second course, striking its own blow for truth with the proposition that "voters are entitled to have the candidates talk about the issues in depth."

The paper focused its coverage on ten key concerns: education, economic development, the environment, agriculture, social services, abortion, crime, health care, taxes, and state spending.[58] Each was the subject of a long background piece in the Sunday paper. Each issue was also charted in "Where They Stand," a weekly feature that gave a brief description of what was at stake, a summary of the two gubernatorial candidates' positions, and then a report on what, if anything, was said that week. For example, the section on the environment noted that Kansas faced new demands on its water supply as current sources dried up. The newspaper treated the positions of the two candidates, Democrat Joan Finney and incumbent Republican Mike Hayden, as follows.

FINNEY
Would increase the state's role in recycling. Has no specific plan. Has not discussed the water issue.
This week: Restated her position.

HAYDEN
Helped pass state water plan to manage resources. Wants private lands more accessible for public recreation. Encourages dryland farming research to

reduce demand for water. Wants to research drilling wells into geological formations deeper than the Ogaliala aquifer.

This week: Repeated his position.

Under the heading "Agriculture" the *Eagle* wrote about the Democrat:

F I N N E Y
Wants agriculture secretary elected by all voters. No other stated position on agricultural matters.

This week: Did not talk about it.

When news was made under this format it tended to be about positions taken, or views clarified. Under "taxes," the *Eagle* wrote:

F I N N E Y
Now is proposing that $460 million be raised by placing a 1 percent surcharge tax on up to 52 categories of goods and services now exempt from sales taxes. Finney would use the money to provide for a 30 percent reduction in property taxes.

This week: Substantially changed her tax proposal Tuesday. Originally had proposed raising $800 million in new tax dollars by placing a 1 percent surcharge tax on up to 52 categories of goods and services now exempt from sales tax. On Tuesday, she lowered that amount to $460 million. Would not say before the election which categories would be taxed. Would use the money to provide for 30 percent reduction in property taxes. Would no longer raise $180 million for state programs—money she has said was necessary to deal with a possible state revenue shortfall.[59]

Several things are worth noting about this scheme. First, any responsible newspaper would report a major change in a candidate's position on taxes. In this sense the *Eagle*'s coverage was entirely conventional. What was different was the conscious display of issues and positions as the major theme of the campaign story. The *Eagle*'s goal was to allow the proper concerns of politics (issues in depth) to shine though in the space provided. Time was also reimagined. "This week: Did not talk about it," is a fact generated by a particular way of sensing political time: as the weekly process by which the choices facing the state are (or are not) clarified by the candidates. The "strategy" approach contains its own conception of time: how the candidates are shaping their images, responding to the latest charges from their opponent's camp, struggling to win as the race winds down.

"Where They Stand" was thus more than a handy voter's guide, although it was also that. Fundamentally, it was an argument for what politics is supposed to be about: public concerns and public debate. It was a powerful use of news space, especially with the threat of a blank appearing under a candidate's name. Deploying this threat was the *Eagle*'s way of being "tough" on the candidates. Toughness, however, doesn't become an end in itself. A candidate can avoid the penalty of white space by cooperating in a dialogue that will help voters make up their minds. The system is publicly announced and the rules are clear: say something meaningful about the key issues, and we'll report it and keep reporting it.

This scheme tried to correct for both the excesses of the adversarial pose, in which a contemptuous dismissal of all public statements is assumed to serve some public good, and the limitations of "balance," in which equal quotation of opposite sides meets the desired norm. The *Eagle*'s approach made a different argument: political talk should address important public concerns, and the press can help. In a post-election survey financed by Knight-Ridder, readers said that the most useful features were the "Where They Stand" box and the in-depth explorations of issues. Horse-race coverage, often touted by journalists as a way to make the story exciting, ranked far down the list.[60]

A further (and more radical) experiment in connectedness came two years later, when the *Eagle* launched the "People Project."[61] If Americans increasingly disdained politics because it didn't seem real to them, then journalism had to start revising its view of what the whole thing was about. Ignoring government and the maneuvering of major players was no answer. But neither could the press avoid the widespread frustration with politics as usual, or the growing conviction that some issues are beyond the system's current capacity. The People Project tried to respond to these facts. It was an experiment with a self-conscious and rather idealistic premise: that journalism could "empower people to take back control of their lives," as Merritt's initial planning memo read. The project began with 192 two-hour interviews with Wichita-area residents, who were asked to speak about their lives and troubles, along with their perceptions of the political process. From these interviews, and from the *Eagle*'s own observations, the following premises emerged, as outlined in Merritt's memo.

    1. People feel alienated from many of the processes that affect their lives. The political process, the education system, the justice system are seen as incapable of resolving anything.

2. People see these issues as interrelated, inseparable and, perhaps, unsolvable.

3. [Their] response is to fall into frustration and anger, to drop out of the processes, to abandon community in a self-protective response, rather than seek solutions which they very much doubt exist.

The idea that average citizens can take back control of institutional structures and social forces may seem naive, even dangerously so. It can lead to a kind of mythmaking, in which the realities of unequal influence are obscured by the charged rhetoric of "empowerment." But from another perspective, journalists have every reason to emphasize the citizen's ability to act, to take seriously the notion of self-government. A story so realistic that it sees through everything risks convincing people that politics is a farce, government a joke, rhetoric a sham, leadership an illusion, change a mirage. This is a journalism that by succeeding becomes defeatist and self-canceling—in a word, absurd. For if all these things are true we don't need journalists and their daily reports. In fact, we don't need politics at all because the system is clearly beyond our control.

Merritt was searching for a way to address this sense of despair without adding to it, on one hand, or whitewashing reality, on the other. In trying to counter public hopelessness, the People Project was not a utopian exercise at all but an open-ended probe for some way to restore journalism's relevance. Merritt outlined the aims of his project as follows:

1. Recognize the frustrations and explain the reasons for them, including the core, often competing values that stand in the way of solutions.

2. Give readers hundreds of places where they can get a handle on problems through the existing, non-government mechanisms.

3. Elicit from readers, and print, their ideas for other mechanisms and solutions.

4. Summarize it all and produce a . . . reprint that would be distributed to non-subscribers through various devices. . . .

5. Encourage, or, with a partner, actively cause continued involvement at various levels.

The People Project became a ten-week package of articles, service features, community events, and "idea exchanges" sponsored by the *Eagle* and several broadcast partners. In a front-page column Merritt announced a "collaborative effort to give shape and momentum to your voices and ideas, with the goal of reasserting personal power and responsibility for what goes on around us." Thus the subtitle of the project: "Solving It Ourselves." For ten weeks, Merritt wrote, the *Eagle* and its two partners, KSNW-TV and KNSS radio, would make the space and time available for "an informed community discussion of critical issues" from which "ideas about solutions can arise, as well as the commitment to carry out the solutions."

The critical issues included faltering schools, crime and the lure of gangs, political gridlock, and the stresses that built up on families and individuals trying to cope with competing demands. Each was the subject of a package of features in the *Eagle,* the bulk of them written by veteran reporter and longtime Wichita resident Jon Roe. Roe outlined the problem and what residents said about it in interviews; then he examined why the issue was so difficult to address, attempting to cut through the surface of conflict to what the paper called competing "core values." By encouraging readers to examine their deepest beliefs (which may of course conflict), the paper hoped to "encourage a search for solutions among people with differing ideas," as Merritt put it.

For each of the major issues under discussion, the *Eagle* published a comprehensive list called "Places to Start," with the names, addresses, and phone numbers of agencies working on the problem—like keeping kids out of gangs. Repeated invitations were made to phone, write, fax, or deliver in person comments and suggestions for change. A series of "idea exchanges" was held at various sites where concerned residents could connect with others like themselves and meet with representatives of community and volunteer groups. A regular feature called "Success Stories" focused on individuals who took the initiative and were making a difference. The paper's broadcast partners produced parallel reports during the ten-week run of the project and provided on-air forums.

The People Project was political journalism in a different key. The aim was to connect people to public life and its full range of civic organizations. Visiting the United States in the 1830s, Alexis de Tocqueville called these groups "associations." He saw them as a distinctive strength of American democracy because they drew people into public causes and gave them a stake in the outcome. The People Project thus drew on a long tradition of political thought, usually called civic republicanism, in which the ideal citizen is engaged with others through a rich web of voluntary associations.[62]

"At the heart of republicanism," writes E. J. Dionne of the *Washington Post,* "is the belief that self government is not a drab necessity but a joy to be treasured. It is the view that politics is not simply a grubby confrontation of competing interests but an arena in which citizens can learn from each other and discover an 'enlightened self-interest' in common."[63] By showing residents of Wichita their opportunities for mutual engagement, the *Eagle* made use of a power rarely visible in discussions of the press: to render the public landscape in a particular way. In this case, it became an open space for concerned citizens willing to learn from each other and get involved.

What were the results? As Merritt later wrote, "Kansas was not free of crime or health care problems and the schools did not visibly improve—nor had we anticipated any of that." There were a few hopeful signs: volunteerism in Wichita schools was up 37 percent when the school year opened. The newspaper's circulation remained flat, but no jump had been expected. In an annual survey by Knight-Ridder, reader satisfaction rose 10 percent, the highest increase in the chain.[64]

Both Wichita projects recognize that beyond information, the press sends us an *invitation* to experience public life in one manner or another. Reflecting on what the invitation should say was the real innovation pioneered by Merritt and his colleagues. The experience should be participatory, the *Eagle* argued. It should propose and deliver a useful dialogue about issues. It should address people in their capacity as citizens, in the hope of strengthening that capacity. It should try to make public life go well, in the sense of making good on democracy's promise. These "shoulds" would eventually form the core of public journalism as a philosophy. As Merritt wrote about the 1990 voter project:

> Something intriguing and promising had happened. We had deliberately broken out of the passive and increasingly detrimental conventions of election coverage. We had, in effect, left the press box and gotten down on the field, not as a contestant but as a fair-minded participant with an open and expressed interest in the process going well. . . . It was also a liberating moment, for me and the journalists at the *Eagle*. We no longer had to be the victims, along with the public, of a politics gone sour. We had a new purposefulness: revitalizing a moribund public process.[65]

In the fall of 1992, this new purposefulness was taken further by the *Charlotte Observer* during its own experiment in election coverage.[66] Like others in journalism, then executive editor Rich Oppel was dissatisfied with press performance in past campaigns, particularly with horse-race polling, which had miscalled a bitter Senate race between Jesse Helms and Harvey

Gantt in 1990. The weaknesses of horse-race coverage were well known; now its biggest strength, the ability to predict the winner, was also suspect.

Oppel and publisher Rolfe Neill were determined to try something different. Meanwhile, the Poynter Institute for Media Studies, which has an educational mission within journalism, was looking to demonstrate that a revised approach was possible. Aware of the progress that had been made in Wichita, the two institutions agreed to cooperate, adding as a partner WSOC-TV in Charlotte. The *Observer* set out to amplify and extend the "new political contract" outlined two years earlier by Merritt and described in strikingly similar language by Broder. In a front-page column titled "We'll Help You Regain Control of the Issues," Oppel announced his intentions.

> David Broder of the *Washington Post* has said voters see no "connection between their concerns in their daily lives and what they hear talked about and see reported by the press in most political campaigns."
>
> We think this is dangerous. . . .
>
> We will seek to reduce the coverage of campaign strategy and candidates' manipulations, and increase the focus on voters' concerns. We will seek to distinguish between issues that merely influence an election's outcome, and those of governance that will be relevant after the election. We will link our coverage to the voters' agenda, and initiate more questions on behalf of the voters.[67]

Oppel's column came clean about the choices involved in campaign reporting. He admitted that politics as strategy was a narrative device that could be drastically reduced. His alternative: a renewed focus on voters' concerns. Oppel acknowledged that the temporal frame—the definition of political time—in campaign reporting was too narrow because it favored "issues that merely influence an election's outcome." He then announced the choice of a new frame: matters of governance that will be relevant after the election. Moving on, he conceded that asking questions is an art that can be performed in several different ways. The one the *Observer* chose was to initiate more questions on behalf of the voters. In the same passage, Oppel implied that covering politics and having an agenda are not mutually exclusive. Thus, "We will link our coverage to the voters' agenda." Finally, he said that a newspaper was entitled to have convictions about politics and that news coverage could follow from those convictions ("We'll help you regain control of the issues").

The search for a "citizen's agenda" began in January 1992 with a poll of one thousand adults (not necessarily readers) conducted by a Knight-Ridder subsidiary and jointly sponsored by WSOC-TV. The poll asked residents not who they would vote for, or what they wanted to read, but what they were concerned about and wanted the candidates to discuss in the upcoming election. Six broad areas of concern emerged: the economy and taxes, crime and drugs, health care, education, the environment, and a general sense that support structures and value systems in family and community life were weakening. These became the citizen's agenda. Five hundred of the poll's respondents agreed to serve on a citizen's panel to help the *Observer* keep its focus on the public's concerns, rather than the machinations of the candidates or the weekly flux of campaign events.

Issues from the citizen's agenda dominated the coverage, with the emphasis on answering questions, explaining the candidates' positions, and exploring possible solutions. Queries from citizens were regularly put to the candidates and campaign staffs; polls and strategy stories were downplayed. Stories were told through the eyes and lives of citizens, relying heavily on readers' phoned-in comments and questions from the citizen's panel. With the citizen's agenda rather than campaign tactics driving the coverage, reporters specializing in business, education, health, and religion were recruited to write political stories. Profiles of the candidates were accompanied by grids comparing their statements and records against the voter's agenda. Campaign speeches were "mapped" against the agenda so that reports focused on not only what was said, or the strategy behind saying it, but what it meant for the problems on people's minds.

Voters emerged as participants in the campaign. Reporters on the campaign trail would ask questions from readers; replies would be published under a regular heading, "Ask the Candidates." Before the state primary, Pat Buchanan was interviewed by eight members of the citizen's panel. Three panel members questioned gubernatorial candidates at a debate on school reform. For three Sunday evenings in October, WSOC-TV featured a televised conversation among citizens, keyed to issues explored in the Sunday paper.

These events reveal another dimension of press power that ordinarily goes unnoticed: journalists determine who counts as a player in politics. By revising its use of this power, the *Observer* crafted a different story about the 1992 election: a tale of citizens, candidates, and public concerns connecting with one another—or failing to connect. Before the initiative began, Oppel said, "If we do campaign coverage this way, it will change the way we do everything here."[68] That remark illuminates the change in thinking in Wichita and Charlotte. By making the citizen's experience the primary reference point, the two papers began to alter the way journalists experienced the political drama as well. The newspapers' quest for politics—their sense of what was worth knowing and why—underwent a shift. The best illustration of it is a story told by Oppel from the 1992 campaign.

> Voters were intensely interested in the environment. . . . So our reporters went out to senatorial candidates and said, "here are the voters' questions." Terry Sanford, the incumbent senator, called me up from Washington and said, "Rich, I have these questions from your reporter and I'm not going to answer them because we are not going to talk about the environment until the general election." This was the primary. I said, "Well, the voters want to know about the environment now, Terry." He said, "Well, that's not the way I have my campaign structured." I said, "Fine, I will run the questions and I will leave a space under it for you to answer. If you choose not to, we will just say 'would not respond' or we will leave it blank." We ended the conversation. In about ten days he sent the answers down.[69]

Seen here are the intricate relations between power and authority in journalism. Clearly, Oppel was deploying the power of his newspaper with his threat to leave a blank space under Sanford's name. But he had another weapon: the renewed authority that came from the paper's inquiry into citizens' interests, and its attempt to make the campaign dialogue address them. These put teeth in the journalist's claim to be "representing" citizens. While the claim is always to some degree rhetorical, it became more and more empirical as the *Observer* found ways to uncover and employ a citizen's agenda. All of which helped make the paper's power play an instance of fair play.

When Terry Sanford explained that his campaign strategy did not include talking about the environment yet, Oppel did not say, "Oh, really? Tell me your thinking on that." This is the dark path that strategy stories enter down. Curiosity is aroused by the insinuation of a clever move, the effectiveness of which can only be appreciated by a savvy reporter. "That's not the way I have my campaign structured" was a subtle invitation to Oppel to enter the universe of handlers and pollsters. By declining this invitation, Oppel stayed within the universe of the citizen. He told Sanford how the *Observer* would be structuring the campaign: as a dialogue on public issues.

By 1992 the seeds of a stronger public philosophy were scattered around in the American press. A critique of press performance was brought forward by the depressing events of 1988. It saw the press as a player, caught up in a system that was making a mockery of politics. Changes were called for, and some big names were doing the calling. David Broder grasped that if journalists are to be seen as actors, it is reasonable to expect from them a kind of agenda, a desired outcome of their actions. Not only should they acknowledge an agenda, they should be able to persuade others—media owners, politicians, critics, the public—that their agenda is a proper one. But what should it be? How can they justify it to wider audiences? What sort of rhetoric should they employ?

These questions confound the profession's normal view of itself. Journalists tend to see themselves as observers; their job is to tell the truth, not to bring new truths into being. Almost all the key tenets in their ethical code emphasize detachment rather than participation: the maligned but still influential doctrine of objectivity, the related emphasis on fairness and balance, the separation between the news columns and the editorial page, the treasured watchdog role, the adversarial stance, the injunction to "let the chips fall where they may." None of these ideas offers guidance to the people Broder tried to address: professionals willing to acknowledge their influence in politics and to use it on behalf of "genuine democracy."

Nor was it journalists alone who declined this challenge. The entire political culture, preoccupied with media "bias," made it perilous to even ask about agendas and outcomes in journalism. Far safer to do as Michael Gartner had done: cling to the observer's position, or contend that the adversarial stance was the only political role the press could play. But there were mounting costs to these attitudes. How long before public confidence in the press evaporated? How long before election campaigns transmuted into something so little resembling democratic choice that nothing journalists did would matter? How long before the entire enterprise of political reporting would come to feel pointless, an exercise in futility, a song for the cynical? Broder knew the clock was ticking: as politics went, so went the press.

Meanwhile, a similar range of problems appeared at the local level. Readers were disappearing. Many of the ties that bind people to their communities were loosening, which meant a looser connection to journalism. Batten caught the essence of it with his awkward phrase "community-connectedness." But here Jack Swift and Buzz Merritt had gone Broder one better; they were experimenting with changes in practice.

If these early gropings were to continue, a lot of work lay ahead. Some of it was practical: how to keep the experiment going among a wider group. Much of it was conceptual: how to find a convincing alternative to the journalist's favorite self-image—the professional bystander, watching politics and public life roll by. This description placed the press outside the action, which was a safe position, but also a weak one, in that it couldn't account for all the ways in which journalism had been incorporated into the system.

In the same article in which she remarked on the immaturity of the American voter, Katharine Seelye of the *New York Times* went on to say: "Modern American culture is loud and adversarial, and politics reflects the culture. And the ever-adversarial, conflict-seeking press helps shape the politics." Trying to be an honest observer, Seelye wound up describing her colleagues as players, people who help shape the scene they also survey. Which left hanging a question: If the press shapes the politics we have, then how can it shape the politics we need?[70]

One thing public journalism became was a reply to that question.

2 In Search of a Different Story

Journalists, Scholars, and the Public Square

In 1990, I sat in a seminar room at Columbia University with a dozen or so newspaper editors and social scientists. The topic of discussion was public disaffection, voter turnout, and related themes. The journalists never had a chance. All the social scientists were steeped in survey research, and they immediately took over, exchanging sophisticated interpretations of polling data as if they were panelists at an academic conference. I have a Ph.D. and took my mandatory course in statistics but had trouble following the discussion; the editors, of course, were lost. Intimidated by this blunt display of academic learning, they withdrew into a collective silence.

I thought the whole scene embarrassing. And I started to wonder: what (besides ordinary rudeness) made it possible for the professors to proceed as if the editors—sitting right across the table—weren't even present? Why did they assume that there was nothing to be learned from six experienced journalists, who put out a newspaper every day, knew their communities well, and had more contact with the rough and tumble of politics than did the researchers? Finally, what was I doing there? I thought I knew something about the subject, but I too remained stuck in silence as the data poured forth.

Here were two professions, both in the business of understanding the world. Yet the journalists weren't able to share in what the academics knew, and the academics weren't trying to know things in a manner that journalists could share. Why? The intellectual historian Thomas Bender offers one explanation. My colleagues were in the grip of what he calls "disciplinary professionalism," the prevailing pattern in American universities for most of the twentieth century. Things were once different, Bender notes. He describes how the founders of the modern research university inherited from the nineteenth century a lofty ideal of "civic engagement." Early graduate schools sought to "train men in the 'mental culture' that would prepare them for careers in the 'civil service,' for the 'duties of public life' generally, or as 'public journalists.'"

Here he is quoting the founders of Columbia's graduate school, which was called the Faculty of Political Science when it was established in 1881. All graduate training was thought to be "political," in the sense that it prepared men—rather, gentlemen—for service to the polity. But as early as the 1890s, the trainees of graduate schools were becoming academics rather than civic leaders. The mission of the professors had shifted "from that of preparing men for public life and toward that of reproducing their own academic selves." Bender connects this shift to the "exhaustion of the humanist ideal of a common civic culture" amid the exploding novelty of a modern society, which gave new status to technical expertise.[1]

Instead of a single faculty of political science, directing higher learning to civic life, the graduate school emerged as a collection of disciplines dominated by the natural sciences and the newly influential social sciences. The distinctive features of today's university—departments and disciplines, training for academic careers, a professional orientation toward scholarly peers— can be traced to this early shift. Bender is careful to add that the civic ideals of the founding moment had their own problems, especially in the exclusion of women from the ranks of "gentlemen" scholars. But what came after was bad, too. The new system severed the vital connection between intellect and public life (which Bender took as the title of his book on the subject). It points to something broken in a world of academic experts: easy intercourse between the scholarly life and the culture's other spheres of mind, including democratic politics, civil service, and journalism.

The problem was not that scholars ignored their duty to the larger society; rather, they reserved to themselves the right to say what it was. Their contributions to the public good "began to flow from their own self-definitions." Professors allowed their minds (and their vocabularies) to develop along a specialized path, which took them deeper into their chosen fields but away from the public square and its broader concerns. A new dynamic was at work: the professionalization of mind. It produced experts who could apply their knowledge through an alliance with decision makers in government and industry. But expertise lost its connection to problems of the whole. An expert was someone who mastered the academic literature and went on to produce more of it. "The academic ideal of the unremitting search for knowledge, whether trivial or not, was born," Bender writes.[2]

This lengthy development helps explain what was happening in the Columbia seminar room. The professors were doing what they were trained to do: sort through the knowledge their discipline commanded. This knowledge was about the public, but it did not arise out of a shared concern for public dialogue or a commitment to improving public culture—topics on which the journalists might have something to say. Seeing no common problem to tackle with the editors, nothing to learn from the journalist's way of knowing, what remained was to analyze the numbers. The academics were in charge of that, and they assumed control of the discussion, which wasn't a discussion at all.

This incident kept me thinking about the work that journalists and scholars might do together. Around the same time, the Kettering Foundation enlisted me in a series of traveling roundtables that brought together a few journalists, scholars, and foundation officials. At the initial meetings, Jack Swift would describe the Columbus experiment and I would expand on what he said, placing his efforts in a larger frame: the troubles in public life, and how they implicate the press. The "Jack and Jay show," as David Mathews of Kettering called it, was an act of persuasion still in its tryout stage when a shocking event struck: Swift shot himself in November 1990.[3]

I had gotten to know him, but of course I realized that I hardly knew him at all. Nor could I fathom the reasons for his act. While Swift was still being mourned, what he had done in his last years as a journalist took on its own life. When Kettering brought David Jones, a top editor at the *New York Times*, into contact with Dennis Dibble, editor of the *Beaver County Times* in Pennsylvania, two ends of a professional hierarchy came together. When David Broder, who joined in these discussions, followed Buzz Merritt, who described what he was doing at the *Wichita Eagle*, two minds moving in similar directions could be heard.

On the surface Merritt was a typical editor from a medium-sized city in the center of the continent, with the plain-spoken style of a man familiar with the horizon. He was more of a brooder than a talker, but when he brooded aloud, his deep and resonant voice—as good as the best radio voices—gave his words a palpable authority. Merritt had grown dissatisfied,

even bitter, with the life his profession offered. In his quest for something
better he was ready to go back to first principles and build up the edifice of
journalism again. He had put more than thirty years into the news business,
starting when he was a teenager in North Carolina. If he couldn't change it
into something he loved, then continuing his career seemed pointless. What
was craft without the romance of craft?[4]

The first time I heard him address his colleagues in a Kettering forum,
Merritt called the *Eagle* "a newspaper in search of an agenda. We believe—
have to take it on faith as this point—that if we can figure out what makes
people connected to their communities and involved, that will tell us some
things about what our agenda as journalists ought to be. My suspicion, and I
guess my fear in some sense, is that we will find out that some of those keys
[to civic involvement] are things we, as journalists, are traditionally not at all
interested in. I suggest we get very interested in them."

H. Brandt Ayers, publisher of the *Anniston Star* in Alabama, offered the
following:

> I have been continually surprised when I have attended the weekly
> question period at my local parliament, the Courthouse Barber Shop, that
> the prime minister of that institution, Jimmy Turner, is better informed
> than my political writers and my editorial group. He has called every elec-
> tion. We have called none of them. He *knows* something. He is not a
> commentator, he is a reporter. He sees a segment of society and sees them
> over time. [He has] a conversational sense of community. What do truck
> drivers think now? What do farmers believe about this set of issues and how
> do they put it?
>
> So why is Jimmy Turner so smart and we're so dumb? We know all the
> organized groups and all the organized groups are what the unorganized
> majority hates. The lobbyists for the insurance company, the spokesmen for
> various causes, they all get to talk to us. They get in the paper. They get their
> voices heard. The unorganized majority doesn't.[5]

By 1993 we were able to plot the perimeter of a discussion that might
lead somewhere. Here is what we had in hand:

- The arguments of Batten and Broder, respected figures who in their
  different ways had called for a rethinking of the journalist's basic task.
  Batten spoke about local newspapers and commercial survival, while
  Broder took aim at the national press corps and its role in politics. Both
  put democracy first; journalism, they said, flowed from it. Both thought

the civic health of the nation should be a bedrock concern for the press. Both went against the grain by calling on journalists to become more proactive. Given their long careers and national reputations, neither could be easily dismissed.

- The experiments conducted in Columbus, Wichita, and Charlotte, which illustrated the arguments Batten and Broder had put forward. These could be seen as the seedlings of a different approach; at a minimum we knew they provoked debate. If we could find other journalists trying similar things, they might learn from each other and begin to generate some momentum.

- The figure of Davis Merritt, a man willing to stand before his peers and tell them they were off on the wrong track. Merritt saw that to get others to experiment he would have to experiment on himself first. He was already doing that when I met him: first, by changing his newspaper, then by reading widely about democracy and citizenship, later by writing a book that tried to convey what he had learned.

- The Kettering Foundation, a think tank headed by David Mathews. A historian, former president of the University of Alabama, and former cabinet secretary under Gerald Ford, Mathews was well versed in democratic theory, knew government from the inside, and was committed to tapping the residual power in America's civic traditions. Kettering was not on the list of big and influential foundations. With headquarters in Dayton, Ohio, it was hardly at the center of things. The usual strategy would be to concentrate on a tightly defined or local set of problems, but Mathews took an opposite path. Kettering's mission was to open avenues to a different kind of politics, one that was "more than what politicians do," as he wrote. Without romanticizing citizens or the New England town meeting, Kettering looked to public deliberation, rather than professional expertise, as the engine for problem solving in a democracy. Reviving deliberation as a practical tool was an immense task, involving a "reconsideration of what politics is, who 'owns' it, and who is responsible for it."[6] Mathews joined in our roundtables with Merritt, Broder, and others; he quickly saw that the journalist's understanding of "what politics is" was ripe for revision. When Swift died and Merritt emerged as a stronger spokesman, Mathews became intrigued with the possibilities. He urged me to devote more and more of my time to exploring them, with Kettering's help.

• The predicament of the American press, an institution that was beginning to lose its way and needed a fresh approach. This offered an opening for discussions that might lead to reform. But that was all it was: a crack in the facade of professional confidence. It meant only that journalists could not be sure of their current course. Persuading them to try something different was another problem, but with Batten and Broder's arguments, Kettering's help, Merritt's example, and some promising experiments on record there was reason to hope. And hope was one item on our agenda.

One hope of mine was to see beyond that scene in the seminar room, where journalists and academics failed to find any common project. Merritt and I were beginning to fashion one, but on a tiny scale: a few one-day meetings. We needed a bigger arena, where many more journalists could come to terms with the drift of their profession. In late 1992, Mathews and I approached the Knight Foundation, seeking a grant that would allow us to build on the work that Kettering had sponsored. Based in Miami, with assets of $800 million in 1993, Knight was willing to fund efforts to improve American journalism, and it was particularly interested in the education of journalists. The foundation was legally independent of Knight-Ridder, but it still had ties to the company, most directly through Batten's membership on the board.[7] It was thus a logical place to turn for a proposal that drew on some of his thinking.

Mathews and I proposed a Project on Public Life and the Press, a vehicle for "going public" with an idea that seemed to be gathering momentum. The project would conduct seminars for journalists, research the relevant experiments, and work out a philosophy for those wanted to move in a civic direction. The project's money originated with journalism—specifically, the Knight publishing fortune. But its ideas could not come from journalism alone. They would have to reach outside the craft for other images of democracy, citizens, and public life. Fortunately, there was a place to go for a more inspired vision: the university, where scholars and critics were doing good work on related subjects.[8]

In 1989, the same year as my Des Moines talk and Batten's speech on community life, a lot of exciting things happened. The Berlin Wall fell, democracy returned to part of Eastern Europe, and Chinese students occupied

Tiananmen Square, erecting an icon of their hopes, the Goddess of Democracy, fashioned after the Statue of Liberty. The inspiration other actors drew from American history caused a host of observers here to comment on a painful irony: with democracy triumphant around the globe, it seemed to be falling into disrepair at home.

In the scholarly circles I traveled—the academic field of media studies—this irony was noted, but noting it seemed almost sufficient. We had our own work to do, the task of understanding media, and while it involved a lot of thinking about citizens and politics, this was a far cry from doing something to reconnect them. Everyone I knew thought the media weren't serving democracy well. But most everyone also felt that deep structural forces were at work: capitalism for one, the privatizing force of American society for another. There was no shortage of theories to explain why the media were the way they were, no dearth of talented critics discussing such developments as the commercialization of culture, the weakening habits of literacy, the rising power of television, or the journalist's constricted view of the world.

As Bender's work suggested, scholarly inquiry could proceed on these subjects without reaching the people who worked in the media complex, or others who worried about its influence. Determining the impact of this colossus is what counted; having an impact was generally discounted, for who could hope to influence such a sprawling and profit-driven system? There was one exception to this attitude: the students we encountered who wanted careers in the media. There, a professor could have a real effect. Whatever hopes we had that our work might make a difference probably rested on classroom encounters with the next generation.

In that same hectic year, 1989, the German philosopher Jürgen Habermas published an English translation of his key work, *The Structural Transformation of the Public Sphere.* The book was part of a wave of scholarly interest in an ideal handed down from the Enlightenment: that through reasoned discussion and open exchange, assisted by a free press, citizens could decide among themselves what direction their affairs should take. This was the sketch of politics implied in the notion of "public opinion," which was received into politics in the mid–eighteenth century. Habermas traced the event to what he called its "carrier" class, the literate bourgeoisie in England and France, which won a place for itself on the political stage by upholding the verdict of public discussion against the traditional authority of kings claiming divine right, or Parliament speaking for, but not with, the people.

Although this eighteenth-century public was small and exclusive, the ideal it promoted—reasoned discussion among informed citizens in public spaces—tended toward the universal. "The public" may have started out as the literate, propertied, and mostly male inhabitants of the eighteenth-century coffee house or salon. But with the drive for universal suffrage in the nineteenth and twentieth centuries, the term expanded to cover the general population in its political capacity. "Public opinion" came to mean the views of the entire nation, not just the chattering classes. At the same time, however, the sphere in which public discussion happened was transformed, as Habermas put it. It became subject to all the pressures of modern publicity: mass advertising, government propaganda, a commercialized press, and the political machinery of a competitive society in which some speakers had vastly more power than others.[9]

Under these conditions, what had become of the original Enlightenment ideal? Students of the public sphere—and there were many in universities during the 1980s and 1990s—entered into heated arguments on this question. To some, the public sphere as sketched by Habermas was a dangerous myth. It had never described our actual history, which was a record of conflict and struggle, not a series of civilized debates. To others the public sphere was still a powerful ideal, admittedly awkward as a description of the contemporary scene, but enormously important as a standard to which a mature democracy could aspire. Most of those who joined in these exchanges agreed that "the public" was not the same thing as a mass audience. Nor could it be equated with a pollster's random sample, or a newspaper's circulation figures. The public ought to be joining in politics—by voting, surely, but also by voicing its views, getting into the game, becoming an actor and discussant. And the public sphere, to be truly public, was not just a "marketplace of ideas." Something more was required.

A public was supposed to be in discussion with itself. Was ours? Its members were supposed to venture into public to participate. Did they? Debate was supposed to turn on the force of the better argument, not the din of the louder voice or the appeal of the packaged slogan. Did this standard still make sense? A public was radically inclusive; if too many were left out or declined to enter, something was clearly wrong. In a society so commercialized, in a political culture so consumed with impression management, in an age of suburban living, technologized experience, and information overload, what had become of "public opinion," which was supposed to emerge from the clamor of democracy with recommending force? Was there any hope for a genuine public sphere, or were we fated to live amid what Habermas called "publicity that is staged for show or manipulation," overseen by an elite class that substituted its own talk for the deliberations of a broader public?[10]

In asking these questions—and arriving at no firm conclusions—contemporary thinkers were resuming a debate that had first emerged in the 1920s, when two of America's most prominent intellectuals engaged in a spirited exchange on the public and its recurrent difficulties. One of the participants had been Walter Lippmann, journalist, social philosopher, and co-founder of the *New Republic,* who was well on his way to becoming the most famous political commentator of the century. Lippmann belonged to a generation of American liberals who were chastened by the events of World War I and its aftermath, especially the ease with which public sentiment had been manipulated by wartime propaganda. In *Public Opinion,* published in 1922, he took a skeptical stance toward the Enlightenment vision of the public.

Lippmann's point of departure was the opaque quality of modern society. The events of our time were huge in scale, complicated beyond measure, and largely inaccessible. Most people are busy trying to live their lives; they have neither time nor motivation to study the "unseen environment" in any depth. Nor do they regularly venture into public for serious discussion. Instead, they rely on hazy impressions and half-conscious stereotypes in forming their views. Politicians knew this, of course. The "manufacture of consent" was their trade and the modern means of communication added mightily to its force. As the Great War and its aftermath showed, public opinion could be engineered by governments trying to whip up nationalist sentiment.

The press was supposed to correct for all these defects by presenting a truer picture of the world. But journalism had to compete for attention against all the other arts of persuasion. Besides, the newspaper was a commercial venture, not a public service; it would inevitably side with the audience and its limitations—the "buying public," as Lippmann called it. And even a steady diet of serious news wasn't sufficient, for "news" was not "truth"; rather, it was a report on events and eruptions, which often misled about the broader currents below.

The whole thing was unworkable, Lippmann declared. It was foolish to expect average citizens to have a reliable opinion on all the issues of the day. The "omnicompetent" citizen was a joke.[11] In 1925, Lippmann went further, calling the public a "phantom," a delusion of naive democrats who refused to think clearly about the matter. Public opinion is "itself an irrational force" that should have no directing presence in political life. "With the substance of the problem it can do nothing but meddle ignorantly or tyrannically." If ordinary citizens have any part to play, it is to offer an up or down verdict at election time ("throw the bums out") or to be mobilized behind a broad shift in direction. "Insiders" are the ones who know about public issues. The bulk of the citizenry remain "outsiders," unlikely and unable to participate in decisions.[12]

Against the soaring rhetoric of American democracy, Lippmann reminded readers of the limitations of the average citizen, the stubborn realities of human nature, the daunting complexity of modern life, and the prosaic facts of manipulation. He put his faith elsewhere, in well-informed experts, who might provide leaders with better and better facts on which to base their decisions. Not popular opinion but a more reliable and relied-upon social science would have recommending force. The public "must be put in its place," he wrote. An exceedingly modest place it was.[13]

John Dewey, by then America's senior philosopher and a fellow contributor to the *New Republic,* replied to Lippmann's *Public Opinion,* which he called an indictment of contemporary democracy, the most effective yet written. But why indict democracy, when what it most needs is improvement? Democracy for Dewey meant not a system of government but a society organized around certain principles: that every individual has something to contribute, that people are capable of making their own decisions, that given the chance they can understand their predicament well enough to puzzle through it, that the world is knowable if we teach ourselves how study and discuss it. Time and again Dewey argued that to be a democrat meant to have faith in people's capacities, whatever their recent performance.[14] In *The Public and Its Problems,* written in 1927, he upheld these beliefs against Lippmann's caustic treatment.

The reason we have governments at all, Dewey argued, is that we live in an interdependent world, where action in one sphere affects the outcome in others. We lead private lives, but we cannot live in a privatized world: our problems are inevitably public, meaning interrelated, and so must our opinions be. A "public" is a name for people who share certain problems and a common stake in their resolution. Publics come into their own when this shared stake is understood and talked about, in a fruitful way.

Public opinion in its genuine form is what people conclude as they come into fuller possession of their problems through intelligence, inquiry, and discussion. Dewey agreed that Americans had a hard time doing so in a complicated world where they were blitzed with misleading messages. As a practical matter, the public was in trouble. But he described it as "inchoate" rather than illusory, unformed but not impossible. It would emerge in its modern guise only if politics, communities, schools, culture, and the educated classes did their jobs well.[15]

The job to be done involved art as much as information, for engaging people in the events of the day meant finding material that not only informed them but touched their souls. Some of the talent that went into selling products and engineering mass consent would have to go to "creation of adequate opinion on public matters," Dewey thought. Unfortunately, he never got beyond this kind of suggestion to describe how the art of presentation might be put to more public use. But if we imagine the force of a great documentary film, a powerful speech like Martin Luther King's "I Have a Dream," or a moment of riveting political television, we can grasp what Dewey meant when he wrote: "The highest and most difficult kind of inquiry and a subtle, delicate, vivid and responsive art of communication must take possession of the machinery of transmission and breathe life into it. When the machine age has thus perfected its machinery it will be a means of life and not its despotic master. Democracy will [then] come into its own."[16]

Lippmann's conclusion was premature and his solution illusory, Dewey felt. Until we had tried to bring the public out of "eclipse," no one could say what its limitations were. Nor could experts, no matter how well informed, substitute for the public's best judgment. How can experts know what the rest of us want? And how can we ourselves know unless we join in serious conversation about the public good? "Democracy must begin at home," Dewey declared, "and its home is the neighborly community." Through the participatory medium of public talk, people learn what they have in common and take ownership of the problems they share. Their experience begins to instruct them, as much as information in the popular press. Public opinion results from this experience. It is a "we" voice, not an aggregate of "I"s, as opinion polling would later have it.[17]

The debate ended with no obvious winner. Lippmann's statement of the problem spoke eloquently to our feeling of being overwhelmed by events and disillusioned by modern politics. (He was also a more talented writer.) In the years since *Public Opinion*, the problems before a modern nation have only grown more technical, harder to grasp for even the educated person, let alone the beleaguered citizen in the street. Lippmann knew of movies and newsreels in his time. Had he observed commercial television at work he might have added several counts to his indictment. And yet his solution—to rely on disinterested social scientists in place of public opinion—seemed drastic, even antidemocratic. A world of insiders (who know about politics) and outsiders (who know little, but vote) seemed to redefine democracy away from the ideal of self-government. How many such revisions were needed before democracy became something else entirely, the rule of an elite adept at manipulating the votes of a distracted populace?[18]

Dewey's faith in public capacities was inspiring, his dream of a more vital public culture unrivaled in its reach and intensity. But he did little to specify how his dream could be made to work.[19] Perhaps the "neighborly community" was the public's best breeding ground, but how were we to reverse the decline of such communities in twentieth-century America? Perhaps there was a way to immerse the public in a deeper understanding of its affairs, but with the machinery of communication in private hands, what were we supposed to do? Overturn modern capitalism?

When I first came upon this exchange, what stood out were its implications for the press: What could journalists reasonably expect of citizens? Up-or-down decisions at election time, or participation in a fuller and richer public life? Was striving for an informed and engaged public an illusion, or was the public merely "inchoate"? If the press wanted to do its part for democracy, should it focus on government and its decisions, as Lippmann did, or should it emphasize the civic climate in which a population may become a public, as Dewey suggested? And what of the recent interest in the "public sphere"? Were journalists just cogs in the system or could they have a hand in strengthening that sphere? These were important questions. While journalists might employ a stray quote from Walter Lippmann, they weren't accustomed to debating the issues his most famous work had left behind. They acted as if the problem of the public had been put behind them, given a sufficient answer in the intervening years.

They were wrong, according to James Carey, one of the nation's leading communication scholars. In a series of influential essays during the 1980s, he helped revive interest in Dewey's work among academic students of the press. Carey described how the public had been "conceptually evacuated" after the disputes of the 1920s. The problem wasn't solved; instead, "intellectual and professional work on the public went into eclipse." In political science the key term became "interests," groups who organized themselves to exert political muscle. Interest-group pluralism, as professors called it, appeared to put the problem of the public on permanent hold.[20] Private interests did battle in the marketplace of ideas and the competition for power. Politicians tried to please the groups they needed to stay in office. Viewed this way, democracy could be said to "work" despite all the difficulties Lippmann and Dewey had identified.

As Carey noted, "interest groups operate, by definition, in the private sector." The stance they take toward public life is "essentially a propagandistic and manipulative one." They maneuver for competitive advantage, try to impress the relevant audiences. The public is not who they are. It is the people whose opinions they try to sway or swing with. "In interest group theory, the public ceases to have a real existence," he wrote. It fades into a "statistical artifact," an audience of "individual opinion holders" subjected to the "pressure of mass publicity."[21] Politics is taken over by groups who try to use popular sentiment, the news media, and the political process to their own advantage. To study politics is to determine "who gets what, where, when, and how," which became the dominant perspective in political science.[22]

The public gets eclipsed in this view, but not because its members are uninvolved; after all, the interest groups are us. But it is "us" as senior citizens, teacher's unions, gun control groups and groups that abhor gun control, pro-Israel Jews and anti-abortion Christians, the fractured, contentious and competitive universe of interests represented at the capital, joined by the lobbyists from Exxon, the telecommunications industry, agricultural combines, the American Medical Association, independent truckers, and thousands of others—all trying to promote their cause within the competitive field of the two major parties.

If politics is organized interests battling it out, how can people arrive at a sense of the common interest? And what about public challenges that aren't represented well in the capital—or at city hall? How do citizens come to engage each other in reciprocal fashion, so that the rising din of interests being defended doesn't drown out the interests we share, the problems we need to solve together? And if professionals and experts do the day-to-day work of politics, how do the rest of us get into the game? These were the challenges that had concerned Dewey and still concerned Carey, among others.[23] And they ought to concern journalists, who operate in the public's name. As Carey wrote: "The god term of journalism—the be-all and end-all, the term without which the entire enterprise fails to make sense—is the public. Insofar as journalism is grounded, it is grounded in the public.

Insofar as journalism has a client, the client is the public. . . . The canons of journalism originate in and flow from the relationship of the press to the public. . . . But for all the ritual incantation of the public in the rhetoric of journalism, no one quite knows any longer what the public is, or where one might find it, or even whether it exists any longer."

Contemporary criticism of the press did not address this difficulty. Critics might try to rid journalism of some of its questionable practices or critique the forms of bias the press exhibits. But they did not focus on the central question remaining from the 1920s, which was how to engage and enliven—rather than merely inform—a genuine public. Carey wrote: "The real problem of journalism is that the term which grounds it—the public—has been dissolved, dissolved in part by journalism." The difficulty now was to reconstitute the public within the journalist's imagination. "How are we going to do that?" he asked.

The American press was typically silent on such questions. The silence dates from the same period as Lippmann and Dewey's exchanges. Like so many other status-seeking Americans, journalists in the 1920s and 1930s were eager to professionalize. University-based training emerged in these years, along with codes of conduct among professional associations like the American Society of Newspaper Editors (formed in 1922) and the group I met in Des Moines, the Associated Press Managing Editors (begun in 1931). In the professional outlook as it took shape, there was little room for Dewey's concerns. Professionals were people authorized to know in place of citizens who were too busy or overwhelmed to know.[24]

The journalist could claim elevated status as an expert commentator (a type Lippmann embodied), as a superior judge of what counted as news (the authority of the *New York Times* begins here), or as a professional "adversary" keeping government in check (most nobly the *Washington Post* during Watergate). In the long interval between the 1920s and the 1980s, these became common aspirations in an increasingly professionalized press. All placed the public at a comfortable distance; all were compatible with Lippmann's skepticism about the average person's competence. Service to a public that was assumed to know little and care less might sound like a contradiction, but it was a manageable one for most journalists, especially given the rise of "objectivity" as official doctrine. It, too, dates from the 1920s and 1930s. Objectivity permits journalists to speak of "informing the public" without worrying about how a public gets formed in the first place. It makes the issue in journalism the quality of information the press provides, not the uses to which people put it. Equally important was the science of opinion polling, which also began its march to prominence in the 1930s. By learning to accept the polls as an approximation of public opinion, journalists "solved" the problem of the public, at least to their own satisfaction. Today the polls offer the impression of a fully formed public on virtually any issue; publish a poll and "public opinion" springs magically to life. As political scientist Benjamin Ginsberg notes, "Poll results and public opinion are terms that are [now] used almost synonymously."[25]

Journalism hadn't really resolved the problem of the public. It had simply moved on. Objectivity and professionalism in the press, along with the transformation of the public into an artifact of opinion research, combined to bury the issues of the 1920s.[26] Clearly there were readers and viewers on the receiving end of the news; clearly they voted at election time and expressed their views in polls. So where was the problem? Scholars were eager to answer, but there were few points of contact between their work and the culture of the press.

The more I read of Carey, Dewey, and Thomas Bender, the more convinced I was that, whatever strengths still held in Lippmann's analysis, Dewey's direction was the better one for now.[27] As Carey would later say at one of the seminars in the Project on Public Life and the Press, journalists could start telling themselves a different story about who they are and what they do. Defending the "public's right to know" before a secretive government, countering the manipulative discourse of the media age, taking an adversarial stance toward anyone in the way of truth—this story, Carey said, "has had a terrific run." It was well adapted to conditions that had held through the 1960s and 1970s. "It's not that the story of the adversarial press is wrong," he noted. Nor was Lippmann wrong in his analysis. Rather, both had become "overadapted." They took up too much space in the journalist's mind, leaving little room for other concerns, like seeing the public into fuller existence.

In recent years journalists have been admitting to themselves that "in our lifetime we've become very powerful," Carey observed. "We shouldn't let anyone know about it, because we're a little embarrassed about having that power. But if the choices are to be powerful or powerless, let's be powerful."

> That's the choice that's been made by journalists . . . being better informed, knowing things that others don't know, always having better facts, better data, better insight. There's a tendency to believe the worst about public

figures and the worst about other people. . . . But what would a journalist be and do if they saw themselves not as someone who informed others or knew more than others—which are both very risky assumptions—but as just someone else who had a voice, one voice in a conversation of many? If there are not a lot of people talking, if you're talking by yourself and you're not hearing anything, then you are no longer engaged in a conversation—and don't believe it's because the people out there believe you, trust you, find you credible, accede to your power. They're more likely to be saying, "The hell with them all. If this is the way the game is going to be played, I'm going to go off in pursuit of private pleasures. I will concentrate on those parts of my life I can control rather than play a game in which I don't have a real role." I think that's the way the relationship has been going.

And how realistic was that? "We've got to cook up a new tale," Carey concluded, a better story about journalism and democracy.[28] Without tossing overboard what was still worthy in the adversarial stance, the revised tale would give citizens a different place in the action, as other people trying to figure out what's going on, discussing events and decisions themselves, joining in where possible, assisted by journalists who talk with, rather than at, them.

In theories about the public sphere, in the work of writers like Carey, and in the reply Dewey gave to Lippmann, stood the outlines of another way of thinking about the public duty of the press. As some in the news trade, like David Broder, began to question their roles in a faltering political system, and as I encountered a handful of others, like Jack Swift and Buzz Merritt, who had begun to experiment with changes in practice, the concerns of the 1920s suddenly seemed alive again.

And so did a way of addressing them. It was to mix Batten and Broder with Dewey and Carey, add Merritt's reflections to my own, find a language that isn't airy or obscure, fashion with it a story, or a sequence of arguments for change, add illustrations from the field, and take the whole thing public, bring it out into the open in as many forums as you can find. As the different story gets around, people react and, by reacting, push the idea along. There was a method here, although I was only dimly aware of it at first. Rather than persuade an entire profession of the soundness of the idea, you multiply the number of platforms from which the sound is heard. You get more people to speak it, and the "it" becomes what they're saying and doing.

This I took to be a more "civic" approach in press scholarship, since it presumed that the scholar's work waited on similar work done by others who were not scholars but equal partners in the inquiry. In settling on such a course, I was borrowing the spirit of America's only homegrown philosophical tradition: the pragmatism of William James and John Dewey. In the pragmatic view, a good idea is good because you can do things with it. The more you can do, the better the idea. Note how different this is from a scholarly field's typical test, where the stronger idea is the one that shows a firmer grasp of the evidence, a more powerful conceptual scheme, a deeper grounding in the academic literature.

A pragmatist, whose job as a thinker is to be useful, not authoritative, judges "strength" by what happens to a notion when it is introduced to the people for whom it is made. *Here's something you can use to get where you're going.* The more people who do use it—what became public journalism—the more they deepen the meaning or "truth" of it. As William James wrote, to realize an idea's practical worth is to "set it at work within the stream of your experience." A successful idea "appears less as a solution, then, than as a program for more work," an "indication of the ways in which existing realities may be changed." He added: "Any idea upon which we can ride, so to speak; any idea that will carry us prosperously from any one part of our experience to any other part," meets the pragmatic test. Public journalism was meant to be something on which some in the press could ride, moving from one set of troubles—their own—to larger problems in the public square.[29]

But you had to start somewhere. From 1990 through 1992, I began operating as what an earlier age had called a publicist, circulator of arguments in advance of a cause. By 1993 the cause had a name: public journalism. Merritt and I began using the term when we got tired of saying "this thing" or "what we're talking about" or just "it." We considered "community journalism," but that sounded small-town. Democracy-cultivating journalism? No. So we settled on public journalism and went ahead. If the first act in going public was to give the idea a name, the second was to put it into readable form. The medium we selected—a published pamphlet, several thousand words in length—had a long and honorable history. We half jokingly called it our manifesto, as if we were sounding a call to arms. Of course, the thing we were trying to rally people around barely existed. At the time, we had one journalist who said he was off on a different approach, and one professor who agreed with him. "Public journalism lives!" we announced. Whether it would or not was an open question—or, as I have termed it, a pragmatic test.

With approval of the grant from the Knight Foundation, we found ourselves in possession of an idea and money to spend on it. Merritt, who was not an applicant for the grant, was enlisted as an unofficial adviser. But in another sense he was the central figure in the Project on Public Life and the Press. The project's aim was to persuade others to move in the direction he was going—not to parrot what Merritt said, but to ask themselves a similar question: how can I find a way of doing journalism that helps reconnect people to public life?

Our "manifesto," an initial statement of purpose, was a self-conscious—some might say pretentious—act, for it openly called others to work we ourselves planned to do. This principle proved to be of enormous value to the idea, which we sought to develop through classically public means: argument, experiment, persuasion, partnership, publicity, debate. All the adjectival meanings of "public"—open, accessible, common, pertaining to the whole—trailed along with the name "public journalism," and we had to learn to take these seriously. What public journalism would eventually become no one could say. There could be no copyright on the idea, no official version, no right way to do it, only better or worse attempts to explain and experiment. Public journalism would have to be owned by all who felt the possibilities in it; and it existed only to give direction to those possibilities.

Our pamphlet tried to express these principles through a rhetoric of urgency. Merritt and I composed a joint introduction.

. . . .

Journalists in the United States are at a critical point in the history of their craft. Threatened on one side by declining readership and new economic pressures in the media industry, they face a different kind of threat from the fraying of community ties, the rising disgust with politics, and a spreading sense of impotence and hopelessness among Americans frustrated by the failures of their democratic system. If this second threat isn't noticed and taken seriously, American journalism may lose control of its future, which is bound up with the strength of public life in all of its forms.

No one knows how the majority of journalists will respond to the challenges ahead. A substantial number are clearly disillusioned about their roles and concerned about the survival of a free press. But wary of binding attachments, suspicious of joining "causes," they may fail to muster any response at all, while the conditions that once gave their work its central importance change drastically or disappear. Indeed, it is no longer unthinkable that a press regarded as unnecessary or merely aggravating could lose its claim on the Constitution—at least in the eyes of the public. Public journalism seeks to respond to this threat, but not by ingratiating itself to a fickle audience, as some have fruitlessly tried. Instead the aim is to fortify the public trust that comes with the special privileges granted by the First Amendment.

Today, the only way for journalists to protect that trust is to strengthen, through journalism, America's civic culture, by which we mean the forces that bind people to their communities, draw them into politics and public affairs, and cause them to see "the system" as theirs—public property rather than the playground of insiders or political professionals. At the level of national affairs and in the life of the local community, the press remains an influential force; and while it is not as powerful as some of its critics suggest, it retains a unique franchise. No other institution reaches as widely across the community in such a regular fashion, focusing daily attention on areas of common interest.

It has long been recognized that the power of the press can be used for good or ill; rarely is it noted that the power itself depends on people's willingness to attend to current issues, take responsibility for public things, and recognize the importance of what they hold in common. Even the most brilliant spotlight can be ignored if what it illuminates is no longer regarded as public property. So it is not only the economy of the newspaper that is at stake when readers turn away; it is the foundation of journalism as a public practice. This foundation—a common interest in common affairs—cannot be secured simply by improving the presentation of news, or attending more carefully to what busy readers want. For unless readers also want to be citizens, journalism cannot meet its public responsibilities. As important as they are, strategies to recapture readers will always be incomplete without another sort of strategy, aimed at re-engaging citizens in public affairs and the life of the community. . . .

We are far from believing that journalists or journalism can cure what ails politics and public life in America. That would ascribe too much power to the press. Nor do we contend that ills and ailments are everything of note in the current scene. That would be cynical and alarmist. Our claim is a more modest one: if changes are necessary for America to meet its problems and strengthen its democracy, then journalism is one of the agencies that must change. That is the conviction on which public journalism stands.
—From Jay Rosen and Davis Merritt, Jr., *Public Journalism: Theory and Practice* (Dayton: Kettering Foundation, 1994)

We had hoped that the entire pamphlet would be a jointly authored piece. But the strain of our different starting places proved too great. So Merritt and I settled for the joint introduction above, then wrote our own versions of what public journalism might be. Mine tried to widen the lens through which the troubles in journalism were seen, in a way that drew on Habermas, Dewey, and other thinkers, without becoming drunk, so to speak—that is, tipping over into a strictly academic discourse.

· ·

Good journalism requires more than good journalists—more even than enlightened ownership, First Amendment protections, and a strong economic base. For without an engaged and concerned public, even the most public-minded press cannot do its job. Thus, the involvement of people in the affairs of their community, their interest in political discussion, their willingness to abandon a spectator's role and behave as citizens—all form the civic capital on which the enterprise of the press is built. To live off that capital without trying to replenish it is a dangerous course for journalists to follow, but this is precisely the predicament of the American press today. It addresses a "public" it does little to help create.

A public is something more than a market for information, an audience for spectacle, or a pollster's random sample. Publics are formed when we turn from our private and separate affairs to face common problems, and to face each other in dialogue and discussion. Whether this turn will be made is always an open question. In a free society, people are free to ignore civic affairs; they can easily distance themselves from discussion and debate. In a busy society, it is often difficult to find the time—or, perhaps, the motivation—to enter into public life. Journalists can recognize these facts without submitting to them. "The public," in whose name all journalists ply their trade, is best understood as an achievement of good journalism—its intended outcome rather than its assumed audience.

Public journalism tries to place the journalist within the political community as a responsible member with a full stake in public life. But it does not deny the important differences between journalists and other actors, including political leaders, interest groups and citizens themselves. . . . In a word, public journalists want public life to work. In order to make it work they are willing to declare an end to their neutrality on certain questions—for example: whether people participate, whether a genuine debate takes place when needed, whether a community comes to grips with its problems, whether politics earns the attention it claims.

Toward specific proposals, particular candidates, the political agenda of this party or that interest group, the journalist's traditional pledge of neutrality remains intact. This pledge is important; it separates "doing journalism" from "doing politics," and keeps the press from trying to dominate the scene. And yet the stance of neutrality draws its meaning from certain conditions: the participation by others in public affairs, the presence of debate and discussion within the community. . . . If silence is heard where dialogue should be, if the vitality of public life dissipates, neutrality devolves into a meaningless pose. It loses its purpose, which is to make a healthy politics possible. Thus, it is no violation of the principle of neutrality for journalists to insist that discussion occur, to encourage broader participation, to help others join in the duties and joys of civic life, to openly advocate an informed but also engaged public.

—From Jay Rosen, "Public Journalism: First Principles," in *Public Journalism: Theory and Practice* (Dayton: Kettering Foundation, 1994)

. . . .

By the time this statement was published in early 1994, the field of activity had widened considerably. Prompted by discussions with James Batten of Knight-Ridder and her own interest in reviving civic life, another foundation president, Rebecca Rimel of the Pew Charitable Trusts, had grown interested in a similar brand of press reform. In early 1993, Rimel asked Edward M. Fouhy, a veteran journalist and former network news executive, to survey the field and recommend a course of action. Fouhy came across the Knight-Ridder experiments in Wichita and Columbus and learned of the Kettering discussions. On the strength of Fouhy's recommendation, Batten's urgings, and Rimel's own ideas, Pew decided to enter the same territory that Kettering, Merritt, and I were exploring with the Knight Foundation's assistance.

In the fall of 1993, Rimel announced a $4.5 million initiative that became the Pew Center for Civic Journalism in Washington. Fouhy was named to run it. He quickly brought in Jan Schaffer, a former reporter and editor at the *Philadelphia Inquirer*, to assist him. Now we had three foundations involved: Kettering, Knight, and Pew. And we added two experienced and respected journalists. In his long career, Fouhy had moved to the center of Washington journalism's crafting of politics into story. He had been a news executive at all three major networks: ABC, NBC, and CBS. In 1992 he was executive producer for the presidential debates. Fouhy knew many of the major players in elite journalism and national politics; more important, he understood the upper reaches of press culture from the inside.[30]

Together, Fouhy and Schaffer could claim standing in the profession that neither I nor Merritt had. They turned this to quick advantage, by pulling into the experiment many broadcast journalists who were urged to join with newspapers in local partnerships. The significance of this move was clear: a cross-media partnership built around civic goals (like generating discussion) declared that competition in the news trade had its limits. There were some things that journalists working for different companies could do together, despite the fact that they were after the same audience. Newspapers and TV stations could complement each other's strengths, even as they competed for good stories.

Some of the partnerships worked well, some didn't. But the fact that they existed at all was due to Pew's farsighted view that broadcast journalism could not remain outside the initiative. When Ed Fouhy talked to broadcast producers, they listened, because he knew all about the pressures they faced. He felt strongly that TV news could do much more for democracy, and he had his own stories to tell in service to that idea. Jan Schaffer had been part of a Pulitzer Prize–winning investigative team at the *Inquirer*. She knew what it meant to go after people with tough, critical reporting. Reporters had a phrase for it: "holding their feet to the fire." Schaffer had done that, to high honor. And she never let her "civic" philosophy run counter to the aggressive style of digging and questioning that had drawn so many talented people into journalism. This made her a most convincing advocate.

The four of us were soon joined by another full-time worker for the idea. Lisa Austin was a former reporter in Wichita under Merritt who also had a degree in public policy from Harvard. Like so many others we would meet in the years ahead, Austin had thought about leaving the newsroom behind because she was frustrated by the narrow range of possibilities. I hired her as research director of the Project on Public Life and the Press, and she quickly made herself into a networking point and idea source for those who wanted to learn more about public journalism—which now had a second title, the Pew Center's "civic journalism."

With Pew's entry, along with Knight's and Kettering's commitment, the idea had gained more than $5 million in capital. It was gaining human capital, as well. Merritt, Fouhy, Schaffer, and Austin were all journalists at heart. They wanted to change their business because it was a business they loved. And they knew many people in the press fraternity. Other institutions soon got involved. The American Press Institute (API) was a leading center for professional development in the newspaper industry. Most editors we met had been to API several times for workshops with their peers. By holding seminars there, the Project on Public Life and the Press could introduce unfamiliar themes in a familiar setting. In addition to API, the Poynter Institute for Media Studies—a think tank in St. Petersburg, Florida, with a similar mission—became active in the field, although it never named what it was doing public or civic journalism.[31]

What had emerged by early 1994, then, was a mix of ideas, people, money, and institutions around a core message:

- public life was in trouble and so was the press;
- a double disconnect had emerged, between journalists and the citizenry, on one hand, and between the American people and their common business, on the other;
- it was time to do something about both problems, in the interest of the craft and the public interest;
- some people in journalism were doing something about it and what they had said and tried was worth contemplating;
- you, too, can join in the experiment, which is the only way it will progress.

Going public with public journalism meant losing possession of it. As the idea became the property of many actors, its properties multiplied. Public, civic, or community-connected journalism—all were floating about—was now a call to action, a story about troubles in the press, a sequence of arguments for change, and a conversation about all of this, unfolding in different venues. It was a Poynter Institute agenda item, a Kettering Foundation project, a Washington-based Pew Center, an experiment in Wichita and other places, a fund for supporting further experiments (which was one part of the Pew grant and would later generate its own controversy).[32]

Here is Fouhy, speaking from experience about change.

. . . .

Like you, I have been a journalist all of my life and until recently never really examined all of the assumptions I had made about what news is, how it is reported, what is the proper role for journalists in a democratic society.

But after spending the last 14 months looking at those assumptions, looking at the state of our society and the place journalists have in it, I have come to the conclusion that we have lost touch with our readers and viewers because our values are badly out of synch with theirs. If we do not change we stand a very good chance of becoming increasingly irrelevant, except as another form of entertainment in a society where there are already many more attractive forms of entertainment.

. . . If we continue to treat our readers and viewers as sheer numbers, demographic groups with greater or lesser purchasing power, instead of citizens who have a need for information so they can make decisions about their communities, then we should expect people to retreat into their own narrow concerns. . . . But consider what that means for our society. We would no longer be able to gather the number of citizens required to make critical decisions. Civic life, essential to self-government, would be destroyed.

—From Ed Fouhy, remarks to Lee Enterprises editors conference, Tucson, Arizona, April 17, 1994

. . . .

In November 1993, Gil Thelen, editor of the *State* in Columbia, South Carolina, wrote to readers about the different story some journalists were beginning to tell themselves. "Newspapers," he said, "are thinking anew about their community roles and responsibilities." Some now realize their "interest in creating public 'spaces' where citizens can intelligently wrestle with the great issues of our day." Thelen wrote of keeping the community "in conversation with itself." He added:

David Mathews of the Kettering Foundation says, "We need more institutions to provide space for the public to shape its initial and individual reactions into more reflective and shared judgments."

This community-focused journalism has a name now, Public Journalism, and it holds a wealth of possibilities: energizing residents to become citizens; reuniting those energized citizens with newspapers, their essential source of information and meaning; using that fusion to reinvigorate communities; reasserting the primacy and legitimacy of newspapers in public life, reimagining a journalism of hope that lifts both readers and journalists.[33]

Chris Peck, editor of the *Spokesman-Review* in Spokane, Washington, was one of the journalists I met after my 1989 talk in Des Moines. In a February 1994 column, Peck announced an experiment with his paper's editorial pages. "Public journalism does not supplant solid, unflinching reporting about the day's events, or the need of the press to hold government accountable," he wrote. But it recognizes an additional task: creating a civic climate in which people can be heard and their concerns can be addressed. The *Spokesman-Review*, he said, was taking a radical step—radical for a daily newspaper. It had abolished the title of editorial page editor and replaced it with two "interactive editors." Their assignment: "reconnecting the editorial pages to the communities this newspaper serves." Peck explained:

> If you have something you want your community to hear, the inter-active editors will help you write and get your views into print.
>
> If there are issues that need public debate, things like consolidating government, or forest management, or low-income housing, the interactive editors will help set up a public forum for these debates.
>
> And, rather that assuming that the newspaper has the right opinion on everything, we've decided to open our editorial opinion columns to opposing views, written either by our staff or others.[34]

This was an initiative that met Carey's urgings, although as far as I knew Peck had not read Carey. Journalism should be imagined more on the model of conversation, Carey had written. "Journalists are merely part of the conversation; one partner with the rest of us—no more and no less. This is a humble role for journalism—or at least it seems so at first blush—but in fact what we need is a humble journalism." When editorial page editors assist people in getting their views into print, journalism becomes a partner in public conversation. When the newspaper's editorials are not the final word on the subject for that day, but just one voice among others, then the more humble journalism Carey had imagined was coming alive in Spokane.[35]

As public journalism drifted, with different names attached, across a variety of screens—newspaper pages, manifestos, conferences, seminars—it began meeting the pragmatic test. Some journalists were finding it useful. They were getting in on the action: sending up their own versions for comment, hearing reactions from their peers, conducting trials and experiments, quoting others whose thoughts were also afloat. From 1994 on, the most important part of the launch phase got under way. In dozens of towns and cities around the country, people began doing public journalism—as the next chapter will illustrate.

Part Two / Practice

3

Applying Practice to Theory

Case Studies in Public Journalism

From 1994 on, I quickly learned that not everyone saw public journalism the way I did, which was fortunate for me because I had only a partial glimpse of it. There were many journalists now contributing to the idea, but it wasn't necessarily public journalism to them—just "what we did in Tallahassee." As I moved among these people, I made the pleasant discovery that I rarely knew what I was talking about. There was always something happening in Dayton or Portland or Norfolk that sent the notion in another direction or showed how thin my understanding of it was.

I mean emotionally thin. Journalists were doing things that felt un-familiar, even dangerous in some of their darker moments. They were also feeling unbound, sprung from traps, alive to a fresh sensibility. For a few, there were moments of self-revelation, when they came to say: "I used to think this way, now I see it differently." But when a reporter for the *Charlotte Observer* stood up at a press conference during the 1992 campaign and said to a Senate candidate something like, "I have a question here from a citizen in Rock Hill," the entire room turned to see who this interloper was. At that moment, we were no longer talking about a "public philosophy," or some other thought maneuver, but a person's standing among peers, a reputation in the balance. We were talking, too, about careers and accomplishments, opportunities to advance, what employers and bosses might think.

My employer was New York University. As far as I could tell, it wanted me to be doing what I was doing: getting grants, writing articles. And even if the deans didn't approve (an unlikely event), I had the luxury of tenure, which gave me far more freedom of thought than the people I was pushing to think freely. "This may cost me my job," Buzz Merritt recalled telling his wife on the evening in 1990 when he decided to drop the conventions of election reporting and start over. He did not know if the executives in his company would approve, if the reporting staff would buy in, if the candidates would revolt—if things would get better or worse. As it turned out, his fears were unfounded. But that didn't make them any less real at the time.[1]

In my role as friendly interpreter, I could always come up with phrases like "start where citizens start" to describe what Merritt and company were doing. No phrase, no speech, no essay or article was going to cost me my job. Instead, my work just got more interesting with the chances a growing number of journalists took. Everything they did was worth thinking about, whether it worked or flopped, made sense or muddied the waters. I knew that articulating a philosophy was one thing, taking it public another. But living it in your professional life, that was something else. Those who did— the editors and reporters—rarely knew what they were doing, although they did know why: public life and the press were in trouble. Their peers watched with a good deal of suspicion. The most prestigious minds in journalism, with only a few exceptions, turned thumbs down on the experiment, using tense words like fraud, menace, cult.

I thought Merritt and company deserved better than that: better criticism, surely, but also a more open attitude from their colleagues. For among the things I admired about this widening group of journalists, their openness impressed me most. They wanted to try another route, and the first turn they made was within themselves. This regularly astonished me. In the university world, people changed their minds all the time. They evolved and matured as their thinking deepened. But they rarely said, "What we've been doing isn't working." Or: "This could cost me my job." My friends in the academy were confident in their institution's public standing, if not always their own standing within it. They had gripes and worries, but they were not concerned about retaining their franchise. Higher education, on the whole, wasn't losing its customers.

But newspaper journalists had begun to feel the franchise slipping away. You once reached 80 percent of your community's households. Now you were down to 55 percent. Sooner or later, the warning would hit. It's not just readers disappearing, it's the *public disintegrating,* at least from our grasp. Not only their place in the profession, then, but their profession's place in the culture was in doubt, from a variety of changes they could not easily control. In this weighty atmosphere—some called it a crisis—fear led in many directions: a defensive crouch, a panicked overreaction, a cool nonchalance that poked fun at any "sky is falling" sentiment. And for some, there came a confrontation with a disturbing fact: the press was failing itself.

Howard Kurtz of the *Washington Post* made the charge in his 1993 book *Media Circus*. He saw "a fatal disconnection, a growing gap between editors and reporters on the one hand and consumers of news on the other."

> My incestuous profession has become increasingly self-absorbed, even as its practitioners wring their hands about why fewer people seem to be listening. I hear this depressing talk every day, in newsroom meetings, in casual conversations, in my colleagues' bitter jokes about toiling for a dying business. . . . Yet we in this business have gone a long way toward squandering our natural advantages. For too long we have published newspapers aimed at other journalists—talking to ourselves, really, and to the insiders we gossip with—and paying scant attention to our readers. . . . Where once newspapers were at the very heart of the national conversation, they now seem remote, arrogant, part of the governing elite.[2]

If public journalism deserved to be called a movement, and in my eyes it did, then it moved in response to Kurtz's warning. The response was hazy, unproven, incomplete. As a solution to the many troubles facing the press, it could not possibly succeed. There were too many troubles, too deeply set. Nor could participants in the experiment feel the confident grip they once had as trained professionals. A degree of mastery had to be lost before anyone could become skilled at public journalism. By "movement," then, I mean precisely this: at a vexing moment in the life of the American press, certain journalists, most of them with long experience, started to cut loose from the mindset that bound them to others in the craft—and enabled them to say, at the end of the day, what their job was. This decision slid them into uncertain territory, where they had to ask themselves: What are we doing? How do we know if we're doing it well?

What they did was only rarely brilliant and not always wise. Some of it was downright dull. But there were many other moments when the light of an idea struck the page of a newspaper because the editor and staff had a daring notion of what to try. They looked to democracy for direction. And while they had commercial motives as well (the survival of their business), they grasped what Harold Evans, former editor of the London *Times,* meant when he said that the challenge "is not to stay in business—it is to stay in journalism." I hung around, picked their brains, asked them to describe their latest adventure, and tried to fit it into my own scheme. Challenging work, but not nearly as difficult as the departure some journalists had made.[3]

In this chapter, I tell five tales of departure, hoping to make clear what was tried and learned by people who no longer knew what they were doing and went ahead with it anyway. They moved the enterprise along, but not by applying theory to practice. Most just started doing things, without worrying too much about conceptual shifts or elaborate redefinitions of their task. The public journalism spirit, if there was such a thing, lay in a messy middle ground between execution and abstraction, craft and consciousness.

There were ideas behind the various projects and experiments that moved in a more civic spirit. Typically, they were ideas embedded in the work, rather than imported from beyond. Digging them out means applying practice to theory, rather than the reverse.

What Do We Do Now? Job Closings and the Dayton Daily News

In a midwestern city, a large defense plant that employs thousands of people in the area is about to close. Clearly, a big story. But how should the story be told? The news is clear enough: how and why the decision was made, the politics in Washington behind plant closings, the likely consequences for the region, the hardships ahead for employees and their families. But if this is the news, it is not the whole story, for in the wake of the news the community has a decision: *what do we do now?* Not "what happens next?" because what happens next may or may not be shaped by what people in the area decide to do. They may do nothing without really deciding on a null stance, especially if the available choices never rise to public awareness.

Here is what John Dewey meant by an inchoate public. It may or may not emerge, depending on whether people pay attention, get engaged. But their engagement depends on other factors: the performance of elected officials, the reactions of business and labor, the strength of civic leadership, the ability of the news media to show what's at stake. Met with the loss of jobs at a big employer, what sort of stance should a local newspaper take? By "stance" I do not mean the view of editorial writers who speak their minds on the opinion page, although that is one option. Far more important is how the newspaper and its style of journalism stand toward the lingering question, "what do we do now?" It can be covered as news, if it happens. But it can also be suggested, modeled, coaxed to life by journalists who say: this is important, and we need to talk about it.

"I'd been one of those who thinks society is best served by journalists who cover the news," said Max Jennings, editor of the *Dayton Daily News,* in a 1995 essay prepared for an industry journal. "I don't think this is good enough anymore. . . . More and more, I'm starting to think that journalists ought to be about the business of making discussion instead of just covering it." A year earlier, Jennings had been confronted with the imminent closing of a nuclear weapons plant and Defense Department supply center that together provided 4,450 local jobs. His newspaper had a choice. It could report the closing and the response of local leaders, if there was a response. Or it could take the initiative by helping to create, within self-imposed limits, conversation about where to go from here.

Creating conversation is what Jennings and his colleagues decided to do. In making that move they crossed into the territory of public journalism, but not because they wanted to be pioneers in their profession. They simply saw the enormous potential in danger of going to waste: highly skilled workers and some promising technology at the plant. So they asked how the newspaper might foster public dialogue "about possibilities for converting the plant's resources and workforce to other use," as Jennings put it.

First, the paper prepared a package of features on the weapons plant and its possible retooling, "to explain to the community and the nation as much as we could about the business potential of the plant." But the *Daily News* also wanted to provide what Jennings called a forum for discussion, so that the community might consider "ways to turn the technologies of mass destruction into peaceful purposes." The editors hoped their efforts would alert local leaders to the challenge ahead. "We were well aware, too, of the enormous problems with what we were talking about," Jennings said. "The Department of Energy certainly had no experience in technology transfer. Many of the operations at the plant are classified. Security concerns restrict normal reporting." Employees would have to join in airing the issues, and the journalists understood how workers were often "ill-prepared to do that."

The end product featured a twelve-page special section intended as both a briefing on the plant and an invitation to further talk. It included profiles of key employees and their phone numbers, should anyone want to contact them about next steps. The newspaper secured unprecedented access to the plant by persuading executives and government officials that it was serious about being constructive in its reporting. It laid out a path that key players could follow to save the business. Through photographs, graphics, opinion pieces, speculative reporting, and the detailed attention it gave to possible courses of action, the *Dayton Daily News* became a catalyst for discussion. As Jennings wrote, "It was a long way from sitting back and waiting for the bureaucrats, politicians and civic leaders to act, then writing about that."

The report was mailed to officials in Washington and distributed as a reprint upon request. One result was that hundreds of businesspeople agreed to tour the plant, discussing its possible conversion with officials there. "Ideas are abundant," Jennings said after the package on the weapons plant was completed. "We'll see what happens." A willingness to be satisfied with this outcome kept him and his colleagues from an excessive manipulation of events. The steps that followed from the newspaper's efforts had to draw their momentum from other actors: employees, executives, possible investors, government officials. The *Daily News* could then resume its role as monitor of a dialogue that evolved away from the journalists who gave the initial push.

In a similar package on keeping a large air force base alive as a source of jobs, the newspaper recruited an architect to complete a rendering of "what the facility might look like utilizing four ideas coming from the community."[4] This exercise in civic imagination tried to multiply the range of possibilities before the community. And it sent a further message: some problems are solvable if we can get our act together; we are not always at the mercy of faraway officials and unstoppable events. By taking the initiative rather than a "not my job" stance, the journalists in Dayton lent support to public discussion without substituting themselves for it.

In the passage below, the business editor of the *Daily News* explains the paper's intentions. He notes in passing that the base should not be counted as the exclusive domain of the federal government but as a community asset, the property of taxpayers who can now consider what to do with it. A sense of civic ownership—toward both the base and the discussion of its future—was thus another animating principle in the Dayton experiment.

. . . .

The business section has been reshaped today to bring you a special report with unusual content and approach.

Our goal is to stimulate public discussion and debate about the future of 165 federally owned acres in Kettering.

The parcel boasts 49 buildings with nearly 2 million square feet of warehouse and office space, roughly the equivalent of two Dayton Malls, or about double the space in the vacant downtown Lazarus department store.

Included in today's presentation are four "what if" multiple uses for what is known as Gentile Air Force Station. They are a minor league baseball stadium, a recycling center, an international inventors' camp for students, and a light industrial and office park.

We also present some of the lessons learned by communities that have converted similar military installations.

This is a different kind of project for us. Newspaper people tend to be more comfortable with reaction—simple reporting of words and deeds.

But this report is pro-active. We are encouraging readers to comment on the ideas presented here by area residents and to offer additional proposals.

We are asking the community to get involved, to discuss a huge chunk of land that belongs to us, the people who pay federal taxes.

This kind of reporting is rare. Today's project, however, is our second such report this year.

In August we looked at how our region might capitalize on the technologies and skilled employees of the Mound nuclear weapons plant. Our intent was to show how private sector jobs and new high tech businesses could be created from Mound. The facility itself is slated to cease its weapons-making operations in 1995.

The approach in today's report is similar. We're suggesting that there can be life after the Defense Electronics Supply Center, the major tenant at Gentile Station, closes down in 1996.

As with Mound, our intent with Gentile is to spotlight the positive. We hope that our report brings about public discussion and a plan for its future.

We also hope that Kettering's public officials and the people managing Gentile Station's transition are open to suggestions from area residents.

Rarely does our community get opportunities to bring ideas to a public forum. The Gentile conversion could be a healthy and refreshing change of pace. —From Greg Stricharchuk, "We Changed Our Ways, Now Let's Talk," *Dayton Daily News*, April 17, 1994

. . . .

In October 1995, the following item appeared in the *Dayton Daily News*.

Kettering's Gentile Air Force Station Reuse Plan took top honors at the 1995 Ohio Planning Conference in Akron in the category of Focused Planning Project awards. The award is given to the project that best displays the fundamentals of the planning process and effective approaches to it. The Woolpert company of Dayton developed the 179-page plan over six months, completing the project in March. The plan calls for Gentile Station to be redeveloped as an office/light industrial business park. City officials expect to take ownership of the 166-acre site in 1997.[5]

From having a problem to having a plan: with assistance from its newspaper, the Dayton area took ownership of a civic challenge and began to move on it. And it was this kind of movement—toward a less inchoate public—that the *Daily News* wanted to inspire. In reflecting on the experiment, Jennings understood the risk his paper was taking: the two packages spoke the sound of possibility, freed for the moment from the usual chorus of doubt. "We'll be aggressive quoting the doomsayers in the future," he noted. "In the meantime, we have created two blueprints as a guide for dealing with two huge community projects." Comfortable in his evolving philosophy, he was able to challenge his colleagues: "Someone's going to have to convince me this is bad journalism."[6]

In a speech to journalists in 1995, Jennings turned more expansive. He spoke of the "downright perilous times" he shared with younger colleagues who were still looking ahead. "After more than 30 years of it, my mind is etched indelibly by experiences only a journalist could have." This gradual "etching," the mark of professional duty upon a labor of love, led him to worry about the future state of the news business, which was undergoing transformation as new kinds of companies—symbolic of the "media"—moved in.

> After all, who are the publishers anymore of newspapers, and particularly, national electronic newspapers? These newest of newspapers are not published by the names you're familiar with in the news business, but by companies such as IBM, Sears, Bell South, Time Warner, . . . and soon, Microsoft.
>
> Are these companies our newest champions of the First Amendment, of freedom of the press? Are they the newest voices for the voiceless? Are they committed to putting the bad guys in jail, to printing stories that may be unpopular with their advertisers, to doing what's right instead of only what's profitable?
>
> I don't know this for a fact, but I'm making an assumption that my contemporaries at . . . the telephone company don't feel the same way those of us in this room feel about our responsibilities as journalists.

In this charged setting—the shifting ownership climate in the news business—Jennings noted a crisis of confidence in the craft. He and his colleagues were "more unsure of our common values than ever before." Enter civic journalism, a term Jennings adopted without pretending that it explained itself or marked any great leap of thought: "I can't imagine a journalism that isn't by definition Civic, and I don't know what civic journalism means. I hope it doesn't mean civil journalism. That's an oxymoron to me." But a moment later he was settling on a provisional definition. "Its proponents, including myself, say that its goal is to 'reconnect' citizens with their newspapers, their communities and the political process itself." Jennings did not shrink from describing the departure involved: civic journalism meant saying "journalists cannot and should not remain detached."[7]

He noted how politics had been faltering while journalists trained a skeptical eye on it. "Essentially, we've let the politicians frame the debates and the issues. We've put the Boys on the Bus to follow them, and while we were preoccupied with this, the issues of real importance of the people were not addressed. The people felt disenfranchised from the political process, so why would they want to read about it?" Public journalism, he hoped, "will allow us to connect readers to American politics in a way that has new meaning and relevance." A telephone company probably wouldn't share this goal. If it can find buyers for an expanding range of information-age products, the firm has no cause to worry if the public's connection to politics wilts. But Jennings was worried, for the simple reason that "journalism is important work," different from the business of media, which felt no obligation to the nation's civic health.[8]

The question "What do we do now?" was thus of equal relevance to communities facing public problems and to journalists coming into the threatening embrace of media companies. The spirit of experiment, the use of civic imagination, the sense of ownership over a public enterprise, taking personal initiative in the way that democracy demands—these were attitudes journalists could adopt toward the troubles in their profession, and toward the communities they addressed.

What was to become of the Dayton defense plants and the people they employed? What would happen to the press and its spirited professionals? Which way for the American experiment in self-government? What do we do now, once we recognize that we're involved? In Max Jennings's mind, these questions were all related; the relationship became thinkable for him through the unfolding philosophy of public journalism.

Race and Dialogue at the Akron Beacon Journal

In May 1992, the acquittal of white police officers charged in the video-taped beating of Rodney King, a black man, touched off three days of rioting in Los Angeles. While scenes showing sections of the city ablaze played on television, other cities struggled to contain outbreaks of street violence. In downtown Atlanta, windows were broken and stores looted in two days of disturbances, leading to an 11:00 P.M. to 5:00 A.M. curfew. In San Francisco, rock throwing, looting, and street fires followed news of the verdict, causing officials there to declare a state of emergency. In Las Vegas, the National Guard was called out after similar incidents, including two shootings. In San Jose, marching students threw rocks at passing cars and police vehicles. In Seattle, crowds smashed windows. In San Diego, snipers fired at police amid other violence. In Madison, Wisconsin, police discovered thirty-six patrol cars and city vehicles vandalized, with notes left on them bearing messages like "Justice for King."[9] And outside the window of my apartment in New York, I watched a parked car get overturned by angry marchers.

What the nation now remembers as the "Rodney King incident" was much more than that. For a few days in May the edge of an abyss showed, and a good portion of the country knew that racial justice was a long way off, despite all the progress that had been made. As long as the divide between the races remained as it was, civil order could not be guaranteed. And for those who looked closely there was another message, startling to some: It was not only blacks who took to the streets; Latinos and whites were there, too. Asians were some of the hardest-hit victims. What was a multiracial America to make of that?

The immediate job of journalists was simply to report what happened: not only the violence in Los Angeles, but other reactions to the trial and the issues that lay beneath it. As the smoke lifted, discussions were dutifully begun in the hope that maybe this time the country could learn something. They made news for a time, as did vows to rebuild South Central L.A., the flashpoint for the anger and destruction. Ted Koppel brought his *Nightline* program to the city and aired the grievances of the black community on national television. Predictably, though, the news media moved on to other stories, including a presidential campaign in which race and the meaning of the events of May were barely visible.

Meanwhile, in Akron, Ohio, editors and reporters at the *Beacon Journal* made a conscious decision not to move on. The memory of May 1992 flashed in their minds as they asked themselves: what can we do, here in Akron? The result was "A Question of Color," a yearlong reporting series that explained in some depth the divisions among blacks and whites in the five-county area the paper served. The series featured statistical analysis of racial disparities, polls showing large gaps in perception between blacks and whites, and group discussions with follow-up interviews, in which residents were asked to speak about their lives and reflect on the racial climate in the region.

The *Beacon Journal* tried to vivify the different worlds of whites and blacks, which meant challenging the notion, common among many whites, that there was no race problem in Akron. As one headline put it, blacks and whites live in parallel realities. Underneath ran a summary of an attitude survey, showing how the two races held vastly different views on a host of questions, from housing and economic opportunities to relations with schools and the police. "The findings are clear," the paper reported: "Blacks and whites in the Akron-Canton area not only remain divided by the color of their skin, but by their perceptions of reality, as well. And it's sometimes hard to tell where reality ends and perception begins."[10]

To a metropolitan area that was 91.5 percent white, the *Beacon Journal* offered facts to contemplate: About 72 percent of whites were able to own their homes, compared with 46 percent of blacks. Eighteen percent of whites had a college education, 8 percent of blacks did. Average household income was $37,143 for whites, $23,164 for blacks. And, the series noted, blacks were losing ground on such measures. Home ownership had fallen 7 percent for blacks from 1980 to 1990, while the rate for whites had remained the same. "While the typical white household here was struggling to make ends meet in 1990 with the equivalent of just $1,000 more in annual income than it had in 1980, the average black household was trying to cope with $1,500 *less* than it had ten years ago." The tale of differences went on:

WHAT THE NUMBERS SHOW ABOUT BLACKS:
- They are far more afraid of crime than whites. Three of four see illegal drugs as a serious problem in their neighborhood.
- Their children are nearly four times as likely as white children to be poor. Half the black children in Summit County are living in poverty.

- Most believe the quality of health care available to them is subpar; nearly half think the schools their children attend are, too.
- They have a far tougher time getting loans than whites. Blacks making $50,000 and up are more likely to be denied loans than whites making less than half that much.

WHAT THE NUMBERS SHOW ABOUT WHITES:

- They are likely to live in isolation from blacks. Two of three live in neighborhoods that are at least 97 percent white.
- They are far more likely than blacks to be upbeat about their economic outlook: Four in 10 see prospects as good to excellent. And they are far more likely than blacks to be optimistic about blacks' prospects as well.
- Most are pleased with the schools their children attend: Seven in 10 say they are good to excellent.
- They are far more likely than blacks to think the police are doing a good job. Three in four say relations are good with the police in their area.[11]

While the *Beacon Journal* wanted to highlight its conclusion that blacks and whites lived in different worlds, it also sought to avoid simplistic analysis. It noted how many students of the subject thought economic class, rather than race, was more of a barrier to poor blacks. It quoted black citizens warning against the "victim" mentality that blamed racism for all problems. Middle-class blacks, doing well, were not absent from the portrait. The paper showed that, on the question of race, there were important differences among blacks, among whites, as well as between the two groups. It also noted how whites will often "go to great lengths simply to avoid the subject." And it described how this "skittishness" showed up in the discussions with area residents.[12]

The *Beacon Journal* was here practicing good, solid, and more or less traditional journalism: Akron was given the chance to hear itself talking about race; the newspaper added information and analysis to put things in wider perspective. It presented hard data, talked to a wide range of ordinary people, mixed in the views of experts and leaders, and drew some firm conclusions, without glossing over the difficulties of the subject or taking a Pollyannaish tone. But as the project moved along, it grew beyond a reporting and listening exercise, for the story told was a stark tale of division and mistrust. "During 12 months of reporting, we found some pretty ugly reality," the paper wrote in a reprint of the series. "In fact, we realized halfway through that we had to show our readers more; that we had to give them at least a glimpse of hope."[13]

Beginning with the second installment of articles in May 1993, the paper began running a coupon titled "Getting Involved: What Can We Do?" It invited civic groups, religious organizations, and schools to suggest projects they could undertake to improve race relations. In a front-page column announcing the effort, publisher John Dotson and editor Dale Allen said they wanted "to do more than just report what is happening." They knew there were groups in the Akron area already at work trying to improve the racial climate. The paper wanted to encourage other "multi-racial partnerships that can work toward common goals." The *Beacon Journal* would serve as connecting medium, putting like-minded people in touch with one another and assisting in their initial discussions. The rest was up to citizens. There was the ethical line the paper found to delimit its involvement in the "hope" portion of the project.

Dotson and Allen outlined their plans:

. . . .

We'll find a place for you to meet. And one of our volunteers will help get discussions going—trying to set agendas and goals for the partnerships. Then the real work begins as the groups seek to achieve these goals.

The goals might be as simple as holding weekly or monthly get-acquainted sessions so more people of different races become friends instead of strangers. Or they might be directed toward specific results—such as helping children of both races with their school work.

So what are the risks?

There may be some. Nothing is ever accomplished without risk. In fact, one of the risks is that the newspaper itself is stepping outside of its more traditional role as reporter of the news and into a role of helping the community repair severed relationships.

We are pledging not to neglect our obligations to report what is going on in our communities. But we do intend to pay special attention to multicultural partnerships that take shape, providing periodic reports to the community on their progress.

We also will report on other organizations that already are working toward racial harmony. And if the paper can be supportive in other ways, we will seek to do so.

—From "You're Invited to Promote Racial Harmony," *Akron Beacon Journal,* May 2, 1993

. . . .

To coordinate the work of making connections, Dotson hired (out of his publisher's office) two community facilitators—a retired clergyman and a retired school principal, one black, one white. Some fifty staffers from various departments at the *Beacon Journal* volunteered to help kick off the discussion for groups that decided to meet. About half came from the newsroom. In December 1993, the paper printed a front-page coupon asking readers to pledge to do something across racial lines in the coming year. A startlingly high percentage of the readership responded—22,000 people for a paper with a daily circulation of 180,000.[14] Their names were printed in a special section in January, so that the pledges became fully visible—that is, "public."

This second dimension of the Akron race project, called "Coming Together," was a more daring enterprise than the reporting series, "A Question of Color." More daring, but also logically related. As their reporting unfolded within traditional journalistic bounds, it began to push at those boundaries. Having awakened Akron to a problem, the newspaper had a choice: Did it want to leave off at the point where a depressing state of affairs was described? Or was there something else it could do, as one of the few institutions that reached across the metropolitan area, spanning the very divisions it had uncovered?

By February 1994, enough civic, church, and leadership groups had responded to the newspaper's invitation that a regionwide planning session could be called with more than one hundred organizations attending. By June, Coming Together was itself an organization, housed at the newspaper, with an advisory council (drawn from the community), a newsletter, and a network. In August 1995 it incorporated as a nonprofit group under federal tax law. Its 1996 annual report noted that "more than 170 organizations representing the arts, business, civic, social, religious and educational institutions belong to the project."[15]

Coming Together moved out of the newspaper into its own offices several miles away in May 1996. One of its officers hosted a weekly radio program on race relations. A special committee worked to draw whites and blacks together in observance of Martin Luther King Day. Churches with predominately black or white congregations held joint prayer sessions and informal get-togethers. Study circles on how to talk about race were held for those who wanted to get better at speaking across the divide. A teenage advisory group coordinated traveling workshops for their peers in high schools across the region. The teen volunteers went from school to school leading roundtable discussions among students about what they could do to improve the racial climate in their own school's setting. Ideas spread from building to building, with some schools joining in exchange programs among students of different races.[16]

For its efforts, the *Beacon Journal* was awarded the profession's highest honor: the 1994 Pulitzer Prize for Public Service. The citation read: "For its broad examination of local racial attitudes and its subsequent effort to promote improved communication in the community." It was the first such award for an initiative that could be called public journalism.

The people at the newspaper didn't necessarily use that term, although some were aware of it. Nor did they think of themselves as joining any "movement." But by taking on a charged issue without waiting for a dramatic event to erupt; by going beyond a description of the problem to an attempt at generating civic action; by using the power of the press to connect citizens to one another (rather than to the newspaper alone); by seeing "hope" as a resource the community badly needed; by giving visibility to those willing to stand up and do something (or at least say they would do something); by sparking discussion and social contact among citizens who might otherwise never meet—the *Beacon Journal* showed that it wasn't neutral about everything. It wanted public life to go well, to yield an atmosphere in which mutual understanding might here and there arise. And it saw no necessary conflict between telling hard truths about the racial climate and making a better climate possible.

Later in its evolution, public journalism would draw a host of critics who thought the idea meant going soft on difficult issues like race. Again and again in meetings with journalists and in published critiques, the "civil rights" question would be aired. Jonathan Cohn, writing in the liberal journal *American Prospect*, was among those who asked it: "What would have happened if the newspapers that pioneered civil rights coverage in the South had practiced public journalism? Would they have taken a more accommodating attitude toward the white establishment? Would they have searched for the 'common ground' of separate but equal?" No one could answer this question for 1963. But the answer in Akron, thirty years later, was clear: it was possible to tell a disturbing story about race and still do something that might remake the story. Without pretending that common ground exists where it clearly does not, journalism could help prepare the ground for more civic engagement.[17]

The vision of Akron "coming together" may sound overly lofty or senti-mental, as if talking about race necessarily meant doing something about it. And taking New Year's pledges could easily be dismissed as weightless sym-bolism. Maybe it was, in some cases. But as the list of cooperating agencies grew, so did the newspaper's achievement. The *Beacon Journal* moved from providing information about the racial divide to making connections across it—a full year after the fires in Los Angeles went out.

Akron's prize drew the attention of the profession to what the journalists there had done. But one thing they did escaped broad notice, although it may have been the most unusual effort of all. In asking the community to sit down and talk about race, didn't it make sense for the newspaper to do the same? After all, it seemed possible, even likely, that a racial divide ran through the newsroom, as it did in so many workplaces. Could journalists exempt themselves from the challenge they had put to citizens?

The *Beacon Journal* didn't think so. So it arranged for two in-house discussions about race—as both a factor in the newsroom and as a theme in daily reporting. Black journalists were in one group, whites in another. The two groups were then brought together to see what would happen when their views met. The seventeen participants, all volunteers, were asked to review two months of news coverage, paying particular attention to crime news, "the subject on which newspapers often hear cries of racial bias." Finally, the paper printed a report on this dialogue, letting the community listen in as journalists wrestled with the same issues that had been treated in the *Beacon Journal*'s reporting: clashing perceptions of "favoritism" in the workplace, the news media's role in deepening racial conflict, the persistence of ugly stereotypes, and so on.

The internal report was headlined "The Struggle for Balance." It was featured on the front page and ran for almost two pages inside.

. . . .

It's a wonder the nation's largest newspapers haven't developed the kind of disgruntled-employee reputation that dogs the U.S. Postal Service.

Find 150 people who thrive on adversarial situations and stick them in one huge room. Crank up the heat of constant deadline pressure under all their private agendas and personal quirks. Let them compete for ink.

Then introduce the question of color.

Given such a volatile mix, it should come as no real surprise that nearly everyone at the *Beacon Journal* would offer you a different spin on how race affects the production of the newspaper—and on what its role *should* be.

Here are the approximate extremes:

A black copy editor points to a story about a husband and wife charged with embezzlement and says the story was downplayed "because this was a white couple."

A white reporter points to a story about a series of unprovoked assaults and says a crucial element was buried because "when black people are beating up on white people, we don't write about it, and when the reverse is true, we do."

In between, you can find almost unlimited gradations of opinion. But almost no one at the *Beacon Journal* would dispute the assertion that race plays a significant role in every aspect of the newspaper's operation, from hiring practices to gathering of information to the way the stories are written, illustrated, headlined and displayed. . . .

The overall opinions are illuminating:

- On the black side, there is a pervasive feeling that, in spite of significant progress in hiring practices, promotion and newsroom policies, the newspaper still is stacked against African-Americans. That's because the bulk of the power remains in the hands of whites, who at worst carry a subconscious bias and at best cannot fully understand blacks. As a result, crimes by blacks tend to be covered differently than crimes by whites.

- On the white side, there is a widespread feeling that the newspaper is trying so hard to be perceived as nonracist that fairness and honesty have suffered, that the truth is sometimes sugar-coated in the name of sociological engineering. Whites point to the presence of a black publisher, a black graphics editor, and, until recently, a black managing editor, and say that white employees feel constant pressure—from editors of both races—to bend over backward to embrace minority perspectives.

What may come as a surprise is this: the level of frustration and anger seems significantly higher among whites.

"A couple of years ago," said a white reporter about his particular assigning editor, "we were told to ask people's race over the telephone (in an effort to ensure diversity in stories). I was never more outraged in my life."

Also highly illuminating is that this type of passion was concealed when the two groups came together.

The stated goal of the meetings was candor. Candor, it was hoped, would lead to understanding, which would help build bridges. To that end, a veil of secrecy was thrown over the project.

- No upper level editors were permitted to watch the meetings or the videotape made of each.
- A white reporter and a black reporter, watching via closed-circuit TV, gave assurances that only one other person, a lower-level black editor, would have access to the tapes.
- No names would be printed without permission.

Still, the sessions seemed to fall considerably short of complete honesty. A series of follow-up interviews, also done with the option of anonymity, proved only slightly better.

Why such reticence, especially among people not exactly known as shrinking violets? As one white reporter put it, "Who knows better than a journalist the consequences of pouring your heart and spilling your guts all over a newspaper?" . . .

The black participants also pulled their punches, to a slightly lesser degree, in mixed company. "You fear repercussions," explained one black employee afterward. ". . . You know there are leaks that go to management."

The irony of this was clear to another reporter: "The very people who want to find the truth in and make sense of the world by getting people to share with us what is in their hearts proved to be more guarded in address-ing crime and race relations in the newsroom than those we decry for lack of candor."

—From Bob Dyer, "The Struggle for Balance: Beacon's Journalists Disagree on Race's Role in News Coverage," *Akron Beacon Journal,* December 29, 1993

. . . .

This *was* candor. Behind the professional facade of the newspaper, its crisply written copy, its tidy graphics, its authoritative reporting, stood a company of journalists who were as divided and angry about race as others in America, and even less open to honest discussion of it. "We're no better, and we may be a good deal worse," is an unusual message to send citizens. But it had to be said, if the newspaper was to become a citizen itself, a creature of the community, and not just its chronicler or judge. The *Beacon Journal* emerged from its self-portrait as a fallible institution, struggling to define what racial justice meant—in news coverage and office politics.

When journalists share with the public their own doubts and divisions about the way the news is crafted, they also acknowledge that it *is* crafted, imperfectly and contentiously, by people who do not leave their experience, their color, or their ideas about race at home when they drive to work. Reporters and editors at the *Beacon Journal* redefined themselves when they chose to report on themselves as participants in the country's racial divide. The newspaper was shown as divided in its soul, but the bigger showing was that it had a soul: there was a human drama there, not just a professional machine holding a mirror up to reality.

The "glimpse of hope" the *Beacon Journal* gave Akron involved more than an invitation to connect across racial lines. There was something hopeful in the way the newspaper presented itself to the community: as a humbled truth teller, finding the facts, but also frustrated in finding a just (or balanced) way of relaying those facts. Sharing the results meant sharing a civic identity with Akron, as one more institution groping for answers to America's most enduring dilemma.

Deliberation and Design at the San Jose Mercury News

Picture a large metropolitan area without a natural center. Many of the residents have come from somewhere else to take jobs in a bustling high-tech economy. Housing prices are sky-high, so people settle wherever they can afford to and commute long distances. They sleep in one community and drive through twenty more to work in another. They shop in a town two exits down the freeway; their kids play soccer somewhere else. At times the whole area seems to be on the go, crisscrossing a territory that can feel more like a space than a place.

Civic identity reflects this scattered and mobile existence. Ask people where they live and they're likely to give any of a dozen names for the area—none official. There is a regional economy, but no polity or government that corresponds to the region and its problems. Public spaces are few in number and rarely populated, unless you count the freeways, which are frequently jammed. Still, life is reasonably satisfying for most who live there, those who are not poor or leading a shadow existence as illegal immigrants. But in public life there is often little to be found. Politics brings the usual frustrations, along with the peculiar difficulties of an area that is metropolitan in size but not a metropolis. It is a collection of "edge cities" around a bigger city for which the airport and sports teams and newspaper are named.

Now picture that newspaper: in this case, the *San Jose Mercury News.* Rob Elder is the editor in charge of the editorial pages. But what he really controls is a public space with great power, which can be put to various ends. But which ends were right for the region? In 1995, Elder began to think hard about that. He ended up redesigning his pages so that the voices heard there might converse in a different way. And he began to experiment with creating civic dialogue beyond the newspaper itself.

Elder's ideas emerged from his own reflections on the press and public discourse, occasioned by wide reading and frequent talks with readers, whom he asked for comment about his pages. In time he concluded that his portion of the newspaper had become too provincial. The paper's institutional voice spoke with wisdom, but it needed to cultivate the wisdom in others. Civic intelligence, Elder thought, could be beckoned from unlikely places; and the institution could "speak" through this kind of action, as well.

He and his staff had more to give the San Jose area than their views on the issues, some letters from readers, and a few opinion columns. They could move outward from their offices, into the vast territory where the traffic merged but ideas rarely met. The newspaper, circulating widely, spanned the boundaries that the cars crisscrossed each day. In the degree that its pages were carefully read, the *Mercury News* stopped traffic and called a sprawling region to attention as a public. Once Elder began to redraw his relationship to that public, he started crafting his own version of public journalism.

His first move was an attempt to create a different kind of dialogue about a hot-button issue. During the spring of 1995, California governor Pete Wilson was claiming heavy news coverage and revving up his presidential bid by declaring support for vast new restrictions on affirmative action. Concerned for the quality of the ensuing debate, Elder started looking for sources of inspiration. He read Daniel Yankelovich's *Coming to Public Judgment,* and he absorbed the idea that complex issues like affirmative action require a period of "working through," a time when citizens can grapple with choices and consequences and clarify the competing values in play. This, he felt, was not happening in California as affirmative action heated up.[18]

Elder spoke with people at the Kettering Foundation and learned more about the National Issues Forums, community-based discussions revolving around a deliberative model of public debate. Then, in cooperation with the public libraries and other civic groups, the editorial pages of the *Mercury News* sponsored a series of public forums on affirmative action policy, held in the evening at local libraries. With Kettering's help, a member of Elder's staff wrote a discussion guide for the affirmative action debate. It laid out the key facts and presented the public with choices that dug deeper than "affirmative action: yes or no?"

Titled "Affirmative Action and Equal Opportunity: How Can Californians Find Common Ground?" the discussion guide was difficult to classify in the language of traditional journalism. It fit neither the news nor the opinion category. And it was not the institutional voice of the *Mercury News*. Instead, the paper tried to frame the issue in a way that allowed more room for honest discussion of competing choices and underlying values. The guide gave a short summary of the problem, including a brief history of affirmative action. It described the rising resentment of those who felt the principle of fair play was being violated, and the likely consequences of a statewide referendum, set for the following year. The referendum (which became Proposition 209 and was approved by a large majority of voters in 1996) would ban most forms of affirmative action in the university system, race-conscious hiring in state government, and set-aside programs that gave some business to minority- and female-headed companies. Under the heading "Questions to Ask About Any Proposal," the guide listed the following:

- Can we create a system that is fairer to some without being unfair to others?
- Is the goal equal opportunity, or equal results?
- Are we talking about a legal problem, an economic problem, or a social problem?
- Does history count?
- What are the values on which we can agree across racial and gender lines? Where can we find common ground?

The guide then laid out three broad choices, or points of view, each including a diagnosis of the problem and what ought to be done to remedy it, followed by what critics say. The first choice was "Treat People as Individuals." It summarized the view of those deeply opposed to affirmative action on the principle that "you can't fight discrimination with discrimination." The second choice was called "Attack the Root Causes of Inequality." It read like this.

. . . .

CHOICE 2: ATTACK THE ROOT
CAUSES OF INEQUALITY

What's the Diagnosis?

The real issue is poverty. The poor are denied an equal opportunity to succeed due to the effects of high-crime neighborhoods, inadequate schools and deficient social services.

Let's focus on the inputs of health and education rather than the using quotas to manipulate outcomes. We can give everyone equal opportunity, but we can't guarantee equal results.

What Should Be Done?

Invest in Head Start, public schools, job training, job creation, health care, social services and law enforcement in underclass areas. Give preferential access to education opportunities to the economically disadvantaged, regardless of race, ethnicity or gender.

Why This Course of Action?

The division of wealth in society is widening. One in four children lives in poverty. Social mobility is an important goal: hard-working people should have a chance to better themselves.

Help should go to the most needy, not to people who can help themselves, and shouldn't be linked to race, ethnicity or gender.

Compassion is the hallmark of a good community: We should help our less fortunate brothers and sisters. If we don't, we'll hand our children a time bomb.

What Do Critics Say?

It won't work. We spent billions on social programs in the War on Poverty and didn't get much for it; we can't afford to try that again.

Group preferences based on class or poverty also would be difficult to implement in education, impossible in the workplace.

It's natural that some do worse than others. Many poor people are not capable of climbing the ladder, no matter how much help they get. Either they lack the work ethic, they're addicted to drugs or alcohol or they have behavioral problems that explain their lack of success.

Society isn't responsible for guaranteeing equal outcomes in life.

—From "Affirmative Action and Equal Opportunity: How Can Californians Find Common Ground?" a discussion guide prepared by the editorial pages of the *San Jose Mercury News*, 1995

. . . .

The third choice was "Enforce Equal Results." There, the diagnosis read: "Inequality created by past discrimination is tearing us apart as a society; this is an urgent problem and progress is way too slow. Discrimination is way too powerful. Minorities and women won't get equal opportunity without government pressure."[19]

The discussion guide was brief, almost telegraphic in style. A careful reader could offer a host of complaints: the writing was rather dry, the summaries of different positions lacked nuance, the possible choices were surely more than three, there was no effort to say whether "what critics say" squared with known facts, and so on. But even granting these weaknesses, there was something subversive about the document. What it offered was not so much "information" or "opinion" but information *about and beneath* opinion. Three options were presented, rather than the usual two. Different diagnoses were seen leading to different conclusions. Different choices proceeded from different values. This was the paper's invitation to Yankelovich's "working through" stage.

"We hoped people would define their own choices," Elder later wrote. "It was the process itself—citizens deciding together what they want for their state and the nation—that was the goal." It turned out to be "farther away, and more difficult to reach, than we knew." The editorial page of the *Mercury News* learned something by holding two dozen public forums with Californians of different ages, races, and class backgrounds. (There were more than one thousand attendees, although some people came to more than one forum.) Because "affirmative action is not a subject which anyone can deal with in an evening's time," as Elder put it, the project partners asked for volunteers from earlier meetings to gather for three more weekly sessions. Part of what they discovered was how frustrating the issue had become.

> Paul Cummins, a black minister, and Joel DeAngelis, a white venture capitalist, found themselves at loggerheads over the importance of individual initiative. Cummins said he didn't know anyone of any color who didn't feel they'd gotten some help at some point in their lives that made a difference.
>
> "My mother sacrificed so I could go to college," he said. "People died so that I could vote."
>
> DeAngelis seemed indignant at the concept. "You're selling yourself short," he said. "You had to step up." He insisted the individual was responsible for his own fate, period.

Another thing the *Mercury News* learned was that the relevant question could not be "affirmative action: good or bad?" because people defined the term in strikingly different ways. To some it meant including qualified minorities in the applicant pool, which seemed to them reasonable and fair. To others, it meant quotas and set-asides, which suggested reverse discrimination. This rendered meaningless a debate framed in familiar and polarized terms: "Do you agree or disagree with Governor Wilson's stand on the issue?" The real divisions lay in contrasting views of what equality and opportunity meant, based in large part on people's life experience. What was valuable about the forums, then, was not the clash of opinion but the opportunity to hear how citizens' lives and personal struggles shaped their beliefs. Elder wrote:

> "Well, you certainly didn't change many minds," a woman said after the last meeting of her group.
>
> That's probably true, but the goal was not to change minds, in the sense of persuading people to abandon beliefs based on life as they have experienced it. The objective was to open all our minds to the different beliefs and experiences of others.
>
> Don Davis, who took part in the Martin Luther King library forums, put it this way: "You think you know the right thing. Then you listen to people, and you don't know what to think. And maybe that's better."
>
> "You read that some people think this, and such and such a percent think that. But when you hear people say it, it really makes a difference."[20]

The forums thus succeeded in taking an artificially clear picture of public opinion, drawn mainly from polling data, and making it *less* clear. "Then you listen to people, and you don't know what to think," as Davis said. "And maybe that's better." It is better, if the paper's goal is not just to adopt an editorial stance on an already polarized issue but to aid citizens in their own deliberations. "So," Elder asked as the initial round of affirmative action forums concluded, "did we find any common ground?"

> I would say yes. But that ground is a rocky landscape. People share a frustration with how unresolved things are, about affirmative action and about race in general. They share a yearning for closure. They share a new and sobering awareness of how many other views exist, and how difficult it is to accommodate them all.
>
> Like many other Americans, they have glimpsed the chasms that sepa-

rate us on questions that involve race. The chasms are wider than many of us knew. They are frightening.

The odd but enlightening result of trying to work through a troubling issue was to convince Elder and his colleagues of what they did not know and were as yet unable to imagine: what's the best way to talk about this issue? "No one—not Bill Clinton, not Pete Wilson, not Jesse Jackson nor Louis Farrakhan, and certainly not the editor of this newspaper—knows precisely how to frame the questions and make the conversation useful," Elder wrote. "I ask your help and advice."[21]

Consider how different this view is from an editorial declaring support for affirmative action, or a columnist who attacks the governor's stand. Elder's view was that taking a position on the issue is impossible—or at least unwise—until the questions are well framed, the conversation's drift and pattern mapped. The job of the editorial page, in partnership with public libraries and other civic institutions, was to make a start on this challenge by seeing what happens when citizens sit down to talk and keep talking. A modest start it was, involving less than a thousand people in the nation's biggest state. But if the means were modest, the aim was large: to experiment with another notion of what editorial pages were for.

Picture for a moment the flow of traffic in a metropolitan area. The image of "flow" describes the feel of much civic experience in our media-fed climate. The news, for example, flows in repetitive cycles that have grown steadily shorter. We can go around the world every thirty minutes with CNN, which suggests that TV itself is a flow experience. Politics, too, can flow by as it fills the public screen: there are the leaders shaking hands, the governor getting picketed, the correspondent standing before the capital with a microphone. Part of what it means to live in a media age is to grow accustomed to this flow, moving past us as we watch, or with us as we shift: from channel to channel, lane to lane. And there is always the temptation to let it all roll by.[22]

Journalism at its best is an art practiced against this temptation. It can halt traffic, arrest our attention, say to us: "here's something you didn't know," or "listen to this amazing story," or "let's think about that." Done well, these pieces stop time, allowing us a glimpse of a world made more intelligible—and thus more available to our civic senses. That's what Elder and his staff tried to do with their discussion guide: call a temporary halt to "news" about affirmative action, and the public rancor that came with it, in order to reframe the issue as a fuller series of choices. By consulting "Questions to Ask About Any Proposal," readers could stop and inquire into their own views on the matter ("does history count?" for instance), while interrogating other views that were out there, circulating around in the flow. The forums held at public libraries were "time-outs" of a different sort: an hour or so set aside for what civic experience too rarely allows—deliberation, face to face, with a common set of facts on the table and the diverse lives of the participants to animate those facts.

Out of the affirmative action experiment and other conversations he had with citizens came Elder's redesign of the space he controlled. Put yourself in his chair: You preside over the editorial pages of a thriving metropolitan newspaper, a powerful voice in a region where few voices speak with broad authority. You have two pages to fill each day, and they carry no advertising. Common practice in your profession tells you what these pages should be. One is called the editorial page, at the top of which is a masthead listing the executives who run the paper, along with its past leadership. Down the left side are the editorials, which are written by individuals but speak in an institutional voice: "we believe . . ." On the right side are letters to the editor, headlined in smaller type. This is where readers have their say. At the bottom may be a signed column by a member of the editorial board—at times, yourself. The facing page is the "op-ed" space. A columnist who is a member of your staff appears here, along with the syndicated writers you publish from among the dozens who distribute their wares nationally. You also feature there opinion pieces generated locally, usually from influential figures in the region, along with the occasional college professor or civic activist.

This, then, is the model you work with as the editor in charge of discussion space in the newspaper. But the model also works on you; it is a medium with a message. The format of the pages prefigures the dialogue, fitting it into slots, directing its flow, deciding when it goes back and forth (or just "forth"). How effective was this form in drawing people in, giving them a voice, helping them work through the deeper questions? How well fitted did it seem to the region it served? These doubts began to tug at Elder. His redesign, announced below, was a series of tentative replies.

. . . .

In the old school of newspapering, an editor wrote his opinion on a brick and tossed it over his shoulder and out the window.

If the brick hit a passerby and made an impact, fine. If it fell unnoticed in the street, that was fine too. The author of the editorial had said his piece; whether the world paid heed was not his concern.

Most editorial pages still reflect that insular attitude. They tell you with gusto what the newspaper thinks. They express mild interest, at most, in what you make of it.

The pecking order is evident in the layout. It's hierarchical: On the left side of a traditional editorial page are the editorials. They speak in a deep voice, with authority. Elsewhere on the page are letters from readers. Smaller type, less space. Pipsqueak voices, by comparison. The remaining space is dominated mostly by professional pundits and staff columnists, although occasionally a regular person sneaks into the mix.

That's how most newspapers do their editorial pages, and with occasional exceptions it's how we did ours, until today. In this new format, we'll still express our opinions vigorously in editorials and staff columns. But we'll also put more emphasis on other views than we did before. . . .

On a typical day, our new approach won't involve hundreds of other voices. But it will often include one or two besides ours, and they'll generally get about the same space as our own editorials. We'll label each "Another View."

These opinions will originate in various ways—in letters to the editor, in local and syndicated columns, in interviews we conduct or in written opinions we invite people to submit.

On our new pages, we'll group material not just by category—editorials here, letters over there—but also by subject. Under a single headline you may find our view, labeled as an editorial, and another view, identified as the opinion of someone else.

These second (and sometimes third and fourth) opinions won't necessarily be the opposites of our own. If we say the world is round, we won't feel obliged to find someone to argue the flat-earth position.

There are some other things we won't do. We won't *always* publish a contrasting view on the same day as our own editorial; with daily deadlines and breaking news, it won't always be possible. We won't publish everything everyone sends us; believe me, you wouldn't want to read the paper if we did. And we won't give up our ability to have the last word. After presenting a range of views on an important ballot issue, for instance, we probably will conclude the discussion by stating or even restating our own opinion.

We're by no means abdicating a newspaper's right and responsibility to take strong positions of its own. But using our voice in a more deliberative manner and by putting increased emphasis on other voices, we hope to make these opinion pages less of a lecture hall and more of a community conversation.

—From Rob Elder, "We're Turning Up the Volume to Raise Your Voice," *San Jose Mercury News,* January 21, 1996

. . . .

In the new design, writers and what they wrote were to speak, not just to readers, but to one another. Elder wanted visual display to mimic the back-and-forth quality of conversation. This meant reducing the "lecture hall" quality of editorial writing, the ex cathedra tone that favored declamation over discussion. Rearranging the pages by subject rather than category ("editorials here, letters over there") may seem like a small, almost technical change. But it was meant to make a bigger point: The *Mercury News* no longer claimed a commanding or fixed position in conversational space. It sought a more fluid role that involved soliciting as much as stating opinion, commenting on other views that were given equal standing—and then letting the comment stand as the paper's view. Without relinquishing its right to speak, the paper tried to enlarge the portion of its pages devoted to the public's speech, and thereby fashion a different role for itself in the sprawling region around San Jose.

Cultivator of civic dialogue, promoter of deliberation amid a fractured debate, partner with other institutions in the "working through" interval— these were some of the aspirations Elder had for his section. Each one spoke to the difficulties of finding civic identity in the scattered, semi-urban climate where the newspaper circulated, the traffic flowed, and politics was so often something scrolling by on television.

Rob Elder found the public journalism spirit in a renewed modesty about what he and his colleagues knew. They knew how to take a stand, have a voice, declare an opinion, and give others room to do the same. What they did not know, but aimed to find out, was how to do the existing political culture, and its atomized landscape, one better.

Revising Convention Coverage in Orange County

On the second night of the 1996 Republican National Convention in San Diego, Ted Koppel, host of *Nightline* on ABC, announced that he and his program were quitting the event, frustrated by the lack of news. "Nothing surprising has happened," Koppel told his audience that evening. "Nothing surprising is anticipated." And with that, he and crew packed up to return to Washington, where the program is based.[23]

Koppel's decision was itself a bit of a surprise. True, television ratings were low (down 16 percent from 1992, with only 22 percent of the audience tuning in), and complaints about the "scripted" quality of the event were routine. But ABC had some three hundred staffers in San Diego and planned to spend more than $10 million covering the Republican and Democratic conventions. Every other major news organization had a team of reporters, producers, and aides in San Diego, bringing the total to some fifteen thousand media personnel.[24] Journalists had long ago concluded that the conventions were little more than advertisements for the major parties, devoid of drama or what they euphemistically called "substance." But still they came, by the thousands, to renew a ritual that had as much to do with the gathering of the news tribe as with the convening of the major parties.

By going home midway through the event, Koppel quit the tribe, temporarily, at least, and thereby exposed the absurdity of its quadrennial rituals—like swamping the 1,990 delegates with its gargantuan presence, reporting ad nauseam that there was nothing to report, entering the convention hall only to watch the proceedings on television. In one sense, then, Koppel and his producers made a courageous move: they took independent action while the rest of their colleagues went along for an all-expenses-paid ride.

But from a different perspective, *Nightline*'s departure from San Diego was a shining admission of defeat. Here was Ted Koppel, perhaps the most gifted television journalist of his time, host of one of the most intelligent and innovative news programs in the medium's history—a program that in 1985 produced the first public dialogue ever between a black leader and a white official in South Africa, and in 1988 persuaded Palestinian leaders and Israeli officials to debate each other on live television, with Koppel perched on a makeshift wall between them—here was *that* Ted Koppel, declaring that neither he nor his staff could think of anything useful to say or do as the Republican Party gathered to make its statement to America.[25]

Because it was scripted for the cameras, Koppel concluded that the convention was journalistically worthless. But what of a journalism that was worthier than the event, a report that gave Americans a better understanding of the Republicans than the Republicans cared to give of themselves? It was hard to believe that this was beyond the capacity of *Nightline* and its veteran staff. So if "the emperor has no clothes" was one way of reading Koppel's early flight from San Diego, "I'm out of ideas" was another.

Dennis Foley, political editor of the *Orange County Register,* had plenty of ideas about what to do with the Republican convention. By trying these ideas out in print, he and his reporters took on a different relationship to the event. They reported what happened, but they also tried to make something of it: an opportunity for citizens to understand in detail where the Republicans stood on the major issues of the day. Foley's planning began with the conviction, gathering in his mind since 1990, that something was deeply wrong with political journalism. In a statement of the problem presented to other journalists, he said:

> Something is wrong when people believe the political system excludes them from access to their own government and that only special interests who give serious money have influence.
>
> Something is wrong when so many people inside the system are cynical and when the voters/citizens are dismissed as unconcerned, unintelligent, and of value only to the extent they can be manipulated.
>
> Something is wrong when journalists are viewed as players in the system—and therefore the enemy.[26]

In Foley's mind these were wrongs that journalists could try to set right, within the limits of their role. That meant redefining what their role was. Political reporters had come to see themselves as watchdogs on the heels of politicians and their professional aides. A typical aim was to get inside the thinking of the pros and behind the facade of impression management. From this perspective, stories about money raising, election strategy, ad campaigns, and the self-serving culture of "spin" convey the reality of politics in the media age. "We could take the position—well, they said or did it. We just report it," Foley remarked. And yet: "We knew, or strongly suspected, that many stories were clashes of spin or outright false. But we wrote them anyway. And we were cynical about campaigns and the people involved with them." If the people within the game were spinmeisters and manipulators, good at their jobs but craven in their intentions, then average citizens were seen as Walter Lippmann saw them—outsiders, always complaining about something. "They just didn't understand or know what we knew," as Foley explained the attitude.

He began to suspect that he and his colleagues were standing in the wrong place. The position they took gave them the same view of the scene the insiders assumed: politics was about money, polls, media manipulation, and out-maneuvering your opponent. "People were angry, sure," Foley observed. "But they were angry at us as much as they were at the political system." Journalists "were part of the inside game" and they were not helping. "This was intolerable and had to change." Candidates and their seers could not be removed from the story, for what they said and did was still important. But the story did not have to be about them. It could be about something else: the citizen's struggle to be heard above the noise the system generated as its skilled operators went to work.

At first, this meant bringing into the newspaper voices of the presumed outsiders. The *Register* opened call-in lines, invited more letters from readers, and printed coupons in the paper asking for people's thoughts on the important issues they felt were going unaddressed—small steps, but well beyond the occasional call from an angry reader complaining about an item in today's news, which had been Foley's primary means of contact with the public. He also began to seek more speaking engagements in the community, where he could explain his thinking and listen to others reflect on the state of politics in California and the nation.

Foley knew he wanted to focus on issues rather than the ins and outs of the game. No simple task, since the issues, as framed by political professionals and interest groups, were so many pieces in the game. To get around this trap, the *Register* needed to do more than invite comment from the outside. So Foley and his reporters began to organize conversations with thoughtful civic leaders and groups of average citizens, in order to provide the paper with a deeper understanding of concerns the system either was not addressing or was treating in such a polarized manner that a majority of people saw no room for themselves.

As Foley put it: "Get ahead of the curve on issues bubbling up to the surface and catch their true relevance from the way real people experience them." The *Register* redirected much of its polling budget, away from snapshots of the horse race to survey citizens about their most pressing concerns. Polling allowed the paper to test what was heard in face-to-face conversation against the best data it could get about the public's priorities. The result, Foley hoped, would be a different kind of expertise in the minds of reporters: reliable knowledge about what mattered to citizens when they turned their attention to politics.[27]

The *Register* did more than ask people about their deepest concerns: it reported what it would take to get them addressed, which meant grappling with the details of issues and likely barriers to their resolution. From school board elections to the presidential race, the *Register* asked itself what kind of questions to candidates would yield the most useful replies for citizens who wanted to make a wise choice. It taught itself to ask those questions. Charts that explained positions in a glance were supplemented with background reporting on the candidates' experience, record of truthfulness, and their success as leaders and consensus builders. This was a different approach to the "character question," because it focused on the public record—building alliances, for example—rather than the private lives of politicians.

Here were some of the principles Foley adopted as he and his reporters tried to address what had gone wrong in political coverage.

> Journalists are . . . responsible both for what they see and for what they do.
>
> It is a journalist's responsibility to reveal the system, help voters understand the possibility of gaining access to and engaging it, should they so choose, to educate, explain and expose.
>
> We can do that in many ways: by exposing its shortcomings, by telling who wields influence and how, by explaining the roles of process and personality and politics on policy-making, by laying out and explaining the choices the public faces in dealing with difficult issues, by helping people understand complex issues, by allowing people to hear voices like their own in discussion, by turning away from the debate between extremes toward deliberation of realistic options, by giving voters a prominent position in the electoral process . . . by encouraging public discussion.[28]

Foley's first principle was the most far reaching: journalists are "responsible both for what they see and for what they do." In other words, what you find depends on where you look. Standing on the inside, glancing out, you are more likely to view citizens as outsiders, target groups, the objects of political technique, largely ignorant of what goes on in the expensive contest for their votes. Move closer to a citizen's perspective, and the scene may change: to politics as an exercise in free choice, a chance to learn and engage with issues. Well executed, this shift could make campaign reporting more useful, more likely to be read. But it was worth doing for another reason: it underlined the principle that elections are public property, not the grim work of a professional class.

In a little-noticed book, *History in Sherman Park*, former *New Yorker* writer Jonathan Schell undertook an imaginative shift of this kind. Reporting on the public's disengagement from politics during the 1984 election season, he decided to narrate his tale from the home of a middle-class family in the Milwaukee neighborhood of Sherman Park. In explaining his approach, Schell wrote:

> In every election season, the candidates, the candidates' supporters, the reporters, the commentators, and others in and around the campaigns pour forth their messages—speeches, political advertisements, press conferences, leaks, articles, editorials—hoping to cast light (or to obfuscate), to clarify (or to muddle), to inform, to argue, to persuade, to charm, to dazzle: to win. I wanted to go to some particular place in America where this bombardment was arriving—where some individual voters were making up their minds whom to vote for as they went about the business of their lives. And, having put myself there, I wanted to look back at the campaigns and their interpreters—and to reflect on what was going on.

Schell's reason for placing himself with a family in Sherman Park was disarmingly simple: in "our system it is the citizens who decide." Acknowledging all the problems with such a statement, he persisted: "So if by going to Sherman Park to talk to Gina and Bill Gapolinsky I was in one sense seeking out people at the bottom of the political hierarchy—people far from the centers of influence and power, on the receiving end of the government's decisions—I was in another sense seeking out the people who, under our system, are at the very pinnacle of power."[29]

Schell wrote as if the votes of Gina and Bill Gapolinsky actually mattered, suspending his knowledge of how elections are actually won, in order gain other knowledge about how politics is experienced by Americans. By moving inside the home to observe how politics arrived there, he could tell a story that returned citizens to their central place in the story. Schell's "as if" method is actually no more fanciful than the insider approach. Reporters who follow a presidential candidate along the campaign trail operate as if the various events planned for their benefit are somehow newsworthy in their own right, and would happen without their presence. But as Joan Didion observed in her 1988 essay: "Among those who traveled regularly with the campaigns . . . it was taken for granted that these 'events' they were covering, and on which they were in fact filing, were not merely meaningless but deliberately so: occasions on which film could be shot and no mistakes made."[30]

It was the emptiness of this taken-for-granted attitude (the convention is just a stage show) that persuaded Ted Koppel to leave San Diego. Party officials, trying to make a flawless impression on voters, sought to control every detail of the event. You're not going to use me that way, said Koppel to the Republicans (and later the Democrats). But the sad result was that *we* didn't get to use him, one of our ablest journalists. Had Koppel been willing to turn around in his imagination and face us—a public increasingly impatient with packaged politics—he might have found other statements to make, using *Nightline* as his forum.

He might have asked, for example, "how did we come to this point?" where fifteen thousand media people gather for an event they regard as mostly meaningless; where the major parties are unwilling to permit anything unplanned to happen, for fear of what might be said about it; where the Republicans and the Democrats, in their efforts to lure the audience to their respective shows, wound up losing the audience to other shows. What else had been lost in the transformation of the conventions into promotional reels? Did it have to be this way? Were there any alternatives? And what had been the role of network journalism—Koppel and his colleagues—in convincing the two parties that an eventless event was in their best interest?

If nothing surprising was anticipated, as Koppel told his viewers, all the more reason to surprise the audience with a fresh approach. Instead of seeing it the way its planners did—as televised propaganda, polished to a shine—why not regard the convention as unfinished and opaque, since it left out so much of what was happening within a turbulent Republican Party? By altering the conventions of convention coverage, *Nightline* might have used those four nights to review the long journey the Republicans (and the country) had taken from the 1964 convention, when Barry Goldwater was nominated, only to be trounced later by Lyndon Johnson, to 1996, when Republican ideas were arguably at the center of American politics. That would have been a statement of another kind: while you're putting on a show for the nation over four nights, we're going to show the nation where you've been for the past thirty years.

To explore these and other options, Koppel would have had to imagine his audience differently: not as people awaiting "surprise" from a convention that was designed to be unsurprising, but as citizens hoping for an *intelligible* politics—one that spoke to their desire to understand, more than their eagerness to be soothed by the Republicans or startled by journalists reporting on dissension in the ranks.

Dennis Foley decided to speak to his readers as citizens. He declared his newspaper's intention to serve them well, whatever the Republicans were serving up for mass consumption. On the same day that Koppel decided to leave San Diego, the *Register* used an entire page to address education concerns, which it knew to be near the top of citizens' priority lists. An extended feature examined how Bob Dole, the Republicans' choice for president, would seek to improve the nation's schools. Headlined "Bob Dole Would Demand More Parental Control and Responsibility in Schools," the article mostly summarized the candidate's views and proposals.

> The schools, in Dole's view, have lost their way in a sea of political correctness and education fads. He scoffs at the notion that some schools dropped the tradition of competitive spelling bees for fear of harming the self-esteem of the losers. He notes with disdain that many colleges—including those in California—are beefing up remedial classes in basic subjects because so many high schools are graduating seniors unable to cope with entry-level university classwork.
>
> Compounding the problem, Dole says, is the sense among many Americans that the people who run the schools won't listen. Between entrenched administrators and politically powerful teachers unions, he says, parents can't get a word in edgewise....
>
> Dole advocates only one major new educational endeavor: a federal voucher program giving low-income families certificates worth up to $1,500 to pay for private-school tuition.[31]

Alongside this story were short passages quoting statements Dole had made about education. On the opposite side of the page a shorter column gave a synopsis of Bill Clinton's views on the subject. In the center of the layout was a profile of two southern California parents thinking aloud about education problems. At the bottom a brief chart explained how federal dollars were spent in the state's public schools.

Viewed on the page, the *Register*'s coverage during the Republican convention seems simple, almost artless. But a better description of it is James Carey's "humble."[32] Rather than try to decode a cleverly packaged spectacle, the newspaper drew a campaign portrait for average people, those with busy lives to lead and important choices to make. Not confused spectators who need tutoring in how the game is played, but citizens with genuine concerns still to be addressed—this is how Foley saw the readers out there. He engaged them as a public, reachable by journalists who were themselves engaged in the search for meaning in politics. Had Ted Koppel sent himself and his producers on that search, he might have returned with something useful, rather than flying back to Washington disgusted and bored.

Civic Framing in Colorado Springs

"Bruce Takes On District 11: Crusader Finds Glitch in Ballot-Question Wording."

This headline ran on the front page of the *Colorado Springs Gazette* in October 1996. The story told of charges by "anti-tax hawk" Douglas Bruce against local school officials. He claimed that they had botched the wording of a bond initiative seeking to raise property taxes for computer equipment and teacher training, among other improvements. Bruce called a press conference to air his charges, the newspaper sent a reporter to cover it, and the result was the sort of story that can be found in almost any newspaper, every day of the week: A controversy has erupted. People are making charges and countercharges. It isn't clear who's right, but it is clear there's a fight.

Bruce's charge was that the ballot measure misled voters by first speaking of a tax increase that would last for five years, beginning in 1996–97, and then stating in the next sentence that the tax would last "through and including the 2001–2002 budget year," which appeared to mean six years. Bureaucratic bungling? An attempt to fool voters? The fight was on, in the pages of the newspaper.

> "If they couldn't count to six, how can we trust them with $235 million?" Bruce asked, referring to the maximum amount of money, including interest, that would be spent on the bond.
>
> [School spokeswoman Tracy] Cooper tossed aside Bruce's accusations and instead fired a salvo of her own.
>
> "Doug Bruce does this every election," Cooper said. "He's just trying to cloud the issues . . ."

Note the metaphors in play here. The lead actor, Doug Bruce, is a "crusader," who is "taking on" school officials. Tracy Cooper, defending her institution, fires a "salvo" back at Bruce, accusing him of precisely what he's charging: confusing the voters. Bruce comes complete with colorful quotes, citing a "multimillion-dollar mistake," noting how "these people can't even count to six," and threatening to file a challenge to the ballot measure with the Colorado secretary of state.[33]

Accounts like this one belong to such a familiar genre in the press that it even has a name: "he said, she said" stories. Journalists know how to write this kind of story. Indeed, they know it so well that they write it almost every day. And as they continue to write it, they keep sending us a message: that perpetual warfare is what politics and public life are about. One of public journalism's aspirations was to find some way of transcending the battleground theme without pretending that politics could be free of conflict and dispute. The problem with "he said, she said" stories wasn't that one side disagreed with the other; it was the premise that such a fact automatically made for news. Disagreement is trivialized when it becomes a technique for winning headlines, because players will always compete for headlines, whether their disagreements warrant it or not. Also, a seemingly innocuous formula like "get both sides" predisposed journalists to look for sides, when there might be other legitimate ways of picturing the public arena.

I will try to suggest one. New York City's Madison Square Garden is oval shaped, and midway up in the stands is a wide aisle that runs all the way around the arena. Whenever I go to a basketball game there, I like to take a walk around while play is under way. As you move along the oval with your head turned toward the game, you notice how the scene changes in appearance. The same players are running up and down the floor, but they look different from each point you occupy on your walk. The court elongates, the lines of force are suddenly reconfigured, the players grow and shrink in size, speeds alter before your eyes, action that seemed fuzzy one moment grows vivid with detail as you wind your way around.

The lesson I relearn through this simple ritual is an epistemological one, as academics would put it. Everyone in the arena has a partial view, although no one's view is obstructed. The game in its totality is as unavailable to Woody Allen, who sits at center court, as it is to the kid from New Jersey way up in the cheap seats. Most everyone in the Garden can see one another, but not what each of the others is seeing—an important point for our amateur epistemologist. Meaning: we can't see the whole situation from where we sit. Even when there's one object, (one game) there are many "objective" views of it, and only multiple perspectives can do justice to this elemental fact of human experience.

The press acknowledges this by including in news accounts the views of officials and spokespeople who disagree with one another. The clash of perspectives ("Cooper tossed aside Bruce's accusations and instead fired a salvo of her own") signals that no perspective is allowed to dominate; this is what is usually meant by "balance." A balanced story is one where the antagonists in some public controversy are heard in roughly equal measure: supporters and critics, Republicans and Democrats, school officials and anti-tax hawks. The news includes these views, but the view it prefers for itself is neither/nor. Journalists wish not to be the judges of who is right or wrong in the disputes they present as news; they associate such reluctance with their duty to be objective and fair. Paul Taylor, a former political reporter for the *Washington Post*, writes about this in his 1990 book *See How They Run*.

> Sometimes I worry that my squeamishness about making sharp judgments, pro or con, makes me unfit for the slam-bang world of daily journalism. Other times I conclude that it makes me ideally suited for newspapering—certainly for the rigors and conventions of modern "objective" journalism. For I can dispose of my dilemmas by writing stories straight down the middle. I can search for the halfway point between the best and the worst thing that can be said about someone (or some policy or idea) and write my story in that fair-minded place. By aiming for the golden mean, I probably land near the best approximation of truth more often than if I were guided by any other set of compasses—partisan, ideological, psychological, whatever. . . . Yes, I'm seeking truth. But I'm also seeking refuge. I'm taking a pass on the toughest calls I face—which may explain why I chose to be a watcher, not a doer, in the first place.[34]

This is a revealing passage. First, it associates truth with the midpoint between extremes. It mistrusts any other kind of lens (partisan, ideological, psychological). It neatly separates watching from doing. And it acknowledges that along with the desire to be truthful and fair is another quest, for what Taylor calls, with high candor, refuge. Journalists try to protect themselves against charges of undue bias by advertising that they have no view themselves; they are steering the story "straight down the middle." For most of them, this is a matter of professional conscience, not just a writing routine.

But Taylor's way of imagining the public world has its defects, too. Return for a moment to my walk around Madison Square Garden. Where is the halfway point in the circle of perspectives the arena affords? Where are the two sides to be set in opposition to each other? Once we begin to see the public arena as a circle (where what you see depends on where you sit) rather than a line stretching from one pole to another, the quest for balance becomes more complicated—in fact, more interesting.

Taylor's approach—which is not really his, but his craft's—helps convince journalists that they are, indeed, avoiding acts of judgment, advancing no view of their own. This is true in some ways, false in others. By "aiming for the golden mean," reporters may refuse to endorse either the best or the worst that can be said about someone. But by writing their stories from the midpoint between opposing sides, they conjure up a world in which opposing sides dominate the scene. Many public controversies can be described this way; but if refuge is what the describers are seeking, as much as truth, there is more refuge available if the arena is habitually seen as a world of polar opposites, with two sides battling to win, both distorting the truth to gain advantage, while the journalist enjoys the advantage of a middle position.

The *Gazette* in Colorado Springs tried to occupy that position in its report on Bruce and District 11. At the time, however, the paper was in the midst of a reporting experiment that moved in a quite different direction. It had decided to use the ballot initiative in District 11 as a canvas on which to practice the art of "framing"—and to play with the possibilities of different frames for the same story.[35]

The experiment grew from the thinking of editor Steve Smith, who had begun to reflect on the automatic decisions journalists make when they write the news under deadline pressure. With little time to think and many facts to include, reporters rely on newsroom conventions absorbed in the course of their training. The rhythm of charge and countercharge is one; it makes the story writable for journalists glancing anxiously at the clock. But it also shapes the way the action is pictured, the selection of lead and subordinate characters, the kind of conflict that will make the story seem interesting, dramatic.[36] All of which is summed up in the notion of framing.

"Choosing the frame for any story is the most powerful decision the journalist will make," Smith said in a talk to fellow editors in 1996. "Identifying and developing alternative frames is, I think, high journalistic practice." Smith wanted to give his staff in Colorado Springs more practice in thinking about the "many possible frames for any story," most of which "fall outside our natural reflexes." He asked how he and his colleagues might frame stories "from the center of the community," rather than setting one pole against another and allowing the journalist to stand as the center. This meant listening to people in a different way—not just for colorful quotes, or the position they were taking, but for the beliefs they held and the stake they felt in the issue at hand.

Shortly after he arrived at the *Gazette*, Smith began discussions among his staff about "public listening," which he defined as "the ability of newspaper people to listen with open mind and open ears; to understand what people are really saying." This sounds banal, until it is set against the highly reductive forms of listening that were already a part of newsroom routine. "Traditional newspaper interviewing tends to involve questioning that leads to a point, that point leading to a quote or a statement or an assertion in a news story." Public listening, said Smith, is more open ended. It suspends the drive for closure that reporters exhibit as they see the clock ticking above their heads at deadline time. If journalists were to expand their repertoire of frames, they would need to listen in a more expansive way.

So he asked reporters and editors to take turns running in-house meetings about changes in the newsroom, to give them experience in a different kind of listening. The routines they had mastered in conducting an interview or posing questions at a press conference would be useless in convening a discussion among their peers. From there, Smith moved to asking staffers to facilitate (without dominating) conversations the newspaper was holding with key stakeholders in the community and groups of ordinary citizens. He required staffers to take turns at a special phone line receiving calls from readers who wanted to comment or ask questions about anything in that day's paper. From 8:00 to 5:00 every day, a different journalist would sit in the chair and handle from forty to sixty-five calls. Some of the calls were mundane subscriber complaints, but many concerned "what is important to readers, and, especially, what is not important to readers," as Smith noted.[37]

Out of all this unroutinized listening, Smith hoped to give his staff a different feel for the community, which might work itself into different frames for telling the community's story. An opportunity to experiment arose with the bond issue vote and a related tax initiative proposed by District 11, in the center-city area of Colorado Springs, where 76 percent of registered voters do not have children in the public schools. A typical approach to such a story would be to explain what was on the ballot, detail how the money was to spent, speculate on the chances of its passage (perhaps through pre-election polls), and report the views of those who were pushing for the initiative, set off against others, like "anti-tax crusader" Douglas Bruce, who were against it.

The *Gazette* did most of that. But Smith wondered how the story would look if it were framed in a more expansive way. So he asked two reporters to go out and talk to people who were considered key stakeholders in the issue before the electorate. His idea was to write the same story with four different frames, and run the four stories on consecutive days leading up to the vote. The perspectives the paper chose were drawn from the many "possibilities suggested by our research, community conversations and one-on-one interviews with a whole lot of folks." One perspective was that of parents with kids in the public school system. Another was teachers, a third, students. The final frame was the view of taxpayers without children in the schools.

The two reporters, Wendy Lawton and Bill McKeown, were then sent back into the community for additional reporting. They built up a base of sixty interviews for each of the articles they wrote. Armed with this knowledge, they asked themselves how the ballot initiative (and the school system itself) looked from the perspectives of the groups they had studied. If what you see of the arena depends on where you sit within it, the reporters had to sit *with* parents, teachers, students, and taxpayers—not only by sitting down with them for interviews, but by imagining how the issue looked from the particular perspective they were trying to capture.

Here, then, was a novel way of interpreting demands for balance, accuracy, and fairness. Instead of balancing the story by framing it as a fight between embittered rivals, the *Gazette* sought a balance among four key perspectives. But even within those perspectives, people were hardly of one mind, so there was also balance to be sought among the conflicting views and values that, say, parents held. While many wanted more money for the schools, Smith said, "You still had parents with children in schools who were going to vote against the bond issue; and their perspective was part of the story . . . what you had was a community of like individuals essentially arguing with themselves about the bond issue."[38]

Accuracy, in this treatment, meant more than getting names, numbers, and quotations right. The paper was striving for a deeper level of accuracy by saying to the community, "This is a complex issue, and there are many ways of looking at it, so view the upcoming vote through the eyes of these people and watch as they wrestle with their own conflicts." A more accurate vivisection, might be one way of putting it. What does it mean for a newspaper to be fair? To Smith and his colleagues, being fair meant being *aware* of the multiple frames that might be placed around the story. It meant choosing these frames carefully, after thinking through the issue at hand and sitting down for dozens of interviews. Fairness came into view, not through a story-writing formula ("aiming for the golden mean"), but by writing the same story four times, giving the entire community a picture of the stage from four different seating sections.

Contrast this method with the spokesperson approach, in which a figure who speaks for the school system or for angry taxpayers offers either the best or the worst that can be said about a proposal. What Smith called civic framing was an effort to put aside the simplicity of such a scheme, which fit the demands of the newsroom—for refuge and ease of production—more than it did the needs of citizens with a decision to make. By bringing the subtle and often disguised act of framing out into the open, among his staff and on the front page of the paper, Smith went public with acts of judgment that normally reside behind the smooth facade of a finished product.

This can be seen in the editor's notes that prefaced each of the articles:

> Editor's note: This story is written from the viewpoint of Colorado Springs School District 11 students and recent graduates. (*Colorado Springs Gazette,* October 30, 1996)

> Editor's note: This story is written from the viewpoint of Colorado Springs School District 11 teachers. (*Colorado Springs Gazette,* October 31, 1996)

> Editor's note: This story is written from the viewpoint of Colorado Springs taxpayers without children in the schools. (*Colorado Springs Gazette,* November 1, 1996)

What, exactly, was the editor noting? That the newspaper was not pretending to be omniscient but describing the varied perspectives it had taken. That there is no view-less view of the issue, but value in multiplying the number of views taken toward it. That journalism involves judgment, which can be worked into the story as a kind of guide to an intelligent reading of it. Finally, that a newspaper can level with its community about the ways of seeing that its reporters have employed and find sufficient "refuge" by disclosing what they are. All this is what Smith meant by civic framing.

The final results were not revelatory, but they were journalism in a different key. Citizens of Colorado Springs had a chance to consider in some depth the concerns of other citizens, not only about the upcoming vote but about the schools and the people who ran them. Administrators were not allowed to dominate the discussion, although their views were included. And the stories managed to convey people's conflicting feelings without use of battleground imagery.

. . . .

It's about skepticism. The feeling—fed by run-ins with young clerks who can't make change or job applicants who can't spell—that public education isn't doing its job. That there's too much featherbedding and not enough teaching.

Taxpayers without children in schools say it's not about turning their backs on other people's children. It's about teaching the basics. Demanding excellence. Getting their money's worth. It's about a perception by many that the present doesn't stack up to the past.

It all adds up to a tough sale for Colorado Springs School District 11 on Tuesday, when the city's largest school system asks property owners for more than $100 million. And rational explanations about how the money will be spent—repairing old schools, building four new ones in the northern part of the city and buying nearly 9,000 computers—might not be enough.

And it's taxpayers without children in the schools—75 percent of the district's registered voters—who will decide the issue.

Chat with these people—retirees in particular—and a pattern emerges. They acknowledge many D-11 schools are crumbling. They concede growth probably means new schools are needed.

But they have some questions, some gripes, some sincere suggestions—and those could color the way they vote.

The rub for the district? Many of the concerns won't or can't be answered by the district's two narrowly focused ballot questions, 3G and 3H.

Take retirees Jim and Ramona Wheeler and David Olson. They volunteer their time to help elementary school students master reading. Their experiences in the GrandFriend program has made them strong supporters of teachers, District 11—and the bond issue. But even they're worried about some of the things they see in classrooms.

"I would definitely want to see a better teacher-to-student ratio," says Olson. "I think sometimes the community expects teachers to accomplish the impossible."

"There doesn't seem to be enough time spent on basics," says Jim Wheeler. "I think the kids either have to have longer hours or more school days."

Retired teacher Doris Loucks, normally a strong supporter of education, has had too many run-ins with vacant-eyed clerks who can't add up her purchases. She, like many others, wonders if the district's plan to spend money for computers will accelerate what she thinks has been a steady erosion in the emphasis on the three R's. . . .

Silver Key volunteers Hank Gendreizig and Ruby Swenson don't doubt for a minute that something needs to be done about aging school buildings. But they suspect there are more than just roofs and boilers that need fixing.

They think classes need to be smaller, kids need a better grounding in the basics, poor teachers need to be weeded out and uninvolved parents need a boot in the behind. . . .

A tough crowd? You bet. Their basic questions: Are our tax dollars being spent efficiently? Will additional taxes correct the problems taxpayers see in public education?

—From Bill McKeown, "Taxpayers Wonder if Schools Do Enough: Many Skeptical About District 11 Bond Issue," *Colorado Springs Gazette,* November 1, 1996

. . . .

When Steve Smith and his colleagues looked back on their story told four ways, they realized that they could have added other frames. What about employers? Religious conservatives? City government and school officials? Arguments could be made for all these perspectives, and probably more. This was one effect of Smith's move toward civic framing. Once the question "how should we be framing this story?" is asked, the habitual frames come under scrutiny. As an important vote neared, reporters and editors at the *Gazette* grew more conscious of their role as scene setters, dramatists, positioners of the people they wrote about and for. Writing the same story four times was not a technique the newspaper could employ for every issue in the news. But by demonstrating that it could be done, Smith and his staff found relief from a tired formula and opened themselves to further reflection on the subtle power of framing.

Coincident with the rise of public journalism were a variety of attempts to reimagine what democratic politics was about, as different thinkers tried to understand in depth Americans' disaffection with the system as it stood. One was Michael Sandel, a political philosopher identified with the "communitarian" school of thought. In his 1996 book *Democracy's Discontent,* Sandel wrote of two concerns at the center of Americans' anxieties for the future: "One is the fear that individually and collectively, we are losing control of the forces that govern our lives. The other is the sense that, from family to neighborhood to nation, the moral fabric of community is unraveling around us. These two fears—for the loss of self-government and the erosion of community—together define the anxiety of the age. It is an anxiety that the prevailing political agenda has failed to answer or even address."[39]

If Sandel was right, then perhaps there was something the serious press could do. It could look beyond the predictable arguments of the major players—which "are unable to make sense of our condition"—and examine the "public philosophy that animates them . . . the assumptions about citizenship and freedom that inform our public life." In the course of this inquiry, journalists might find new tasks for themselves that met the anxieties of the age. Sandel writes of a "formative politics," one that equips citizens to be actors with others, as against a procedural view, which assumes that the system is simply there, and we either work it to our advantage or drop out. To him, democracy as self-government "means deliberating with fellow citizens about the common good and helping to shape the destiny of the political community." It "requires a knowledge of public affairs," but also a "sense of belonging, a concern for the whole, a moral bond with the community whose fate is at stake."[40]

When the *Dayton Daily News* asked its community "where do we go now?" following the shutdown of two large local employers; when the *Akron Beacon Journal* said in the wake of the Los Angeles riots, "There must be something we can do, here in Akron, about our race problem"; when Rob Elder of the *San Jose Mercury News* learned to see the editorial pages as a place for "working through" heated issues; when Dennis Foley and his reporters at the *Orange County Register* looked beyond a prepackaged Republican convention to where issues met up with people's troubles; when Steve Smith and his colleagues in Colorado Springs experimented with civic framing; when, in dozens of towns and cities across the country, a similar spirit of invention took hold, something was happening in the press that touched again on the American experiment in self-government.

To borrow Sandel's terms, reporters and editors were finding a "formative journalism" to go with his formative politics. They were asking themselves what it meant for the newspaper to be a good democrat. This demanded a different kind of commitment from journalists, who could not pretend they had no stake in how the story turned out. After all, they were citizens, too, inclined no longer to forget this fact or will it away.

Does It Help the Citizen Decide?

The Intellectual Journey of the *Virginian-Pilot*

One newspaper more than any other took the idea of public journalism and moved it several stages ahead. At the *Virginian-Pilot*, headquartered in Norfolk, the enterprise found a home—an organization that learned how to experiment on itself. From 1994 on, the *Pilot* found the tools it needed: a vocabulary for sparking change, models and templates that redrew the newspaper's place within the community, readings on democracy and civic life that applied to daily journalism, staff retreats where people could think and argue together, and a spirit of inquiry that brought this work forward into print.

The experiment in Norfolk did not reach everyone; nor was it a fully coordinated effort. Rather, scattered parts of the operation changed as a new language entered the atmosphere. The people most involved tried to let others in on what they were doing and thinking. Enough got the drift to turn the *Virginian-Pilot* into a kind of learning machine, as the following tales are meant to suggest.

Does It Advance the Conversation?
New Rules for Candidates and Journalists

A September evening in 1995. With election season just under way, dozens of cars pull into the parking lot of the *Virginian-Pilot*. Candidates for state legislature, some accompanied by their aides, emerge for a meeting with journalists. It is not a press conference or a round of endorsement interviews. On the agenda are the rules of the game: what will count as news during the upcoming campaign, and the treatment the candidates can expect as the paper goes about its reporting. The *Pilot*'s editors have come to some broad conclusions about revising the ritual. The changes will affect their own journalism, the newspaper's interaction with contenders, and perhaps the campaign itself. That is why the candidates are there.

Tony Germanotta, an assigning editor at the *Pilot*, introduces himself as "the person who will be making some of the decisions on what goes into the newspaper." He notes that in conversations with citizens the paper uncovered a lingering frustration with both candidates and journalists. "They told us they were not getting much out of the old way we did it," he says. "The horse race, the bickering, the mudslinging, that didn't inform them when it came time to go into a voting booth."[1]

The *Pilot*, he adds, will be basing its coverage on a citizen's agenda, a list of priorities culled from interviews and roundtable discussions with area residents. The agenda has been vetted by journalists and tested through survey research; the staff is reasonably confident that it includes citizens' deepest concerns and the major problems facing the state. On the list are such issues as taxes and spending priorities, creating new jobs, crime and public safety, the quality of public schools, and the atmosphere of partisan bickering that has overtaken Virginia politics. Items on the citizen's agenda will be reported in depth during the campaign, and candidates will be asked for their views on each of the major issues, to be summarized later in a voter's guide distributed the week before the election.

In deciding where to focus their news coverage, Germanotta and his colleagues have settled on a simple rule: Does it help the citizen decide? Does it advance the conversation? He tells the candidates that the editors aren't about to "cut any deals with you tonight." Nor are they seeking approval or giving out advice. "We're not going to tell you how to run your campaign." The goal is to explain the paper's plans, answer questions and get an initial response. "We're in the process of learning this," he adds. To underline their determination to be open and aboveboard, the editors declare that the meeting is on the record. They can be held accountable for anything they say.

Other details are spelled out. The *Pilot* will solicit questions from voters and then phone the candidates for their responses. Personal attacks and manufactured controversies will be downplayed, unless they involve levels of deception that illuminate a question of public character. Strategy stories and coverage of who's ahead will not be as prominent. The paper plans to publish a regular list of candidate forums and debates, so that citizens who want to attend will know where to go. For the first time, it will set up a site on the World Wide Web containing voter information, including links to the candidates' Web sites, if they have them.

After listening to the *Pilot*'s plans, the politicians ask questions, mostly about the citizen's agenda and the paper's priorities. Someone wants to know if explanatory reporting about major issues would be constrained by the public's existing, and often vague, grasp of public policy. (The answer is no.) How do I get an op-ed piece into the paper? (Call the editorial page editor; we don't control that space.) As the discussion continues, candidates and journalists find themselves in agreement that education issues are profoundly related to concerns headlined as crime, that both are related to job creation, and that citizens often see them this way. Both groups puzzle aloud about the difficulty of examining intricate problems of public policy without over-simplifying on one hand or swamping people with details on the other. "I don't envy you," says one candidate when he considers that challenge from the journalist's perspective.

A few of the politicians try to curry favor with the newspaper, praising its new plan, warming to the reporters who will be covering the campaign. Editor Cole Campbell interjects. "We do not think of you as our customers," he says. "We think of you as our suppliers. Our primary customer is the citizen, and if it suits the citizens' needs, we will print it." The general tone of the meeting is civil and businesslike. No deals are cut, few speeches made. The candidates seem to grasp the rules and the logic behind them. Several say they welcome the change, others just want to know how it might affect them. The editors go out of their way to call what they are doing a first attempt. When they sense that they have answered all questions, they end the meeting and everyone goes home.

Later that election season, the *Virginian-Pilot* went out and did exactly what it said it would: center its coverage on the citizen's agenda, downplay personal attacks that might have become distractions, reduce the emphasis on politics as strategy, and produce a voter's guide including the candidates' answers to seventeen key questions drawn from the paper's understanding of citizens' major concerns.

Treating Readers as Citizens: The Newspaper Gets Audited

April of 1995. Dennis Hartig, deputy managing editor of the *Virginian-Pilot*, gives a talk on public journalism to the local League of Women Voters. He explains how his paper is trying to treat readers as citizens rather than spectators, which means emphasizing what people can do about public problems, other than read the news and shake their heads. League members listen with interest, ask a few questions, and thank Hartig for his time.

Without telling the newspaper, the League then convenes a series of meetings in which members discuss whether the paper is achieving its announced goals. The group decides to conduct an audit of the *Pilot*'s crime coverage for the month of May, to see if citizens are indeed being addressed as potential actors. The audit shows that some stories succeed and others do not. A report on vandalism, for example, includes a "How to Help" guide, which shows citizens what they can do. But an article about the increase in child abuse doesn't say how to detect and report cases of suspected abuse.

The League prepares a report on its findings, noting that public journalism can be a way to "support, encourage, and inform citizens' participation in government." But talking the talk is not the same as walking the walk, it observes. "The *Virginian-Pilot*'s commitment to this approach must be evaluated before it may be declared a success; citizens must examine its implementation and outcomes." In studying the paper's crime coverage, League members were "looking for information that would lead to knowledge, and to power," the report said. "They were looking for articles that could lead citizens to further action, and to solutions." The report ends with mixed findings: The *Virginian-Pilot* has made "great strides in public journalism by opening citizen dialogue, and pointing the way to citizen action," but it "could do more to inform readers of the grassroots organizations and institutions that deal with specific issues." One member notes how crime news is frequently disabling: "The feeling of being powerless against crime is reinforced when all you hear about is crime. To empower people, we have to see a complete picture of crime in the community—the crime, the victim, the arrest, the criminal justice system, rehabilitation, and reconciliation."[2]

The League then sends a copy of its study to the *Virginian-Pilot*—the first that the newspaper has heard of it. Editor Cole Campbell responds with a Sunday column headlined "League Takes Us at Our Word, Studies Our Effort to Serve Citizens Better." Campbell summarizes the report's major findings and quotes from passages criticizing the paper and a few that praise its efforts. He adds that the *Pilot* is "rethinking its coverage philosophy" in response to some of the League's suggestions. "Thanks for the report card," Campbell concludes. "We'll keep working to improve our marks."[3]

Core Values and Key Questions: A Public Journalism Retreat

A spring weekend in 1995. I travel to Norfolk with my colleague Lisa Austin, research director of the Project on Public Life and the Press. We're there to join in a two-day retreat with forty editors and reporters from the *Pilot*. The goal is to introduce a wider group to some of the thinking behind public journalism, in a beachfront hotel removed from the hectic atmosphere of a daily newsroom.

For several weeks prior to the event, the staff has been preparing itself, reading from a packet distributed to all participants and including selections from Alexis de Tocqueville's *Democracy in America,* an essay by James Carey on the press and public life, the work of political scientist Robert Putnam on the decline of civic participation, excerpts from Daniel Yankelovich's *Coming to Public Judgment,* some of my writings, and the thoughts of other authors on the state of politics and citizenship in America. In-house seminars have been held for those who want to discuss what they have read in advance of the retreat. Editors and reporters have been asked to annotate or critique stories, using what they have gathered so far about public journalism. In a fine display of newsroom sarcasm, the staff has already renamed the event "the lockdown," because no one will be allowed to go home on Friday or Saturday night; hotel rooms are booked for all.

The primary participants are editors and reporters whose work touches on public life, but they are joined by a few outsiders to the newsroom. Beyond myself and Lisa Austin, these include Bruce Bradley, vice president and general manager of the newspaper, who later became its publisher; Louis Hodges, a scholar at Washington and Lee University who specializes in professional ethics; and Patricia Richardson, a local citizen and director of a leadership group in the Norfolk area. The visitors have pledged to do the readings as well; Richardson would later write about the event in the newspaper.

The retreat is designed around a few "core values" and "key questions," drawn from the assigned literature or aimed at common assumptions in the craft. The core values include:

- seeing readers as citizens and starting where citizens start;
- imagining public life as a conversation;
- deliberation as a key to problem solving;
- journalists as exemplary citizens.

The key questions are:

- How do we make public journalism vital reading?
- How do we use public journalism to hold citizens and the community accountable?
- How do we maintain our independence and engage the community in solving its problems?
- How do we make public journalism fun and fulfilling to do?

As with any group of journalists, the *Pilot* staff has doubts and fears about an implied overhaul of the paper's principles. Many are openly skeptical. Those of us with an idea to promote—Lisa Austin and I, along with some editors and a few committed reporters—have to push ourselves to be clearer. Just what are we suggesting: how to do a better job, or how to define a different job? If public problem solving is politics at its best, is politics at its worst to be slighted or somehow ignored?

Members of the Richmond bureau, who cover the state capital, emerge as the toughest questioners. They are among the most experienced and talented journalists on staff. They compete with correspondents from the state's other major newspapers and the *Washington Post*—where some of them may want to work someday. If public journalism takes over at the *Pilot*, how will their work stand up against the competition? Will they come under some mandate to take a more civil tone, perhaps by going easier on politicians?

It is up to Cole Campbell, the boss, to address these fears. And he does, pledging to force nothing on the Richmond bureau that its members don't regard as an improvement. But he also argues with doubters, asking them to give their own view of the drama of politics and where the citizen's place lies. One vision of the press, stressing the watchdog role above all, collides with another, in which the journalist's job is to help people get their deepest concerns addressed. One view of politics, as perpetual conflict between rival parties, meets a different view: politics as civic participation, deliberation in public, and community problem solving.

As these differences get aired, public journalism drifts in and out of focus. It gets sharper for some, murkier for others. Problems of trust burst into view, as some sense a fad or formula about to be imposed on them, despite the editor's promise that nothing of the kind is in store. In any newsroom, certain journalists are the most respected figures among their peers. Since colleagues are sure to be influenced by what these opinion leaders conclude, they play a key role at the retreat. Some hold fast to a traditional approach. But others remark on how the old ways of doing things—crime coverage that flows downward from cops, political news that starts with city hall—seem to be less and less effective.

At one point, a deputy managing editor who is African-American notes that she has heard little about the minority groups that she feels are underserved by the newspaper. Until that issue gets addressed, she says, all talk about reconnecting with citizens sounds like empty rhetoric to her. Campbell halts the proceedings and asks for a round of ideas on how the *Pilot* can better reach the disaffected citizens in minority communities, many of whom have given up on the paper.

Later, the participants split up into work groups that try to discern how public journalism might be worked into education coverage, local and state politics, crime news, or women's and family issues. Some of these go well; others sputter to a halt. At dinner on Saturday night, I sit down at a table with a few political reporters and Campbell, who is trying to get them excited about a different metaphor for election coverage. He sketches in rough outline a "job candidate" model, in which the contenders for office would be treated as applicants for public posts, complete with job descriptions, résumés, letters of recommendation, and other features that would help voters focus on the choice of whom to "hire." As I join in, the reporters listen and argue back, resisting some of our wilder notions but absorbing the idea that all forms of political journalism rest on a mental picture of how politics and democracy are supposed to work. This we count as progress. And in 1996 the job-candidate metaphor became a major tool in the *Pilot*'s election coverage.[4]

Over drinks and in one-on-one dialogue in the evening, I can see where public journalism stands with the people of the *Pilot*. Not surprisingly, it stands everywhere: Highfalutin nonsense to some, undistinguished common sense to others. An exciting turn of mind, a dense stew of unfamiliar terms. A new orthodoxy coming down from on high, a challenge to the old ways moving slowly into sight. There is no consensus, no conversion; the native skepticism of an experienced staff remains intact. But there is also a lot of lively chatter, and a good portion of it is about journalists and what they are for.

The retreat, then, is an experiment on the mind of the organization: If we put the idea into play, will people play around with the idea? If we ask them to read serious thought on politics and democracy, will they work their way toward the press? (Indeed, will they read it at all?) If we offer a thesis—that public life is in trouble—will they trouble themselves with the consequences? If we call public journalism a work in progress, will people do the work that might make for progress? Or will we simply frustrate them further with vague injunctions to "hold citizens accountable," without making clear what that means? And if our preferred method is intellectual persuasion, what will it take to persuade journalists who find honor in their traditions, satisfaction in their routines, a lot of good in what they are doing now?

Cole Campbell has an idea of what it takes. He ends the retreat with a talk to his colleagues (later fashioned into a column for the paper) in which he traces the development of his own philosophy. He began his career, he says, with an image of the reporter as investigator. "Here the journalist aggressively covers—or uncovers—what happened and tells readers about it." This view treats the rest of us as a client of the newspaper, equipped with reliable information and professional advice so that we can make intelligent decisions. Journalism serves this client. Campbell then came to appreciate the storytelling model, in which a human character faces a troubling predicament and tries to resolve it. This approach sees readers as spectators, "showing them what happened and hoping they will experience an 'aha!'—a moment of revelation" into human nature or present reality. Readers want these moments: good stories, well told.

The third image Campbell calls a conversational model, his term for public journalism. Here, "the journalist works to give readers a way to talk about the news—among family, friends and associates, and among members of the larger community." The audience is regarded not as clients receiving a professional service, or spectators to a compelling public drama, but as actors, "people who have a stake in the news, who want to see the possibilities behind often troubling developments, who want to participate in solving shared problems." Campbell then heads for the intersections. He describes the fact-finding, storytelling, and conversational models not as warring philosophies but as component parts of a "three-legged stool." As he later puts it, "All three legs are needed to keep superior journalism upright." Without investigation, we are missing key facts. Without storytelling, the facts lack a human drama to animate them. Without conversation, the story is consumed privately, when it should be a prelude to public activity.[5]

Campbell's talk ends on a personal note. "My daughter is twenty years old," he says, "and I want her to live in a democracy. Right now I have my doubts." Whatever one thinks of the three-legged stool, it is difficult to doubt his sincerity at this moment, for there is emotion in his voice, the sound of an editor taking a risk in front of his staff and his boss. The retreat itself was a bit risky. It could easily have snared us in our own pretensions. Or, by pressing people together in an atmosphere of ideas, it might have left them with a renewed sense of possibility. Both probably happened, and a lot else besides. Because the weekend seemed to demand a lot of work for an uncertain payoff, the organizers had heard a good deal of grumbling beforehand. Afterward, the editors told me, some in the newsroom who hadn't been there felt miffed. "Why wasn't I invited to the lockdown?" they said.

Tuning into Citizens: Conversation as a Reporting Tool

The summer of 1994. The *Virginian-Pilot* is invited to join a statewide partnership to report on crime and parole issues. Governor George Allen is about to propose that the legislature abolish parole in Virginia, and the state's major newspapers want to combine forces to examine the question in depth. A few *Pilot* editors and reporters—call them early adopters—want to test their understanding of public journalism, particularly the use of what they have come to call "community conversations."

They have a hypothesis. If they are actually doing something different, then they should be able to add something to the partnership's reporting that would not otherwise be present. The Virginia newspapers joining the *Pilot* are fairly traditional in their outlook. If public journalism can supplement the series, without provoking a needless debate over high principles, then the editors will know that what they've been trying to teach themselves can enrich statewide political reporting.[6]

The background to this field test is another experiment the paper is simultaneously conducting on itself. Earlier that year, the newspaper had enlisted the aid of the Harwood Group, a research firm headed by Richard Harwood, who specializes in the art of listening to citizens as they grapple with complex public problems. In 1993, Harwood had distilled the lessons of his firm's experience into a report titled "Meaningful Chaos: How People

Form Relationships to Public Concerns," published by the Kettering Foundation. The report asked, what allows people to find personal meaning in public issues, to see their own stake in policy debates? The answers came out of Harwood's long experience in listening to a diverse group of citizens discuss politics around a table, where they can join in the give-and-take without excessive steering toward a particular proposal or poll-tested appeal. Among the conclusions:

- People want to find the *connections* among issues in the public arena, rather than treat them as isolated or self-contained controversies.
- They employ their own *experience* in discussing public questions—not just self-interest, narrowly defined, but lessons drawn from personal encounters and a lifetime of learning.
- Talk to them long enough and citizens show a desire for *coherence* in public dialogue, an intelligibility that would allow them to see the "why" and "how" of a problem as well as the "what." This is something they don't often get from the current flood of news and information.
- People insist on *room for ambivalence* if they are to join in public discussion, an "opportunity for fact-finding, listening, testing of ideas, and figuring out what they believe and how they feel." Frequently this safe space is absent in the partisan battleground that politics has become.
- *Emotion* comes out when citizens get engaged; without a means for expressing the intensity of their views, they find public discussion arid and uninteresting.
- A formidable barrier to civic engagement is the *inauthentic* feel of public discussion, much of which doesn't ring true to people's experience, sounds inflated or hyped, or feels deadened by the language of experts.
- People want a sense of *possibility* before they will get engaged; they need to believe that progress can be made, that they can participate effectively.
- Often, there are individuals who become *catalysts* in citizens' lives, leading them to take a greater interest in public affairs—a family member, neighbor, or friend who sparks a feeling that "getting involved" is worthwhile or the right thing to do.
- People grasp the importance of *mediating institutions*—churches, schools, neighborhood groups—that provide a place to come together, talk, and learn to act.[7]

Rather than simply preach these lessons, Harwood teaches his clients how to discover such factors at work in their own conversations with citizens. Beginning in early 1994, the *Pilot* tries it out with the newspaper's "public life" team. Self-named, the team brings together reporters who had earlier been assigned to cover local politics at the city hall and town council level. Editor Cole Campbell decides to use this group as a proving ground for the work of Harwood and some ideas in public journalism. Beginning with a vague desire to listen more carefully to citizens, the team learns to make use of "community conversations," which bring together a dozen or so local residents to spend an evening wrestling with an issue prominent in the news.[8]

At first, the team does not know what to do with the results. Printing a transcript of the talk is easy enough, but it makes for dull reading. Team members soon discover a different use for the deliberations. Instead of hunting for convenient or colorful quotes, they try listening in depth as people do what Harwood says they often do: search for connections among issues, find "room for ambivalence," apply common sense and their own experience to the problem, speak with genuine emotion, and toss aside packaged politics or the numbing discourse of experts. Just listening to people doesn't sound like much of an insight. But it proves to be harder than conducting a standard interview. The *Pilot* reporters have to abandon their search for the provocative one-liner and their casual assumptions about the average Joe or Jane. Citizens are heard wrestling with conflicting priorities, getting beneath the back-and-forth of policy debates to their own doubts in the face of difficult choices, voicing their hope for resolution, asking for a more honest, authentic public dialogue. The journalists also note that when the meeting ends, people just keep talking, right out into the parking lot. The hazy notion of "engagement" takes vivid form. *They don't want to stop.*

With an intuitive sense that there is something knowable in these conversations—significant, if not scientific—the public life team tries to work this knowledge into its reporting. Perhaps they can find (or frame) stories that connect better to citizens' deepest concerns. With this in mind, team members Tom Warhover and Tony Wharton come to the statewide parole project with a plan: to crisscross Virginia holding community conversations with reporters from other newspapers, in hopes of hearing something unavailable to other ways of knowing about crime, parole, and punishment. Warhover decides at the outset that expectations for public journalism's influence on the project will be kept low. "Just ten degrees" is how he describes it: a slight turn in the partners' angle of vision.

From earlier talks with citizens about crime, Warhover and Wharton believe they know something: to begin with parole, and the governor's proposal to abolish it, can be counterproductive. It encourages a rehearsal of "time to get tough on crime," a sloganeering style that might work to win elections but does not win journalists any new insights. Citizens could fall into this discourse as easily as candidates and consultants; journalists could always let them. Better to wind up at the governor's proposal after a detour through people's more thoughtful reflections on crime, punishment, and the wider problem "no parole" was meant to solve.

So Wharton and Warhover set out across the state on their listening jaunt, joined by members of the *Pilot*'s capital bureau. They invite some of their partners to the conversations they arrange. What do they hear? Horrific tales of crimes against loved ones, neighborhoods gripped by fear, and feelings of decency coarsened into attitudes that were harsh and unforgiving toward career criminals. But they also hear some hope for answers and occasional empathy for the lives caught up in crime. In general, Virginians seem to support Allen's call to abolish parole. They want convicted criminals to serve their time, and they don't mind adding: "All of it." But that is not all of it. As one participant says, "If that's all we do, we'll be here again in ten years talking about this all over again." Wharton later writes in summary of what was heard:

> Virginians said there had to be a parallel effort to keep the next generation from turning to crime. In defiance of all political pundits' labels, they were not "conservative" or "liberal" on this issue. They wanted crime punished. They also wanted society and government to reach out to young people and even the convicted felon with efforts to get them on the right track and keep them there. Nobody was interested in "rehabilitation," which we quickly saw was also a buzzword with little meaning left; but they wanted education, and boot camps, and programs for single parents, and better day care, and good jobs. Punishment, they said, must be paired with prevention . . .

Next, Warhover and Wharton learn that their colleagues at other newspapers are hearing echoes of the same sentiment. The partners agree to add a fifth installment to the parole project treating the "next generation" theme, which is now seen as integral to the issue—whether or not it is prominent in the governor's proposal and the upcoming debate in the legislature. With the prism turned ten degrees, political reporting now includes what politics as usual may be avoiding: a view of crime and punishment that goes well beyond the pros and cons of abolishing parole, or its prospects for passage in the state capital.[9]

Harwood's work was here coming to life. When citizens get engaged with an important public question, they look for connections: for example, between punishment and prevention. They want to move forward to possibilities: what about the next generation? They jettison what sounds inauthentic: buzzwords like rehabilitation. They carry strong emotions into the room: grief and rage, but also a desire to save another kid from going bad. They don't want to be placed in the political system's boxes: are you a liberal or conservative on crime? They seek room for a variety of convictions, some of which may conflict while others cohere into a nuanced view of the problem: yes, we have to get tough with criminals, but an equally tough chore is to give young people a decent chance in life.

That same summer, Tony Wharton discovers a further yield from his listening exercise.

> I had been in community conversations that summer where two women talked about their experiences with horrible crimes in which loved ones had been murdered. One thing that had struck me was the incredible human drama and power in their stories, and how easily it was cheapened by journalists and politicians alike talking about crime. I also saw the complexity of their feelings about crime, not the one-dimensional victim's cry for revenge that is so often depicted.
>
> I faced the reality of this within a few months, when I saw these two women again at a press conference held by Virginia Governor George Allen, out promoting his parole abolition plans. Allen was using Dale Pennell and Dorothy Soule simply to politically support his program. He was not interested in the complexity of their feelings and in fact, had not talked one-on-one with either woman. His staff had lined them up.

It would have been easy enough to just report what happened at the governor's press conference. Many reporters would say, "and that's all you should do." But Wharton knew there was a missing piece, and he got it from citizens—people around the state and his interviews with two Virginians who were lifted onto the public stage. They had become symbols in a political play, but they were also citizens with something to say. And what they were saying had its own integrity, not to be trifled with: not by Allen, the politician, not by Wharton, the journalist. In writing the story, Wharton felt challenged "not to simply trip up Allen by using the women's other statements against him." His responsibility to Pennell and Soule was "to let the story clearly state that they supported Allen's plans." Here is how his account begins.

> One by one, the four respectable, middle-aged women told their hair-raising tales of brutal crimes committed and punishment cut short.
>
> In front of Gov. George Allen and an enthusiastic crowd of his supporters on the steps of the courthouse Friday afternoon, the four went on to firmly endorse his plan to abolish parole. . . .
>
> The four were part of a well-orchestrated string of appearances by Allen, Attorney General James Gilmore and a host of political allies across the state in an effort to persuade the General Assembly to approve Allen's plan.
>
> What some of the women said afterward—but Allen did not hear—is that they consider his proposal a good beginning, rather than the entire answer, to solving the crime problem.
>
> "First," Soule said, she wanted to make one thing clear: "I am for the governor's recommendations, very much so. Something has got to be done."
>
> "However," she also said, "we have got to reach these kids in the home. We can't wait. We have to see to it that these single parents take parenting classes."[10]

The lesson: By tuning in to the sound of politics as it comes into public possession, the *Virginian-Pilot* taught itself how to learn from citizens and deepen the yield on its reporting. Just ten degrees was all the adjustment needed.

The Skills of Democracy:
Walter Lippmann, John Dewey, and Cole Campbell

September 1995. Cole Campbell finds himself at the podium before several hundred peers at a Washington symposium sponsored by the Pew Center for Civic Journalism. In the hierarchy of the craft, Campbell is a man from the provinces. Many in attendance are in the Washington press corps; they want to see if there's anything to these lofty visions of reconnecting with citizens and cultivating democracy coming from places like Wichita, Charlotte, Dayton, and Norfolk.

Campbell, one of their guides, is an editor with a talent for seeing things whole. His office says a lot about him. It is always piled high with books, from the latest management treatise to academic works on politics and social trends. Several times on visits to Norfolk I hear from him about some exciting new study by a philosopher or social scientist—published in the scholarly fields I try to monitor myself. The titles he gives me are good and on topic, so I am grateful, but also curious about what he draws from his reading. One thing he has concluded: no revision of the journalist's role in democracy is complete unless some democracy comes to the newsroom. As much as possible, he wants his reporting teams to be self-governing; he looks for ways to devolve more decision making to them, without pretending that he's no longer in charge as the top-ranking editor.

Campbell is part intellectual, part editor at a daily newspaper. Which is not to say he's smarter than his peers, just more curious about the world of ideas and comfortable at higher levels of abstraction. Here he is at the Pew Center's conference, reflecting on the exchange between Walter Lippmann and John Dewey, then transposing the ideas there into the daily world of his newspaper.

. . . .

Four score and minus seven years ago, in 1922 our intellectual father Walter Lippmann brought forth his contention, a new notion, skeptical about liberty and dubious of the proposition, that all men are equal to the task of self-government. Now we are engaged in a great newsroom war—testing whether Lippmann's notion or any notion so skeptical and dubious should still endure.

Greetings from the *Virginian-Pilot*, where circulation is relatively flat and profits are strong . . . where objectivity is mostly intact and rascals still get driven from office by the newspaper, and where the editor is humbled daily.

In *Public Opinion*, his seminal work on American media and politics, Lippmann declared, "The common interest very largely eludes public opinion entirely and can be managed only by a specialized class." Lippmann sharpened his view in his 1925 sequel, *The Phantom Public*. "Only the insider can make the decision, not because he is inherently a better man, but because he is so placed that he can understand and can act. The public must be put in its place so that each of us may live free of the trampling and the roar of a bewildered herd." . . .

Walter Lippmann was a rare presence in American journalism, a Harvard-educated intellectual who rose to power as an editor of popular publications, including the *New Republic* and the editorial page of the *New York World.* . . . Even today identification of journalists with professionals and insiders, as opposed to citizens, pervades newsroom cultures.

Given Lippmann's intellectual legacy and our predilection not to reflect on it, there is little wonder many journalists scorn new initiatives to connect with citizens as pandering to the public.

This debate began 70 years ago when Lippmann was challenged by his contemporary and intellectual peer, John Dewey. Dewey argued that people talking to each other are capable of attending to common interests and public decisions. Dewey said, "The printed word is a pre-condition of the creation of a true public, but it is not sufficient. People must engage each other in conversation about issues in the news."

This is the whole debate in a nutshell, according to James Carey of the Columbia School of Journalism. Carey says that: "To Lippmann, the journalist is an eyewitness trying to describe what the insiders are deciding to a passive public whose only real role is to vote the rascals in or out."

To Dewey, the journalist is, at her best, a catalyst of conversation, and insiders and citizens alike are active participants and partners in that conversation. The conversation in the end is the medium of democracy, not newspapers.

So what does all this theory have to do with life in the newsroom of the *Virginian-Pilot*? Most fundamentally we believe that vital journalism cannot exist without vital democracy, and that vital democracy cannot exist without vital journalism. . . .

We have learned that, to improve our work and revitalize our craft, we must live in two worlds—the world of ideas and the world of action. We have begun to peel back the layers of our unexamined newsroom ideology to learn what frames our view of public life. We are coming to realize that deliberative democracy may hold more possibilities than representative democracy, and that covering democracy one way can be just as legitimate as covering it another.

We have gone immediately into the field reporting and writing our stories in new ways, not as special projects but as daily field tests. And we have begun to build a deliberative newsroom, where journalists are taking charge of their shared professional destiny.

We have discovered a more powerful kind of accountability, beyond the scared, deer-in-the-headlights, freeze-frame of the exposé. We are learning to hold citizens accountable, not only in asking them during conversations to reconcile their beliefs with contradictory evidence, but also asking them to spell out what they believe to be their responsibility for the health of the community.

And we have begun to hold ourselves accountable to our communities by publicly explaining why we're covering stories the way we are. . . .

We have done all this in the pursuit of a big idea that was a gift to us from Davis Merritt, Jr., editor of the *Wichita Eagle*. Buzz Merritt defines a successful community as one in which the people know what's happening and take responsibility for it. This . . . is where a kind of new idea enters the debate: We're all comfortable as journalists with the first half of that, which is making sure people know what is going on. What is new to us is exploring our role in how we can help people take responsibility for it. We use our story-telling and investigative skills to help citizens know what is going on, but we don't want them to feel like a passive audience or dependent clientele, so we are developing a third set of skills, the skills of conversation, deliberation and frankly democracy to help people take responsibility for what's happening. . . .

I'd like to close with John Dewey, who said something that was very powerful and really hard to get my mind around. In 1916 he said, "Society exists not only by transmission or by communication, but it may fairly be said to exist in transmission or in communication." In other words, our society exists only as we share it with one another, as we transmit its values, communicate its values and what is happening. If that profound thought is true, then I think we, as communicators, have a huge responsibility to reflect upon what our role is in that transmission, in that communication. And I daresay we cannot do it effectively from a detached position.[11]

—From Cole Campbell, remarks to the James K. Batten Symposium on Civic Journalism, Washington, D.C., September 13, 1995

. . . .

"Covering democracy one way can be just as legitimate as covering it another." This describes what the men and women of the *Virginian-Pilot* were learning as they put public journalism into practice in Norfolk.

Understanding Public Life: The *Pilot's Intellectual Journey*

August 1995. A group of reporters and editors from Norfolk is invited to a seminar at the American Press Institute in Reston, Virginia, sponsored by my project. They are there to describe the intellectual journey of the

Virginian-Pilot for colleagues from other newspapers, along with a few academics and interested observers.

About the term "journey" the *Pilot* people are unembarrassed. They have a clear sense of where they started and what propelled them from one stage to the next. The story they have to tell is public journalism coming alive in another way: as a learning curve for the people involved. Journey One, then, is out in the field, doing stories, editing pages, and planning other tests of public journalism as a practical tool. Journey Two is more internal. It takes place in the newsroom's mind: the space between people where an understanding of the journalist's job gains root, amid other ideas about politics and public life.[12]

So here is the team from Norfolk, about to take the floor and tell us where they've been. They could start the story almost anywhere, but they choose the autumn of 1991, when a new management regime assumed command at the *Pilot*—the pre-Campbell era. Senior newsroom leaders are asked to articulate a mission for the paper. They do and it includes a telling phrase: "Our responsibility," the senior staff declares, "is to identify conflict and air it."

Reflecting back on other common metaphors in use in 1991, the group in Reston identifies the following: Journalism was seen as police work, hunting down the bad guys. Politics was a contest, featuring politicians as combatants. The reporter thus became a detective, digging into the wayward dealings of shady characters and returning with an investigative story. The citizen's job was to be a consumer of these reports, rather like the analysts at an intelligence agency, deciding what to make of them.

A second and equally powerful metaphor came from another direction: literature. "If not an investigative story, then it must be a yarn," says the *Pilot* about its thinking in 1991. A strong narrative, with vivid characters, human passion, and climactic moments, was prized. But as the team gathered in Reston notes, traditional storytelling in journalism, even when effective and absorbing, often turns people "into an audience of one"—the Reader. This will come to trouble the *Pilot* when Campbell and his staff begin to redirect some of their thinking. For a reader is a solitary figure, leafing through the newspaper at home. That same person can also be seen as a citizen, an identity held in common with others—whether they are neighbors on the next block, residents of the region called Hampton Roads, members of the Commonwealth of Virginia, or fellow Americans.

In its habitual forms of address, shouldn't journalism speak to all these identities—including the shared, civic ones—instead of always locating the audience in isolation, as the Reader, the Voter, the Consumer, or the proverbial Person in the Street? The "public" in public journalism starts emerging for the *Pilot* in these early doubts about the image of the audience in the mind of the machine, which is what a daily newspaper is. It remakes the world of current events every twenty-four hours. But for whom? For a public imagined in what way?

And also: for what? Second thoughts surface around 1991's blunt declaration: "Our responsibility is to identify conflict and air it." Is airing conflict a worthy mission, good for its own sake? Certainly the clash of interests, personalities, and parties is part of a noisy public square, which is the kind democracy expects. But reporting on conflict doesn't tell you what your reporting should accomplish. Noting the persistent complaints from readers about an excess of "bad news" and bias in the news columns, *Pilot* editors and reporters wonder about the "distorted mirror of life" that the paper presents: conflict is news because news is about conflict. This makes sense to journalists more than to the people they serve: "If our readers don't trust our view of the world, then how long will it be before they completely stop relying on us for facts about the world?"

The editors feel a different sense of urgency coming from the business side: people don't seem to need the newspaper the way they once did. With so many other sources of news available, the newspaper has to work harder to deliver a useful product. There is the anxiety of the counting room in this question: where are our customers going? But there's also something for the craft to confront: shrinking market share means a smaller portion of the public is being addressed. The argument for change is deepened, the team says, by a "trickle of democratic literature" through the newsroom and by an "instinctive sense" that the paper's journalism is "not making a difference." Investigative stories that win prizes and meet the craft's definition of excellence often fail to make permanent change: the stories are done, and a few years later the same corruption and abuse is seen.

From these reflections comes a kind of collision with ingrained "habits of the journalistic mind." The team in Reston summarizes them as follows:

Habit: We do journalism independent of readers
The challenge: We can't do journalism without citizens

Habit: Fairness as contrasting points of view.
The challenge: Fairness is conveying multiple, overlapping points of view.

Habit: An informed citizen needs facts to decide.
The challenge: An informed citizen needs conversation to understand.

Habit: The tyranny of the [either] or.
The challenge: The ambiguity of the "and."

During four years of thinking, reading, and experimenting on themselves, the *Pilot* moves from one way of viewing people to another. In 1991, readers were seen as a passive audience, on the receiving end of the news. By 1995 they are understood as active participants, partners with journalists in fashioning an understanding of events. Citizens once regarded as "political consumers" are treated as potential actors and the "primary stakeholders" in (some) stories. In 1991, candidates for public office were viewed as the "black hats" or "political merchants," akin to used-car salesmen in their attempts to pull the wool over the public's eyes. By 1995, the *Pilot* is trying to see contenders for office as job candidates and "proponents of choices." Leaders, the people in power, were at one time considered the decision makers, those who set a course for the community. Public life was about what they were saying and doing. The *Pilot* in 1995 tries to treat leaders as the people who carry out decisions that rest with citizens themselves.

A changed view of other civic actors leads to a remodeling of the journalist's job. At the outset of the *Pilot*'s travels, journalists were the agenda setters, using their power to goad the political class into action. They functioned as information brokers, selling verifiable facts, and private eyes, digging up dirt. They told compelling stories. By 1995, journalists are also seen as "connectors," putting scattered publics in touch with one another. They create and cultivate a public space, the pages of the newspaper, into which citizens are invited. They remain watchdogs, but not just of government; citizens, too, can be held accountable. Finally, the journalist is viewed as an exemplary citizen, trying to lend some dignity to public life, treating the affairs of democracy as serious business, rather than a game or a hustle.

In Reston, the journey taken by the *Pilot* is described as incomplete, still evolving, unevenly distributed among the staff. It is hardly the case that everyone thought one way in 1991 and another way four years later. Rather, these shifts in outlook are what public journalism has grown to mean in the imagination of a core group in Norfolk. As the story goes on, the team describes, under the heading "The Journey to Understanding Public Life," how it got from one key concept to another.

. . . .

1. From Starting Where Readers Start to Public Listening.

We began by wanting to see the world the way readers see it, which led us to discover we needed to learn new ways of listening. To say "let's stop the horse race coverage" begs the question: So what then is our coverage about? Starting where readers start means learning how they form connections to public issues. It also means seeing readers as more than just consumers—that their connection to public life, and therefore the newspaper, comes as citizens.

Public listening means to listen beyond the conflict; to listen for where people are torn, what connections they make between issues, what possibilities they see in making a difference, etc.

2. From Public Listening to Deliberation.

As we listened to people talk to each other, we discovered that they learn from each other through deliberation. Listening in different ways to the public led us to an amazing discovery: that when people grapple with an issue together—when there is truly a dialogue and not simply debate—they learn from each other. And, when it works well, new points of view, new choices emerge.

And that led us to deliberation: the place where people move beyond snap judgments and into this muddy, messy "working through" period that ultimately can lead to a more informed "public judgment."

3. From Deliberation to Framing.

As we observed people deliberating, we saw them approach issues in new ways and discovered the power of framing. Witnessing these new realities from community conversations must change your concepts of what the story is about, if you're listening at all.

We frame stories all the time, albeit without thinking about how we do it or why. Story "angles" or ideas are simply the icons that should click on deeper questions. What is the frame that drives these story ideas? How are we positioning the players?

4. From Framing to Engagement.

As we learned to frame issues from citizens' perspective, citizens began to get more engaged in dealing with the issues. When we begin to frame our coverage from where citizens start, they in turn begin to see a place at the

table. That in turn leads to hope for making an impact—the key induce-
ment for people to engage an issue.

5. From Engagement to Social Capital.

When citizens become actively engaged, they contribute to a region's social
capital. Social capital, according to Robert Putnam, is the equivalent of
economic capital. The human relationships that make up society—the associations, the church groups, the voluntary organizations—form an intangi-
ble network that supports communities.

6. From Social Capital to Public Life.

When social capital increases, public life is enriched. With social capital,
people learn the arts and skills of exercising their freedoms and responsibilities. That leads, we think, to a healthier public life. And journalism
achieves its true symbiosis: Journalism cannot survive without a healthy
public life; public life cannot survive without healthy journalism.
—From the Norfolk *Virginian-Pilot,* presentation at the Project on Public Life and
the Press seminar, American Press Institute, August 14, 1995

. . . .

For each of these steps, members of the team cite the articles, books,
speeches, and reports that informed their thinking and allowed them to see
where the paper's journey to understanding public life was leading.[13] By presenting a journal of their intellectual travels, the group from Norfolk was
putting public journalism into practice. But it is "practice" of another kind:
not the daily task of newspapering, but the conscious act of imagining what
the task is all about. The *Pilot*'s core group of thinkers learned to see their
job in a more civic way and then used the lessons of experience—and the
"trickle of democratic literature"—to deepen their understanding. Viewed
this way, public journalism advances whenever journalists remodel the idea
as they go, conjure it up in a form they can use. In these steps toward a more
civic mind, public journalism was experienced as "movement" by the people
who made it go.

Helping People Participate: Public Journalism on the Page

In early 1997, after Campbell has left to take the editor's chair at the *St.
Louis Post-Dispatch,* a new feature is introduced in the local news section of

the *Pilot*. The prime mover is Dennis Hartig, who became managing editor with direct supervision over the daily news product. Hartig wants to bring public journalism principles alive in daily reporting, to get beyond the "project" approach. The device he employs is a different kind of page, to appear three times a week. One of these is about crime and public safety, another reports on politics and public affairs, a third concerns education. The idea behind them lies in the "civic nature of the questions the pages pose," as Hartig explains. "What do people need to know regularly that will enable them to participate more effectively in the public life of their community?" The new pages carry no advertising. They mix traditional investigation and computer-assisted reporting with features derived from earlier work in public journalism and some of Harwood's teachings.[14] In the center of the page is usually an in-depth story, a data-filled chart, or an explanatory tool that helps readers get a handle on an important public problem and see where it presently stands.

On March 4, 1997, a Tuesday, this section charts the steady decline in violent crime rates in each of the five cities the paper reaches. "Many people believe the threat of violent crime in Hampton Roads is on the increase, but the opposite is true," the paper explains. "In 1996, the rate was the lowest of any year during the 1990s. The rate has dropped almost every year since 1991." In a note to readers, Bill Burke, the editor of the public safety team, writes of the paper's plan to use database reporting to give a truer picture of crime: "How often are crimes committed in Hampton Roads? Who are the victims and who are the perpetrators? . . . How often do the elderly fall victim to crime? Where are the hot spots for drug sales in Hampton Roads?"

The *Pilot*'s approach here is intended to offset the distorted impression left by television news, with its nightly litany of crime footage that takes no notice of overall trends while suggesting, in increasingly lurid fashion, that danger could strike anyone at any time. Burke writes:

> We hope these reports will help in some way to make sense of crimes that seem to occur randomly and chaotically. If patterns can be shown, it becomes clear that they are not so random, not so chaotic.
>
> And it's easier to combat crimes if there are ways to anticipate where they occur, and when, and to whom. . . .
>
> This page will . . . also include stories about people who are weary of acquiescing to the criminal threat—like the hundreds of people in Portsmouth who two years running have participated in citizens' "crime summits."

At least partly because of those efforts, the violent crime rate in Portsmouth fell last year for the first time since 1983, and the drop was precipitous: 29 percent.

The page will also provide information about the criminal justice system: how courts work, what magistrates and bail bondsmen do, how likely you are to be selected for jury duty, how you can form a neighborhood crime watch.[15]

News about a murder or rape would still appear in other sections of the newspaper, but in this spot the declared purpose is to give people a handle on the crime problem, to allow them to chart its progress, place the danger in proportion, and get involved in creating the civic asset called pubic safety—for instance, how to make tenant patrols in public housing work, how to act against obscene phone callers, how to help out a friend or neighbor who's been a crime victim.

On Wednesdays, the focus is on politics and government. The center section might track the progress that local officials are making on outstanding problems, like bringing more jobs to Portsmouth, the poorest city in the region; balancing growth with the concerns of existing residents in Suffolk, including how the city council has voted on six key proposals for future development; a program for sidewalk and sewer repair in Norfolk that asks residents to petition the city for improvements and then contribute to the cost, an idea now faltering for lack of funds; the Virginia Beach city council's "to do" list, meaning its top priorities for the year—which emerge from a yearly retreat for council members—along with a summary of where each issue stands. The politics page also features quick rundowns on what various municipal bodies are doing, so readers can keep abreast of decision making at that level. To help citizens become more active, early versions of the page explain how to speak effectively at a council meeting, how to appeal the tax assessment on a home, how to report unsightly blemishes on a block, like a house with overgrown grass and weeds or a lot littered with abandoned appliances.

These pages, then, try to offer a report on public affairs designed for the citizenry's use, a space where civic problems and priorities can come into clear view, so that people might take action—public officials as well as ordinary residents. The goals are to make issues more comprehensible and to show that there is work to be done, decisions to be made, opportunities to get involved. Readers learn about problems—and what's being done. They can see what's faltering, but also what is working. They keep up with public institutions, follow along as the drama of public life unfolds, like they do with the sports pages. But they can also get into the game.

Helping out on this last goal is the job of reporter Mike Knepler, who is asked to write a column called "Neighborhood Exchange" for the Wednesday page. Within the circle of people at the *Virginian-Pilot* who set to work on public journalism, Knepler had a special feel for the idea. Unassuming and nonaggressive in person, with an elliptical speaking style lacking the sharp edges of newsroom chatter, he was easy to overlook in a noisy gathering of journalists. On my visits to Norfolk, several of his colleagues point this out. "Mike is the one who really understands this stuff," they tell me, "and he's the one doing it."

Knepler built his own model of journalism from other ideas he had about the American political tradition. Then he went out into the community to test the model with the people he interviewed and hung around with. He was renowned at the *Pilot* for knowing about life in the neighborhoods and among the array of civic groups, councils, clubs, and meeting places where people got together, talked about issues, and led public lives. The "politics" that filtered up from below was Knepler's expertise—and he had found it well before public journalism found him.

I first understood this when he greeted me in the hospitality suite at the *Pilot*'s 1995 retreat. He had a thought to venture about the First Amendment. If we want to understand where the press intersected with public life, he said, freedom of assembly should be the focus. Knepler thought it was the citizenry's right to join in public activity, to gather and form associations for their own purposes, to speak and be heard by fellow citizens—it was all that, the fruit of liberties secured by constitutional law—that gave other laws about freedom of the press their importance, both to journalism as a profession and to him as a professional.

He saw the newspaper as a public space, not a professional domain. Citizens gather there and journalists help them exercise their rights. By reinterpreting the First Amendment tradition to begin with freedom of assembly, Knepler arrived at his own brand of public journalism, which employed the space of the newspaper to ease entry into other locations where readers could become citizens and make their own contributions. "Hands off the press" had meaning, he reasoned, only when people put their hands *on* the press to make for themselves a fuller public life.[16] Here, then, is his initial "Neighborhood Exchange" column, in which he describes what he wants to accomplish: a public space where people who have ideas—and those who need ideas—might gather, with a journalist's assistance.

. . . .

How does your community group help keep neighborhood sidewalks free of litter?

Looking for a way to boost attendance at civic-league meetings?

Can your organization attack problems, such as juvenile delinquency or the need to move welfare recipients into the work force?

Welcome to the *Neighborhood Exchange,* a new feature in the *Virginian-Pilot.*

Several times a month, this space will highlight problem-solving efforts by groups and individuals. It will recognize valuable public work performed by citizens, but it can also be a place for you to exchange ideas.

For example, a Virginia Beach group has an innovative program for teaching teens to settle disputes without resorting to violence. This column could help spread the ideas to other Hampton Roads neighborhoods.

It could work the other way, too. Chesapeake neighborhoods may suffer from illegal dumping. We'll describe the issue here and ask other communities to respond with ideas that worked for them.

Hampton Roads has no shortage of great ideas and civic energy. There are efforts by people at every level of our community. Here are a few examples:

- Chesapeake civic activists wanted more property-code enforcement, especially in aging Norfolk. But they didn't want to punish fixed-income home owners. So the Chesapeake Council of Civic Organizations now musters volunteers and raises money to help with home repairs.
- Residents of Norfolk's Lafayette-Winona, Colonial Place, Berkley and Ghent are doing architectural inventories of nearby houses and buildings. The information will help the neighborhoods become state and national historical districts, which could bring tax credits.
- Virginia Beach residents Julian Aiken of Plaza Apartments and Jacqueline Greer of Pecan Gardens West discovered that they had the same worries for the well-being of teen-agers in their neighborhoods. To give the kids a positive activity, they created a basketball league.

You get the idea. And you have the ideas. We'd like to hear about them for possible columns.

Also let us know of neighborhood problems that have you stumped. Maybe someone else has an idea that you can build on. Together, we won't have to reinvent the wheel.

—From Mike Knepler, "Where You Can Swap Ideas on Community Problems," Norfolk *Virginian-Pilot*, March 19, 1997

. . . .

As public journalism was slowly integrated into the *Pilot*'s daily routine, it became easier to practice but harder to spot. This, in fact, was a goal: to dissolve the idea into habitual ways of working, to talk less about the philosophy and more about the journalism to be done with it. But behind the new habits that emerged were different ways of thinking, and it was possible to keep them in view as the diffusion of the idea proceeded apace.

I conclude this tale with some words from Dennis Hartig, taken from the *Pilot*'s internal newsletter. In early 1997, he responded as follows to a question posed by the newspaper staff.

. . . .

Q. What is the status of public journalism?

A. I've largely abandoned the phrase because it has been so poisoned by the debate among journalists. But its ideas and values are alive and well and all around you. In the *Pilot*'s Statement of Purpose we see our journalism described as work that improves the community. That's public journalism.

Our strategy describes the *Pilot* as a newspaper that not only contains the news, "but *what it means to you and to our community.*" Fulfilling that phrase that's in italic requires an intimate knowledge of the community, knowledge that can be obtained through the practices of public journalism. Some, like framing and identifying stakeholders, are common tools of public journalists. These tools have been most evident in our coverage of three elections in the past year.

Some aspects of public journalism are behind new features to be launched next month. For example, we will have several features that give readers coherent progress reports and assessments of public concerns, public institutions and public authorities. This is "public" journalism because it enlarges the number of people who can keep score and raise intelligent questions. This will help more people participate in the civic life of their communities.

In our coverage of controversy, we do public journalism when we spend most of our time and talent reporting not on insults and images, but on the underlying issues and ideas that matter to people. This kind of journalism frees people to think, talk and participate more effectively. This is what political and public affairs reporting is supposed to be about. Americans are telling journalists to get back to basics. This is becoming more frequent in our daily report.

We do public journalism when we define politics as the way this community's problems are identified and dealt with, not as a horse race or mud wrestling contest. Every time we edit our stories in a way that helps readers to see not only their self-interest, but also their stake in the broader well-being of the whole community we are enlarging the public, and strengthening it. We invite our readers to think in "public" ways.

We have nothing to fear from public journalism. We should be alarmed instead about the loss of a "public" identity in our communities.

—Dennis Hartig in "Continuous Information," the *Virginian-Pilot*'s internal newsletter, January 14, 1997

. . . .

5 Doing Less Harm

Public Journalism as Personal Tale

As the people who collected around our different story began to reflect on their careers and the dissatisfactions they felt, they came upon moments when their view of what they should be doing changed. These personal stories are part of the literature of public journalism. They tell of a crisis of purpose among professionals who could no longer continue on the course they were following. So they began a new course, the search for a "purpose beyond telling the news," as Buzz Merritt wrote.[1]

Merritt's travels began when he started to question what is perhaps the supreme value in the culture of the press: the ethic of "toughness." He had been in Washington during the Watergate crisis and felt what most of his colleagues felt. "We celebrated," he wrote. Not the resignation of Richard Nixon but the "reaffirmation of the intent of the First Amendment" was cause for cheer in the press. Watergate proved "that even a runaway administration of enormous power and guile could be called to account by tough, determined authority." But an event "that should have been a plateau from which the profession moved on to even greater heights turned out to be a peak," Merritt observed. From the height of its power and influence, the press learned to look down on a political world that now seemed full of Nixons. "The journalistic norm became 'we catch crooks.' Small-bore Whatever-Gates won the profession's plaudits and awards. Scalps on the belt, particularly government scalps, were the sign of rank and the measure of testosterone at gatherings of the tribe. The democratic process, superbly served by Watergate reporting, was devalued by the onslaught of self-indulgent journalists-cum-cops."

Investigative reporting continued to prove its value in exposing abuse and corruption. But it also shaped what journalists came to value above all else—"the relentless uncovering of wrongdoing, no matter its ultimate importance to the public or the great scheme of things." The triumph of Watergate gave new shape to the profession's image of itself: "the journalist as folk hero, the astute political analyst as media star." Merritt recalled a scene from ten years after Watergate, when Nixon, eager for a return to public life, gave an address at the American Society of Newspaper Editors convention in Washington. He watched with bemused detachment as Benjamin J. Bradlee, executive editor of the *Washington Post* and "the consummate Watergate tough guy," table-hopped around a room that regarded him and his colleagues as heroes. With Nixon prepared to take the stage, a small demonstration took place.

> After lunch, as the editors shuffled their chairs to face the still-empty stage, Bradlee and [his wife, Sally] Quinn arose at their center-ring table that was now the focus of a thousand pair of eyes. Leading their tablemates, they wound their way half the length of the great hall and out the double doors, leaving a starkly empty table directly in front of where Nixon would stand.
>
> If Nixon was aware of the demonstration by the *Post* people, he gave no sign as he took the stage to warm applause by the remaining editors. Standing on a bare stage with only a single floor mike, with no intervening or protective podium, no lectern for support or shelter, without notes or other aids, he delivered a brilliant 45-minute lecture on foreign policy and domestic politics. It was an astonishing, nearly inhuman display of grit, the man with perhaps the greatest burden of public humiliation possible facing, totally without physical or psychic protection, hundreds of those who participated in his humiliation.
>
> Absent, of course, were the people from the *Post*.

At the time, Merritt labeled the stunt "bush league." But he later came to a different judgment. "I see it now as merely sad," a theatrical display of "toughness for its own sake." Nixon's own toughness in standing unprotected before the press was a good deal more impressive than the staged walkout by the *Post* editors. As he reflected on this and other distortions in the culture of the craft, Merritt began to redefine what toughness ought to mean in journalism. "The ultimate tough story, the ultimate scandal," he wrote, "is that America's public life does not accomplish the long term goals of the American people."[2]

In published commentary and seminar settings, self-described public journalists or those simply curious about the notion told how they had arrived at the conclusion that something needed to change. Some of these stories could be conveyed in a few sentences. They might talk of the reward system in the press and a larger sense of public duty. As Marty Steffens, then an editor with the *Dayton Daily News,* put it, "I am a managing editor who keeps thinking, Pulitzer, Pulitzer . . ." But were the people of Dayton well served by the drive to impress a national jury of her peers? Steffens started to ask herself, "is there a greater good out there?"[3]

Jeanine Guttman, an editor at the *Portland (Maine) Press Herald,* was one of those who felt the glamour of covering Watergate. As a student journalist at Kent State University, she and her colleagues had played a starring role in a remarkably similar drama: an investigation that found "they were selling degrees" in the business school. The resulting scandal forced the president of the university to resign. "When I left school I wanted to put people in jail," Guttman said. "That is what I was trained to do. It took me a long time to realize that there was something more than that."[4]

For Vikki Porter, the turning point came at age forty, when she left the profession, unsure if she would ever come back. During her two years away from the business—which Porter described as "my mid-life crisis"—she read the newspaper as a reader and sensed something missing from it. "I was not as an individual reflected in those pages," she said. Returning as the editor of a small-circulation paper published by Gannett, the *Olympian* in Olympia, Washington, she found herself under a company mandate to address such problems. After stripping away the "corporate packaging" around the readers-as-customers mantra, she saw an opportunity to return to the mission that had once drawn her to the craft.

Twenty-five years earlier, she had been "naive enough" to seek in journalism the chance to join in "building or rebuilding a country." To reaffirm that belief, she sought the editorship of a small paper, where her own sense of community might matter again. Olympia appealed to Porter as a sophisticated, educated market, where people regularly pressured the staff to do better. "And I was able to return to the West"—significant, she said, "because I have always thought of the West as a place where there are still opportunities for new ideas. And there is a populist nature [there] that makes communities a little more vibrant and open to this kind of discussion." By which she meant rethinking the newspaper's role in civic life, a discussion that could not be confined to the newsroom itself.[5]

Like others who joined in the inquiry, Frank Denton, editor of the *Wisconsin State Journal* in Madison, was influenced by the Kettering Foundation's *Citizens and Politics: A View from Main Street America* of 1991. (The report, by Kettering's count, drew more than three thousand inquiries from journalists.) Denton said he was struck by the account of a pervasive mistrust of all major institutions, but even more so by Americans' eagerness to include the press in that category. "That is what really got me: they put us in with the other big institutions," he said. "It should not have surprised me, but it really knocked me off my pins for a while."[6]

Denton's reaction is not hard to explain. In the afterglow of Watergate, journalists had learned to think of themselves as our heroic representative before wayward institutions of government. If they were now fencing more and more with public officials, trying to get behind the public facade, it was self-evident—to people in the press—that citizens were the final beneficiaries. Struggling against the manipulations of elected leaders and the foot-dragging of bureaucrats meant being for the public and its right to know. But citizens didn't necessarily see it that way, and this proved to be an important discovery. By continually locking horns with public officials and defining public service through this adversarial relationship, the press was little by little detaching itself from the average American's deeper concerns.

Frank Caperton, editor of the *Indianapolis Star*, spoke of the shock of finding that others no longer view you the way you view yourself. Journalism had once appealed to him as a chance to show "passion for the underdog" and "exercise a little hostility to authority," he said. But he now had to live with the irony of being seen as an authority himself. "I thought when I was a young reporter that it was transparent to people in the communities where I worked that I was on their side. What I discovered increasingly over the decades is that they did not view me as on their side. In fact, today, increasingly they view me and the newspaper I edit as a kind of spectator that does not care . . . that to us at the newspaper it is a matter of indifference whether or not the Indianapolis public schools work and succeed and educate children."[7]

This growing sense of distance struck many participants as intolerable. Jon Roe, a reporter for the *Wichita Eagle*, told of the day he realized "that I could and generally did spend my entire working day without moving from my desk and my computer and my telephone except to go get Diet Cokes and M&Ms." This disturbed him. What disturbed him even more was the knowledge that "my assigning editors were happy" with the arrangement, because "as long as I was sitting at that desk I was being productive." He wrote stories that matched his editors' expectations, but increasingly his own expectations were not met. "If indeed I was being productive," Roe wondered, "then why did I feel so cut off from the community I was covering, which led to a second question: was I indeed covering that community at all?"[8]

Roe's lament seems to suggest a simple remedy: get out of the office and find out what's happening! Hearing such tales presented as "turning points," critics of public journalism might react with incredulity: "Come on, getting out of the office and talking to people around town—that's just good journalism. You don't need a movement for that." But this would miss the point of Roe's story. Sitting there at his desk, munching his M&Ms, plugged into the power structure via telephone, he was doing good journalism as it had come to be defined. Newspaper people still felt the romance of "shoe leather" reporting—hitting the streets, knocking on doors, getting a personal feel for the facts. But they tended to practice the art of institutional reporting: flipping through the Rolodex, reaching the right spokesperson, getting the quote they needed to make news, all at a widening distance from the people they were making it for. Roe and others came to an alarming conclusion: they could succeed at journalism and fail at its essential task—to help citizens cope with the public dimension of their lives.

Dennis Hartig of the *Virginian-Pilot* discovered that something had changed in the public's response to the newsroom's best efforts. Reporters and editors used to "get really excited about a story and our whole community would be excited," he recalled. Gradually, though, he and his fellow editors noticed that what impressed journalists did not "seem to have that wave effect through the community." Part of the reason, he thought, was declining circulation at the *Pilot*—from a high of 80 percent of households in the 1980s to under 60 percent in 1994. The loss of circulation gave the newspaper less power in the Hampton Roads area. It also weakened an important civic asset: a public forum that once reached across a region in which five municipalities were embedded. "So it is really essential for us to be able to maintain a mass medium status," Hartig reasoned.[9]

Frustration with election coverage led to feelings of impotence for some journalists, including Peggy Eastman, a political reporter for the *Cape Cod Times*. "I went through two election cycles with one of the most difficult congressional candidates that the world has ever produced," she related. He was a man who understood that by attacking his opponent he could control the newspaper's reporting agenda. "I was just going crazy because all I was doing was chasing him around from press conference to press conference and checking out his wild accusations against his opponent. I just felt like I was on a leash like a little dog, and I went to my editor and I said, 'He is going to run a third time and we have got to do something else; we cannot let this man run our election coverage the way he has been doing it.' "[10]

Ending this cycle required an alternative starting point for campaign news, as John Dinges learned. As the editorial director of National Public Radio during the 1988 campaign, Dinges realized how "we were led around by the nose by the candidates" and their campaign managers. He began thinking of ways to detach NPR's coverage from the narrow aims of the candidates and their advisers, which raised an intriguing question: whose agenda do you serve? Dinges found his answer in the idea of a citizen's agenda, "getting ourselves back into the communities" and starting election coverage from there. He said he was also struck by the "very unhappy professionals" he found at NPR. The discovery that "people are not taking satisfaction out of what is a wonderful news product" was a clear sign that "something is wrong."[11]

A similar feeling of emptiness at the core of a prestigious operation was heard in the comments of Dennis Farney, a reporter for the *Wall Street Journal* who attended one of the project's seminars. When he joined the *Journal's* Washington bureau, Farney noticed something odd. "We would have these staff conferences where we would sit around discussing ideas for our Washington Wire column, which runs on Friday mornings," he remembered. "And it struck me that a . . . strange thing was happening here. We were discussing . . . how politicians would pull the wool over the eyes of the ordinary voters, and how they would maneuver to look good, and that is what we were doing the items about. And we were almost never talking about outcomes."

Farney later persuaded his editors to let him remain in the Washington bureau but operate out of Kansas City. There, he could report on gathering trends in America's midsection as people looked toward Washington—or away in disgust. Analytical pieces with a Main Street feel were his attempt to break the Beltway patterns that frustrated him. But even in Kansas City, the codes of serious reporting had come to seem confining, given the results he sought.

> I have to say I feel stifled at this point. I feel trapped despite all the freedom I have, trapped to some degree by the conventions of journalism. . . . I'm finding that I would very much like to focus on solutions, but I find it very hard to transcend the polarization, the one side against the other kind of stories that typically emerge. . . . I find it hard to figure out a way to transcend issue stories, to go beyond that. In short, I feel that the system is fragmenting, society is fragmenting, journalism is fragmenting with the proliferation of ever more types of journalism and outlets for journalism.[12]

Farney did not become a "convert" to public journalism, but he did see how it responded to a problem that concerned him personally: the futility of politics as usual and the narrow range of responses available to the press.

Mike Phillips, editor of the *Sun* in Bremerton, Washington, ran up against those limits early in his career. He believed then in the righteous power of investigative reporting, a method that virtually defined "public service" for Phillips and his colleagues. "We were very proud of all the rotten public officials we ran off," he said. The turning point came during a meeting at a public library in an impoverished black neighborhood in Broward County, Florida. Phillips was there with others from his newsroom to talk with community leaders about a project that would help their neighborhood. Or so they thought. The journalists were looking for a list of targets for the investigative reporting they were determined to do. "We wanted to make sure we didn't neglect any social ill or any injustice that needed to be exposed," Phillips said.

> And after an hour of conversation, one of the community leaders said that he wanted to talk about this a little differently and asked if we would be willing to listen . . . to a really different approach. Then he said, "Let me tell what we think we need from your newspaper. We think that they're never going to give us decent roads and they're never going to do anything about crime in our neighborhood and they're never going to give us sewers and they're never going to give us running water that works. What we need from your newspaper is to pick it up for our young people, pick it up every day and see some example that would lead them to believe that they can succeed in life by being something other than an athlete or a drug dealer or criminal because that's all they ever see."[13]

There are two ways for journalists to interpret this tale. In one hearing, the neighborhood leader is fed up with negative news and wants the newspaper to tell uplifting stories. That sounds suspiciously like a demand to whitewash reality, and journalists react with immediate alarm whenever they feel this message coming down on them. But Phillips drew a different lesson, equally alarming, which was that he and his fellow journalists had no idea what kind of "public service" this particular public needed. What they had instead was a standard method for doing good: to investigate and expose. But it was premised on the assumption that, once exposed, social ills will be corrected by the larger community. To the people in southern Broward County—poor, black, and in many ways powerless—the journalists were the ones whitewashing reality. They had marched in with little real knowledge of the neighborhood to expose things that weren't going to change with further exposure.

The way Phillips heard it, "We think they're never going to give us decent roads and they're never going to do anything about crime" was the neighborhood's way of saying: you are drastically out of touch. Before you try to do good here, listen to the people who live here, because we have some ideas about what's needed and they don't necessarily match yours. "It takes a pretty good ego to be in this business," Phillips said. "It took a long time for me to be willing to admit that what we had to do should be done in partnership with the community."[14]

Again and again as people described a more citizen-centered journalism, we heard this line coming back to us: "But that's just good reporting." Usually it was spoken in a tone of frustration. A practice that sounded traditional ("listening to citizens") was being presented as somehow novel. Even more irritating to some was talk of a "movement," which was imagery foreign to the profession. Journalists didn't join movements; in fact, they didn't join anything—except other journalists, in the sense that common practices were extremely common, at times almost uniform across the craft.

The peer culture of the press, a remarkably effective teacher, told its members how to get inside political life and find the "real" story. Metaphors drawn from war and sports (and to a lesser degree, theater) helped organize the mind of the press, and when individual journalists went out to report on public life they borrowed that mind. But its contents were stored as conventions, not concepts. American journalism rarely paused to ask itself whether "public life as battleground" was a metaphor well chosen. Instead, the metaphor seemed to choose *for* journalists, directing their vision toward certain scenes and away from others. All this went on at a subterranean level, since the discussion of controlling images and root metaphors wasn't a part of press culture. The results were often subject to criticism: the press "blew" this story or mishandled that, it was unfair here, needed to improve over there. There was plenty of self-examination in journalism—more, in fact, than a mistrusting public knew. But the critiques left off at the point where journalists drew their maps of the public world, conjured up politics in the peculiar shape they tended to give it.

Public journalism was trying to put forth a different map. But when we sketched our alternative image of political life, centered more on citizens, journalists frequently compared it not to the controlling metaphors in the mind of the press but to the residual self-image most of them carry: as old-fashioned shoe-leather reporters who know the issues, stick up for the little guy, and ask the questions on people's minds. These ideals were close to the hearts of the people we were addressing and close enough to the "civic" rhetoric we were speaking to produce an exasperated reaction: "This is just good journalism!" Which really meant: "We already believe that, we already do these things—why are you talking as if we don't?"

Getting past this sticking point required the testimony of seasoned professionals who felt the craft had drifted away from the ideals at its core. One of them was Stan Cloud, who in a long career had been a national correspondent, White House reporter, Saigon bureau chief, and Washington bureau chief for *Time* magazine. In 1995–96 he directed the Citizens Election Project for the Pew Center for Civic Journalism. In remarking on changes in election coverage, Cloud noted that at some point in the late 1960s or early 1970s, the press corps shifted its gaze "from what candidates said and did on the stump to what was going on in the so-called smoke-filled rooms."

The new goal was to get beyond the facade of politics, as Theodore White had in his best-selling series of books, *The Making of the President.* Journalists were intrigued by White's ability to tell the story behind the story, and this led them backstage, to where the strategic arts of politics were practiced. "The problem with such coverage, however, was that it was not very helpful to voters who had to choose one candidate over another," Cloud wrote. White's books appeared after the election; they were never intended to inform the electorate while it still had choices to make. By 1972 White had begun to regret his influence on the political press. He "would have been horror-stricken to see what election coverage has become in the 1990s," Cloud observed.

Cloud continued his story of drift in the following opinion piece, framed as the wry confession of a seasoned professional. By showing how political coverage had gotten off track, he was able to describe civic journalism as both a clear departure from current practice and a return to an honorable tradition. Which turned out to be the best answer to those who shouted, "that's just good journalism." Yes, said Cloud, but let's be honest: it is not the journalism we've been doing.

. . . .

First, a confession: I, a former card-carrying member of the National Press Corps, have sinned. I have engaged in "horse-race" and "fuselage" journalism, I have written stories that focused more on campaign tactics than issues. I have interviewed political aides and consultants as if they, and not the voters, should decide the content, if not the very outcome, of an election campaign. I have pretended to know what the country wanted, when in fact I had little or no idea because I had not really done the hard, precinct-level reporting from which such knowledge might stem.

I am truly sorry and I humbly repent.

So should anyone who is similarly sinning today, for it is clear to me that we who are privileged to call ourselves political journalists have a great deal to be repentant about.

The bad habits of what I call "know-it-all" reporting have become so ingrained that many of us have actually begun thinking of them as principles. It is hardly a principle of good journalism, however, to write or broadcast primarily for ourselves, our colleagues and our sources; or to shape our stories in terms of conflict between extremes (abortion is an excellent example), instead of attempting the more difficult task of reflecting the doubts and confusion in the middle; or to employ an arcane jargon—"spinmeisters," "tracking polls," "soft money," "media buys"—that alienates our "audience" and drives it away.

Yet today we are doing all of this and more, and our "audience" is moving away in droves.

Civic journalism is, in part, an attempt to replace these bad habits with what are really nothing more than the basics of good reporting: shoe leather, a decent respect for the opinions of others, and a commitment to provide citizens with the information they need to meet the obligations of their citizenship.

—From Stan Cloud, "Confessions of a Sinner," *Civic Catalyst*, April 1996[15]

. . . .

For public journalism to succeed, it could not limit itself to journalists, for there were many others who conceivably had a stake in the idea. These included people outside the press who were concerned about the repair and revival of civic life. Nancy Kruh, a staff writer for the *Dallas Morning News*, investigated these disparate developments in a series called "The We Decade: Rebirth of Community," published in her newspaper in 1995. In the essay below, she addresses readers of the *National Civic Review*, most of whom are not journalists but people engaged in community "revitalization." Something was happening in American democracy, she noted, and only a small piece of it had touched journalism.

. . . .

Public journalism could be viewed in the context of a larger movement. It is a movement that has spawned millions of participants; a national dialogue among social scientists, policy makers and legislators; lively discussion on the pages of alternative publications. It is steeped in the issue that now preoccupies this increasingly frustrated nation: How should the country's public business be conducted? And it is a movement that remains virtually uncovered by the mainstream media.

How could this happen? How could a profession devoted to news gathering be so out of touch? We are failing to identify this societal shift through our own small piece of it: public journalism. It's as if we haven't yet figured out that if the editor's kid has the flu, maybe there really is a flu epidemic. . . .

My interest in the story began two years ago when I was watching the local television news. In three consecutive stories, citizens were in one way or another trying to fight back against social excesses. The juxtaposition of the stories caught my eye in a way that, individually, each report never would have done. I couldn't help but wonder, is something bigger going on here?

At first I think I asked the question out of my own concern as a citizen of this country. What American doesn't have the same unsettling feeling that something is wrong with the way we are doing our public business? Soon, though, the question became a matter of professional curiosity. Was there a story here? I talked to my editor, then put out a few calls around the country to see if anything was worth exploring. Within three or four phone conversations, I had found the iceberg's tip. It would take months more work—and collaboration with more than a dozen of my colleagues—to get a clear picture of this complex and often elusive story.

At the moment, the movement goes by many names. The new citizenship. Civic democracy. The citizens' movement. The civic revival (or renewal) movement.

It is not like any other experienced by contemporary Americans, mainly because there is no clear target or enemy other than our own collective failure at effectively tackling the myriad social issues confronting the country: housing, health care, education, crime, employment, racism, family stability, the environment.

But in other, significant ways, it fits our understanding of social movements. People are moving to the same rhythms, simultaneously and independently. In community after community, they are taking the same new steps and talking the same new language as they try to deal with an assortment of problems. Rather than fighting until one side remains standing, they are seeking consensus and common ground. Rather than relying on experts or blue-ribbon commissions to figure things out, the everyday people who are most affected by the problems are mapping their own solutions. Rather than accepting traditional barriers, such as race and class, they are pulling together—not out of kinship or charity—but out of necessity.

They are rejecting the country's modern tradition of isolating issues in order to deal with them. Instead, they are understanding and responding to the interconnectedness of the problems (health affects education, which affects employment, which affects family, which affects crime, which affects health, and so on), and in turn, the interconnectedness of solutions.

But this isn't just a movement about procedural change. Perhaps most important, this is a movement that seeks a new social compact.

The public sector is rejected as the answer. So is the private sector. The two sectors combined aren't it, either. The only thing that will work—so say the voices of this movement—is an equal and concerted effort from all three sectors of society: public, private and civic.

The civic sector, the "civil society": It is the sum of churches, schools, civic and nonprofit groups, clubs, unions, news media—yes, the news media—and all the other nongovernmental institutions that serve as society's connective tissue. Once, this was a concept that held the pulse of the nation. Now, we're conditioned to look at each entity as an isolated special-interest group.

This way of viewing public affairs is the fallacy we've bought into as contemporary journalists. In fact, we are not passive bystanders. We are active participants in this democracy. It is now up to us to come to terms with all that this role means. . . .

> Once we journalists stumble into this relatively unexplored region of
> our profession, we not only change the way we look at ourselves, but we also
> begin to expand the way we look at our mission. We not only cover the
> politicians, but the populace; not only the crises, but the opportunities; not
> only the differences, but the commonality; not only the mired society, but
> the society in motion.
> —From Nancy Kruh, "Public Journalism and Civic Revival: A Reporter's View,"
> *National Civic Review,* winter–spring 1996

. . . .

The initial carriers for the idea of public journalism were newspaper
editors who had become frustrated with the way their organizations worked.
They were the leaders of newsrooms, but they were also, in a way, the most
distant from the action. Editors don't write the news; reporters do. And there
was no way to order anyone to write and report in a different fashion. Nor
was it easy to teach people how to "do" public journalism because it was not
in essence a technique; it was an attitude about the use of other techniques:
the basic tools of listening, interviewing, gathering facts, framing stories,
weaving narratives. The inherent fuzziness of the idea and the lack of a
rulebook for public journalism were a constant source of frustration to
reporters who grasped the goals and caught the spirit of the movement, but
wanted clearer guidance on how to proceed. We could and did remind them,
"It's an experiment," but the smarter ones grasped that this was a way of
saying, "We don't really know what to tell you."

More than once I had reporters say to me words to this effect: "It's easy
for editors and professors to wax philosophical about civic journalism, but
we can't report on a philosophy." They were right, of course. But the discomforting fact was that we had no formula, only our feeling that a journalism
more helpful to civic life was within reach. Reaching it would have to be
the work of reporters willing to give themselves headaches when they sat
down to translate the idea into questions they could ask, stories they could
write, using what Merritt vaguely—but accurately—called a different set of
reflexes.[16]

Such sketchy thoughts are a long way from a newswriting formula. But
they made sense enough to Karen Weintraub, a reporter for the *Virginian-
Pilot,* who began to work these principles into her own way of doing journalism. Here, she reflects on the version of public journalism she understands
and tries to practice.

. . . .

Part of my working definition of civic journalism is to do less harm than conventional journalism.

What exactly does that mean? It means I try to frame my stories to focus on what's real and relevant to people, on the things that will encourage citizens to take action rather than discourage them from caring. . . .

That puts a burden on me to make clear when and how people can get involved—even if it's as simple as including a phone number or the time and place of a City Council meeting. . . .

Because I view civic journalism as a philosophy rather than a tool, it doesn't make sense to me to use it solely for projects or campaigns. That's like saying I'm going to have journalistic ethics only during election season or when working on a series. For me, the power and importance of civic journalism is the way it has transformed my relationship with readers, but that wouldn't have happened if I had only used it in half a dozen stories. . . .

I was in a church last Dec. 26 when I got an interesting lesson in civic journalism. I was there to cover another installment in a long-standing story about City Council efforts to buy up an historically black neighborhood and turn it into an industrial park.

The residents felt the city was trying to buy their heritage for insultingly low prices; the council members believed the city needed the jobs the industrial park could bring.

Sitting in a back pew, I started to play a mental game. As one speaker rose, I tried to really understand the emotion and passion she was displaying to the council. Then, when I thought I had an idea of where she was coming from, I switched sides, and tried to hear her words as if I were one of the council members sitting at the front of the room. When the council members spoke, I did the same thing with them.

And all of a sudden I realized that they had no idea what the other one was saying. The council members' view of the situation totally precluded them from hearing the citizens; and the citizens were completely deaf to the arguments of the council members. Instead of just remarking on this to myself, as I would have done before civic journalism, I made it the crux of my story.

The piece that appeared in the paper described why the council members were so hard of hearing and what it was about this group of citizens that made them both so passionate and so uncaring of another point of view.

I think the story I came up with was far more interesting than the "Two sides clashed last night" piece I could have written, and it was far more truthful. Yes, the groups clashed, but it was more than a screaming match, it was a fundamental miscommunication I thought the public needed to know about.

The other thing that happened when I wrote the story that way was that I stopped seeing the residents and property owners as victims. Instead of portraying them as the people who were being run over by that mean-ol' City Council, I was depicting them as active participants in the process, as people with a point of view that could not be ignored. Doing that made me realize how often I had made people like them into the powerless victims of the process, instead of actors in their own right.

I don't think one story like this can change public policy or opinion on an issue that's already dragged on for most of a decade, but as I continue to cover it with this approach, hopefully, each side will begin to see a little more of the other's point of view and the reading public will understand the true implications of their city's policy. To me, those are worthwhile goals.

—From Karen Weintraub, "Doing Less Harm," *Civic Catalyst*, October 1996

. . . .

In addition to the editors, reporters, and scholars who took time to reflect on the idea, there were publishers who took an interest in public journalism's development. Since their primary duty is to ensure that the enterprise returns a profit, publishers make easy targets for the journalist's fear that business imperatives will overwhelm public service in the press. But many publishers show a keen grasp of the newspaper's public charter and their communities' problems.

Here, Joel Kramer, then publisher of the *Star-Tribune* in Minneapolis, speaks to readers about professional ethics and the challenge of making public life work.

. . . .

You might think that the media are among the forces dividing and fragmenting our community. And you'd be right, at least some of the time. Excessive negative coverage of government, for example, can breed cynicism that makes people unwilling to serve or even vote. The news-is-conflict model can overemphasize differences and underemphasize the possibility of solutions.

But the media also help unite us. They give us a place to talk together, and a vocabulary to use in the discussion.

I gave a talk a week ago to a group of lawyers, entitled, "Would you want your child to grow up to be either a journalist or a lawyer?" My conclusion was that, notwithstanding low public confidence in both professions, you could certainly lead an ethical life in either. But ethics are just about the rules of the game—doing things right. More important, I said, was the purpose of the profession—doing the right things.

In journalism, an increasing number of people are asking whether the right thing is to be disinterested, detached observers who tell people what we think they need to know, with no concern for consequences. Proponents of the traditional detachment call it a public service; detractors call it arrogance. An alternative view, that journalism must focus on what readers want, is praised as more caring but criticized as pandering or marketing.

Personally, I favor a third concept, sometimes called "public journalism," which holds that the journalist's role should be more active: to persuade people to accept the challenge of public work, instead of retreating into cynicism, despair, tribalism or privacy, and then to help people do that public work. This is public service without arrogance, and caring without pandering.

I challenged the lawyers to think about their own profession's purpose. Law preserves order. It protects life, liberty and property. These are noble goals, but increasingly, law seems to be about fighting.

If you view the legal system as a boxing ring, most of the energy around legal ethics has gone into making sure the fight going on in that ring is fair—no razor blades in the gloves. The handlers and referees are the experts on those questions, and have led the way.

But is boxing good for society? Is fighting between adversaries for a winner-takes-all purse the best way to resolve disputes? Should I have to step into that ring every time someone challenges me to a fight, no matter how frivolously? Are our businesses, governments and even individuals absorbing so much pounding to the body in those rings that they have little energy left to create more life, liberty and property? Why isn't the legal community leading the effort to answer that kind of question?

You probably have your own opinion about the roles of both journalism and law in the life of our community, but I'm more interested in this question: What about the work you do? Does it contribute to making the community a better place for all of us to live? With all the other things on your mind, do you ever even think about your work in those terms? . . .

Take a chance. Get a group together in the office to talk about the

purpose of your work. If your place is anything like ours, you won't get unanimous agreement. But maybe you'll ignite a change for the better.
—From Joel Kramer, "Ask Yourself If Your Work Makes the Community a Better Place," Minneapolis *Star-Tribune*, October 16, 1994

. . . .

"Maybe you'll ignite a change for the better." Or maybe you'll make things worse. Cheryl Carpenter, assistant managing editor of the *Charlotte Observer*, found herself in the middle of a public journalism initiative that frightened her. It was the newspaper's "Taking Back Our Neighborhoods" project, which tried to alter the pattern of news coverage in some of the city's high-crime areas. The *Observer*'s effort involved meeting with citizens in these neighborhoods to understand how they saw the problem. Its goal was to portray the depth of the difficulties citizens faced in high-crime areas, and to focus attention on what needed to be done—by city officials, by the residents themselves, and by the larger community. Here, Carpenter reflects on her experience and what it meant to her.[17]

. . . .

I learned by doing and the journey happened while I was doing it. What I started out with was a pain-in-the-butt project that I felt overwhelmed by. I was saying to myself, "What is this? I do not understand what we are doing and I have real apprehensions about how it is going to work." That went on for a really long time, that conversation with myself.

Then I got past the "we do not know what we are doing" and I said to myself, "This is scary. I don't like it. It is scary and it is testing me in ways that I have not been tested before. And it does not feel right." Then it went from there to, "Something is happening." It was "something is happening *in this room,*" a room where I was talking to citizens, and then after the meeting, I thought: Well, something is happening to *me,* too.

But I did not have time to think about it. I just knew something was happening, and I was still scared. But it was a fear that turned exciting rather than dreadful. I kept trying to figure out why this was so tough; and a couple of times in my career—everybody has this—you get tested, you know? Maybe you have to fire someone. Maybe you have to do a hard thing, or maybe your character has come under fire and you have to defend it, or your news judgment.

This was a test for me. I mean, it was a defining test. It told me who I am as a journalist and who I wanted to be. If you are in it, you will understand this. You will be in the middle of it and it will feel as if you evolved and didn't mean to. It will feel like something happened and you lost control.

So then I went from "something is happening in this room and to me" to, "what is our responsibility as a newspaper?" Is that not funny? I have been in management a long time, but I never really thought about that. What is my responsibility in *this* newspaper and *this* city? I have discovered a few things I am and a few things I am not and a few things I want to be. So, if I had to recount my light bulb it was *this is bigger than I thought it was.* It is not just about civic life, it is about democracy, which gave me the profession I love. I am a watchdog and I am a storyteller; and I believe in using those roles to return power to my power sources, the citizens of this democracy. I was a run-and-gun journalist. I was a night cops editor. I was blood and guts. I was: "get the bad guys." And I still am.

Then I became a student of storytelling and learned about dramatic narrative and foreshadowing. And I still am. Now, what [do] I do with those skills, in a deeper, broader sense?

—From Cheryl Carpenter, remarks at the Project on Public Life and the Press seminar, American Press Institute, August 15, 1995

. . . .

When Carpenter says she had never really thought about her responsibilities as a journalist, what she means is that she allowed the profession to do her thinking for her. She thought what others thought: our job is to get the news, get it right, tell stories to make it compelling, and "get the bad guys." Her extended encounter with citizens and the quest for a different kind of crime coverage so disrupted the smooth demeanor of the competent professional that she felt frightened and probably angry at having to work out for herself (under pressure) an answer to the question What are journalists for? From it emerged a new definition of herself as a professional, which incorporated the old definition—finding the news, telling the story, getting the bad guy—under a broader banner: "using those roles to return power to my power sources, the citizens of this democracy."

Part Three / Reactions

6

Journalism Is What It Is

Critics React to the Experiment

"Excuse me while I run screaming from the room."

So wrote David Remnick, a former correspondent for the *Washington Post,* commenting in the *New Yorker* on the rise of public journalism. Remnick was reacting, in part, to the mission statement of the *Virginian-Pilot's* public life team, which read: "We will revitalize a democracy that has grown sick with disenchantment. We will lead the community to discover itself and act on what it has learned."

These were lofty sentiments, a bit overblown, perhaps. But what was it about them that drove Remnick up the proverbial wall? The reporters at the *Pilot* were simply describing their aspirations. It may have been hubris to state that a newspaper could revitalize democracy and lead the community to act. But surely there was hubris in "All the News That's Fit to Print," the slogan that appears on every edition of the *New York Times.* It's hard to imagine that Remnick ran screaming from the breakfast table when he saw that in the morning. So perhaps it was not the lofty tone of the *Pilot's* goals that so irked the *New Yorker* writer, but the goals themselves, and what he imagined the results would be. As Remnick went on to say: "If a few papers want to hold forums with their readers, bully. But why abandon the entire enterprise of informed, aggressive skepticism—even in its current [depressed] state—in the hope of pleasing an imagined public? When journalists begin acting like waiters and taking orders from the public and pollsters, the results are not pretty."[1]

Compare these lines with the remainder of the *Pilot* team's mission statement: "We will show how the community works or could work, whether that means exposing corruption, telling citizens how to make their voices heard, holding up a fresh perspective or spotlighting people who do their jobs well. We will portray democracy in the fullest sense of the word, whether in a council meeting or a cul-de-sac. We do this knowing that a lively, informed, and most of all, engaged public is essential to the healthy community and to the health of these newspapers."[2]

Now listen to Remnick again: "Once an editor starts responding to every cry of 'What about my needs?' the front page will read like a community shopper, and the news from Sarejevo will come in the form of A.P. briefs back near the want ads. Like it or not, part of the job of a great editor is to listen to public desires—and then, if necessary, act against them. The alternative is to scare oneself out of existence and accelerate the race to a no-newspaper town."[3]

Read against one another, the passages above show a clash of self-definitions at work. The reporters at the *Virginian-Pilot* had been asked by their editor to deliberate on the goals they shared. For the half dozen journalists in the room, it was the first time they had considered the matter in the company of their colleagues. "Our first exercise was to write down everything about Campbell that made us angry," they recounted. Then they got to work: "We admitted to ourselves, and said out loud, that we wanted nothing less than to fight the forces of apathy and disengagement that seemed to be driving people away from public life."

Acknowledging to one another that their aim was not just to do good journalism but to improve democracy *with* journalism felt to them like a breakthrough. And in a way it was. It broke with conventions in the craft that placed the public on the receiving end of the news, reading what the journalist wrote. By relocating the public in their imaginations, bringing it closer to what they were trying to achieve, they also brought themselves closer together as a group. "With that, the reporters present agreed that they believed in something, namely, democracy," wrote Tony Wharton, a member of the team.[4]

David Remnick believed in something, too: keeping a proper distance between a professionalized press and a fickle, distracted, yet overly demanding audience. Greatness in journalism meant the courage to defy a public insufficiently committed to the "enterprise of informed, aggressive skepticism." Journalists were supposed to be engaged in public service, Remnick said. But if they interpreted the phrase too literally and became servants of the public, "acting like waiters and taking orders," their work would lose its purpose, which was presenting the unvarnished truth, not "pleasing an imagined public."

Whenever journalists reacted to public journalism, they revealed themselves on the question, what are journalists for? To bring about this result was part of the point of going public with the idea; and in this sense, at least, the press got the point. Journalism did journalism to public journalism, and the results were almost always instructive. Critics contributed the way good critics do: they warned about possible dangers and raised hard questions for proponents to consider. In this chapter, I describe the most frequent objections to the idea, and I reply from my perspective inside the movement.

A good place to begin is with the remarks of Rem Rieder, editor of the *American Journalism Review,* who in 1995 spoke to a conference of journalism educators. He presented what he called "the critics' multi-count indictment" of public journalism. Rieder was careful to say that he was neither an enthusiast nor an opponent, although he did feel that "something fundamentally unhealthy" had entered the relationship between the press and the public. How to repair it was another matter, and this is where criticisms of the movement became relevant. Rieder's list reports the most common complaints against public journalism.

. . . .

Public journalism is nothing new. It's what good papers have always done. Good reporters and editors know what matters to their readers. They're in touch with their communities. What's happened is that many papers have cut back on their staffs. They don't have reporters on the street. So public journalism cranks up all these town meetings and focus groups and pizza sessions to find out what readers and viewers care about. But if they were doing their jobs they would already know. You don't need a movement to do this.

The emphasis on positive stories or success stories is nothing new. Gene Roberts [then of the *New York Times*] talks about his days when he worked for the *Goldsboro News-Argus* in North Carolina and the paper recognized the region was too dependent on tobacco. So Roberts wrote story after story about farmers who had found ways to thrive without tobacco. Again, just good, traditional journalism.

Public journalism is a marketing ploy. It's a way to build circulation and advertising by catering to readers, finding out and giving them what they want, wrapped up in fancy rhetoric about restoring public dialogue and saving democracy. Look at who its biggest boosters are: the nation's two largest newspaper companies. Gannett, long known for its commitment to high profits, and Knight-Ridder, moving increasingly in that direction.

It's a way to make beleaguered editors and publishers feel good, feel that they are loved. You're never going to please everyone in this business. If you do tough stories you are going to make people mad, even when the stories are right on target. In fact the best service you could do for a community is identifying problems and abuses that need to be solved. Public journalism is a nice fuzzy way of wrapping yourself up in the community and avoiding the hits that come with doing your job correctly.

It leads to boosters rather than hard-edged watchdog reporting. One of the tenets of public journalism is that conventional journalism is too confrontational, too conflict-driven. Public journalism stresses the need to build a public consensus. The fear is that it will lead to softer coverage that will make communities feel better about themselves and focus less attention on misconduct and malfeasance.

Editors are abdicating their responsibility if they rely so heavily on residents to help them set their priorities. Editors are professionals. Readers are not. The editor's job is to know the community, decide what's important, to shape the newspaper's coverage. One reporter was quoted as describing the process this way: "It's like turning surgery over to the patient."

Crossing the line. It's fine to recommend solutions and campaign on the editorial pages. But there's a danger when you crusade on the news pages. Some fear a return to the bad old days of William Randolph Hearst, when the newspaper was a vehicle to implement its own agenda. They fear a juggernaut that can ram a program down the community's throat. They express concern about public journalism campaigns in places as diverse as Bremerton, Washington, and Columbus, Georgia, where in the view of many the newspaper became too intimately involved in civic affairs.

It's widely known that sagging credibility is one of journalism's most serious problems. And rather than help solve the problem, critics fear public journalism will exacerbate it. If a newspaper or television station is the driving force behind a community project, no matter how worthy, who is going to believe that it will cover that project with balance and objectivity? In reporting on public officials, we often say that the appearance of impropriety is a problem even if no impropriety has been established. Even in the absence of proof of skewed coverage, there will be the public perception that the news organization is protecting the project it has embraced so vigorously. What if problems emerge: cost overruns, misconduct, conflict of interest? We all know how the situation changes when the publisher is on the board of the committee deciding to build a new stadium, or the parent company is deeply involved in the drive to build a new civic center. At many papers these stories have the kind of high-level attention, not to say interference, that they wouldn't have if the company wasn't involved. That would be magnified exponentially if the newspaper or TV station or media company is the major player. . . .

And if that's overstating the involvement of the newspaper or TV station in public journalism efforts, what is all the excitement about? When you do a major series on a problem, you conclude with a large installment or two about how the problem might be solved. Then you weigh in with aggressive editorials. Isn't this the traditional approach first-class news organizations take to helping the community better itself? Why do we need a new movement to do this?

It's not a journalist's role to usurp the political process. Journalists should inform. Then the people and their representatives should decide how they want to proceed. . . .

Newspapers have their hands full trying to solve their own problems. It's no secret that the newspaper industry is plagued by sagging circulation. With increasing competition from new media, papers are flailing around finding a new formula to keep readers and win new ones. They desperately need to figure out how to get young people to read them. They should concentrate on doing their primary job, informing people, more successfully. . . . How can they fix society as a whole if they can't even solve their own problems?

The evangelical tone. Even if you buy the analysis, the alienation of the public from the media, is this the only solution? There's sometimes the implication in the remarks of public journalism advocates that this is the one true way to proceed, that it's either embrace public journalism or journalism is doomed. For some people, that's a serious turnoff. Tallyrand once said of something he didn't approve of, "It was not only a disgrace, it was a mistake." Well, I'm not sure this qualifies as a disgrace, but tactically speaking, it may well be a mistake.

Public journalism has also emerged as a force on the editorial page, nowhere more dramatically than in Spokane, where the *Spokesman-Review* has dramatically increased public participation, and has abolished the position of editorial page editor, replacing it with a couple of interactive editors who help whip the public's pieces into shape. Here's what some of the critics have had to say about this development:

It's another instance of dumbing down the newspaper. This should be one place left for intelligent, serious, informed opinion, not fluff. They cite point-counterpoint editorials about the merits of zucchini. Says one Spokane staffer: "There are a lot of people out there who don't know what they're talking about. . . . Where else [besides the editorial page] am I going to get informed opinion?"

Many editorial page highlights have been principled stands that fly in the face of local public opinion: courageous support for civil rights in the South, lonely opposition to the Vietnam War. Editorial pages should lead the moral charge.

—From Rem Rieder, remarks to a panel discussion at the Association for Education in Journalism and Mass Communication convention, Washington, D.C., August 11, 1995

. . . .

Nothing new. A gimmick that draws attention away from cutbacks that have led to poor coverage and a dissatisfied public. A marketing ploy by an industry desperate to retain market share. A misplaced longing among editors who want to be loved. An invitation to go soft. An assault on the profession's prerogative to judge what's important. A call for advocacy journalism, which would usurp the political process and further erode public trust. A distraction from the basic task of covering the news, difficult enough without adding the duty to repair society. An arrogant and preachy movement that pretends to have all the answers. A recipe for dumbing down the newspaper and backing away from courageous stands that defy popular opinion.[5]

So read the indictment against public journalism. What can be learned from these charges? First, they were useful in noting the risks that accompanied the idea, among them: lending ideological cover to a downsizing industry, getting the press too entangled in politics, neglecting the basics, getting carried away with the charged rhetoric of reform, eclipsing the distance required for honest truth telling, reducing the news to the lowest common denominator. These were real dangers. Some, no doubt, had been realized in the hundreds of experiments that unfolded around the country.

Pointing out the risks was a genuine service to the idea; but critics were typically saying more than "beware." They were saying be done with public journalism, since the dangers outweigh the possible benefits. And between the lines they were saying something else: The press already has an adequate understanding of its place in the public square. It understands politics and civic life well, knows its role within them, and needs no insights from would-be reformers. That is one reason Rieder asked, more than once, "Why do you need a movement to do this?"

It is striking, then, that amid all the criticisms of public journalism, no competing notion of reform was put forward. Instead, critics fell back on "tradition" as the best answer to problems in the press: the traditional separation between news and opinion, the traditional caution against getting too involved, the traditional imperatives of independence and detachment, the tradition of hard-hitting investigative reporting. But hadn't these failed to prevent journalism from losing its audience, losing public trust, losing effectiveness—in general, losing its way? That, at least, was the argument public journalism was making. No one knew if the movement was going to succeed. On the other hand, no one knew whether the press was going to survive its many difficulties, either. But the dangers of doing nothing were rarely weighed against the risks in exploring public journalism.

In this sense the movement was literally about moving—getting started on changes in thinking and practice, shifting priorities around so there was some room to learn and grow. Critics, by contrast, often declared themselves against movement, period. Here, for example, is Paul Greenberg, editorial page editor of the *Arkansas Democrat-Gazette,* condemning public journalism with an assertion that the old ways are better.

> It is always a temptation in any business, including newspapering, to start doing new things poorly instead of the old things well. It's so much easier, and novelty seems to attract Americans in a way quality no longer does. Especially if the new departure can be packaged attractively.
>
> Thus the laundry that can't iron a shirt properly may go in for same-day service, minor repairs and valet parking. Now some newspapers—excuse me, media—are toying with what is called public journalism instead of the old-fashioned kind.
>
> . . . This new fad and plague will pass, but before it does, public journalism will have done its part to chip away at the always-precarious credibility of American newspapers. And the always-fuzzy line between reporting the news and making it will have been crossed again.[6]

Michael Gartner was one of public journalism's most outspoken critics. His career had taken him to almost every level in the profession: page-one editor of the *Wall Street Journal*, top editor of the *Des Moines Register*, president of the American Society of Newspaper Editors, president of NBC News, publisher of the *Ames (Iowa) Daily Tribune*, columnist for *USA Today*. So he spoke with some authority when he warned his colleagues about the emergence of public journalism, which he described as a "menace." Gartner agreed that times were tough. But the remedy was to go back to basics. Those who had lived through earlier periods of doubts and despair had "discovered and rediscovered and rediscovered again that newspapers need news," Gartner said.

He was offering this reminder to the annual meeting of the Society of Professional Journalists because, as he said, "I think you—and, especially, your bosses—are being lulled and conned by this thing called public journalism," which went against everything the press was supposed to do. "Newspapers are supposed to explain the community, not convene it. News reporters are supposed to explore the issues, not solve them. Newspapers are supposed to expose the wrongs, not campaign against them. Reporters and city editors are not supposed to write legislation or lead campaigns or pass moral judgments. They're supposed to tell the truth. And God knows that's hard enough to do all by itself."

Reporters are now running about trying to solve problems rather than explain them; newspapers are writing laws rather than exposing wrongs; journalists are becoming moralists and judges rather than truth tellers. All this contradicts what journalism is. Newspapers should do "what their names imply," he said, and that was simple: "To *Herald*, to *Mirror*, to *Chronicle*, to *Register*, to be a *Tribune*, a *Clarion*, a *Bulletin*, a *Journal*. Or, to use the name of my favorite newspaper, a weekly in Linn, Missouri, an *Unterrified Democrat*. Papers aren't Conveners or Soothers or Legislators or Involvers or Consensus-makers."

Here Gartner tapped a powerful belief in the culture of the press: the news mirrors the world as it is, reporters tell it like it is—without being cowed by the consequences. These ideas are evoked by the honored names of American newspapers, he said. Of course, he neglected to mention other names that honored different ideas, like the *Springfield (Missouri) News-Leader*, the *Maryville (Missouri) Daily Forum*, the *Awatonna (Minnesota) People's Press*, the *Atlanta Constitution*, or, my favorite, the *Cushing (Oklahoma) Citizen*. The spirit of the American press was alive in these titles, as well. Gartner put aside these competing strands in press tradition to portray public journalism as a foreign presence smuggled in from outside:

> Now, all this would be OK if it were just a fad—just another way for journalism professors to get articles published so they can get tenure or just a repackaging of an old idea into new academic jargon to shake loose foundation grants.
>
> It is that, of course, but I fear it is more.
>
> I fear that the people who are touting this really believe it, really believe that newspapers should be like a branch of government—holding hearings, like council members; or writing legislation, like congress members; or leading campaigns like political candidates; or nabbing crooks, like police officers.[7]

To journalists like Gartner and Greenberg, the press was in trouble because it was changing too much, abandoning protections that had taken years to put in place. The way to survive was to protect these traditions against oncoming fads and dangerous interlopers. That was their view. Public journalism offered a different attitude: the spirit of experiment, which was "tradition" read another way.

In many passages in his voluminous works, John Dewey argued that an experimental outlook was central to the American idea of democracy. The United States themselves were founded on it, he said. By putting into practice the ideal of liberty and the design of federalism "we have been, as it were, a laboratory set aside from the rest of the world in which to make, for its benefit, a great social experiment." In another essay Dewey wrote: "Be the evils what they may, the experiment is not yet played out. The United States are not yet made; they are not a finished fact to be categorically assessed." The freedom of the press clause in the Constitution was part of the experiment, which meant that the press itself could be seen as a laboratory of democracy, a proving ground for ideas on how a diverse nation could communicate with itself about public business.[8]

In the beginning were the noisy newspapers that sounded the alarm and helped mobilize the population during the break from Britain. They were followed by commercial journals for the trading class and a party press dependent on political patrons. Abolitionist papers argued the case against slavery. In the 1830s, the penny press found a mass circulation and an entertaining formula for a bustling commercial society. The so-called yellow press followed, including the legendary swagger of William Randolph Hearst—a political figure as much as a publisher. In the twentieth century, the professional model remade American journalism by emphasizing objectivity and the separation of fact from opinion. Starting with radio's arrival in the 1920s, broadcast journalism emerged with the power to assemble a vast audience copresent in time. Then the professional model was itself remade with the growth of an adversarial mentality after Vietnam and Watergate.[9]

Of course, this brief sketch leaves out a great deal: the underground press that allowed subterranean currents to surface, foreign-language papers that eased the immigrant's entry to a new world, small community papers that knit neighbors together, the labor press that energized and informed workers in their struggle to organize, the black press that gave African-Americans the word, national magazines that distributed news, views, and pictures across the land. All these enterprises arose as containers or forms for the practice of journalism. All were experiments with the free press clause in the Constitution. And what they experimented on was the country the Constitution created.

The ideals of democracy on which the nation was founded, the tools of communication as they multiplied and improved, the churning markets of a competitive and expanding economy, the shifting tides of American politics and parties, the changing demands and desires of citizens, the egos and talents of the people involved: with these and a host of other conditions journalism has been experimenting since the early days of the republic. Viewed from this angle, "journalism" is an extended elaboration on the idea of democracy, a laboratory set amidst the real world, where a free people can find the means to convey its thoughts, inform and entertain itself, put centers in touch with margins, and cohere around common concerns.

This longer view of journalism implied an alternative understanding of the First Amendment and its free press clause. Among those who tried to articulate it was James Carey, who, by the time public journalism arose, had been crafting the ideas behind it for some twenty years. A vital public culture is not the automatic consequence of a free press, Carey asserted. Rather, the prior existence of a rich public life is our only guarantee that the free press clause will work in our favor, that journalism will actually improve the body politic. A journalism "independent of the conversation of the culture, or existing in the absence of such a conversation" will soon become a "menace to public life and an effective politics."[10]

To most journalists, independence is what the First Amendment is all about. The press is singled out for special protection because its independent status is what keeps a free people free. For Carey, the First Amendment is about those people and the common life they create for themselves. The republic was founded on a hopeful image of what public life could be, codified in the First Amendment freedoms we praise so lavishly. Carey interprets them this way: "The amendment says that people are free to gather together without the intrusion of the state or its representatives. Once gathered, they are free to speak to one another openly and freely. They are further free to write down what they have to say and to share it beyond the immediate place of utterance."

From this Carey derives the deepest purpose of journalism, which is to amplify and improve what the rest of us produce as a "society of conversationalists." Public conversation is "ours to conduct," Carey wrote. It must flourish in the country at large, in our politics and the way we relate to one another as strangers who are also citizens. When "the press sees its role as limited to informing whomever happens to turn up at the end of the communication channel, it explicitly abandons its role as an agency for carrying on the conversation of the culture."[11]

Carey had a different view of what the free press clause was for. His emphasis on citizens who are "free to write down what they have to say and to share it beyond the immediate place of utterance" did not conflict with "hands off the press." Rather, the first principle is what justified the second. Not "information" provided via the press, but enlivened conversation—cultivated by journalists and conducted by citizens—lay at the heart of the First Amendment tradition to which all Americans were heir. And the country had been reworking this tradition since the moment of its birth.

The spirit of experiment that animated public journalism thus had long roots. Although critics often claimed the mantle of tradition, a deeper and more compelling tradition was to keep the experiment going as times changed and new problems presented themselves. Journalism, in this way of thinking, is a variable. Its forms are not fixed, its aims are inconstant, its meter and method vary with time and place. But for many in the press, the very notion of experiment seemed objectionable. Journalism's task was simple and clear, its methods well defined. A typical comment along these lines came from Joe Rigart, an investigative reporter at the *Star-Tribune* in Minneapolis. "If we really care about helping people be better citizens," he said, "we should put the money and effort into our main task: finding out what's going on and informing people about it."[12]

Michael Gartner thought this the main task, as well. He said he had tried to grasp what public journalism was about by borrowing the file of a friend who collects such material,

> and I pored over it. And I'm still not sure what public journalism really is—I hear people call it "democracy-enhancing journalism," an awkward and bizarre phrase, or "journalism that cares about solutions," or "journalism that encourages the flourishing of public life" or "journalism that seeks to redefine and learn a different set of reflexes."
>
> Frankly, I don't know what any of that means. But like Potter Stewart and pornography, I know public journalism when I see it.
>
> And I'm beginning to see it everywhere.
>
> And I think that's just awful.

Gartner pronounced himself mystified by the idea. Enhancing democracy, nourishing public life, aiding in the search for solutions to public problems, changing the reflexive attitudes of the profession—these phrases were mere gibberish to him, and there was a touch of pride in his inability to discern their meaning. Gartner appealed to his colleagues' mistrust of abstractions, their self-image as practical people who don't need fancy terms and newfangled ideas to do their jobs.

Having denied to public journalism any weight or sense, he went on to reject what he saw as the results, one of which involved the unusual case of the Unabomber manifesto, the rambling diatribe of a killer who vowed to keep up his bombing campaign unless the text was printed. The FBI persuaded the publishers of the *Washington Post* and the *New York Times* to agree to the demand, in the hope that wide distribution of the manifesto would help identify a suspect—which in the end is exactly what happened. The Unabomber decision, Gartner said, was "public journalism run amok." So was the *Akron Beacon Journal* "asking in its news pages for church and civic and social organizations to volunteer with projects to help improve race relations." This "new journalism" was bad journalism because it "will ultimately cost the newspaper its most precious asset—its credibility."

He added that he was in favor of listening harder to readers' concerns and explaining to the public how newspapers operate. Journalists should be more attentive and less defensive, he said. "But I also think we should be objective." Taking stands was fine for the editorial pages, "where you are supposed to argue and lead and rant and rave." But in the current "cycle of tough times" scarce resources were unwisely diverted "into these projects with a cause, these stories with a view, these campaigns for a solution." This is not what people need. "Readers need facts, facts about their towns, their schools, their city councils, their zoning boards, their neighborhoods." They do not need experiments.

> I've said enough about the new journalism. I probably should have come out and said, "I don't like it, I don't trust it, I don't think it's right journalistically or morally or philosophically or any other way." And then shut up. . . .
>
> I just want to add one thing: As I read about the new journalism, I saw references to journalists who wanted to change the world.
>
> That is not the role of newsroom journalists.
>
> If you want to change the world, become a teacher or a politician or a missionary or an editorial writer.
>
> If you want to explore the world, to explain the world, to expose the world, become a reporter.[13]

What's most illuminating about Gartner's treatment of public journalism is not the totality of his dismissal, or the severity of his claim that news reports offer nothing but facts. It's his static view of what journalism is. More than a traditionalist, Gartner declared himself an essentialist. The news is what it is: a record of events. Reporters are recorders and that's that. Newspapers aren't conveners because they aren't. Reporters may explain and expose, but no civic purpose beyond that is allowed. In this cramped and ahistorical vision, the links between investigative reporting and the political reformers of the 1920s era disappear; a common image of the press as the Fourth Estate or "fourth branch of government" is wiped away. And the many journalists who, when asked why they joined the profession (a question I often posed to them), answered "to change the world" or "make things a little better" are denied membership in the fraternity. Civic-spirited journalists who experiment with the power of the press can only ruin the institution, for the results are known in advance: an automatic loss of credibility.[14]

But how could anyone know this with any certainty? Consider the case of the Unabomber. By publishing his screed, the *Washington Post* and the *New York Times* were hardly embracing public journalism. They remained foreign, even hostile, territory for the idea. But they joined in its spirit in one important way: by recognizing themselves as something other than just chroniclers of events. The two papers acknowledged a duty to the nation (and in a sense to human life) that went beyond the standard duties of journalism. And as Gartner warned, they did lose credibility—with journalists, many of whom were dismayed by their decision. (One, in fact, was Davis Merritt.) But did the American people trust those institutions any less as a result? Was there any significant public outcry? Did advertisers drop out? Did readers revolt? And when a suspect in the bombings was arrested (after his brother read the manifesto and recognized the mind at work), did the complaints of journalists about lost credibility resonate with anyone but journalists?[15]

"So they got away with it," some in the press might concede. "But what about the next nut who comes along?" Then another decision will have to be made. The first, after all, was an experiment, a risky venture with an unknown outcome, undertaken in the hope that some good might come of it. To deny the institution such measures is to doubt its capacity for mature judgment while evacuating its moral imagination, its ability to arrive at different ideas about what's right under shifting circumstances. In commenting on public journalism, many critics defined the experiment by the disastrous outcomes they imagined, as if the experimenters themselves could not anticipate the same problems and learn from their experience if things went awry. A *Columbia Journalism Review* article described the typical fears public journalism seemed to evoke: "A newsroom that would seek to market itself as the community's pal, meanwhile, is the kind that could reflexively refrain from doing anything that might offend that community. *Newsday*'s editor, Tony Marro, is proud of a series his newspaper did in 1992 on segregated housing patterns on Long Island. But the series brought some of the most vicious reader reaction Marro says he has seen in his career. 'If we went out and said, "what are your concerns?" this would not have been one of them,' he says. 'A lot of time people don't want to talk about the most important stories.' "[16]

John Seigenthaler, a respected figure in the press, raised similar concerns in a lecture series honoring Elijah Parish Lovejoy, an abolitionist publisher killed by a pro-slavery mob in 1837. The *Boston Globe* reported:

> "The conflict to me is obvious," said Seigenthaler, former publisher of the *Nashville Tennessean*. "This new movement includes the suggestion that journalists poll their communities to determine what readers want to read and see and hear—and then follow the graph lines.
>
> Seigenthaler added: "I shudder to think what the public response would have been had Lovejoy conducted a poll on the question of abolition and adhered to the findings."[17]

Both complaints show the imagination of disaster at work. Strengthening the connection to the community will mean marketing yourself as the "community's pal." Taking a poll will spell enslavement to public opinion. Asking people "what are your concerns?" will mean limiting the news to only those concerns. Listening more carefully to citizens will mean surrendering to their sensitivities, pandering to their prejudices. If you do public journalism, you won't do any other kind of journalism. And in the end, you'll lose your nerve, "abandon the entire enterprise of informed, aggressive skepticism," as David Remnick wrote.

All these outcomes were imaginable, of course, and that was precisely what made them avoidable. When in 1995 the *Akron Beacon Journal* decided to prod community groups toward greater engagement across racial lines, it had to decide where being supportive ended and reporting the news resumed. An impossible quandary? Not to Dale Allen, then the paper's editor. "We told these groups: 'If you're doing something that backfires, we're going to cover that, too.'" Would it be awkward for the Akron paper to report on dissension and bumbling in civic groups the paper had also helped motivate and bring together? Perhaps. But solving that problem was another part of the experiment, another opportunity to learn.[18]

An experimental attitude is anti-essentialist. It respects tradition, but not as a tablet showing fixed commandments. And it asks for patience in evaluating the worth of any new practice, for what looks dangerous at one moment might draw a different reaction as the work unfolds. Compare the following accounts of an initiative at the *Wisconsin State Journal* in Madison. Titled "City of Hope," it was both a reporting project, in which the newspaper investigated untreated problems in the community and discussed them with citizens, and a kind of leadership roundtable, convened by the *State Journal.* Elected officials and other movers and shakers were asked to sit down with the editor and his reporters to discuss the paper's findings and what could be done about them—if the people with power could only cooperate better.

Editor Frank Denton knew he was taking a risk, stepping outside his traditional role, by convening the group. But he was also convinced that the newspaper might do some good by connecting Madison's leaders to the wider concerns of citizens and the facts uncovered in the paper's reporting. So he went ahead. In February 1995, the *New York Times* reported on the Madison effort.

The Mayor of Madison, Paul R. Soglin, said he was troubled by the methods being used by the State Journal in one of its most visible public journalism experiments, a long series called "City of Hope," which has explored problems of crime, poverty, racism, and unemployment in the region. . . .

One result was that the group called together by the newspaper convened a "jobs summit" to develop an economic development strategy for the area.

Mayor Soglin says the experiment has been awkward. The *State Journal*, the most powerful editorial voice in the region, has been "wearing two hats" by reporting a story it helped to create, he said. And Mr. Soglin says he worries about the "top down" nature of a process in which a group selected by editors, rather than by voters, is making policy proposals.

But mostly, he said, he worries that by mixing the roles of creating the news and reporting it, the newspaper may get too much power.[19]

Eighteen months later, *Governing* magazine also took a look at the Madison project. Its article described the usual objections to the notion of newspaper as convener. It then noted how the mayor's views had evolved:

Madison Mayor Paul Soglin says public journalism has made a difference. After the *Wisconsin State Journal* ran "City of Hope," a series of articles on urban problems, businesses effectively assumed responsibility for financing a city program to provide "job coaches" for at-risk teenagers, and the "leadership group" agreed to develop "career ladders" to help people advance beyond low-paying jobs. Moreover, while Soglin says he initially was concerned about the newspaper setting the agenda in the leadership group meetings, the newspaper has limited its role to that of a facilitator. And in one notable case, civic journalism actually thwarted the newspaper's own political preferences: After the newspaper ran a series of articles and held town meetings on how to deal with suburban sprawl, voters elected a new slate of county supervisors who favored land use controls, even though the newspaper had endorsed the pro-growth incumbents. "I am convinced their land use project changed the county board," Soglin says.[20]

Could a leadership group convened by the newspaper become a tool for imposing the paper's agenda on the city? Yes, that is a danger. But the same paper, using good judgment, can also learn how to restrict its role to that of facilitator for the discussion, and earn the trust of participants by remaining an honest broker. Can a newspaper with a pro-growth editorial stance manipulate the public meetings it convenes to favor that stance? It could, if it wanted to risk the wrath of those who can see through such bald tactics. But it could also restrict itself to reporting on the problem and supporting public discussion about it, letting the political process take over from there. If the outcome conflicts with the urgings of the editorial page, so be it: that's democracy at work. Meanwhile, the credibility of the paper as a broker and convener of discussion would likely improve with such a result.

Perhaps the earliest civic journalism initiative was the effort in Columbus, Georgia that led to the founding in 1989 of the citizen's group United Beyond 2000. It tried to press a lethargic leadership into confronting long-term problems that had been uncovered by the newspaper's reporting. Many in the press—and more than a few who identified with public journalism—thought the paper erred badly by permitting staffers to be involved in the new organization. Billy Winn, who was one of those participants, later agreed with that assessment. But he had other things to say as well. Looking back on the project in 1994, he felt it had achieved something.

> Winn says the project had enormous support and accomplished a great deal. "It was exactly the right thing to do at the right time," he says. "We have $171 million in civic improvement underway." Even today, when he gives speeches in Columbus, people still ask when the *Ledger-Enquirer* plans to revive Beyond 2000.
>
> "If I personally had to do it again," says Winn, "I certainly would have no reporters have anything to do with the task force." But he will still cross the line into activism. He believes that if you care about your community, as he does, it's impossible to stand by passively reporting on its deterioration and do nothing.[21]

"If I had it to do over again . . ." An experimental approach tries to learn from mistakes, as Winn did. Compare this with "It will ultimately cost the newspaper its most precious asset—its credibility." To assume, with Gartner, that public trust is automatically lowered by initiatives like those in Madison or Columbus is to judge in advance the outcome of a venture that might be better known by its results—and by what gets learned. Mayor Soglin was willing to do that and changed his mind about "City of Hope." Gartner and many of his colleagues were not.[22]

By forcing these attitudes forward, public journalism illuminated just how conservative the press could be about itself, and how suspicious it was of anyone who spoke too passionately about reform. This surfaced most clearly in a recurrent motif in press commentary: the depiction of the idea as a new religion, complete with true believers and traveling evangelists. *American Journalism Review* headlined its first article on the movement "The Gospel of Public Journalism." Reporting on what she called "the hottest secular religion in the news business" (a line that was recycled by several others), Alicia Shepard portrayed Buzz Merritt and myself as itinerant preachers inside a tent.[23]

Rosemary Armao, who quit the *Virginian-Pilot* around the time public journalism entered the paper's vocabulary, said the idea had devolved into a "cult." "It was like being born again in Jesus," she complained. "If you hadn't experienced the conversion, you just couldn't understand."[24] A reviewer of the first public journalism textbook, written by Arthur Charity, took a similar line in *Editor and Publisher*.

> What Charity makes clear, although [he is] apparently not aware of it, is that public journalism is a kind of new age cult or rather, an old-fashioned religion.
>
> In espousing its own doctrine and a special political correctness, it spawns a hierarchy equivalent to archbishops and bishops among editors and in the ranks, preachers, evangelists, elders and deacons.
>
> All the stages of a historic religion are here, for better or for worse.
>
> First comes a sense of guilt. He talks of journalists waking up to the fact [that] community and social and political problems are not being solved.
>
> He harbors a mea culpa feeling that somehow journalists are to blame if only in not living up to their potential force as the fourth estate.
>
> After guilt comes confession. Public journalists "must, in short, get real with themselves."
>
> They must know they have sinned and make a clean slate on which faith can build.
>
> A conversion experience is important. "They must see the public with new eyes," he says.[25]

Public journalism's enthusiasts may have been asking for such satirical treatment, especially with our frequent allusions to a "movement." But something else was at work in the imagery of evangelism and a cultlike fervor: the idea was being denied the status of an experiment. True believers entertain no doubts. A cult is built on the certainty that it is right. It cannot operate by trial and error or learn from its mistakes, because indoctrination, not inquiry, is the aim.

Through the assorted images and labels that got attached to it, public journalism became a story the rest of the press could tell itself about itself. If the reformers were dizzy revivalists preaching sin and salvation, then the remainder of the craft looked secular and rationalist, almost scientific by comparison. The apparent conflict was not between one press philosophy and another; it pitted religious zeal against sober skepticism, a rising cult against cooler heads, a confused and confusing band of reformers against those who were clear in their purpose and needed no movement to give them direction.

No charge was more commonly leveled at public journalists than the one captured by the word "advocate," or, an equivalent term, "activist." A related count was typically included: that opinion would be mixed freely with news as public journalists pursued their chosen causes. These rebukes warned of turning the newspaper into an ideological instrument. In a pair of columns, Lynne Enders Glaser of the *Fresno Bee* defined public journalism as "a means of delivering information, sometimes liberally punctuated with opinion." She continued:

> Proponents say it would empower people to act on public issues and promote causes that are right and good.
>
> Under public journalism, mainstream newspapers would move from the traditional role of observer/reporter to bridge builder/convener to advocate/newsmaker.
>
> "Advocate" is the key word.
>
> Public journalism, say proponents, would reverse the national apathy. Yes, they would cast objectivity aside, but the outcome would be worth it, they say.
>
> It's about "community connectedness."
>
> Opponents might answer, "Hogwash."
>
> First, they'd say, there's little new involved here. Good papers traditionally have involved their readers and, at least in the last three decades, they have done so through focus groups, reader representatives, reader surveys, polls and other means that are being treated as new ideas under the tag "public journalism."
>
> Second, opponents would say, it's bloody dangerous to open the news columns to editorial opinion, no matter how right or good the cause.[26]

William Woo, then the editor of the *St. Louis Post-Dispatch*, also found the essence of the idea in a call for political activism:

In every example of public journalism, the foremost principle has been that the newspaper and its journalists can no longer remain detached; that they must be involved and activists. The underlying assumption is that through community or democratic action, a newspaper may recapture the worthiness of purpose and relevance that traditional, detached journalism has frittered away—and also, as we shall see, replenish its depleted revenue stream.

Editors sit on public boards or commissions or action committees. Newspapers are becoming the conveners of their community, the master of ceremonies of the new democracy. Journalists no longer serve or inform the electorate; they become it.[27]

Actually, there were no editors who, in the name of public journalism, joined public boards or commissions. At least, I never came across any; and Woo did not cite any names. In a handful of cases—Madison was one, Columbus, Georgia, another—there were editors who helped pull together civic leaders or citizen's groups to create a forum for discussion. There were legitimate questions to be raised about such efforts, in which the editor was a key actor. But Woo's aim was to define public journalism by the mythical figure who "sits on the commission that is promoting a particular point of view on the matter." Paul Greenberg went even further, comparing the aims of public journalism with the uses of the press under Soviet communism.

Pravda, having come to a sad and thoroughly deserved end, American newspapers are now being hectored by the usual saints to follow its sterling example—and further blur the always-tenuous boundary between news and opinion. The right issues not having been addressed, this new media-ocracy will see that they are. And once again it will be done in the name of The People.

. . . Public journalism, as opposed to the real kind, blurs a lot of essential and useful distinctions—distinctions between news and opinion, and between people and the press. It reduces journalism to politics by other means.[28]

Public journalism did, in fact, speak of a political role for the press, but not as just another interest group with a partisan agenda and the means to advance it. Charity tried to explain the difference in his book.

Helping citizens to act is the final straw for many critics of public journalism. . . . Journalism's one protection against arrogance—its one claim on the public trust—is its refusal to get involved. Giving that up, it will inevitably careen down the same slippery slope as demagogues and spin doctors. It will end up speaking only for citizens it agrees with, and cheerleading civic action in which it's improperly involved.

Actually, public journalism has a golden rule—an ethical line—every bit as sharp as mainstream journalism's rule . . . : *Journalism should advocate democracy without advocating particular solutions.* This rule isn't so different from the conventional rule as it might seem at first glance.

Newspapers already recognize that certain democratic norms are essential for the news media to play their social role, and they feel no qualm about championing these norms, on the news pages or off. Take free speech, for example. No paper would hesitate to advocate the First Amendment, nor think twice about throwing its full resources into the First Amendment's defense. This is because, unlike abortion rights or aid to Russia or presidential candidate X or ballot initiative Y, the First Amendment is a sine qua non of informed public debate. Public journalists, looking at citizens' anger and apparent apathy, have simply asked themselves what other sine qua nons have gone unrecognized and unchampioned so far.[29]

Proponents of public journalism were trying to see the craft as a political art and the press as a political institution—rather than seeing both as somehow outside the sphere of politics. In *Democracy on Trial,* published in 1995, philosopher Jean Bethke Elshtain made a similar observation on the political character of the public schools. "Education always reflects a society's views of what is excellent, worthy, and necessary," she wrote. "These reflections are not cast in cement like so many foundational stones; rather, they are refracted and reshaped over time as definitions, meanings, and purposes change through democratic contestation. In this sense education is political, but being political is different from being directly and blatantly politicized—being made to serve interests and ends imposed by militant groups."[30]

What Elshtain says about education as a civic art was true for journalism, as well. Although journalists may cultivate the stance of the outsider, the work they do is a reflection on—and also a reflection of—the broader political culture, and it naturally has a role in shaping that culture. When Ed Fouhy, another proponent, called public journalism "an attempt to reclaim the central role journalists must play in enriching the life of the community," he was recognizing for the press what Elshtain observes about the schools: both are political institutions, and both are endangered when they become too politicized.[31] And both have a public purpose that can never be "cast in cement," for the public they behave purposefully toward is a dynamic, living thing.

Moreover, with the enormous influence the mass media have assumed in political life, the press is repeatedly incorporated into politics, as politicians and others react to what they know journalists do. The scholar Phyllis Kaniss tells an instructive tale in *The Media and the Mayor's Race.* Kaniss tracked press coverage of Philadelphia's mayoral contest of 1991, interviewing all the major participants, including the candidates and their staffs. She describes how in designing a campaign any competent candidate had to factor in the behavior of political reporters, such as those at the *Philadelphia Inquirer,* the city's major daily. About the thinking of Democrat Ed Rendell, the eventual winner, she writes:

> At a journalist's newspaper like the *Inquirer,* political reporting no longer meant reporting what the candidates said about issues of substance. Even though Rendell planned to focus his campaign on the issues, generating position papers on all the city's problems, he knew those positions would not get much ink. Instead, the reporters would analyze why the candidates said what they did. Or worse, they would not even report what the candidates said, at least not in any comprehensive way, but rather would pick out an isolated sentence here and there with which to stir up controversy where none existed, to make the election more interesting.[32]

Rendell understood how he could be hurt by two predictable themes. One was the charge that he would not get the black vote as a white candidate competing against black Democrats in the primary. The other was the appeal to journalists of the "outsider," in this case a prominent attorney named Peter Hearn who was making his first bid for elective office. Both issues draw the interest of reporters who are interested only in certain things. According to Kaniss,

> there was only one way that Rendell [and his advisers] could counteract this. They would appeal to the media's preoccupation with the horse race and reporters' unquestioning reverence for numbers. They would use polls. Reporters don't want your housing program, Rendell would say, but they love to talk about polls. And so Rendell and his media strategists determined at the outset of the campaign to use polls to their advantage. They would try to make it seem that Peter Hearn was a total longshot, that nobody thought he was a credible candidate, and that he wasn't making any headway with the public. And they would use polls to show that Rendell

would get a sizable chunk of the black vote. . . . [They understood] that being the best known—and generally liked—meant that you could dominate the polls early on. And they knew that those polls would be picked up by all the political reporters in town.[33]

It is hardly news that politicians try to work the press to their advantage. Nor is it a scandal that they sometimes succeed. What Kaniss demonstrates in rich detail is that the routines of political journalism—its obsession with polls, strategy, winning and losing—have contributed to weaknesses in public dialogue, as candidates and advisers react to what they predict journalists will do. Everyone in the game understands the press as a player; any candidate (or reporter) who overlooked such a fact would be at a major disadvantage. Again, no scandal there. What's troublesome is the *quality of play* the press brings on by its own mode of participation—its relentless insiderism, its weakness for cheap drama, its narrow focus on winning as the one true story of politics.

To call the press an actor, then, is to say that its actions in viewing the scene have consequences that double back to shape that scene. This is not an overly complicated thought. But it does spell trouble for a simplified view of the press as fact finder. Placed inside politics, the press has to decide what to do as an intelligent agent, which need not mean being anyone's shill or press agent. Buzz Merritt's proposition that "voters are entitled to have the candidates talk about the issues in depth," which was central to the election experiments in Wichita and Charlotte, was not central in the 1991 Philadelphia mayor's race. Why? Because journalists, as players in the campaign, did not try to make it so.

Professional lore insisted, against every sort of evidence, that the press was a political innocent, uninvolved in the events under its scrutiny. That is why Dave Tucker, city editor of the *Inquirer,* could separate himself from public journalism by saying, "This stuff about becoming a part of the story and the reporting about yourself is . . . for the birds."[34] According to Kaniss, this is exactly what the *Inquirer* did in 1991: it reported on a Rendell campaign that was shaped from the outset by the paper's predictable interest in poll results and the horse race. The *Inquirer* and its routines were part of the story even before the story unfolded. But were they a useful part? Did they serve a compelling public purpose?

According to its many critics and chroniclers, public journalism's most dubious demand was for journalists to "get involved." But a more disruptive demand was to lift the journalist's existing involvement into clear view. Acknowledging what everyone already knew—the press is a player—the movement went on to ask, for what and for whom should the press be playing? The answers offered were certain broad public values that might be political in nature but would not politicize the craft or prevent it from speaking the truth: civic participation, deliberative dialogue, politics as problem solving, public discourse that starts where citizens start and connects to their deepest concerns. How to translate these priorities into everyday journalism, aggressive and alive, was the practical problem the experiment tried to solve. What seemed to work in Charlotte might be unworkable in Philadelphia; what the community welcomed in Columbus would be absurdly out of place in New York.

Neutrality was not to be abandoned in this approach but relocated, for there were many ways to find a neutral position in the drama of public life. One was the neutrality of the observer in the press box, another the neutrality of the referee keeping order on the field of play. There was the neutrality of the critic or analyst, judging the scene from a distance, but also the neutrality of the catalyst, persuading people to engage one another, then stepping back. The reporter's role was a neutral one; but so was the convener's. Those involved in public journalism were not pursuing partisan agendas or tossing aside the virtues of an independent press. They simply wanted to experiment with different styles of neutrality, a point that eluded their most vocal doubters.

By declaiming against the movement's supposed belief in advocacy, you could stand in favor of objectivity, as Michael Gartner did, or against opinion in the news columns, as Lynne Enders Glaser and Paul Greenberg did. You could warn, as Dave Tucker did, against becoming part of the story, thereby suggesting that the story unfolded without you. You could caution, as William Woo did, against journalists who became "master of ceremonies of the new democracy," while ignoring the role they played in the existing ceremonies—which might not be "master," but surely wasn't "sideline observer," either.

Here, then, was another illuminating event in the flood of criticism the idea encountered: public journalism permitted some in the press to reclaim their innocence at a time when the press needed to own up to the fact that it was more and more implicated in politics. If there was anything radical about the movement it was the disturbing force of this admission. "Who's kidding who?" asked Teresa Hanafin, an editor of the *Boston Globe,* at a conference on civic journalism in 1995. "You know, it's the reporters who have access to the governor, who go and play golf with the mayor, have dinner or drinks with the political handlers, the movers and shakers in the communities. And we are players. And I see [civic journalism] as an attempt to diminish our role as players and make us more facilitators and to increase the role of everybody else in the community, just ordinary people, to be the real players, which is what they should be."[35]

What should journalists be playing for? A system in which everyone gets to be more of a player, said Hanafin. It was one of the better answers public journalism had to offer.

Describing the press as inevitably "involved" in political life was one thing: defending the kind of involvement civic journalism imagined was a different task. Here, the aim was to confront basic questions of purpose—to ask, again, what are journalists willing to be for? What kind of relationship to our democracy do they seek? Most journalists saw themselves as information providers and watchdogs over government. These self-images imply a particular view of citizens, as well, although that view is rarely made explicit.

The citizen is typically imagined by what he or she lacks: first, information about complex public matters with which to make intelligent decisions, and, second, the opportunity to question public officials and hold them accountable for what they say. These are things journalists have, and so their job is to supply them. The prohibition on involvement springs in part from these demands: how can information be trusted, how can the check on power be respected, if journalists get mixed up in political causes?

That question can be heard in the following passage from an *American Journalism Review* article, "The Real Public Journalism," describing the skeptical views of staffers of the *Philadelphia Inquirer.*

Many Inquirer editors say true "public journalism" is not what the movement proclaims. Rather, it's what the Philadelphia paper does so often—taking a complex issue and explaining how it affects the reader. "You get people's juices flowing," says Lois Wark, an assistant managing editor. "You get them concerned enough to hold their legislators' feet to the fire. This is public journalism."

Real public journalism, says Wark, is the paper's three-part series last fall exposing the old-style patronage shop run by Philadelphia's powerful registrar of wills. Or the paper's massive five-month effort to prove a state Senate election was stolen though ballot fraud.

. . . The fraudulent ballots were discovered by old fashioned shoe-leather reporting, knocking on doors and asking questions. "The company said, 'We don't care what it costs, how many hours [are] involved,' and they freed up people to do nothing but the story," says Inquirer columnist Steve Lopez.

What if the Inquirer had followed the public journalism initiatives of the Boston Globe or Wichita Eagle and in its news pages had urged people to vote? "If we had been part of the move to encourage voter registration, we would have found ourselves smack dab in a scandal," says Tucker. "The question then would have been, 'What was our role in this?'"[36]

From this angle, citizens are well served when the press digs up information that would otherwise remain hidden—by the complexity of public issues or behind the veil of secrecy that allows corruption to flourish. What prevents democracy from working, then, is public ignorance of policy matters and political chicanery that remains hidden from the public eye. Thus, the "real" public journalism amounts to aggressive reporting that explains and exposes.

One of the attractions of this view is that it permits the journalist to serve the public while retaining a considerable distance from it. The reporter who is skilled at explaining complex issues becomes immersed in those issues, reconnecting with citizens through their identity as readers. The intricacies of public policy are brought home to people through hard facts, explanatory prose, and the newspaper's delivery truck. The citizen's job is to read and comprehend, and then carry this understanding into the voting booth, where democracy gets enacted. In the exposure model, the citizen's job is to read and get outraged enough to demand reform, which is typically accomplished by legislatures and public bodies acting on what appears in the paper.

Both types of journalism—explanatory and exposure—can coexist with a view of citizens that sees them as lazy, inattentive, and immature. Some critics of public journalism were quite candid in displaying such attitudes, which at times verged on contempt. Here is Susan Rasky, a former *New York Times* reporter, explaining her objections to an election project in the San Francisco bay area that tried to put "voters' voices" at the center of news coverage.

. . . .

At a less critical juncture in California's political and economic evolution, such pseudo journalism might be safely ignored as just another dumb marketing gimmick or media fad. What makes it noteworthy and troubling, however, is its emergence at precisely the time when economists, academics and influential business groups are coming out with some of the most thoughtful and provoking analyses of what ails California.

Just when the policy wonks are crunching the relevant numbers and beginning to usefully frame the kinds of difficult policy choices that will have to be made if the state ever hopes to prosper again, the newspeople who could best use this information to enlighten political debate are being asked to take their reporting cues from a woefully ignorant public.

It is neither fashionable not polite—let alone politically correct—to suggest that the *vox populi* may not be all it's cracked up to be. But the dirty little truth that emerges in voters' "voices" is well known to political reporters, political scientists and above all to the politicians themselves: Citizens generally want very contradictory things from those who govern. And that's not just different groups of voters with conflicting ideologies or partisan preferences. *Vox populi* journalism is at its perversely instructive best when a single voter, asked to tell the candidates what's really wrong with California, manages to embody all the contradictory policy desires in one glorious burst of spleen venting.

For lack of a better description, the "consensus diagnosis" on California points to a serious long-term decline in the kinds of productive investments—schools, transportation, other infrastructure—that are absolutely critical to job creation and economic growth.

. . . No candidate in his or her right mind makes a stump speech out of those kinds of policy questions. But reporters conversant with them at least have a fighting chance of offering the public some context for judging what the candidates are really saying or not saying when they babble about getting California back on track.

—From Susan Rasky, "The Bottom Line," *California Journal,* May 1994

. . . .

Here, informed and skeptical reporters take the place of "a woefully ignorant public" by asking the tough questions citizens are unprepared to ask—either because they don't understand what the policy wonks have already figured out, or because they want so many contradictory things from government that all they can manage is spleen venting when handed the microphone. Rasky's critique of public journalism burdens the movement with a naive belief in the divine wisdom of the average person, which a skeptical journalist must expose as a fiction. Second, she imagines that the ignorant citizens of California, treated to a political dialogue that panders to their thin grasp on reality, can nonetheless emerge as informed and critical voters by election day, if journalists will only explain to these unfortunate souls how things really work. Third, she groups savvy journalists with policy experts as the ones who are committed to truth in politics, while manipulative candidates and manipulated citizens dwell in a world of fantasy and cliché.

Wasn't there a danger of romanticizing citizens in the rush to give them a larger role in political coverage? (There was.) Wasn't there a role for policy experts and skilled reporters in grounding political debate in up-to-date facts? (There had to be.) Wasn't it incumbent upon citizens to sort through their conflicting values and desires before they made a decision? (Yes.) Wasn't it true that candidates often pandered to the fantasies and prejudices of inattentive and wishful-thinking voters? (They did.) And shouldn't journalists try to see through these tactics and let voters know what's really going on? (They should.)

Among the answers public journalists found as they struggled with Rasky's doubts were these:

- People need to see themselves and their priorities reflected in the news, or they will tune it out. But starting where citizens start doesn't mean ending where citizens end. The trick is to begin with citizens' concerns as a grounding for political coverage, and then move on from there to sophisticated news and analysis that responds to those concerns—even if the candidates are not responding.
- Experts are an invaluable aid to a public faced with tough choices. The guiding principle, however, should be "experts on tap, not on top," for even the most sophisticated grasp of policy will matter little to citizens who can't get engaged in an issue. Helping them get engaged is part of the journalist's job. Adding expertise comes later.
- People need space and time for working through—that is, deliberating about—tough policy choices. The press too often disables or dismays the public by reporting on public life as a battlefield, where opposing armies agree on nothing. Journalists need to find more imaginative ways of illustrating conflicting choices, the values that lie beneath them, and the

consequences that follow. If this doesn't happen in the normal run of political life, the press can ask where it does happen and how a more deliberative discussion can be aided and brought alive.

- People generally sense when they're being conned. They may not have all the facts and figures at their fingertips, but they are well aware that political advertisements, for example, are not the whole truth. They have a healthy mistrust of election-year rhetoric, and they need more from journalists than sophisticated accounts of how politicians are trying to manipulate them.

- Seeing through things doesn't always mean seeing them well, or whole. The deepest challenge in political reporting is not to strip the veil from a system that citizens already mistrust, but to help them find a way back into it, through journalism that touches their deepest concerns, appeals to their latent desire to reconnect, and helps them get involved in public life so they will see the point of being informed about it.

- And as Teresa Hanafin reminded her colleagues, "I think it's an indictment of the media, the fact that there are many readers, many citizens, who are not as well-informed as they should be."[37]

Of course, the ability to summarize these lessons—drawn from several years of experiment and reflection—does not mean they were all incorporated into the project Rasky was criticizing. The journalists in the Bay area were early participants in the experiment, and their fumbling, even their naïveté, was part of the learning curve. Rasky's view of them as starry-eyed romantics, or mouthpieces for an ignorant and lazy electorate, revealed the excesses of a professional stance in journalism that was capable of dismissing citizens in the name of serving their interests.

As David Remnick of the *New Yorker* put it, "Like it or not, part of the job of a great editor is to listen to public desires—and then, if necessary, act against them." Rasky seemed to go further: why bother listening to people who know so little, and behave so childishly? What's most revealing about her argument is that it can accommodate almost any level of public estrangement, political demagoguery, and professional cynicism. There seems to be no point at which these corrosive trends call on journalists to take a step back and reconsider what they're doing. Democracy sputters along in its depressed state, but journalism can still shine as long as it keeps its distance from the disaffected and deluded citizens it is nominally pledged to serve.

This is a kind of surrealistic fantasy, in which the press can somehow perform its public duties in the absence of a genuine public for which to perform. Adopting the tone of the sober-minded realist, Rasky spoke the dream of a craft that could free itself from the very conditions—an engaged and alert citizenry—that gave news its meaning. Citizens vent their angry spleens, candidates bluff and bluster, elections come and go. Meanwhile, public problems deepen and the horizon of possibility shrinks. But journalism, properly insulated and professionally done, remains a fine service to the republic.

Public journalism became an experiment upon the press as much as a movement within it. Responses often illustrated the ingrained and reflexive attitudes that prevented the profession from responding in a more daring fashion to the troubles in American democracy. Among these attitudes were an essentialist view of the journalist's task that afforded little room for experiment; a narrow reading of press history that allowed tradition to speak against reform and renewal; a frozen image of what journalists were for that disabled civic imagination in the craft; a quest for innocence amid the entangling forces of the media age, which disallowed any view of the press as a political actor with decisions to make about the aim of its actions; a desire to keep a firm distance between the press and a navel-gazing public, from which the serious professional had much to fear.

None of this means, of course, that public journalism had the right answers and critics the wrong motives. On the contrary, most of the hostility seemed to spring from an honorable desire to protect the press against misguided notions that, in the eyes of critics, would cause it to abuse its power, confuse its mission, or exhaust to no worthwhile end its shrinking resources. Those who saw public journalism this way had a duty to speak up about it—and speak they did. Even at their most derisive, the critics always admitted that there was something serious at stake here, an attitude for which the movement had to be grateful if it also wanted to be graceful in moving forward with the hard work of reform.

But by picturing the experiment in the shape of their worst fears, many critics overlooked the fact that the people involved had the same fears, along with an additional one—that if they stood fast, doing "traditional" journalism day after day, the tradition they loved might die a gradual death, or cease to matter to the thing that mattered more: democracy as a way of life.

7

The *New York Times* and the *Washington Post* on Public Journalism

One Sunday in October 1993, an extraordinary article appeared in the *New York Times Magazine*—extraordinary for what it said about the state of politics and journalism.

The author was Michael Kelly, a former Washington correspondent for the paper who had covered the 1992 presidential campaign (he later moved on to the *New Yorker*, then briefly became editor of the *New Republic*). In the *Times Magazine* piece, his ostensible subject was David Gergen, the media adviser, pundit, and consummate insider, described as a "master of the game." But the real subject was how something called "image" had become "the sacred faith of Washington," making a mockery of politics. Gergen, who had just joined the Clinton White House, typified this development. Now Kelly undertook to critique it.

In scalding terms he described the shared assumptions of the nation's professional political class: the "pollsters, news media consultants, campaign strategists, advertising producers, political scientists, reporters, columnists, commentators," all of whom had come to believe that what a politician is and does are not important. "What is important is the perceived image of what he is and what he does." In this view, politics "is not about objective reality, but virtual reality. What happens in the political world is divorced from the real world. It exists for only the fleeting historical moment, a magical movie of sorts, a never-ending and infinitely revisable docudrama.

Strangely, the faithful understand that the movie is not true—yet also maintain that it is the only truth that really matters."

The nation's capital has become "a strange and debased place," Kelly wrote, "the true heart of a national culture in which the distinction between reality and fantasy has been lost." Fully implicated in the debasement was the national press corps. "Obsessed with the appearance of things," journalists have made themselves "susceptible to the machinations of the image-makers." The press "has become as faddish as a teenager, vacillating in its attitudes toward the powers that be, going from bubbling enthusiasm to hysterical anger, from cheering all that the President says to denouncing all that the President does."

The press pack, as Kelly called it, rewards with glowing coverage the clever image, the well-turned phrase, the effective manipulation of the news media. The pack then "exacts a perverse revenge by seizing on the slightest misstep, the smallest deviation from the perfect image." Here Kelly offered as evidence some of his own dispatches for the *Times*. In May 1993 he had reported on a perception that President Clinton, who had arrived in Washington with the image of a New Democrat, "has come to look very much like the same old—liberal—thing." This and other "bits of fatuousness" he had written were attempts to "fashion reality out of perceptions" and keep the game of images going.[1]

The argument was not new. The outlines were there in Daniel Boorstin's 1961 book, *The Image*. In 1975, Jonathan Schell documented the dangerous consequences of image politics in his account of the Nixon era, *The Time of Illusion*. Later, during the two terms of Ronald Reagan, the importance of image management—the art of seeming "presidential," especially for the cameras—became conventional wisdom in Washington circles, and a host of journalists noted how successful it was for the Reagan White House. Kelly was thus elaborating on a familiar theme. But there was something different about the *New York Times*, the nation's preeminent newspaper, allowing one of its own reporters to compile such an damning indictment. The elite of the elite press was charging itself with a profound dereliction of duty.[2]

Along with the rest of the political class, journalists had forgotten one of the most basic requirements of a democratic society—an on-going commitment to "live within the truth," as the Czech hero Václav Havel put it in his famous essay "The Power of the Powerless." Attempting to dramatize how deep the corruption of spirit had run under Soviet-style regimes, Havel described life in the captive nations of Eastern Europe as "living within a lie." There, the lie began with the state and penetrated down to the level of a greengrocer, who might place in his shop window a placard showing some official propaganda slogan. The grocer didn't believe the slogan, Havel suggested; what mattered to him was avoiding trouble with the authorities. So he participates in the Big Lie simply by doing what everyone else does.[3]

Havel and the Big Lie weren't what was on Kelly's mind, but he was describing the political life of the American capital in eerily similar terms. Any effort to live within the truth had become pointless in Washington and its journalism, for while everyone knows that the "movie" isn't true, everyone also believes that "it is the only truth that really matters." The press corps was joining—and knew it was joining—in a destructive trend, by defining normal politics as the perfection of images and normal journalism as commentary on that. By failing to expect something better—of itself or others— the press was making cynicism a fact of life, rather than an attitude toward some of the more dismal facts. "A lot of people, even in Washington, look upon all this with regret and even horror," Kelly wrote. One of them may be David Gergen, or maybe not. The piece ends with Gergen's statements of regret over the rise of image politics, cleverly undermined by Kelly's insinuation that the regrets may be the image master's latest image.[4]

A curious scene confronted the reader of the *New York Times* that Sunday. On one hand, political life stood revealed as fraudulent in its normal condition. The assumption that politics was about issues and problems, ideas and ideals, could not be trusted, said Kelly. By adapting to this fact instead of resisting it, political journalism had lost its own grip on the real. It was now a reflection of the weird sense of irreality that had overtaken Washington. On the other hand, this was nothing to get excited about. Kelly's indictment seemed to suggest the need for a change, maybe even an urgent call for reform. But neither he nor his editors saw it that way. Describing the scene in what the magazine called "writing of unusual power and quality" was enough. Kelly and the *Times* were taking an observer's stance toward a story that directly implicated them.[5]

Note, then, our predicament as readers: If we accept the Kelly account as true, then the news from Washington can be discounted as either trivial (little "bits of fatuousness") or concocted (a "magical movie of sorts"). Short of the perverse pleasure we might take in watching a counterfeit spectacle unfold, paying close attention to politics will bring no reward because it is not about anything but calculated perception. In fact, the more political news we absorb, the less we know about anything outside the dubious business of image making. If, on the other hand, we do not accept the report as true, if we see it as exaggerated in some fundamental way, then we still have to face the fact that Kelly and his editors see things this way. But what do they propose to *do* about "a national culture in which the distinction between reality and fantasy has been lost"? Is it possible to practice serious journalism in such a culture? It is possible to have a serious politics?

All this can be avoided with a pose of ironic detachment. Irony is what Kelly showed toward his own behavior: *look at me playing the game like everyone else.* Irony is the tone he took toward Gergen, the image master, trying to cope with what he had wrought: *or is this merely another image?* To an intelligent citizen who accepts what the newspaper is reporting, an ironic shrug is the proper response: *the emperor has no clothes, but admits it.* No doubt Kelly and the *Times* appeared honest to themselves by acknowledging their complicity in the cult of image. Where they deceived themselves was in thinking that acknowledgment was enough. The issue of what it would take to change the press disappeared from a view of the press that argued decisively for change.

Not long afterward, though, in March 1996, *Times* columnist Maureen Dowd was critiquing a new book by James Fallows that, among other observations, charged the press with fueling public cynicism. Dowd saw fit to quote her colleague Michael Kelly on "a mistaken revisionism" that pictures "a golden time in which the press did a better job explaining government and policy than it does now." In fact, said Kelly, "The press does a better job and the public is hugely more informed about what's going on in Washington than it has ever been—and being hugely more informed does have a tendency to make one a little more cynical."[6]

In 1993, Kelly had thought the national press was cooperating in the cynical reduction of politics to a contest of images. Two and a half years later, his outlook was different: journalists, he said, were more effective than ever at explaining government policy. Cynicism was the residue of reporting's hard-won truths, a mark of accomplishment, not a cause for alarm. What had happened in the interval? Had the national press somehow seen the light and remade itself? If so, the *Times* had missed it and so had all the journalism reviews.

One thing that had happened was the rise of public journalism to visibility on the national stage. In March 1996, Dowd in her column and Kelly in his quote were taking aim at Fallows, whose book *Breaking the News* deepened the same indictment Kelly had sketched in his 1993 article. But Fallows had gone beyond lament to prescription, spotting in public journalism a potentially promising move toward reform. Dowd and Kelly were having none of it. Nor were most of the other voices that spoke on the subject in the *New York Times*. And many did speak, in a fashion that revealed how they saw their own journalism as much as the new variety arriving from the provinces.

As I will later show, writers at the *Washington Post* had a more nuanced view of the movement and its central claims. I will begin with the *Times*, and then move on to its chief competitor. The contrast is illuminating, and so are some of the similarities.

Public journalism officially entered the newspaper of record on October 3, 1994, in an article by William Glaberson in the business section of the *Times*. The piece had its origins a few months earlier, at a lunch I had with Glaberson at his request. The lunch meeting was just a conversation, as he put it, an opportunity for two minds to meet. But we both knew it was something more: the first contact between public journalism, that fledgling player in the press game, and an institution that could greatly affect the player's standing.

The *New York Times* could do almost anything it wanted with a recent development—ignore it, make news of it, condemn or applaud its appearance. But whatever it did would matter greatly. For among the most attentive readers of the *Times* are other journalists, who take cues, as much as news, from the newspaper of record. The editors of the *Times* thus "edit" many publications other than their own: they are a hidden presence on the front pages of hundreds of other newspapers, and their influence is heavily felt in network television, which is far more likely to investigate what the *Times* has already covered.

Other journalists are in fact the ideal audience for the editors in New York, since they know how to read the paper for the full variety of messages it conveys. The notion of story "play," for example, is understood at one level by the reading public: the big news is on the front page, the smaller items inside. But another interpretation is available to editors and producers. Because they scrutinize many sources of news (the wire services, competitors to the *Times*), they also "read" what the paper is not covering. The newspaper's judgment that this or that is newsworthy generates for the *Times* one of its surest sources of power: elevating events and themes to wider attention. While all news media do this, when the *New York Times* does it all other news media notice.

A national bestower of legitimacy is a force to be reckoned with, and anyone who does not know how to reckon with it ought not to be playing the legitimacy game. For the *Times* is acutely aware of itself as a force in the culture. A. M. Rosenthal, the former executive editor of the paper, recalled how he had once grumbled to colleagues that people were always picking on the *Times*. "Then I reminded myself of the reason and I did not feel bad at all," Rosenthal wrote. "We are prestigious, elite and influential, that's why."[7] Suffice it to say that the picture Glaberson absorbed at our lunch was important. The intricate task of framing the story—a kind of contest among the reporter, his editors, and his sources—would begin that afternoon at the Knickerbocker Saloon in Greenwich Village. My job was to influence the story's framing, but this did not require any cunning strategy. Indeed, the more calculated my explanation seemed, the less effective it would be, for any experienced reporter has his crap detector permanently on high, and Glaberson was experienced and sharp.

I had to concentrate on two things. One was to elude some of the associations my "professor" title carried. Nothing is more immediate cause for dismissal than losing a reporter in the fog of academic analysis. So my first task was to stay within journalism's analytical categories, to talk the news industry's talk. Task two was to persuade Glaberson that public journalism was a "story" and would seem so to his editors. The idea had to be conjured up in newsworthy shape: as an emerging trend, but also something that cut against conventional thinking. Glaberson investigated this by presenting me with the arguments and objections most of his colleagues would make. He would judge the seriousness of the idea by how those challenges were handled.

In time, Glaberson got interested in the story, particularly the fact that national notice had not yet come to public journalism. The angle he used to make news of the movement was "problem solving" as something that ought to concern more journalists. At our lunch, I stressed repeatedly that this did not mean the press could itself be the agent for solving problems; rather, it had to be more helpful to citizens and communities in that task. This distinction made its way into Glaberson's reporting, but it was glossed over by the headline writer—not an uncommon event.

"A New Press Role: Solving Problems," read the header over Glaberson's article. But the text told a different story: that some newspaper editors were "experimenting with coverage aimed at provoking people to get involved in public issues." Rather than emphasizing conflict," these journalists "want news coverage to spur people to find solutions to political and community problems." He also introduced themes that would come to dominate the debate over public journalism: "Some news professionals say the experiments are dangerous because they are shifting the role of the journalist from observers to participants in community events and come close to a kind of boosterism that hurts the credibility of the press. And the critics say it is sometimes difficult to tell the difference between public journalism, which may be motivated by some noble aims, and marketing schemes intended to pander to readers."

The article went on to describe the movement's origins in disgust with the 1988 campaign; the election projects that try to "capture what citizens, rather than experts and politicians, see as important"; the concerns about rising public cynicism and the "declining interest in traditional journalism"; and the perception of journalists as insiders, more attuned to professionals in politics than the public's concerns. A photograph of Buzz Merritt appeared with the article, over a caption quoting his description of public journalism, "a new way of seeing our job in the context of public life." Merritt also spoke of an "attitude, a mind shift" among people attracted to the idea.

My own role in the story was to serve as a focal point for the critics of public journalism. In a metaphor that appeared often in the years that followed, I was termed "an evangelist of public journalism" who "travels the country warning journalists that traditional news organizations are in peril." The religious imagery allowed for subtle associations with extremism to creep in: "Mr. Rosen prescribes some solutions that even many journalists who are experimenting with public journalism find unpalatable. He often suggests that traditional journalists' claims to objectivity are not only mythical but also crippling and should be abandoned."

While some journalists were receptive to such a message, Glaberson wrote, others were skeptical of "some of the more controversial ideas," like the presumed attacks on objectivity. One quoted was Maxwell King, editor of the *Philadelphia Inquirer*. "The traditional rules about the distance and impartiality of reporters from their subjects are a key source of our strength," King was heard to say. "It is crazy to break those rules, and there is no reason to break those rules." Glaberson later added, "The more journalists at prestigious news organizations express reservations, however, the more Mr. Rosen and some of his allies condemn them as dinosaurs." Bill Kovach, curator of the Nieman Foundation at Harvard, a former Washington bureau chief at the *Times,* and a respected figure in the press, was also "troubled by talk of abandoning objectivity," as Glaberson put it. But Kovach described the experiment as an "effort to make journalism more useful to a self-governing society." With that thought the story ended.[8]

Glaberson's report was about as fair and accurate as we could expect. He had misconstrued, however, a key point that Merritt and I had tried to make: The press was already a player in public life, already involved in hundreds of ways that journalists like Michael Kelly took for granted. Had that point been emphasized, the danger cited by critics ("shifting the role of journalists from observers to participants") would have made less sense, for we did not accept "observer" as a useful description of the press in its actual role, nor did we see "participant" as a label that applied to public journalists alone.

The tension between one description of the press (actor, artist) and another (observer, fact gatherer) was central to public journalism as an idea. But it was difficult to inject into the *controversy* over the idea, which would frame the way most journalists saw it. It mattered, then, that this tension was missing from Glaberson's story. Highlighted instead were the clashes between reformers and traditionalists; between those "who have campaigned in their news columns" and skeptics said to be dubious about promoting causes. The view of journalism as inevitably a participant in public life made its appearance only in highly coded form: my belief that "claims to objectivity" are "mythical" and "crippling" and should therefore be dropped.

Here I had the unsettling experience of opening the *New York Times* to learn something "new" about my own ideas. It had never been my view that objectivity has no place in the belief system of the press. Nor did Glaberson feature any quotations from me to that effect. But the misunderstanding was not a surprise. The whole topic was tricky terrain because objectivity meant so many things in the press. Some of them amounted to self-delusions; others were invaluable because they put the journalist on the side of truth.

Following our lunch, I mailed Glaberson a copy of a talk I had given on the subject at Kovach's Nieman Foundation. There I had called objectivity a myth, but I had also noted that at its core were some key principles: "the notion of a disinterested truth, the wish to separate doing journalism from doing politics, the principled attempt to restrain your own biases, looking at things from the other person's perspective. These are important values for all of us, and particularly for journalists. You can't just wave them away by saying, 'objectivity is a myth.'" The solution to the puzzle of objectivity, I suggested, "lies with another important term—democracy." Journalists might redescribe their role in the political system, to take account of the actual influence they had in events and to respond to some of the troubles in the public square, in which they were implicated. If democracy was in trouble, journalism was in trouble; and public journalism was a way of saying to the press: get involved in *that*. Don't use objectivity as an excuse to ignore the problem.[9]

Absent this understanding, public journalism would be stamped an activist philosophy, a license to push causes that journalists favored. The next label applied would be "advocacy" journalism. With these scare words attached, the idea would go down to defeat. So I wrote Glaberson a note, urging him to examine again my objectivity talk to see if the views there matched what he had written. A month or so later he called to say he wanted to do an interview on the subject, which would be published in question-and-answer form. Of course I accepted; here was a chance to greet the beast in its proverbial belly. The *New York Times* was the citadel of objectivity, home office of the idea. If part of the point of public journalism was to interrogate (in public) fundamental beliefs in the press, then doing the interview would be doing public journalism, even though Glaberson said he would ask no questions about that.

With the terms established, Glaberson came to my home for the interview. Before he turned on the tape recorder, an odd moment occurred. Everything would be on the record, he said. I agreed. But there was one restriction: "You can't talk about the *Times*." We both knew the reason: the *Times* tries to avoid speaking of itself in its own pages. The interview, already a departure from Glaberson's usual reporting, would be harder to get into print if it pointed to the newspaper itself as evidence. This, in fact, was part of the regime of objectivity: the observer must be the one observing, not the one observed. Excluding the *Times* from a discussion of objectivity made as much sense as an interview about the American theater forbidding mention of the word "Broadway." But Glaberson was simply informing me of a fact, not inviting a debate. If I wanted to do the interview, these were the rules. Here, then, are the results.

. . . .

Jay Rosen, a journalism professor and director of the Project on Public Life and the Press at New York University, is a press critic who often draws criticism from reporters and editors by saying that journalism needs to rethink its fundamental canon: objectivity. Mr. Rosen sat down last week for a conversation about the way the press uses, or abuses, the claim to objectivity. Here are some excerpts:

Q. What is journalistic objectivity?

A. It is the value of fairness, which is extremely important. It's the ethic of restraining your own biases, which is also important. . . . It's the idea that journalism can't be the voice of any particular party or sect, which is also very important. All those things are very honorable, very important. What is insidious and crippling about objectivity is when journalists say: "We just present you with facts. We don't make judgments. We don't have any values ourselves." That is dangerous and wrongheaded.

Q. Do you think we make judgments?

A. Of course. And I think you think you make judgments all the time. . . . I don't think the kind of bias journalists are usually accused of—ideological bias, personal animus—is generally worrisome. Far more subtle and more dangerous are the conventions of journalism: the ways in which journalists go about dividing the world, framing public life for us, picturing the world of politics. There are values and assumptions hidden in those decisions that are extremely important to name and to debate, and I think, at this point, to change.

Q. What is behind that framing?

A. In every area of coverage, from politics to sports, there are these kinds of lenses. When we talk about politics and public life, the frames journalists employ are very identifiable and narrow. There is, for example, the strategy lens: seeing everything through the eyes of the tactician. There is the emphasis on winning and the game aspects of politics.

Q. And what does that have to do with objectivity?

A. Objectivity officially declares that none of this goes on because, officially, the description of what journalists do and what they ought to do is present facts.

Q. And is that not what we ought to do?

A. That is not a description of what's possible in journalism. When journalists say, "All we do is present the facts," that is misleading.

Q. Do we mislead intentionally?

A. Sometimes, to avoid criticism, yes. To escape from discussions about your craft, yes. To sever the conversation about journalism and its values from the rest of the political culture, yes. Journalism doesn't admit that criticism is legitimate. One of the most powerful things about the declaration "I'm objective," is the hidden corollary: "You're not."

Q. Who's you?

A. Everybody but the journalist. So everybody who comes at the press with a dissatisfaction, with a complaint, or even with an idea, is seen by journalists as subjective. And those who are "subjective," who are interested, who have a stake, are almost by definition unqualified to pass judgment on the "objective" operation of the press. So one of the most insidious effects of objectivity is that it created a world in which journalists can live without criticism, because they're the only judges of what's objective.

Q. But isn't that one of the reasons journalism exists, to be a third party, the Fourth Estate?

A. If you're saying good journalism is independent journalism, I agree completely. However, I also believe that an objective press has to be in conversation with the rest of the country and the political culture about what's a good lens to take.

Q. But the reality of the rest of the culture is that it's highly partisan and the press ought not to be.

A. Ah, but see that view of "everybody else but us is highly partisan" is itself an artifact of the ideology or doctrine of objectivity.

Q. Isn't it the case that there's a great deal of partisanship?

A. Yes.

Q. And don't you need somebody who is not partisan to provide the information so the partisans can function?

A. Yes, you need an independent source of information in politics. The issue is: How should we describe what this independent institution does? If we describe it simply as providing facts, we're going to miss a lot of what this institution does. . . . The political drama given to us by the press is dominated by professionals in politics, by insiders, by discussions of strategy and technique and manipulation. It is almost exclusively a story of conflict and controversy within the political class, and it is increasingly out of touch with the rest of the country and out of step with the problems we face as a democracy.

Q. The press often feels it should stay as far out of the story as possible, doesn't it?

A. That is a fantasy that journalists have about themselves. If you look at Washington political culture, journalists are completely involved in that culture in a whole variety of ways. They are constantly involved in what gets on the public agenda, who's getting attention.

Q. What would you call the role the press plays in politics?

A. I would say the press is framing the story of public life for us in a particular way. It's inescapable. It's in the nature of what they do. And it's not working. . . . It's not working for citizens.

Q. And the press won't admit it?

A. They won't admit it because they would face a very different criticism of what they do, which they don't know how to deal with. It would require them to rethink a lot of their most basic assumptions, and it would require them to take a certain basic level of responsibility for how we conduct ourselves as a public society. At the root of objectivity is the wish to be free of the results of what you do.

—From William Glaberson, "Press," *New York Times*, December 14, 1994[10]

. . . .

It isn't every day that a great institution presents a discussion of its ruling doctrine. For the *Times* and the fortunes of public journalism, however, the curious thing is that the points established here were more or less ignored in further commentary on the idea. The story line Glaberson had employed in his first article—getting involved versus remaining detached, supporting causes versus remaining independent, abandoning objectivity versus remaining objective—governed the way the paper treated public journalism from here on.

Glaberson returned to the subject in February 1995 with a short article billed as a "progress report on a new kind of problem-solving journalism." It described the efforts of the *Wisconsin State Journal* in Madison. Frank Denton, the paper's editor, spoke of the shift in emphasis he was after. "Our journalism is not here to fry people—although we fry people all the time," he said. "Our main goal is helping the public find solutions to problems."

As part of the paper's "City of Hope" series, Denton had taken the unusual step—unusual even within the climate of public journalism—of inviting public officials and influential figures in the community to periodic meetings at the *State Journal.* There they would hear from reporters and editors about the paper's findings when it went out into the community to research problems of crime, poverty, racism, and joblessness. This violated a traditional rule: do not give officials advance warning of what will appear in print, because they will pressure the paper to change the story and gain the impression that a right of review exists, a dangerous precedent.

Applying the "controversy" lens, Glaberson featured the comments of Denton's counterpart in Madison, Dave Zweifel, editor of the competing newspaper, the *Capitol Times.* "Mr. Zweifel said he thought the concept of public journalism and the movement that is growing up around it have made some journalists lose sight of the most important traditions of their profession. 'My idea of public journalism,' he said, 'is finding out what is going on and raising hell about it. But I don't think I should go down to the mayor's office and hold his hand.' "[11]

Aside from brief comments in stories devoted to other subjects, the next sustained scrutiny was a column in the *Times Magazine* in May 1995. Titled "Fix-It Journalism," it was the work of Max Frankel, the paper's former executive editor—a certified heavyweight whose views would be noted across the country. Shortly before the column appeared, Buzz Merritt got a call from Frankel. Merritt tells the following story: Frankel phoned to say he had a few questions about public journalism. The first was, "What's your agenda for the city of Wichita?" Briefly taken aback, Merritt said he had no particular agenda for Wichita and felt puzzled by the question. Frankel replied that according to his understanding of public journalism, a newspaper proclaims an agenda that it tries to push in the news pages. This was a serious misreading, Merritt suggested. As the conversation continued, it appeared that Frankel's grasp of public journalism was so different from his own that Merritt finally said, "Look, I've just written a book on the subject. It's about 130 pages. It'll take you two hours to read and I can have it on your desk tomorrow morning." Frankel's reply: "No, thank you." And Merritt's name did not appear in Frankel's piece.[12]

"Fix-It Journalism" began with Frankel recalling how Iphigene Ochs Sulzberger, a "daughter, wife and mother of newspaper executives" at the *Times,* grew alarmed in 1943 when she sensed "an appalling ignorance of American history" among college graduates. She then used her influence to get the paper to conduct a survey of the situation. It found that only 18 percent of colleges and universities required courses in American history. The news prompted changes in many college curricula, and the *Times* won a Pulitzer Prize for its work. Frankel told this story to show that newspapers have long used their influence to "promote civic virtue."

But the new movement called civic or public journalism wants something more, he said: to "cure" the community of "political disaffection" by refashioning the news into a "more deliberate act of citizenship, dedicated to the solution and not just description of social problems." Those Frankel called "the true devotees of civic journalism" would scoff at Mrs. Sulzberger's "willingness to settle for a few articles that only incidentally shamed college deans into action." As Frankel wrote: "The ardent civic journalists of today are not content to tell it like it is. They want to tell it and fix it all at once. They would summon those college deans to a conference and make them either defend their neglect of history or promise prompt remedial action, with front page punishment or reward. Also invited to the conference would be legislators and foundation heads so they could be badgered into providing the funds to endow the necessary new chairs in American history."

As examples of the "fix-it" mentality, Frankel took note of the "Children First" campaign at the *Detroit Free Press,* which tried to prod the community to aid poor children in the wake of numerous street shootings; the *Charlotte Observer*'s "Taking Back Our Neighborhoods" project, in which the newspaper teamed up with a local television station to search for ways to help the most crime-ridden sections of town; an economic development conference sponsored by the Bremerton *Sun* in Washington State; and an attempt by the *San Jose Mercury News* to stimulate voter turnout in one section of the city.

Two "valid lines of criticism" have been aimed at public journalism, Frankel wrote. First, if the goal is simply to reconnect the news to ordinary people's concerns, then public journalists "are only doing what they should have been doing all along." In other words, there is no novel or challenging idea here, only a reminder of what journalists do when their work is properly done. If, on the other hand, public journalism means an emphasis on "solutions" and "connections," this will likely "distort the news agenda, devalue problems for which no easy remedy is apparent and end up compromising the paper's independence."

The reply to all this fell to me, as the man said to offer "philosophical justification" for the movement: "In response, Rosen has argued that 'objectivity' in reporting is an illusion and that even the quest for fairness and balance in news articles can obstruct the truth or understanding of it. But his debunking of some journalistic clichés hardly justifies a new ideology that holds journalists duty bound to stimulate and organize public opinion and action." Frankel's conclusion: Public journalism's attempt at "organizing solutions" is either a formula for disaster or a distraction from the more important task of reporting the news. "American journalism sorely needs improvement," he wrote. "But redefining journalism as a quest for a better tomorrow will never compensate for its poor performance at explaining yesterday. Reporters, editors and publishers have their hands full learning to tell it right. They should leave reforms to the reformers."[13]

Frankel's column drew a sharp reply from Neil Shine, publisher of the *Detroit Free Press,* whose "Children First" project was derided as "fix-it" journalism. In a column for the *Free Press,* Shine asked: at what point did the traditional attitude of detachment amount to a kind of civic neglect?

. . . .

In more than 45 years at the *Free Press*, I watched while we turned our newsrooms into strategic hamlets from which we lobbed salvos of news to our readers, confident that if our mission was to provide them with information, we were acquitting ourselves honorably.

Mostly what we told them is that things were not going well. Our daily message to them was a litany of problems they needed to confront—crime, violence, poverty, racism, homelessness, hunger, abuse, neglect, apathy.

Every now and then, we would peer out from behind the barriers we had erected between them and us to reinforce our suspicion that things were, indeed, not going well.

And then, citing tradition or policy or both, we retreated to the comfortable isolation of non-involvement.

Give people in a free society enough information, we reasoned, and they will be able to challenge the problems that confront them and, sooner or later, overcome them.

As for us, leave us out of it. It's not our job. There is a certain solace to be found in detachment, something journalists figured out a long time ago.

But in the past few years, more and more of us have been wondering: if it's not our job, then whose job is it? . . .

For years, perhaps decades, we had been reporting on the outrages committed against Michigan's children. We told our readers that for tens of thousands of children, abuse, neglect, and the prospect of violent death were part of the fabric of their lives.

We chronicled the shootings and ranked the dead in age groups. We updated the numbers in every new story so that those who cared knew, every time they saw the score, that they were losing and nobody, including the *Detroit Free Press*, seemed interested in helping them win.

Our movement, through Children First, to a more active involvement in the lives of the children of the community we serve changed all that forever.

If, by doing it, we crossed some imaginary, self-imposed boundary, then it is a line we should have crossed long before we did.
—From Neil Shine, "If We Don't Do It, Who Will? A Newspaper's Role Must Go Beyond Simply Reporting the Day's Events," *Detroit Free Press*, May 28, 1995

. . . .

In writing that the "debunking of some journalistic clichés hardly justifies a new ideology that holds journalists duty bound to stimulate and organize public opinion and action," Frankel had said something significant, since the official fiction in journalism declares the news an ideology-free zone. If the former editor of the *New York Times* wanted to argue that the existing ideology of the press worked just fine, this was a welcome event. Perhaps someone could get him to say what this ideology was, where it came from, why it was still effective, how and where it applied. These were subjects journalists often declined to discuss, fearing the swamp of personal bias. Better to stick to official doctrine: ideologies are what others promote and journalists avoid. One of the few willing to speak candidly on the subject was Paul Taylor of the *Washington Post,* who wrote the following in his book *See How They Run.*

> Most of us remain, in our collective self-image, tribunes of the people. Despite our better education and breeding, our instincts remain populistic and our habits of mind are shaped by what Lionel Trilling once described as the "adversary culture." We see problems more readily than solutions; we side with the little guy against the establishment; we are progressive reformers, deeply skeptical of all the major institutions of society except our own. "Comfort the afflicted, and afflict the comfortable," reads the adage that hangs on many newsroom walls. It is a goad to anti-institutional journalism.[14]

Taylor's description of Progressive-era ideology in the press was one many scholars of the press would recognize.[15] But it was not common currency in the profession, which meant that certain questions rarely got asked. Anti-institutional journalism had its virtues, but was it the answer to a public climate in which few institutions inspired any public confidence? What did journalism have to say about making them work again? What about siding with the "little guy" (or as journalists put it, Joe Six-Pack): might there be a hint of condescension in that? And if the press remained deeply skeptical of all the major institutions but its own, as Taylor said, how long could it afford this uncritical attitude?

Public journalism was trying to ask such questions. But this part of the idea would remain invisible if the profession continued to deny that it had an ideology, or that it saw itself as a progressive institution. "Leave reforms to the reformers," Frankel had said. Taylor believed that American journalism had never done that.

In January 1996, a major event affecting the public standing of the idea unfolded. James Fallows, then the Washington editor of the *Atlantic,* published *Breaking the News: How the News Media Undermine American Democracy.* Fallows was well known among elite journalists in New York and Washington, and his book received wide attention. Its major themes echoed almost point for point the critique on which public journalism was based:

- "Americans believe the news media have become too arrogant, cynical, scandal-minded, and destructive."
- "Year by year, a smaller percentage of Americans goes through the trouble of reading newspapers or watching news broadcasts on TV."
- The press establishment, "still in the denial stage," has been unable to "deal with outside complaints honestly enough to begin the process of reform."
- "The best known and best-paid people in journalism now set an example that erodes the quality of the news we receive and threatens journalism's claim on public respect."
- Journalists more and more "present public life mainly as a depressing spectacle, rather than as a vital activity in which citizens can and should be engaged."
- The press has drifted into a destructive pattern: "The less that Americans care about public life, the less they will be interested in journalism in any form."
- "Many journalists have noted the crisis in their profession, and a number of them have begun reform efforts."[16]

This last observation referred to public journalism. Earlier in his career, Fallows had written about the Pentagon's agonies after Vietnam and the American auto industry's troubles following the Japanese invasion. In both cases, he found big institutions unable to acknowledge destructive patterns bred by their own corporate culture. Reformers who saw what was happening were ridiculed or ignored by those at the top.[17] Fallows saw a similar dynamic at work in the American press, and as he asked others about reform efforts, he kept hearing of public journalism. So he investigated, and wound up with a concluding chapter titled "The News and Democracy." It presented a short profile of the movement and some of its key ideas.

During his collegiate days Fallows had absorbed the exchange between Walter Lippmann and John Dewey on the nature of the modern public. In *Breaking the News,* he wrote: "Today's journalistic establishment has tried harder to meet Lippmann's challenge—the need for expert accounts of complicated issues—than it has to accommodate Dewey's concern about the impact of journalism on democracy. Reporters operate as experts, or at least insiders, in their field, and they often act as if their real audience is made up of the other reporters or government officials they consider their peers."

In Fallows's view, Americans' frustration with journalists "comes from the problem John Dewey identified: the public's sense that it is not *engaged* in politics, public life, or the discussion that goes on in the press." Lippmann's warning—that modern life created issues too complicated for citizens to grasp—was powerful and prescient. "Yet Dewey's fear, that democracy could not function well if citizens feel estranged from political life, touches a more profound modern concern." Estranged from the political system "because they feel they have no control over it and that it has no connection to their lives," citizens find only further estrangement in the news, which treats politics "as a game to be played by insiders and pros."

Arresting this downward spiral would take much more than an improved press. Politicians and the public would have to change their attitudes and demand more from each other. "Journalists could, however, recognize how much they are contributing to a mood of fatalistic disenchantment," Fallows argued. This would be the first step in the hard work of reform, which involved "making it easier for citizens to feel a connection to their society's public life." In a critical sentence, Fallows explained what he meant by an attitude of denial. "The truth that today's media establishment has tried to avoid seeing is that it *will rise or fall with the political system.*"

His reasoning was provocative: If people see no point in paying attention to politics, then to get them to pay attention, journalism will have to transform itself into something else: entertainment. But the press cannot hope to compete with the entertainment culture, with its lurid diet of celebrity news and sensationalism. In flunking the *political* test before it, the press will fail commercially, as well. Thus: "Today's journalists can choose: do they want merely to entertain the public or to engage it?" If they opt for entertainment, they will keep doing what they're doing—painting public life as a sorry spectacle, a game of "who's up and who's down," a public comedy played by villains and fools, scored by journalists who believe themselves above it all.

"But if journalists should choose to engage the public," Fallows wrote, "they will begin a long series of experiments and decisions to see how journalism might better serve its fundamental purpose, that of making self-government possible. They could start with the example set by public journalism and work on the obvious problems and limits of that model." Fallows's enthusiasm for the movement was reportorial in nature. He had conducted an analysis of an institution in crisis, and found in one corner of it people who were asking the right questions and trying to respond: "As was the case with the military reformers, their efforts have been scorned by some of the most powerful leaders of the current establishment. As with the military reformers, they do not have the complete or satisfying answer to all of today's journalistic problems. But, like the military reformers, they are more right than wrong."[18]

Prominent in the book's indictment of the elite press was a detailed account of the dubious practice of "buckraking"—wherein big-name journalists pontificate on television and boost their lecture fees, which can run as high as thirty thousand dollars. Fallows had named names and come down hard on the corrupting influence of televised punditry. He expected the book to bring a counterattack from those in Washington identified as the worst offenders. Familiar with the egos and the money involved, he prepared himself for a nasty war of words. To his surprise, the attack on buckraking brought little resistance. Many in the press were similarly alarmed; the buckrakers, it turned out, had few defenders among their peers. *Breaking the News* drew fire for a different reason: its suggestion that public journalism might be a place to start for those who wanted to improve the press. For Fallows, this response was surprising. He had simply tried to listen with a sympathetic ear "to people with ideas about correcting what was wrong," as he later put it.

> Not all their ideas were brilliant or practical, and they did not agree among themselves on every point. . . . Little did I imagine that a respectful hearing for the public journalism case would be by far the most controversial and criticized aspect of my argument. I don't mean criticism by "civilian" readers, of course. I am referring only to in-house criticism from the most powerful institutional voices in our business—the editors and retired editors of our leading papers, those who view their duty as safeguarding journalism's independence.[19]

The American press can absorb almost any volley of criticism aimed at its performance. Journalists know they often mess things up in their rush to complete the "daily miracle." They are aware of their tendency to run in packs, to sensationalize a story, to overdramatize conflict; and they have learned how to cope with the charge that their biases often show in the news. But Fallows had gone a step beyond the critique of performance: he had challenged the premise that journalism and democracy stood in relation to each other as observer and observed. In his treatment (as in ours), the press was seen as a political institution, its fortunes rising and falling with the health of the democratic system.

"Issues that affect the collective interests of Americans—crime, health care, education, economic growth—are presented mainly as arenas in which politicians can fight," Fallows wrote. Anyone who grasped this criticism at the level it was offered would reach an unavoidable conclusion: issues presented in one way could be presented in another. Arenas in which Americans could talk and reason together, rather than watch politicians fight, were within journalism's power to construct. But did the press care to use its power this way?

The force of this question—coming from a Washington journalist with a strong reputation—was far more unsettling than Fallows's complaints about greedy pundits and their mindless predictions. Taken seriously, *Breaking the News* was nothing less than a call to action, grounded in a sober acknowledgment of failure: "The institution of journalism is not doing its job well now. It is irresponsible with its power. The damage has spread to the public life all Americans share. The damage can be corrected, but not until journalism comes to terms with what it has lost."[20]

What it had lost was a sense of public purpose strong enough to inspire the needed reforms. By finding at least some of that sense in public journalism, Fallows made himself a traitor to the culture of the elite press, which believes that whatever corrections may be needed can be located within the culture itself: in objectivity and the adversarial attitude, in the usual demands for truth, accuracy, and fairness, in the pledge of nonpartisanship and the prohibition on supporting causes. By going outside the culture—to John Dewey, Wichita, Norfolk, NYU—for a different understanding of journalism's public mission, Fallows invited an attack he had not foreseen.

Howell Raines, editorial page editor of the *New York Times*, led the charge. In a signed column, Raines drew attention to what the header called "The Fallows Fallacy: A Plan for Turning Reporters into Lackeys." Raines said the author was right about the pundits and their misbehavior. "It is when Mr. Fallows turns from diagnosis to prescription that he becomes a fount of dangerous nonsense." The problem lay in the author's background and priorities. Fallows had gotten his start at the *Washington Monthly*, a policy magazine. He had also been a speechwriter in Jimmy Carter's White House, where he absorbed a view of the press that, according to Raines, put government rather than journalism first. "Career journalists judge the worth of their work by how well it serves the intellectual needs of the readers," Raines wrote. "Journalists influenced by early political employment are more apt to judge journalism by whether it makes life easy for candidates and officeholders and promotes the formulation of sound public policy."

Fallows was a policy person, not a press hand. He did not grasp the ethical tradition that mainstream journalism had developed since World War II, which "calls on reporters to forswear partisan advocacy, to be indifferent to the fortunes of individual candidates, to be agnostic as to public policy outcomes, to be dogged in the collection of information for its own sake." Fallows mistakenly believes that readers "will be better served by reporters who see themselves as civic stenographers" (Raines's term for public journalists), who are "dedicated to promoting worthy policies and well-motivated politicians." The book poses an "insidious danger, and that is that reporters and editors become public policy missionaries with a puritanical contempt for horse race politics." The unruly ceremonies of the campaign trail bring the "wisdom of democracy" alive. Through the "clarifying vitality of unrestrained debate" the public gets an education.

"The participation of mainstream print journalists in this process as skeptical observers is a high, venerable and independent calling," Raines wrote. "Mr. Fallows's case for abandoning that calling may be well intended, but it is poisonous to the values of the newsroom. If journalists follow his prescription, their readers will truly have reason to blame their press for undermining democracy."

By choosing to take public journalism seriously, and by regarding the press as an institution that, as he wrote, "will rise or fall with the political system," Fallows provoked Raines into personal attack that said: Jim, you're no journalist. Raines went out of his way to deny any view of the press as a civic actor. Journalists are indifferent and agnostic. As skeptical observers, they strive for a radical independence that grants them license not to care about public policy outcomes. As Raines saw it, *Breaking the News* was a brief for turning reporters into political hacks, beholden to candidates and causes. The book was the work of an intruder, not a professional concerned about the drift of his craft.[21]

As Max Frankel's treatment had earlier shown, one way the elite press sought to contain the disturbance caused by public journalism was to draw the lines of conflict between center and margin. In places like Wichita and Norfolk, would-be reformers may be spouting dangerous nonsense. But in

Washington, New York, and Philadelphia, tradition held: an independent, objective, and skeptical press remained scrupulously uninvolved in politics. Fallows had upset this portrait by offering, from Washington, where he lived and worked, a vaguely sympathetic portrait of the editors in the provinces and what they were trying to do. And he coupled it with a critique of the prestige press as a player in public life. Views like his were impossible to contain within a center-margin portrait of the controversy. Frankel tried to ignore this fact. Raines dealt with it by marginalizing Fallows. But not all of their colleagues were so inclined.

In an op-ed column responding to Raines, Richard Harwood, a former editor at the *Washington Post* and a career newspaperman, took exception to any view of the press as agnostic and indifferent toward the outcome of public struggles. Such phrases may be "well established in the defensive rhetoric newspapers employ when the practices of contemporary journalism are brought into question," Harwood observed. "But if Raines is suggesting that these precepts are faithfully adhered to by the 'mainstream press' and its journalists, then he and I are living on different planets."

Good journalists try to keep their partisan feelings in check. But a good newspaper cannot operate without "social and community values," which are shown in what it chooses to highlight or ignore. Thus: "It is simply not credible or intellectually defensible to argue that the reporters and news editors for the networks or for newspapers such as the New York Times were 'indifferent' and 'agnostic' about the policy outcomes of the civil rights struggles in the South in the 1960s, that they cared nothing about the outcome in Vietnam, or that they care nothing today about the outcomes of the quests of women, homosexuals and other groups for full acceptance in society."

Journalists, said Harwood, have long honored newspapers that "took on slumlords, worker exploitation, rapacious monopolies and utilities, drug lords, the criminals of Teapot Dome and Watergate." Could this be called agnosticism? The *Times* itself "has been, in a journalistic sense, a leading patron and arbiter of high culture and the arts." Its own "social and political values are easily discerned in its pages." No scandal there, Harwood added. "Those are public-spirited things to do and are not inconsistent with the spirit of 'civic journalism.'"

Consciously or not, critics of the movement often seem to contend "that the only true and legitimate journalist is a strange species of citizen who betrays himself and his 'calling' if he harbors notions of civic responsibility or cares about the purpose and impact of his work." Fortunately for democracy, such creatures are rarely seen, Harwood concluded. The title of his column in the *Post:* "The Legitimacy of 'Civic Journalism.'" This was noteworthy because the previous year he had written in the *Post* of his misgivings about the movement, which were more or less those of Max Frankel. Here was one member of the elite press who, upon further examination, had changed his mind. As far as I could tell, this did not happen at the *Times.*[22]

Howell Raines was not the only one at the *Times* who reacted to Fallows. It figured that Frank Rich—a former drama critic who closed many a show with a negative review—would have a hard time seeing the press as uninvolved or agnostic. His column on *Breaking the News* was generally supportive, although he stepped carefully around public journalism, avoiding the term itself. Rich wrote: "A true reformer, [Fallows] ends on an upbeat note as he cites how more newspapers might turn to public service journalism—the in-depth examination of issues that affect our lives rather than the relentless fixation on the scandal, crime or political horse race du jour. . . . You don't have to be a media-basher—indeed, you can be a press-card-carrying media bashee yourself—to appreciate that the media are missing the story of their own role in compounding the alienation and anger that define the destabilized political culture of our time."[23]

A year after his first column on the subject, Max Frankel returned to it by contesting a key sentence in *Breaking the News,* in which Fallows had written: "Today's journalists can choose. Do they want merely to entertain the public or engage it?" Frankel's response was: "By allowing a choice only between *entertain* and *engage*, Fallows leaves no room for the customary journalistic ambition to *inform* and *instruct.* He wants newspapers to 'engage' by means of 'public journalism,' a fashionable new creed that asks newspapers not merely to depict social problems but to lead the community in seeking their solution. Standing apart from social activity, he contends, is an irresponsible pose of 'objectivity.'"

Frankel stood up for the "American tradition of confining preachments to the editorial page," which had always been "the place—the proud place—for newspapers to engage and crusade."[24] Asked to comment on public journalism for the *American Journalism Review*, Frankel, like Michael Gartner before him, pronounced himself mystified. "I've never understood it," he said. "I've read all the theory on it. Some of it sounds like good old fashioned reporting. Some it sounds like getting into bed with the promotion department and that's unfortunate. Some of it sounds downright political."[25]

Downright political: that was one thing the *Times* was not going to admit into its view of itself or of the press as a whole. In a mostly positive review, Christopher Lehmann-Haupt of the *Times* wrote: "For Mr. Fallows, the way to involve the public more responsibly lies in a newly-developing movement called 'public journalism,' in which newspapers and television shows define the important issues to be covered, like the environment or race relations, instead of relying on political consultants and spin masters to dictate to them." This was an odd summary, since it left citizens out of the picture altogether. Lehmann-Haupt raised the usual questions about objectivity, noting Fallows's contention that "the world covered by the establishment press is no more objective" than one defined by the ideas of public journalism. "But what [Fallows] neglects to consider here is the latitude such journalism might leave to a less responsible editor. And in any case, isn't a journalist who defines a theoretical world beforehand less likely to be objective than someone reporting on empirical reality?"[26]

Here was a *Times* man staking a claim, not to radical independence, as Raines had written, but to a kind of radical *innocence*. Journalists operating in traditional fashion do not make narrative decisions or frame facts. They are merely "reporting on empirical reality." Public journalists, by contrast, are not in quest of reality. They want to "define a theoretical world beforehand" and then do the reporting that confirms it. Only public journalism leaves "latitude . . . to a less responsible editor." Traditional journalism is latitude-less, apparently because its rules prohibit editors from making any judgments at all. It seemed remarkable that Lehmann-Haupt, a book reviewer by trade and thus more familiar with the intellectual currents of the age, could mount such a claim to epistemological purity. But there it was.

Noting Fallows's contention that a corrosive cynicism had overtaken the Washington press, columnist Maureen Dowd (whom Fallows had criticized) saw no cause for alarm. The real danger was in the author's eagerness to leave untouched the public relations veil government drops over its policies.

> The modern history of the Presidency—from the Bay of Pigs to the Gulf of Tonkin from Watergate to Iran-contra—illustrates why reporters must look behind the veil. The veil is not especially democratic, and journalism is supposed to be the opposite of boosterism.

We don't need Mr. Fallows's version of "public journalism." If you want to appreciate the role of journalism in a democracy, go to the Vietnam Memorial. I walk along the black wall, as it grows taller with names, and I think about how the men running the country sent so many young Americans to their death because they were driven by ego to insist on the veil, to lie and lie to the public.

"Americans," Dowd wrote, "did not become disillusioned because the press distorted the workings of government but because the press exposed the workings of government." In another column she added: "Now people calling themselves 'public journalists' make a career denouncing us unpublic journalists. They say we're cynics. (In fact, we're stoics.)" Persisting in the face of carping criticism that blames the press for almost everything is "my profession," Dowd declared. "And I'm going to keep at it because this is what keeps me and my fellow pathological truthtellers alive."[27]

In the hands of Dowd and Lehmann-Haupt, the contrast between public journalism and the established creed amounted to fictionalizing versus truth telling. On one side stood the public relations veil and the peddling of a predefined theoretical world. On the other side, "pathological truthtellers" and their accounts of empirical reality. Framed this way, was there anything to debate? When Iver Peterson, who took over the press beat in 1996, wrote of "public journalism techniques that blur the traditional distinction between reporting and editorializing," or when Francis X. Clines of the paper's Washington bureau defined civic journalism as "the self-advertised responsibility to root out good news," was there anyone in the press likely to be in favor of such? When a nameless editorial writer for the *Times* spoke of the damage to the credibility of the press wreaked by "the fad for intellectually flaccid 'civic journalism,'" was there any (tasteful) way to reply?[28]

In 1996, Eugene Roberts, the legendary former editor of the *Philadelphia Inquirer* who was then managing editor of the *Times,* gave a lecture on "corporatism versus journalism." His theme: "It is time, high time, that newspaper corporations become subjects of debate and be held accountable for covering the communities they serve. Meanwhile, they are managing their newspapers like chain shoe stores, with no sense of being important community institutions with highly important responsibilities to the public." For Roberts, the issue was not philosophy but money: the managers of the large newspaper chains were cutting back on staff and space. The public was losing confidence in the press because the press was losing the resources it needed to do an adequate job. Public journalism just papered over this fact with a lot of high-blown rhetoric.

> It is sad but true that some newspapers are failing their communities by under-informing them, while proclaiming all the while that they believe in something called "public journalism." So-called "public journalism" has become a fad, even a movement. Not all of it is bad, but much of it has more to do with public relations than with journalism. It often involves "connect-ing" with the public by staging town meetings and community policy seminars and in engaging in glad-handing.

Roberts said he believed in public journalism himself. But his definition meant "covering public meetings, not sponsoring them." It meant "inform-ing the community thoroughly and diligently about all aspects of commu-nity life." This required no rethinking of the journalist's task, just the money to accomplish it. "Pretending to care about a community while cutting back on newshole and staff and, thus, information, has a lot to do with P. T. Barnum and hocus-pocus," he charged. "But it doesn't have much to do with journalism and public responsibility." So much for public journalism and its message to the press. Roberts called it a fad, but he came close to saying it was a fraud, perpetrated by companies that had no intention of serving their communities well. Invisible in his treatment were all the editors who had come to the conclusion that their craft was dangerously adrift, and their fran-chise disappearing because of it. Did their arguments make any sense? Were they misguided or just confused? Had they sold out? Roberts did not say.[29]

Looking at the entire episode, the critical factor in the *Times*'s treatment of public journalism was the refusal to allow into serious discussion any image of the press as a purposeful institution, one that tries to accomplish something beyond providing news and remaining skeptical. A language of alarm accompanied this move. It charged public journalism with supporting causes, wiping out the distinction between news and opinion, threatening the journalist's independence, promoting the fortunes of individual candi-dates, "defining a theoretical world beforehand," relinquishing the habit of doubt, indulging in a mindless boosterism.

Against this danger the *Times* spoke a preferred language of innocence: it talked of objectivity, fairness, skepticism, lonely truth tellers, the enduring quest to "tell it like it is," and the stoicism required to do so. There was no place in this scheme for the journalist as a player in public life, although here and there one could find admissions from *Times* people that the press was just that. Kelly's 1993 essay was one. Another was Katharine Seelye saying that "the ever-adversarial, conflict-seeking press helps shape the politics" we see today. But such observations remained unassimilated into the paper's view of itself, and that was one reason public journalism got the reaction it did—in general, thumbs down.[30]

Among commentators at the *Washington Post,* a more intricate act unfolded. The *Post* was not in any way "for" public journalism. In fact, Leonard Downie, the executive editor of the paper, became one of the movement's earliest and most visible critics. He spoke often about crossing the line into activism and the public journalist's dubious support of causes. But others at the *Post* took a different view, not so much in favor of the movement as worried about the same things that concerned the civic journalists.

Sentiments virtually identical to Max Frankel's were not hard to find among the *Post's* writers. When a new work by scholar James Fishkin praised the thinking behind public journalism, Jonathan Yardley, book critic for the *Post,* noted that if the movement "encourages the press to focus on issues . . . it is most welcome." But Fishkin and others tend to "carry this further into advocacy and direct involvement in public affairs." Yardley wrote: "This is the hardest part of his argument to accept, at least for a journalist of considerable seasoning who believes that what the press must strive for is not participation, which ends up as partisanship, but disinterested reportage and commentary. This is an old-fashioned view of the press, and perhaps it is less valid in this new age; but no one has yet made a persuasive case against it."[31]

In fact, the case against it had been made by others at the *Post,* including the paper's distinguished roster of political writers. Trying to tell it like it is, they could not avoid describing the press as one actor among others in a system that wasn't working. One of these writers was Paul Taylor, an accomplished political reporter who began to reflect on what he had witnessed in his work. In *See How They Run,* his 1990 study of presidential campaigns, Taylor took an ecological view of the subject. "The premise of this book," he wrote, "is that the political dialogue is failing because the leading actors in the pageant of democracy—the politicians, the press, and the voters—are bringing out the least in one another."

Taylor told story after story explaining how the press had become an agent of influence in the campaign. In 1988, for example, one reason journalists were so obsessed with character issues was the large number of candidates competing for their attention. "Somebody had to prune the field," he wrote, "to 'get rid of the funny ones,' as one 1988 campaign manager put it." There were too many choices, too much information to present, and "the culture was too apolitical" to sustain interest in such a large number of candidates. "With the party bosses out of the equation, there was a huge vacuum at the front end of the process. Who would screen the field? The assignment fell to the press—there was no one else."

It was simple candor that argued against Yardley's old-fashioned view of the press as straightforward observer. Tasks like screening the field, weeding out the "funny ones" and using the character question to do it were clearly a kind of participation in politics. An occasional effect of the journalist's entanglement in the process—unintended, but real—was to exclude the public from decision making. Taylor described the early exit of Gary Hart and Joseph Biden, contenders for the 1988 Democratic nomination who withdrew after especially harsh scrutiny by a press pack employing the character theme. The sinking of Hart and Biden, he noted, came "months before voters had any chance to ratify or overrule the unsparing portraits of them drawn by newspapers and television." The view that journalists took of the pageant depended on the way they defined their task. "We see our job as a daily struggle to expose wrongdoing, watchdog power, right wrongs," Taylor wrote, adding that the "psychological make-up of most journalists" leads them to view the world—and shape the news—in a certain way: "What attracts us to our line of work is not only the chance to observe but the chance to expose. . . . Reporters strain mightily to see things clearly and whole. But we also define the world by its unfinished agenda, and in so doing we cannot help but see mostly bad news."[32]

All these observations fed into Taylor's ecological view of the press, the public, and the political system. The leading actors influenced one another, which meant that journalists could not stand apart from the downward spiral in national politics. In a 1992 essay on that theme, Taylor noted how the elite press "has become a carrier as well as a chronicler of the prevailing discontent with public life." Along with the rest of us, journalists help make politics what it is. "For quite some time now," he claimed, "the public square has been more like a vicious circle. The fakery of the candidates (whether through attack ads or through empty promises, on the order of 'Read my lips: no new taxes') begets the cynicism of the reporters and voters, and the cynicism of the reporters and voters begets fakery and attack politics, because those tactics work best when the public is poised to believe the worst about the candidates."

Turning to the question of what journalism can do to improve things, Taylor left no doubt that he and his colleagues have a role. They cannot "leave reforms to the reformers," as Frankel would later advise. For with the waning power of political parties, "journalists have increasingly become players in a political contest in which they also serve as observers, commentators, and referees." The news mattered and the news was something they *made*. Taylor could be disarmingly clear on this point. "Political stories don't just 'happen' the way hailstorms do," he noted. "They are artifacts of a political universe that journalism itself has helped to construct."

Taylor showed how journalists favor two main story lines: "the search for the candidates' character flaws and the depiction of the campaign as a horse-race, full of ploys and surprises, tenacity and treachery, rising action and falling action, winners and losers." The "master narrative" in campaign reporting reflects too many of "journalism's bad habits." The challenge now was to find a way to "improve the political discourse."[33] Changes "must come from within the hearts, minds and souls of journalists." He called for a better master narrative with more room for serious public talk, a clearer rationale for when to cross the zone of privacy in reporting about candidates' personal lives, and some effort by journalists to overcome their ingrained cynicism by trying to improve public dialogue.[34]

Although he was willing to offer these suggestions, Taylor had already quit the political beat by 1992. In 1996 he went further and resigned from the *Post*. At age forty-six, near the peak of a dream career, he left journalism to pursue an idea that might make the system work better: challenge the major networks to offer free television time to presidential candidates during the campaign season. If the contenders could escape from the limitations of sound-bite news and ad-speak, perhaps they would say things of genuine import, and journalists would have something more meaningful to report. Taylor raised foundation money (from the Pew Charitable Trusts) and turned himself into a self-described public-interest lobbyist, on a crusade to improve the "language of politics and the habits of journalists." In a press release he wrote, "Surely we can find a way out of the vicious cycle in which all the great actors in the pageant of democracy—the citizens, the candidates, the journalists—bring out the least in one another."[35]

Taylor's journey led him to quit the profession in order to serve the ideals that brought him into it. Those attracted to public journalism had come to similar conclusions, but they chose to remain and seek reform from within. Like Taylor, they had grown alarmed at the rapid deterioration of public life in the 1980s. Like him, they could not avoid the conclusion that journalists were implicated in democracy's discontents. This movement—from growing alarm to the conclusion, "we're implicated," and on to suggestions for reform—also described the journey of David Broder, a man of unique stature in journalism as the *Post*'s lead political writer for almost a generation. Speaking at a 1995 conference on civic journalism, Broder framed the question before the group: "What responsibility, if any, does a news organization have for the quality of civic life in the community?"

Broder said he had come to this question a few years earlier, "not as a matter of theory but out of considerable personal pain and anxiety." His discontent had a simple source: "I love politics. I love reporting on politics." But he now found it difficult to ignore the "rising chorus of complaint about our political system and the people in it." Interviewing voters door to door, as he had for many years, Broder heard a deepening cynicism and a voice that verged on despair. Americans had come to believe that all politicians were crooks, who "don't give a damn about the people who put them there."

One crystallizing event for Broder was a rueful one: some of the best young reporters at the *Post*, "people who we wanted to enlist in our political coverage," had asked to be excused. (One, in fact, was Paul Taylor.) This refusal to follow in his footsteps struck hard at Broder. Approaching sixty, he saw in front of him "a repudiation and a rejection of everything that I had thought was important." As he glanced ahead to his own retirement, and back upon his thirty-five years in journalism, he said: "I did not want the [obituary] on my generation of political reporters to be some smart-ass remark that for 40 years we reported everything that was happening in American politics except that public support for the system was collapsing."

So in 1990–91 he came to some conclusions. The first was to drop the defensive pose and admit that people had good reason to be frustrated with the press. His own experience in "door-knocking" had led Broder to trust in the common sense of Americans, who "don't make terrible misjudgments very often." A second conclusion: end the insidious "collaboration" among reporters, campaign strategists, and media advisers, which yielded a savvy style of analysis informing "them, the public, how easily they, the voters, were being jerked around." A third: redefine rights of ownership over the campaign season, away from political professionals and toward average citizens. Spend enough time with voters to understand their concerns; then "use the clout of news organizations"—the power of the press—to pressure the candidates to respond in a more genuine way.

All of which led him to the civic journalism movement. By organizing forums and voter registration drives, making themselves into catalysts and conveners, some journalists had taken his idea "several long steps beyond the point where I sort of dropped it off." Broder had watched these experiments "with great interest and sympathy" and had been impressed at times with the results. He also felt some skepticism, grounded in his conviction that "the essential role of the news organization is still the informational role." He wouldn't go as far as others had gone. "But given the evidence of civic decay around us, given the scarcity of organizations with the resources to help revive civic participation, I think it is a healthy exercise for some news organizations to be experimenting in novel ways to try to re-establish the bonds between the leadership of the community, the state and the nation, and the citizens."

This was not a time when journalists could afford to be complacent, he warned. Representative democracy was in trouble, and might in time yield to plebiscite forms that, in Broder's view, posed a serious threat to liberty, including liberty of the press. "But we will not thwart that trend or move-ment simply by writing columns or editorials." Journalists could help make the representative system work again, by strengthening their own links to citizens and, if possible, working to close the gap between the public's needs and the deeds and words of politicians. It was not necessary to agree on the best way to meet this challenge, "but it is vital that we act on the knowledge that the challenge is real."[36]

In its tone of urgency, its call to action, its placement of the press as a player within politics, and its recentering of journalism around citizen's concerns, Broder's address was of a piece with much of the thinking behind public journalism. Where his own views diverged from some of the move-ment's riskier experiments, he took an open stance: they're experiments, he said, and we need more of those. By conveying his sympathy for representa-tive government, as against other expressions of the democratic impulse, Broder made it clear that his ideas about the press flowed from other convic-tions he had about politics, democracy, and the citizen's proper role in the system. This was a far cry from the agnosticism of Howell Raines.

Finally, and most powerfully, he grounded his call to act in an un-abashed tone of reverence: "I love politics. I love reporting on politics."

Emotions lay behind those words, not only love of craft and love of democracy but pain and sadness toward what had become of our public life. Broder was not a man to allow the professional imperative of detachment to harden into cynicism, or snuff out his feelings of regret. He implicated himself and his colleagues because he *felt* implicated, and by doing so set an example of civic professionalism that could inspire others, whether or not they called themselves civic journalists.

The *Post's* E. J. Dionne is one of those rare journalists with a Ph.D., in political science. An outstanding reporter who became a *Post* columnist, Dionne spoke at one of my own project's seminars and at a 1995 conference sponsored by the Pew Center. There he expressed his "huge enthusiasm for the people who are hard at work on public and/or civic journalism." He said he had many questions about how it could work in practice. And he noted how "all of us who are sympathetic with this enterprise" had grown to believe that "our democracy is actually going to hell in handbasket."

Dionne spoke of a crisis in his profession: "We're not sure what it is we do anymore." The press had moved from a partisan ethic in the nineteenth century to an ethic of objectivity in the second half of the twentieth, and now to "an ethic that is neither partisan nor objective." It was an "ethic of skepticism," which had its own problems. "The danger of this ethic is that it can make journalism increasingly disconnected from the obligations it has to promote a healthy democratic debate and actually engage citizens in that debate."[37]

In *They Only Look Dead,* published in 1996, Dionne sketched a subtler portrait of journalism's difficulties. On one hand, the line between "information and rumor, fact and opinion" was breaking down, in part because newer media (talk shows and the like) were rife with ideologically inflected speech that mingled baseless assertion with provable claims. Another problem was that serious news was more and more attitude driven. As Michael Kelly observed in his essay for the *New York Times* in 1993, the news now treated perception as a kind of reality, and offered a cynical slant on a political culture preoccupied with impression management.

As the culture of politics and the culture of journalism merged with the newer media forms, the airing of public controversies got livelier but also emptier. "The liveliness is in some sense artificial," Dionne wrote. "It involves people tossing epithets and one-liners at one another as weapons." This combat ethic was visible on television shows like CNN's *Crossfire,* which was mostly a parody of argument. A genuine journalism of controversy would have its advantages, Dionne observed; but that was not what was emerging. We were losing the journalism of fact and gaining a phony journalism of confrontation and insult. "Without either information or reasoned debate, there is—cynicism." Dionne showed how a concern for traditional values in journalism—truth, fairness, evidence, accuracy, information—was compatible with the concerns voiced by public journalism.

> On the one hand, there is a need to resurrect a concern for what's true—to draw clearer distinctions between fact and opinion, between information and mere assertion, between flip predictions and reasoned analysis. At the same time, there is an urgent requirement that the media take seriously their obligation to draw people into public debate, to demonstrate that the debate is accessible and that it matters. Journalism, in other words, needs to be conscious simultaneously of its traditional "professional" imperatives and of its obligations to making democracy work.

Like Taylor and Broder before him, Dionne placed the press inside politics as a powerful institution that might employ its influence in a more constructive way.

> No one elected the press, yet the press is now an intimate part of everything having to do with elections. The press is not there to make political decisions, yet everything the press does helps shape those decisions. The press does not exist to represent the citizenry, yet in fact reporters do believe they represent citizens (or at least their interests) when they probe and question and analyze and pontificate. The press, radio and television have no obligations to Democrats and Republicans. But they do have a powerful obligation to worry about their role in the functioning of a democratic republic.

Dionne was asking his colleagues to consider whether they had aided or undermined America's search for a workable public life. "Journalism is under sharp attack now precisely because the public (and most journalists) suspect that it is not promoting a level of public debate that matches the seriousness of the choices the country confronts," he wrote. A great debate lay ahead about the proper role of government and the kind of society we were to become. "If Americans in large numbers sit out this great debate and decide that politics has nothing to do with the problems at hand, and nothing to do with them, the whole political class—and perhaps *especially* journalists— will have failed." Writing in the tradition of civic-minded reform, Dionne argued that the press could not meet its duties merely by observing the scene before it, although scrupulous observation was still important. Something more was required: a press that "sees public life not simply as a realm of combat but also as the ground on which citizens can engage in a common search for understanding."[38]

Taylor, Broder, and Dionne had a boss at the *Post*. He was Leonard Downie, the paper's executive editor, who had a very different view of the press and public life. Even more than Raines of the *New York Times*, Downie, when he thought about the press, tried to remove it from the sphere of politics—and even from society itself. So complete was the separation in Downie's mind that public journalism had almost no hope of entry. But neither did the ideas of Taylor, Broder, and Dionne. "No matter how good the end is— building a new stadium, creating new parks, cutting down on air pollution— it makes it impossible for newspapers to report on those things with complete detachment and credibility if the newspaper's involved with those projects," Downie said in 1996. "Our role is to gather information and present it to our readers, not be the stage managers or the participants in the events."[39]

Downie was fighting an imaginary opponent—those who favored advocacy journalism in service of a cause, like creating more parks. More interesting was his understanding of what good journalism required. Downie fit the category of purist, but in a particularly vivid way. In his mind, the press was not only detached from the sphere of politics, it was separate from the larger society—or needed to be. He deliberately sought a position as an outsider, removed even from the category of citizen. It was a fascinating movement of thought: starting with the usual imperative of objectivity, Downie derived a philosophy of civic exile, the best position, he believed, for a responsible editor.

I first became aware of his thinking on this subject when I read a column he wrote during the 1992 campaign. It explained to readers that the newspaper's recent endorsement of Bill Clinton would have no effect on its coverage of the campaign. The "opinion-making and news coverage functions of the paper are kept completely separate," Downie wrote. Recognizing that journalists are people who "cannot be expected to cleanse their professional minds of human emotions and opinions," he noted that the *Post* wanted its reporters and editors "to come as close as possible to doing just that." He then added, "In the most extreme effort of this kind, I no longer exercise my right to vote."[40]

Most journalists are content with a philosophy that says: we keep our personal feelings out of the news. Downie was after something more, for himself and his staff. In his view, a principled journalist keeps personal feelings and political convictions at a clear distance, not only from the news, but from the *self.* Thus his preference for journalists who come as near as possible to cleansing "their professional minds of human emotions and opinions." Downie thought this a desirable state—never to be reached, but always to be sought.

In a panel discussion in 1989, he had elaborated on his position, which involved more than a personal prohibition on voting. Speaking of issues like abortion, he said he wanted his staff to get their opinions and feelings "out of their system if they're going to work for the Washington Post." Not out of their stories, out of their system. He said he was undecided himself about abortion, and could see the "moral strength" of both sides. "I'm going to strain as hard as I can to not have feelings about these things," Downie said. "I don't want to decide it in my mind." In his quest for news that was completely free of bias, he would refuse to come to a personal judgment on the question. Not only that, he regretted that "some members of my staff have opinions about it."

Downie's personal rule against voting had a similar logic. As an executive at the *Post,* he could influence all areas of news coverage. "I do not want to have to decide whether George Bush or Michael Dukakis should be president," he said (acknowledging in an aside that his wife and children disapproved of his position). He was careful to add that the *Post* did not impose this rule on the staff; everyone was allowed to vote. And Downie was aware that his policy sounded odd to others. "But I think it's odd to be a journalist," he said. "I think we're very different from other people. I feel very different . . . an outsider to my society and I think that's part of my great strength to my approach to my job."

This view—that the principled journalist dwells outside society—extended to Downie's ideas about the press as an institution. He rejected "the theory of social responsibility of the press." Rather, he believed in "the independence of the press from society," which he considered "Thomas Jefferson's idea . . . what the First Amendment is all about." The Constitution's gift of radical independence, not only from government but from the nation at large, meant that journalists had to relinquish something in return. What they surrendered were "certain other rights they have as individuals in pursuit of this larger right, freedom of the press." Thus, the *Post* prohibited many forms of political activity, which was not unusual among newspapers. And Downie prohibited himself from voting, which was unusual.[41]

In a 1994 panel discussion in Philadelphia, Cole Campbell and I sat down with Downie and Richard Aregood, a Pulitzer Prize–winning editorial writer, then working for the *Philadelphia Daily News*. Downie put forward his case: He said he approved of seeking insights from discussions with citizens about their concerns; he liked voter's guides that gave the candidates' stands on key issues; and he supported solid research on solutions to public problems. But none of those things were original to public journalism; each was just good reporting, the kind the *Post* was already doing. The new movement "crosses the line for me when the newspaper and its editors and reporters become actors on the public stage," he said. Public journalism oversteps the bounds of good reporting "by forcing candidates to participate in dialogues with voters, by staging campaign events, by deciding what good citizenship is and forcefeeding it to citizens and voters, by pressuring citizens to register and vote when, as I say, nonvoting can also be viewed as an honorable and honest way to participate in the democratic process."

Downie also said that "too much of what is called public journalism appears to be what our promotion department does at the *Washington Post*," but "with a different kind of name and a fancy evangelistic fervor." He agreed that there was too much horse-race coverage of politics, that "reporting on the political system should not be shaped primarily or solely by politicians, political consultants." The better newspapers, including the *Post*, had already recognized this and were moving in the right direction. There was no need for a movement, he argued, to improve journalism.

What characterizes public journalism is the next step, he argued, where "you set up joint task forces of journalists and citizens to decide to do things in a community." To make a decision to "cross that line and accomplish X" is fundamentally wrong, Downie declared. "It is arrogant, it is mistaken, it is not our constitutional function." He acknowledged the existence of an "agenda-setting that comes willy-nilly from providing people with information and making judgments about information." In that limited sense the *Post* did operate as a political force in the capital, but it worked hard to ensure that its news judgments were not influenced by personal bias or "communities of sources and friends."

In my own remarks to the conference, I said that public journalism asks the press to "view the scene the way people start viewing the scene." But if the reforms ended there, nothing much would change. A newspaper that was "no more than a mirror, reflecting people's prejudices and half-baked ideas back to them, would be useless." The idea was to begin with what citizens value in politics, what they want to see addressed. That meant shifting from one set of priorities, derived from institutional actors, to "another set of actors, citizens who are supposed to own politics in the first place."[42]

Of course, what I should have done was quote back to Downie the words of Paul Taylor and David Broder. Afterward, I could only wish I had been so well prepared. Campbell and I did what we could to describe public journalism as a shift in the master narrative, toward the deeper concerns of citizens. Downie and Aregood did what they could to challenge the notion, as Aregood put it, "that this is somehow something miraculously new." They tried to focus the debate on "crossing the line" into activism. A year later, Rem Rieder, editor of the *American Journalism Review*, assessed the results: "The apotheosis of the public journalism faceoff as blood sport came at last year's Associated Press Managing Editors convention, when *Washington Post* Executive Editor Leonard Downie, Jr. and editorial page legend Richard Aregood, he of the withering one-liner, eviscerated public journalism's defenders in the Thrilla in Phila."[43]

Leonard Downie's philosophy, while fascinating in its quest for a position beyond politics and removed from society, rarely spoke to the idea of public journalism, at least as I understood it. He wanted to contest those who favored advocacy in the news pages, most of whom, he said, were academics "risking the terrible prostitution of our profession." More significant, perhaps, is that Downie didn't speak to the observations of Taylor, Broder and Dionne. In fact, he openly contradicted them. What sense did it make to call journalists outsiders to American society when, according to Taylor, they have become "lead players in a culture of disparagement?" Or when, according to Dionne, "the press is now an intimate part of everything having to do with elections?" If Downie believed that the *Post*'s job was merely to gather and present information and no more, how did he handle Taylor's insight that the press constructs the campaign story by employing its own master narrative?[44]

Or consider this: If journalism and participation were logical opposites, what did Downie make of Broder's observation that "we have colluded with the campaign consultants to produce the kind of politics which is turning off the American people?" If Downie felt that the First Amendment separated journalists from government and society, could he accept Broder's notion that the press ought to help reconnect politics and government? Or Dionne's conclusion that if Americans sit out the great debate ahead of them, then "the whole political class—and perhaps *especially* journalists—will have failed?" Or Broder's warning in 1990: "We cannot allow the [November] elections to be another exercise in public disillusionment and political cynicism." Or finally, this ringing passage from Broder's pen: "It is time for those of us in the world's freest press to become activists, not on behalf of a particular party or politician, but on behalf of the process of self-government."[45]

These were questions that almost never got asked in the often heated debate over public journalism. Downie did not have to recognize how some of the movement's key ideas resembled his own staff's thinking about the journalist's role in public life. The glaring conflicts between, say, Taylor's perspective and Downie's were submerged in various press accounts and public arenas. Downie appeared often as a critic of public journalism; but Taylor was never seen as a critic of Downie. This is just one way in which the wrangling over public journalism reflected the weak tradition of debate within the culture of the press. There was a debate to be had—among the minds at the *Washington Post*—about the press and its influence on public life. Instead, it was played out in shadow form, through the variety of positions taken toward public journalism and its animating ideas.

One of Downie's more intriguing positions was that journalists have no business "deciding what good citizenship is" and forcing that view on readers or listeners. This, I thought, would make for a fine debate on the limits of neutrality in the press. Can journalists really avoid coming to *any* conclusions about citizenship and what it involves or requires? Downie appears to say so, but he must have arrived at such conclusions himself by editing a powerful newspaper in the nation's capital. Simply by reading the *Washington Post*, anyone can detect the following convictions at work: A good citizen is an informed citizen. Good citizens get both sides of the story and decide for themselves. Good citizens follow foreign affairs. Good citizens like a range of opinion to sample in the morning. Good citizens grasp the difference between "news" and "analysis."

Shall we denounce Downie for force feeding these beliefs to innocent readers of the *Post*? We could, but that would be rather uncivil. What we ought to discuss, after all, are competing views of citizenship and how they may lead to different forms of journalism. Downie had his theory of what a good citizen is, and that view was properly reflected in his newspaper. Public journalism was offering a different view. (For example: good citizens take the trouble to vote.) Others in the press probably had their own alternatives. Let the best view win! But this is exactly where the debate did not go, in part because of a successful act of denial implied in Downie's philosophy. To claim that journalists have no business deciding on good citizenship was like saying that university professors have no right to define what an educated person is. But they do have that right. In fact, they have a responsibility to think the matter through, since everything they do for students depends on it.[46]

We can credit Downie with this, however: he was willing to have on staff people who, when they spoke their minds, did not agree with him on journalism and its civic duty. Equally impressive was the way he pursued his ideas to their logical conclusion. If he really felt that the press at its best was an outsider, then, if he was going to be consistent, he had to remain outside the voting booth on election day. There is considerable honor in this sacrifice of democracy's most basic right. Downie was a man determined to behave in accord with his own beliefs. There were others, however, who shared his values but came to a different conclusion.

One of them was Joann Byrd, a former editor at the *Herald* in Everett, Washington, who succeeded Richard Harwood as ombudsman of the *Post*. She pronounced herself, in a column from 1995, a traditionalist at heart. "I equate independent, disinterested reporting with the salvation of the planet and was the last journalist in America to concede that human beings cannot be objective," Byrd wrote. "I think journalists shouldn't even sign petitions. And I think a newspaper has no business deciding what's good for a community until it asks." But she also considered civic journalism a good thing, an extension of the newspaper in "forum mode," where it "enhances citizens' understandings of one another and their common interest."

In Byrd's view, some public journalism projects seemed to be journalists causing news, in a greater degree "than we purists approve of." It is no help "to have the paper acting as a booster or champion of its own agenda," she warned. But the movement's deeper goals can be upheld apart from some of the more troublesome experiments. Journalists need to be able to "stand back, take the long, broad view" if they want to serve the entire community. Civic journalism could accomplish that by turning the newspaper "into an ostentatious vehicle for the community's conversations." In her formula: "The community decides what to talk about; the newspaper provides the encouragement and the means." This would include traditional reporting that relied on the knowledge and judgment of the staff. "A newspaper that immersed itself in facilitating would surely seem less arrogant and self-serving; a paper acting as a microphone for all perspectives could not be accused of bias," wrote Byrd. In short, there were ways around all the familiar objections to public journalism, if reformers were careful to put the community's concerns ahead of their own, seek out a wide range of views, and rely on good old-fashioned reporting.[47]

Byrd was especially interested in the journalist's narrow view of conflict. Her tale proceeded through the same logical steps that drew so many editors into public journalism, and that also characterized the musings of Taylor, Broder, and Dionne: first, recognize a problem in public life; then, acknowledge the press as part of the problem; then, seek to experiment with changes in routines.

The problem: "The public agenda has become a mountain of conflict—complete with fragmentation and isolation and bickering and special interests and clashing values." The inclusion of the press: "This is not surprising when practically all news stories, in detail or theme, are about conflict." As Byrd wrote: "News is good vs. evil, the status quo vs. change, what happened vs. what we wanted, humans against the environment, conservatives vs. liberals, and so on. If conflict is the model, journalism is instinctively in search of the opponents, and routinely—and efficiently—measuring the breadth of a story by outlining the edges."

It was important in this kind of story to also praise what was praiseworthy in an otherwise troublesome pattern. Thus: "Let us hasten to note that conflict is often an accurate story with no intervention of reporting. And there's nothing wrong with debate over serious social issues. There's a chance that journalism raises the currency of conflict, actually encouraging people to draw lines in the sand they might not draw. But conflict is real." And the news should reflect it. But the quest for reality in journalism had to include the (very real) possibility that the news was helping to exacerbate conflict.

> The world portrayed in newspapers has the players crouched in rigid, self-serving corners, prepared for someone to win and someone to lose, and positions being communicated via loud, disruptive, sometimes violent media events.
>
> And after years of seeing unrelenting conflict, the pile of apparently intractable problems on the public agenda now looks immense, distant, impossible. People come to think combat is the natural order of things, and they feel powerless. A lot of them retreat.

Which led Byrd to the experiment. She called for an enlargement of the journalist's task.

So the time has come to get some things off the agenda. While continuing to cover the world's conflicts—which journalists are obligated to do—journalism can do that by recognizing solutions and agreement and cooperation as "news."

Instead of only piling on conflicts, journalists can make it hard for a problem to get on the agenda without being followed by a search for common ground, an effort at mutual understanding, attention to remedies.[48]

In remarks at a conference on public journalism in 1996, Byrd, no longer with the *Post*, tried to bring the strength of Downie's position together with the insights of public journalism. She began in a deliberately opaque fashion: "Journalists believe their greatest value derives from being outsiders. Public journalism thinks it's time journalists admit they are insiders and that acting like outsiders is suicidal. The public consensus is that journalists are outside insiders. I think journalists should be inside outsiders. Are there any questions?"

What her first two sentences meant is clear enough: here is the apparent divide between traditionalists and reformers. Her third sentence referred to a growing hostility toward journalists as insiders who operate outside the citizenry's vital concerns. Thus, "outside insiders." Byrd wanted to retain the value of the disinterested observer—for her, journalism's deepest promise—while overcoming some of the excesses of that pose. She also wanted to keep the newspaper out of the business of directly mobilizing citizens. Her opaque opening yielded to a strikingly clear conclusion:

In my variation on public journalism, somebody outside the journalism assembles the public. Actually, I've got faith that the public would do that automatically. Journalism would facilitate the conversation in the community. We would stay with it as long as the community stayed with it. Which is likely to mean through resolution. That's a lot longer than we usually stay with anything. We would be insiders because we would be responding to and working for our communities. But our inside job would be the resident outsider. We would be the disinterested voice, the dispassionate mirror, the troublemaker, the inside outsider. Just like we promised.[49]

Geneva Overholser, former editor of the *Des Moines Register*, took over for Byrd as the *Post*'s ombudsman. And, like Byrd, she tried to mediate between the best ideas of public journalism and the strengths of the journalism she knew and loved. Writing in the wake of the same civic journalism conference where her colleagues Broder and Dionne spoke, she thought "the movement might just be coming of age. Newspapering, it has begun to seem, might be able to learn from this interesting exercise while largely avoiding its more unsettling effects."

Public journalists saw the criticisms of traditionalists like Downie as "so many straw men," Overholser wrote. "Acknowledging that you care about what happens in your community—and acting in the newspaper as if you do—doesn't require that you shed your journalistic principles." This was indeed what many in the movement were saying. But Overholser had a question for us: "If that's true, then why the need for the new package, new language—the movement? Why not take the best of the thinking it has included, the questions it raises and bring them squarely back to traditional journalism? There is plenty of fodder there for answers to these questions, a fact that the new thinkers seem to have overlooked."

All journalism is about service to the public, Overholser wrote. "To present as newfangled notions the idea of service to community or concern about average citizens is inaccurate." And it would alienate potential supporters. The problems in the press had to do with practice, not principles, for the right principles were already there in the journalist's creed. "If we have been concentrating overmuch on the negative, then we must renew our commitment to tell the whole story, to be accurate and comprehensive." In other words, this was a course correction, not a reformation; and the maturity of the movement lay in recognizing that fact. Overholser put it succinctly: "Journalism needs strengthening, not repudiation."[50]

There was wisdom in Overholser's column—and generosity, too. Whether we could have arrested the attention of the American press without talking the language of reform, without being regarded as something "new" on the scene, without advertising ourselves as a movement—that is another question. I tend to doubt it. Still, Overholser had done the idea a favor. Like Joann Byrd, she pointed the way toward its eventual success: to dissolve back into the tradition from which it arose.[51]

Part Four / Lessons

8 Design Flaw or Driver Error
The Hazards of Going Public

In his many lectures and informal talks to journalists, James Carey would try to give listeners a feel for conversation as an ethic; a way of entering into the world at a useful angle. Stealing a thought from the critic Kenneth Burke (with due credit), he would say: "Life is a conversation. When you enter it is already going on. You try to catch the drift of it. You exit before it's over."

Conversation, for Carey, was simultaneously a better way to live, a better way to think, and a better metaphor for journalism. The journalists he most admired were those who could say: "This is the best we could do in figuring out what the hell was going on today—here it is! Do you have a better idea?" Then they listen for a response.

Here's my best guess, what's yours? Journalists could behave this way toward citizens; professors could take this stance toward journalists; we could all stand in a "conversable" relationship to one another, Carey suggested. Trying to learn from him and others who took a similar approach (like David Mathews of Kettering), I gradually formed ties with journalists who were trying their hand at public puzzles of one kind or another. They told me what they were doing or thinking and I told them what I found in it.[1]

Of course, I had another role: defending or explaining public journalism to those not involved in it. Often on these occasions I would hear myself introduced as a "guru" of the movement. I did not care for this term, although I recognized that there could (sometimes) be good humor in it. But who went around saying to themselves: what I need is a good guru? Journalists,

251

especially, were unlikely to flock to such a figure, since working themselves into meditative trances rarely sounded to them like a hot time. "Guru." The term was either derisively meant ("Yeah, enlighten us . . ."), or it said: You know what this public journalism thing is, so tell us about it.

Well, I did know—in my own way. What mattered more was getting into fruitful contact with theirs. As an intellectual style, the conversational approach was difficult to master; and I faltered at it. Turning people off by coming on too strongly, alienating potential supporters with inflammatory rhetoric, sounding clueless to three-quarters of the room—these were semi-regular lapses. Journalists sympathetic to the basic message would sometimes call and yell at me for making their job harder after my latest newsroom visit. "You really lost a lot of people when you said . . ."

On top of these failures came the problem of succeeding in a regrettable way. Inevitably, some of those who were enthusiastic about public journalism began doing things that were dubious or even devious. This was one of the hazards of going public with an idea: the trouble caused by those who like the sound of the thing and carry it off in crazy directions. No tale of public journalism's circulation through the press can avoid such episodes, because the doubtful uses to which the notion was put were tests, of a kind—as significant in their way as the other experiments I have discussed. Both said something about what was in the proposals we floated. I am not the best person to chronicle the wrongheadedness or abuse of public journalism. I was far too involved in saying it was right for the times. But there were times when I saw for myself the hazards in the idea, and a few stories can at least be told about that.

At dinner one evening before one my talks to journalists, I listened at length to a news director from one of the leading television stations in town. Let's call him, for purposes of this tale, Tom Moore from WXYZ. Tom said he was all for civic journalism (his term), and he went on to tell me how his station practiced it. I was eager to hear him. Here was a news executive who had declared his commitment to what I was championing myself; I wanted to know what it meant to him.

This was data gathering, of a sort. Once the notion of public journalism is out there, other notions of what it's about rise up and compete with yours. They become part of the action. Putting an idea into play means you lose control over it, as a referee does when he tosses the basketball into a player's hands. Of course, we wanted to see others take the ball and go. The more people who say, "I'm doing some civic journalism," the more action there is around the idea: more discussion, more experiment, more trials—and more errors.

That's why I leaned in when Tom Moore of WXYZ started to talk about his brand of civic journalism. Moore said he loved the "town meeting" part of it. He held them frequently around the city and presided over the events himself. Getting out with the public had done nothing but good for the station, he added. This told me to be alarmed. There was nothing easier to phony up than a televised town meeting, with "real people" employed as props. In fact, many of Moore's meetings weren't televised, but it was a television attitude he took with him. I gathered as much when he told me about his routine: he would head into different neighborhoods, give a speech on the station's news philosophy, and answer questions from a waiting crowd. "You hear stuff," he offered, cheerily.

WXYZ's town meetings were far from what I imagined as civic journalism; but that didn't matter. The important information was coming from Moore. What he was getting by going "out into the community" would tell me what he was seeking, which is what I wanted to know. As it turned out, Moore had heard the usual gripes about television news and some deep-seated anger from people who felt ill served. All of which can be instructive for a news director with open ears. But Moore was much better at talking than listening, and as he continued to describe the good results he was getting, he started to hint at some of the commercial motives behind his ventures into public. In a slightly conspiratorial voice, he then let me in on a trade secret.

His choice of where and when to stage these town meetings was a careful one, Moore said. During the periods when the Nielsen ratings service was out in the field measuring the audience for television news, he planned at least one event in the zip codes where the Nielsen company's diaries were distributed. These diaries were detailed logs kept by TV-watching families, part of the data the firm gathered to rate the most popular shows. Everyone in the industry knew about the Nielsen families, and Moore said it was possible to find out where they were clustered. When he did find out, he went there for one of his civic journalism exercises, in hopes that a diary-keeper might show, someone from the same family, or someone who might know the family. They would come away with a favorable impression of his station, he suggested with a wink.

I sat there speechless: this was civic journalism? To Moore, it was. The fact that he was telling me his trade secret was weird enough: did he think I would find it a worthy innovation? But that he was doing it was worse: an open-and-shut case of public journalism as public relations, not a different story for the craft, but a cover story for a naked attempt to manipulate the ratings. Not even to *get* good ratings, but to seem like you're getting them by tipping the instrument your way.

Well, I should not have been shocked. The ratings mania in television was known to all. Critics of civic journalism had warned about ill-intentioned moves like these. Tom Moore had proved them right. In absorbing his tale, I didn't get into an argument with Moore that evening. As I said, he was a poor listener, the sort of man who took up all the space in a dinner conversation. I should have said, "That isn't civic journalism to me." But the larger trouble was: how many more Tom Moores were out there? And what do you say about their dubious advocacy of the idea, when you're one of the idea's chief advocates?

I had tried to avoid this problem by staying away from local television in most of my travels, even though it had tremendous power and reach. Colleagues and supporters often reminded me that TV drew the larger audience for news. Newspapers, they said, were in a steady decline. I knew that, but I also knew that a different kind of decline was under way in broadcast journalism. By the early 1990s the commercial imperative had so overtaken the industry that there simply wasn't much journalism left. TV news was increasingly under the command of another institution—not journalism, but the media. This other entity had its own formula for the production of news: the largest audience at the lowest possible cost.

That was news to nobody. But it was also what "news" now meant for lots of bodies—or eyeballs, as viewers were called in the programming business. Deregulation during the Reagan era and the enormous profits that could be won in local news were gradually leading to the abandonment of the public service ethic that had given birth to television journalism in the 1960s.[2] A kind of hypercommercialization had set in, enforced through narrow and pessimistic—distinctly Lippmann-like—assumptions about the audience. People are ill attentive, blasé about everything, and unlikely to invest much time or effort unless immediately hooked by dramatic images, violent themes, celebrity names, or some other attention-getting device.

Despite the pressure to remake the news along these lines, there remained some pockets of excellence, especially at the major networks. But at local stations the philosophy "if it bleeds, it leads" was rapidly becoming the industry standard. In one sense this was old fashioned sensationalism, the same genre that had been selling newspapers for several centuries. Ordinarily, however, the more sensational a news source, the less credible it seems to audiences and advertisers. As scholar Philip Meyer points out, supermarket tabloids like the *National Enquirer* are bought, read, and enjoyed by millions. Whether they are believed or not is another matter. The absence of any major consumer products in the tabloids' ad pages suggests the trade-off involved when "your lead headline is 'Housewife Impregnated by Sheep Dog.' "[3]

But the curious thing about local news as a television genre is its ability to indulge in rank sensationalism (or "tabloid TV") and remain credible enough to generate ad dollars. What seems to make this possible is the para-personal relationships viewers develop with local anchors. Amid the calamities on the streets, the smooth delivery and friendly demeanor of the anchor is familiar and stabilizing. Reenacted nightly, the anchor's role brings the station a kind of visceral credibility: these are people I know. For newspapers, the product—not the people—must prove credible. Trust earned through reliable newsgathering is far more expensive than finding a credible performer for the role of anchor. "If it bleeds, it leads" lowers TV's production costs even further, since reality, as it were, can furnish the truck crashes, house fires, and spectacular arrests that, along with the anchors, make the genre go. Odd as it sounds, a kind of "news without journalism" was possible on television.

Phyllis Kaniss discovered this when she studied the news media's treatment of the 1991 Philadelphia mayor's race. "Local television reporters didn't have the time to investigate any public official's performance, and they knew that their producers and news directors wouldn't want the results even if they did," she writes. "What the higher-ups liked in the newscast in the way of local government coverage was personalities and emotion and drama. They were particularly enamored of good guys and bad guys, local heroes and villains. The more simplistic the image, the better."

Critics need to be careful here. Vivid personalities and high drama appeal to journalists working in any form, and there is always a temptation to hype the story at the expense of a complicated and less exciting truth. But Kaniss describes something different: a refusal to investigate what falls outside the simplest dramatic frame. If the mayor's race didn't fit the producer's formula for luring a reluctant audience, then it just wasn't worth the time. "Increasingly disdainful of the issues," she notes, "the TV stations were demanding more and more that there be a guarantee of drama and barbed exchanges before they were willing to commit cameras—much less one of their ever-dwindling reporters—to cover a campaign event."

To see the quest for a large audience as inimical to good journalism is shortsighted and a bit silly, for the public *is* a large audience, and public affairs deserve the attention of as many people as possible. But when news becomes hypercommercialized, ratings conscious in every detail, the possibility of doing journalism at all may vanish into broadcast air. Kaniss suggests that this point had been reached in Philadelphia: "It was the sad fact of life in local television news that increasingly the job of the reporter was not to seek out information about the candidates—whether qualifications or performance or proposals or plans—but rather to figure out how to fold each day's media events into a couple of ultrasimplified story lines."[4]

Seeking a wide audience for the story of our common life is different from reducing our common life to the few story forms that seem to guarantee a wide audience. That is service to the media alone. While it is true that the notion of public service never held complete sway over commercial broadcasting, or for that matter the daily newspaper, it is precisely the incomplete sway of the commercial drive that makes journalism possible at all. And that possibility was the one disappearing from many television newsrooms by the 1990s.

It was a depressing fact, as Kaniss suggests, but it demanded recognition. The media had in many cases overtaken journalism and put in place its own brand of news. I had talked with some TV people about this, and endured my share of lectures from busy news executives, who would counter anything I said about civic purpose with, "That's nice, but you have to understand the commercial pressures we're under." I did understand. And that is what made me wary of TV news: it was populated by the Tom Moores of the world, who could easily degrade public journalism into gimmickry or worse.

On the other hand, the idea had been taken public. It was already out there—to circulate around and either degrade or improve the craft. If what happened to it was abuse, misappropriation, gimmickry, then didn't this count against the wisdom of the notion? By avoiding TV newsrooms in my public appearances, I was avoiding the whole problem—not really facing it. As Mike Hoyt of the *Columbia Journalism Review* observed, the rhetoric we were speaking had room for maneuver in it. We had designed it that way, so that journalists might enter at many points on the arc from cautious and traditional to adventurous and reform-minded. But there was another arc to worry about: it ran from principled devotion to professional standards and the public interest, on one end, to cynical flouting of those standards with a "public interest" cover, at the other.

"With a few twists of the semantic dial," Hoyt wrote, "public journalism can become public posturing." He was right. And right again when he added: "But so can other forms of journalism. When such lines are crossed— as even civic journalism's supporters concede they will be, at least on occasion—does that point to a fault in the philosophy or merely an editorial lapse? Design flaw or driver error?"[5]

I began to ask myself this question in 1994, when I received a call from a reporter at the *San Jose Mercury News,* who wanted to inform me of the paper's latest public journalism initiative. It turned out to be an effort to improve voter participation in a district where a high percentage of immigrants and poor people typically led to low turnout. The project seemed ill conceived, because it singled out a particular population. Why favor one district over another and justify charges of undue interference in the election? After all, everyone knew poorer voters were likely to vote for the Democratic Party. The reporter was clearly wounded when the man he had phoned, a self-described champion of public journalism, had no praise or constructive advice. But the project went forward and public journalism took some well-deserved knocks in the San Jose newsroom.[6]

Design flaw or driver error? I had to wonder as I learned of cases like the one-district voter drive at the *Mercury News.* The best response, I thought, was to spread a nuanced understanding to more and more of the working press, so that people could apply high standards to anything they heard presented as public journalism. But at what point does a co-creator of an idea turn against his—and others'—creation and begin criticizing what it has wrought? I didn't know. And not knowing was a hazardous condition, as I learned when a stunt of a different kind was visited on public journalism by a media giant, the Gannett Company.

Gannett was the largest newspaper chain in the country and consistently among the most profitable. In a 1995 advertisement that ran on the front page of a leading trade journal, *Editor and Publisher,* the company declared: "We believe in 'public journalism'—and have done it for years." The text told how some newspapers around the country had launched "community leadership" projects, which were being loosely defined as public journalism. "To those newspapers we say welcome aboard," the advertisement read. "Congratulations to all newspapers that are expanding their community leadership role. We're sure that your communities will discover what Gannett communities have known for some time: Public journalism is good journalism. And it's at the heart of Gannett journalism."

The ad went on to document fifty such efforts in the previous year, which, according to Gannett, were representative of projects regularly undertaken across the company. The papers mentioned ranged from the *Elmira Star Gazette* in New York to the *Detroit News*. Some of the work described in the ad moved in the general direction of public journalism and probably did some good. But other efforts Gannett promoted were more reminiscent of "advocacy" journalism, especially in the way they took up causes directly. The Elmira paper, for example, had "spearheaded a drive that raised $200,000 to bring the city-owned baseball stadium up to the standard to keep the [local minor league] baseball franchise in the city."

In 1994, I had begun to use the phrase "proactive neutrality" to describe civic initiatives that got people engaged without doing their work for them. The Elmira project was a long way from that. Advocacy was a better term for what the paper had done: let's lead the effort to get money for a new stadium. It might work, or it might not. But stadium fixing was not the idea we had floated in any form I could recognize.

With this ad, Gannett was doing a complicated corporate dance, which illustrated other dangers in going public with an admittedly fuzzy idea. The ad was simultaneously hailing public journalism, and saying: we've been there all along, so how innovative can it be? It was bolstering Gannett's claim to public service by praising its own papers as community leaders, while also borrowing whatever legitimacy clung to the upstart movement and its ideas. In linking the company to public journalism, the ad put teasing quotation marks around the term, as if to say, "we don't need the name, we just do the thing." And with its breezy invitation to others ("welcome aboard"), the promotional stunt was meant to say: we're the leaders here, with fifty innovative projects in the last twelve months. The "heart of Gannett journalism" beat proudly before the rest of the craft.[7]

My heart sank when I saw it. A heated exercise in hype, the advertisement also undertook a kind of intellectual operation on the idea, redefining it as "community leadership," which could easily mean taking the community where *you* wanted it to go. This wasn't the point I and others were trying to advance. Declaring "we're leaders in this community and our job is to lead" could preempt the difficult work of uncovering civic concerns, then asking yourself: what kind of journalism might meet with those concerns? But that was just one of many problems. Another was the Gannett Company's dismal reputation as one of the homes of market-driven journalism, a corporate ethic ready to dispense with public values for the quickest return on investment.[8]

Gannett was a business first, an outpost for journalism second. While this might be said of all newspaper companies—even the family-controlled dynasties where the pressures from Wall Street were not as great—the distance between first and second priorities at Gannett was wider than in most companies. And the control exercised by corporate headquarters was notoriously tight. The result: It was often difficult to practice serious journalism in the more than eighty towns where the chain held papers, in part because the company consistently moved its editors around, as if to prevent them from sinking other roots—into the community, for example. Loyalty to "Gannett journalism" is what accumulated when other loyalties were given scant room to grow.[9]

In his widely read book *The Media Monopoly*, industry critic Benjamin Bagdikian wrote, "Gannett Company Inc. is an outstanding contemporary performer of the ancient rite of creating self-serving myths, of committing acts of greed and exploitation but describing them through its own machinery as heroic epics." Citing Bagdikian's critique, journalist Richard McCord noted how in "speeches, advertising campaigns, and articles in publications such as *Editor and Publisher*, Gannett touted traditional virtues in public while dismantling them in private." After seeing the company in action and reviewing many legal cases against it, McCord left no doubt where he stood: Gannett was evil incarnate, up there with major polluters and tobacco companies as an emblem of corporate venality. There were many journalists who felt the same way, perhaps a majority of the craft, including some I met who once worked for the firm.[10]

So having the Gannett logo attached to public journalism—even somewhat sarcastically—was bad news for the idea. The impression would linger: "public journalism . . . oh, that's a Gannett thing," which was precisely the co-opting aim of the ad in *Editor and Publisher*. Still, the thousands of journalists who worked for the chain were not evil people; it was to them and their colleagues in the press that our idea was addressed. Was it possible to interest thoughtful professionals employed by Gannett in a version of public journalism that gave civic values their due? Could journalism, in their newsrooms, win out over media? Or should these people be dismissed or ignored, because they worked for a firm with such a dubious reputation?

I didn't think they should be exiled, which is why I included a handful of

Gannett editors, those who seemed most open to civic thinking, in my own project's seminars. And several months after the company's ad appeared, I accepted an invitation to address Gannett editors and publishers at one of their annual meetings. Doubtful about the company's intentions in embracing public journalism, I wanted to say something that would challenge the self-congratulatory tone in the ad. But I also wanted to reach the journalists in attendance, who, more than most employees of newspaper chains, felt the sharp conflict between the public values of their profession and the bottom-line mentality for which Gannett was known.[11]

At the time, the headlines were dominated by the deadly bombing of a federal office building in Oklahoma City and the arrest of a leading suspect in the case, Timothy McVeigh, who was later convicted of the crime, the biggest mass murder in U.S. history. I used him as my jumping off point.

. . . .

Timothy McVeigh, if he has done what we think he's done, alerts us to the dangers of neglecting the real work of democracy—which is not passing laws, or pulling levers, or publishing the news. No, the real work of democracy is living together, despite our differences. It is solving problems in the absence of a Big Brother, or a Judgment Day, or a Magic Bullet that will solve them for us.

If I tell you, then, that politics and public life are the heart of democracy—and of journalism—I am pointing to the stark presence of their alternatives. The alternative to a politics that works is not a politics that doesn't, for that situation cannot endure. The eventual alternative is violence. When public life falls apart, we cannot retreat to the safe space of the private. For no place is safe, which is the "news" sent by terrorism, particularly domestic terrorism. . . .

If there are no rewards for participating in public life, if there is no story into which people can insert themselves, if there is no hope of joining a conversation that might get us somewhere, if there is no point in membership, then the prospect we face is to become a nation of drifters, seeking from private motion that sense of progress that public life is supposed to provide when it works well. Well, it isn't working at present, and that means journalism can't work, either.

It seems to me that a large and influential company like Gannett, which is a home for so many serious journalists, can ask of itself what it should also be asking of local communities: Are we telling the story of our public life in

a way that invites people in, and gives them a task? Are we doing everything we can to improve public dialogue so that it meets its deepest challenges—solving problems, coping with difference? Are we trying everything we can try to engage those who are cut off from the community? Are we serious about proving that politics can work for citizens, and are we demanding from people that they behave as citizens if they want politics to work? Are we behaving as exemplary citizens ourselves—listening well, working with others, claiming our rights as members of a community who also have a responsibility to the whole? Are we investing in public life, or, leery of such a commitment, are we practicing the great American art of public relations?
—From Jay Rosen, remarks to Gannett Company editors and publishers, Roslyn, Virginia, May 10, 1995

· ·

As a challenge to the corporate minds at Gannett these remarks were rather mild, aiming for a glancing blow at best. They could even be heard as praise for the "community leadership" approach. In retrospect, I thought I should have been far tougher—for instance, on the habit of shifting editors around so often. My role as publicist for an idea conflicted here with another duty of a professor: to defend civic values against their willing violators and speak truth to power, as academic critics often said. On the flight back to New York from National Airport, I rewrote my remarks in my head. But that is where the tougher version remained. "We believe in 'public journalism'—and have done it for years." The Gannett Company could go public, too. When it did, I felt a lot less comfortable in the company of my own ideas.

These tales of alarm and lapses in judgment—Tom Moore's tactics at WXYZ, watching the *San Jose Mercury News* go off in a disquieting direction, seeing Gannett twist public journalism its way—were part of the adventure of public journalism. Not the heart of it, I would say, but not a mutant strain, either. "Design flaw or driver error?" Perhaps a better way of putting it is to recognize a few perils in going public. Ideas will be co-opted and watered down for use. Experiments will go awry and occasionally do more harm than good. Rhetorical fires, once set, will race out of control. Speak a civic tongue and commercial interests, chasing profits, will pick it up. Media will borrow legitimacy from journalism with no intention of paying it back. Put your message into play and it will return to you in distorted form.

Or: It is one thing to think about the public sphere, another to enter into it.

9 What Was Public Journalism?

The Idea in Built Form

In 1982, the critic Leslie Fiedler asked "What was literature?" knowing, of course, that literature in some form would go on. In a similar spirit, we can ask what public journalism was, while recognizing that it still is—out there, under development.[1] Some initial answers, then: Public journalism took five forms.

- First, it was an *argument*, a way of thinking about what the press should be doing, or, as I have termed it, a different story about journalists' predicament and the general state of public life in America. The story went something like this:

  Journalists would do well to develop an approach that can (1) address people as citizens, potential participants in public affairs, rather than victims or spectators, (2) help the political community act upon, rather than just learn about, its problems, (3) improve the climate of public discussion, rather than simply watch it deteriorate, and (4) help make public life go well, so that it earns its claim on our attention. If they can find a way to do these things, journalists may in time restore public confidence in the press, reconnect with an audience that has been drifting away, rekindle the idealism that brought many of them into the craft, and contribute, in a more substantial way, to the health and future prospects of American democracy.

- Public journalism was also an *experiment*, a way of doing journalism that corresponded to the argument and was tried in hundreds of communities across the country, as journalists attempted to break out of familiar routines and make a different kind of contribution to public life.

- It was a *movement*, a loose network of practicing journalists, former journalists who wanted to improve their craft, academics and researchers with ideas to lend and studies that might help, foundations and think tanks that gave financial assistance and sanctuary, and other like-minded folk who wanted to contribute to a rising spirit of reform.

- It was a *debate*, an often heated conversation within the press and with others outside it about the proper role of the institution at a time of trouble. This debate was about the wisdom and dangers of both the argument and the experiment. Because it was largely conducted by the press, it also revealed some of the habits of mind that public journalism was trying to question in the first place.

- Public journalism was an *adventure*, an open-ended quest for another ethic in the press. The adventure had no fixed goal, no central office, no clear formula for success, no sharp boundary between itself and other varieties of civic work, and no limits on who might join in. Most of all, no one really knew where the quest might lead. Of course, I am being somewhat romantic when I call it an adventure, but there was romance in the idea, too. Among certain journalists, love of craft met a renewed love of democracy. The two hit the road together, not knowing what they would find.[2]

By becoming an argument, an experiment, a movement, a debate, and an adventure, public journalism emerged into what architects call "built form." It is one thing to imagine what buildings and urban spaces can be. It's another to bring imagination forward into houses we inhabit, places we can go. So it was with public journalism. As an idea or argument it appeared as one thing, in built form another. The variety of experiments that appeared on newspaper pages, the national movement and lively debate that grew up around the notion, the news articles and commentary that appeared in print and other venues, the spirit of adventure among people who committed themselves to the idea, the variety of institutions that became involved—all show the idea etched into public space. If we ask, then, what public journalism was, one answer is the five forms it took, listed above. But there were others, for which another set of terms is required.

A climate of mind. When people who are scattered about a profession, aided by others outside it with similar aims, begin to convene and confer;

when they learn from each other's experiments and come together to reflect on what they are doing; when a style of thinking and a way of working merge under a common name; when some journalists and what they are doing become the subject of reporting and dispute among others who are watching the experiment, we can point to the emergence of a widening field of mind, where ideas and possibilities are in play.

In 1995, Cole Campbell, then editor in Norfolk, said that he and his staff were pursuing "a big idea," which he called "a gift to us from Davis Merritt, Jr., editor of the *Wichita Eagle*." (Merritt had earlier visited the Norfolk newsroom.) "Buzz Merritt defines a successful community as one in which the people know what's happening and take responsibility for it," Campbell said. Journalists in Norfolk felt inspired by this vision and wanted to figure out what it meant for them, which is what I mean by a climate of mind. Through seminars, weekend retreats, on-site visits, panel discussions, and other forms of exchange, public journalism became a learning environment that stretched from newsroom to newsroom.[3]

Those outside the movement but interested in it also contributed by giving their advice and criticism. When Mark Jurkowitz, media critic of the *Boston Globe*, pointed to a "great middle ground of observers" who applaud the goal of reconnecting with citizens but worry about "letting the public drive the journalistic mission," he was illuminating one of civic journalism's challenges: how to reach people who were neither critics nor supporters with better arguments that addressed some of the relevant fears. "Journalism needs strengthening, not repudiation," said Geneva Overholser of the *Washington Post*. This was fair warning to the idea's advocates: don't trash the profession in the name of improving it. Jurkowitz and Overholser were part of the climate of thought that surrounded public journalism, although they did not place themselves under its banner.[4]

A style of commitment. Recall the words of Max Jennings, who, as editor of the *Dayton Daily News*, said he was beginning to think that journalists ought to be making discussion instead of just covering it. Making discussion implies a commitment to doing it well, which means pursuing certain virtues. To the journalist's commandment against undue interference in political life Jennings added a second priority: the production of a civic asset, genuine dialogue, to go with an honest and accurate report.

Gil Thelen, editor of the *State* in Columbia, South Carolina, spoke in a similar vein when he coined the term "committed observer." He used it to describe a newspaper that promised continuity of interest to those involved in public discussions, if the discussions showed some promise. Commitment and observation are traditionally seen as opposites in the press. By combining them into one ethic, Thelen's phrase opened room for a fresh approach. The drive to remain detached from all civic activity was joined by another imperative: giving sustained visibility to public talk when it might lead somewhere.[5]

Thelen's committed observer and Jennings's desire to make discussion happen are just two examples of the different style of commitment that public journalism encouraged. Other editors, like Merritt in Wichita, decided that urging eligible voters to use the ballot box was something the newspaper could do without compromising itself. Inviting citizens and community to groups to work across racial and ethnic lines, as the *Akron Beacon Journal* did, was an attempt to create an improved public climate: we'll give you a place to meet and provide the coffee; the rest is up to you. "One thing we should be willing to stand for as journalists is high quality public dialogue," said Tom Hamburger of the *Star-Tribune* in Minneapolis. "Not only should we call for quality, we can go on to advocate it and suggest ways to bring it about." In general, public journalism tried to enlarge the range of permissible goods to which the press might commit itself, while retaining safe distance from partisan causes, political parties, and special interests.[6]

A disturbance in the hierarchy of influence. Imagine a cultural pattern in which the life of the America theater begins on Broadway and radiates outward from there. People flock to New York to see the most exciting and original plays, critics review them, and the productions move outward from Broadway to regional theaters, which present their own versions. Now picture another pattern, more like our present one, in which original plays are written and produced in regional playhouses or university settings, and later become the dramas featured in Broadway's best houses. Action that once flowed from center to margin now moves in the opposite direction. This reversal of flow also means that a cultural monopoly is breaking down. New York has to look outward for new and exciting work, where others once looked to New York.

Something like this—not as dramatic or complete—happened with public journalism. Ideas and experiments began to flow from Wichita, Dayton, Norfolk, Colorado Springs, Portland, Charlotte, and other places where editors read the *New York Times* and *Washington Post* and said to themselves, "We're doing something different." Matt Storin, editor of the *Boston Globe*, caught the essence of this shift in a 1996 address to civic journalists. Storin made clear his deep respect for the *Times* and the *Post* as national newspapers with a strong commitment to public service. "Still," he said, "I wonder if they are in the best position to judge what the editors in Wichita, Sioux Falls, Charlotte and Kansas City and elsewhere deem as their proper role in communities."

The *Post* was the dominant newspaper in a government town, where politics and daily life were virtually synonymous. The *Times*, to be frank, was an elite paper. If the *Globe* reached the same proportion of the Boston area that the *Times* did in New York, Storin said, his circulation would drop to 170,00 from about 500,000. This was not a slam at the executives at the *Post* or the *Times*. "As good as these newspapers are," said Storin, "I think it hurts our business when we only look to those rather unusual publications with their specialized audiences and let them influence what flies for the rest of us."

Criticism from New York and Washington was fine, he added. It ought to continue. But "we editors in the hinterlands" should "do whatever we think it best to reach out to apathetic citizens" and show the way to solving problems, Storin said. Boston's sophisticated market and the *Globe*'s richly talented newsroom were not quite the hinterlands, but he had made his point: Forget about influencing the *Times* and the *Post*. They are different animals. But don't allow yourself to be limited by their influence, either.

Influence beginning to flow from margin to margin, while the center responds with criticism and scattered support, was an upset in the traditional hierarchy of the American press. The usual pattern was quite different. "Most of what gets noticed in our business," Storin said, "is what is read in New York and Washington with the exception of when one of the rest of us does something wrong." The movement for civic journalism redirected this flow—without, however, reversing it. Wichita did not began to instruct New York, but Wichita did suggest to Charlotte another way to do election coverage, and Charlotte looked beyond New York for inspiration.[7]

A passage between journalism and a broader current of reform. During the years of public journalism's gradual emergence, another and larger movement was taking place. Theorists of American democracy, civic organizations that tried to engage people in public life, foundations looking to make a difference, local leaders and activists searching for inspiration—all began to reexamine what democracy was and how it could be strengthened from the bottom up.

There was no single name for this development, no central agency directing it. Many strands of thought could be found within it, and what it inspired moved in multiple—at times, conflicting—directions. But there were some overarching themes, chiefly the attempt to find a more participatory politics that focused on problem solving, citizen deliberation, and a quest for the common good that was more than the sum of individual preferences.

Books like Benjamin Barber's *Strong Democracy*, E. J. Dionne's *Why Americans Hate Politics*, James Fishkin's *Democracy and Deliberation*, Jean Bethke Elshtain's *Democracy on Trial*, Robert Putnam's *Making Democracy Work*, and Michael Sandel's *Democracy's Discontents* addressed these core themes. The "communitarian" movement—inspired by Sandel's writings, the work of Robert Bellah and his colleagues, and the efforts of scholar Amitai Etzioni—was a further expression of the same impulse.[8]

Organizations like the National Civic League and a network it helped to found, the Alliance for National Renewal, used phrases like collaborative problem solving and civic renewal to describe their aims. They went to work on bringing these phrases alive, mostly by reaching out to citizens at the local level. Politics for People was the title David Mathews of the Kettering Foundation gave to his reflections on a related problem: finding a responsible public voice that can better inform politics. Around 1995, Kettering joined with other foundations in thinking through an approach called civil investing, a long-term strategy that would try to build civic capacity—the resources people have for solving their own problems—rather than "fix" things through an influx of grant money and a demand for quick results.[9]

A report prepared for the Rockefeller Foundation in 1995 found thousands of civic groups involved in what it called community revitalization. Some were formal organizations with boards and professional staffs; others were looser in form. "Many of revitalization's actors come from the progressive and liberal traditions of American life," the report read. "But initiatives to build and rebuild communities definitely cut across partisan lines, to include groups like the National Center for Neighborhood Enterprise and the Empowerment Network, associated with the Republican Party. The Heritage Foundation's *Policy Review* regularly reports on grassroots community revitalization and empowerment initiatives."

The authors of the report grouped public journalism with a wide range of revitalization efforts, under the theory that all partook of the same spirit: a desire to make room in public life for citizens, whose problems were going unaddressed through more traditional means. Most of the initiatives were local, although they sometimes spread through national networks of like-minded folk. Among the developments seen as similar in aim were

- "urban partnerships" bringing together leading actors in the community to tackle outstanding problems;
- "collaborative community problem solving," in which groups without matching agendas find a way to cooperate where their interests overlap;
- "leadership development" groups that identify emerging leaders and encourage them to put their talents to civic use;
- efforts at conflict resolution that experiment with new ways to settle disputes and avoid the spiral of escalating mistrust;
- community service, in which the spirit of volunteerism was being revived among students and others;
- deliberative discussion forums, which were drawing citizens into face-to-face dialogue about public issues;
- neighborhood and community associations, growing in number around the country;
- civic work by churches and other religious institutions, which had become more vital to communities as government funds dried up;
- and, finally, public journalism, described as a "promising opening for the reassertion of the journalists' responsibility to help create an informed and problem-solving citizenry."[10]

These varied developments point to another thing public journalism was: a passageway between an experiment in the press and the efforts of other social thinkers and civic actors—all of whom thought that politics and civic life could be improved, all of whom were at work on the problem. "What does it take to make democracy work?" was a question being asked all around the contemporary scene. "And what is the role of the press in making it work?" was a piece of the puzzle the movement added.

An intersection between press and academy. When trained intelligence traps itself too narrowly within an academic field, other fields of mind may suffer. This, I think, had happened to American journalism. The university was quoted often by the press, but how often was it consulted as the news media assembled its moving picture of the world? Where were the teams of journalists and scholars working together on the best portrayal possible? Or the points of exchange between the richest thinking in the university and the most ambitious reporting? On class, culture, economic trends, political divides, taxes, schools, families, welfare, health care, and a host of other common concerns, both the press and the university had things to say. But they rarely collaborated to produce a richer public narrative.

Why should this be so? Reporters and professors do not work the same way, but they are, after all, in the same business: trying to understand what's going on, struggling to comprehend the public interest, arguing about the proper lens to put on their viewfinders. Reporters could always tap the university for expert knowledge or a colorful sound bite, but these were brief encounters, not a regular meeting of minds. Public journalism made an attempt at overcoming this divide. Its efforts were limited in scope and involved a small group of people; but they led to a traffic in ideas that moved both ways.[11]

A large body of scholarly work on how the news media habitually frame issues, for example, began to inform the thinking of some editors and reporters, as they struggled to improve their lens on the contemporary scene. "Framing the news" thus moved from its spot in the academic literature to a more public setting—the newsroom, which began to understand its own rituals using tools of mind that professors had long employed. Steve Smith of the *Gazette* in Colorado Springs was one editor who encouraged his staff to think aloud about civic framing and experiment with the results.

This flow went in both directions. Harry Boyte and Nancy Kari, two scholars writing on the theme of public work, were able to tap public journalism to illustrate what they had in mind—another model of democratic politics that gave more room to citizens. Academic theorizing, valuable in itself, was here enriched by the activity of journalists who were putting related ideas into practice. In *The Voice of the People,* a book about deliberative democracy, political scientist James Fishkin could discuss the people in public journalism who had taken the principle to heart. Boyte and Fishkin were just two of the scholars who joined in seminars of the Project on Public Life and the Press, where their work drew an enthusiastic response.[12]

Meanwhile, a number of journalists were led to reflect on the argument in the 1920s between Walter Lippmann and John Dewey about the nature of the modern public. James Fallows in *Breaking the News,* Buzz Merritt in a column for readers in Wichita, and Cole Campbell in remarks to a civic journalism conference were among those who re-joined a debate that had rested for years on campus library shelves. Why did this matter? Because the university and the press were two vital public resources that might improve each other, if the proper points of contact could be found. If journalists were resuming a discussion that scholars had kept alive, both institutions might benefit.[13]

As Dewey wrote in 1927, a "genuine social science"—one the entire

society could use—would not confine itself to scholarly and technical journals. It would also shine through in the daily press, where "learned books
and articles" can "supply and polish tools of inquiry." The knowledge that a
public requires to arrive at sound judgments "must be contemporary and
quotidian," not lofty and abstruse. The press was current, dealt with daily
life, and reached a broad audience. Social science was more patient in its
inquiry, sought a deeper grasp of current patterns, and appealed to trained
intellect. The ideal form of intelligence, Dewey thought, would combine the
strengths of each. Journalism and scholarship needed each other; and an
engaged public needed both. In the movement for public journalism some
journalists and some scholars found they needed each other to get where
they were going: toward a workable understanding of our common life, and
how best to communicate about it.[14]

What was public journalism? I have tried to describe it in built form. It
was a climate of mind, a style of commitment, a disturbance in the professional hierarchy, a passage between journalism and other attempts to
strengthen American democracy, and a point of contact between the press
and the university. It was also an argument, an experiment, a movement, a
debate, and a kind of adventure.

If all these were public journalism, what did they accomplish? Our usual
approach to that question is to talk about effects. Did voter turnout rise
when journalists did more to engage people in the issues? Did readership
increase at newspapers that learned how to start where citizens start? Did
communities have an easier time reaching resolution or finding the will to
act on common problems? Did the political climate improve because the
news media tried to play a more constructive role? What scattered evidence
we have cannot answer these questions in any definitive way. Only a handful
of social scientists have tried to assess the effects of public journalism. Some
of the results have been encouraging, others have not.

In "Civic Lessons," a 1997 report funded by the Pew Charitable Trusts,
researchers interviewed residents, community leaders, and journalists in four
cities where significant work was under way: Charlotte, San Francisco, Madison, and Binghamton, New York. Among the report's findings:

• Public awareness of civic journalism initiatives in all four cities was high.
  In Madison, the "We the People" project brought together the *Wisconsin
  State Journal,* Wisconsin Public Television, Wisconsin Public Radio,

and WISC-TV, the local CBS affiliate. The partnership sponsored a series of televised forums featuring citizens who deliberate together on current issues, backed by intensive newspaper reporting on the same themes. According to a random survey, 52 percent of local residents were aware of "We the People." In Charlotte, a startling 84 percent of those surveyed knew of the "Taking Back Our Neighborhoods" project, the yearlong effort by the *Charlotte Observer* and several broadcast partners to study the causes of crime and prod the community to act. In San Francisco, a more crowded media market, 40 percent of respondents were aware of "Voice of the Voter," an attempt to center election coverage on citizen's concerns. In Binghamton, 51 percent knew of "Facing Our Future," a cooperative effort by the local newspaper, three broadcast stations, and the State University of New York at Binghamton to stimulate community-wide discussion on rebuilding the local economy.

- Those who knew of these efforts generally gave them high marks. From interviews with local residents, the researchers concluded: "Citizens exposed to civic journalism want more such reporting." In Madison, 62 percent said "We the People" had gotten them to think more about politics. In Charlotte, the figure was 59 percent; in San Francisco, 49 percent; and in Binghamton, 53 percent. The study also asked whether people aware of the projects felt they "wanted to be more involved in making this city a better place to live," as a result of what they had seen and heard. In Madison, 64 percent agreed with the statement; in Charlotte, 78 percent; in San Francisco, 47 percent; and in Binghamton, 67 percent.

- Following its creation in 1992, Madison's "We the People" project had sunk deep roots in the community. The researchers found that the name had become a verb in local parlance: "The partners have all been approached by civic leaders asking them to 'We the People' a given issue. The term occurs repeatedly in both public and private settings." As reflected in this common usage, "We the People" began to be seen as a public asset with tangible benefits to the community.

- In Charlotte, "Taking Back Our Neighborhoods" focused its initial efforts on the Seversville neighborhood, a predominately black community struggling with a high crime rate and frustrated by the lack of response from the city. Reporters spent six weeks on the streets of Seversville talking to people about crime, its causes, consequences, and what might be done. Two public meetings where held so that journalists could get a better handle on how people saw the problem. "On the spot, more than 60 residents signed up to participate in a new Crime Watch in Seversville—a number that quadrupled within weeks." In July 1994, the *Observer* published an exhaustive report on its findings, which consumed almost seven pages. It portrayed what life what was like for the people there and included a "needs page" that outlined what the neighborhood could do to combat rising crime and what the city might do for Seversville. The broadcast partners ran similar reports. This pattern was repeated over the next six months until the project had profiled ten neighborhoods and their needs. By the spring of 1995, according to the researchers, the Charlotte project had "inspired more than 700 groups or individuals to volunteer to help" and "moved several local law firms to file public nuisance suits, pro bono, to close neighborhood crack houses." Focusing on the inner city, "Taking Back Our Neighborhoods" also "raised awareness of the City Within a City among people who previously knew little or nothing about that part of town." The project "prompted residents of the neighborhoods covered to discuss their common problems and join forces on behalf of better services." And it "stimulated a wide-ranging group of residents to cross racial lines and class boundaries to begin working together in new ways."

- In all four cities, researchers found that the public journalism approach "typically had less impact within the newsrooms involved than in the community at large." At times, the projects were seen as top-down efforts driven by news executives. In Binghamton, there were doubts about management's commitment to the enterprise, even among those who were enthusiastic about "Facing Our Future." The report stated: "Newsroom critics at all sites asked why outside funding [from the Pew Center] was necessary for the news organizations to undertake projects that were being promoted as central to their organizational mission."[15]

In a report sponsored by the Poynter Institute for Media Studies in 1996, researchers Deborah Potter of the Poynter Institute and Philip Meyer of the University of North Carolina studied what they call "citizen-based journalism" across twenty different markets. They first surveyed newspaper journalists in all these regions to determine who among them planned to use public journalism principles in their coverage of the 1996 election. Some did; some did not. This allowed the report to rank papers by their intent to do more citizen-based reporting.

The researchers then interviewed local residents in the twenty markets before and after the election (along with a control group that was questioned only after the vote, to adjust for any changes in behavior that might result from the experience of being interviewed twice). Potter and Meyer also studied the content of the newspapers' election coverage, to see if a determination to practice public journalism showed up in the kind of news offered to citizens. Among their findings:

- Newspapers that had intended to practice public journalism ran more stories devoted to policy issues and fewer that mentioned horse-race ("who's ahead?") polls.

- Citizens in the high-intent cities learned somewhat more about the presidential candidates during the course of the campaign than did citizens in regions where public journalism was least in evidence.

- More frequent mention of horse-race polls did not affect people's interest in the campaign or their knowledge of the candidates. This contradicted what the authors called a "cherished belief" among some public journalists that such polls "distract voters from the substance of the election and keep them from learning about issues."

- Citizens were asked, "Would you say the news media are run by a few big interests looking out for themselves or that they are run for the benefit of all the people?" Most of those interviewed across all twenty markets said that a few big interests prevail. But in the ten cities where the commitment to public journalism was strongest, mistrust of the news media was weakest, although this could not be traced to election coverage because the findings did not change much during the 1996 campaign. Nonetheless: "Media bashing declines as citizen-based journalism increases, even after the effects of party, age, race and education have been filtered out." Something that public journalists were already doing before the election may be involved, the report suggested.

- As Potter and Meyer wrote: "In theory, citizen-based journalism should increase the rate of voter turnout and other kinds of political participation. We found no such effects."[16]

In May 1997, the Pew Center released a report on the effectiveness of public journalism during elections. It studied the efforts of the *Record* in Bergen County, New Jersey, during a hard-fought Senate campaign in 1996. For nine weeks, the *Record* devoted fifty-four full pages to issues-based coverage that attempted to frame the Senate contest as a constructive debate, rather than a shouting match. In surveys and focus groups after the election, a series of findings emerged, most of which showed that the paper's efforts had little effect in a public climate saturated with negative ads and candidate attacks. Among the report's findings:

- Discussions with readers after the election left the editors "feeling stunned and somewhat shaken" that impressions left by the campaign "seemed to have been shaped mostly by the candidates' commercials," not the newspaper's efforts.

- Only 19 percent of readers could recall seeing "Campaign Central," the title the *Record* gave to its initiative. A voter's guide to issues and positions did better; it was remembered by 43 percent. Still, 44 percent of the newspaper's audience named television as their most important source of campaign news.

- Readers of the *Record* did not reach the end the campaign with more knowledge than readers of other newspapers in the state. Just 42 percent of the paper's readers could name either Senate candidate after the election.

- The *Record*'s readership was no more likely to vote, to join in discussion about the election, or to care who won the seat vacated by Senator Bill Bradley on his retirement.

Viewed from the perspective of effects, these were plainly discouraging results. From another angle—the spirit of experiment—the *Record*'s efforts and its follow-up research contributed greatly to the enterprise of public journalism. They suggested how difficult it was to make a dent in a media environment overtaken by television and political advertising. They showed that voter's guides were among the most useful products journalists could offer during a campaign. They raised important questions for further study, such as: "Was *The Record*'s public journalism coverage 'blunted' by the continuation of conventional campaign stories elsewhere in the paper?"[17]

In any genuine experiment, discovering what doesn't work is as important as learning what does. As results come in, new and better experiments may follow. The point is not to succeed in every attempt, but to keep trying. Taken together, the studies highlighted here show public journalism in midcourse. Some of it was clearly working; some was not. In general, citizens seemed to respond; but this was not always the case. There were initiatives that reached deeply into the life of the community and changed people's expectations of the press. There were others that passed with little effect.

A different way to judge what mattered about public journalism is to examine the professional culture of the press, which took deep root in newsrooms, trade journals, industry conferences, and debates among the high priests of the craft. This culture also lived in the shared beliefs and daily habits of the press tribe, which was an anxious tribe through much of the 1990s. Doubts and misgivings emerged over a range of problems—commercial pressures, technological change, public anger, collapsing standards, and a diminishing sense of high purpose.

If the 1988 campaign began a period of self-scrutiny on these themes, the same worries were present ten years later, when the country endured the investigation and impeachment trial of President Bill Clinton. The perception of a disconnect between the class of journalists and the concerns of ordinary Americans became an article of common sense—a news story in its own right—during the long struggle. Profound questions about political character, the fate of the public sphere, and the zone of privacy were unavoidable, not only in mainstream journalism but in the nation at large. Nothing was settled by the acquittal in Clinton's trial. Rather, everything seemed more unsettled.[18]

But this was a kind of progress. There could be little doubt that journalists were implicated in the politics of scandal, although it was equally clear that many other forces were at work. If the zone of privacy was going to erode further, everyone knew that the press would be involved. In the coming years, reporters either would or would not be asking about such things as the sex lives and marriages of candidates. They either would or would not be trafficking in rumor. Whatever decision they made was sure to matter at almost every level of public life. But would they arrive at a conscious choice, or allow the drift of things to decide for them? Here, I think, the movement for public journalism made an important contribution. It did not have a proven answer for all the perplexing questions brought by scandal politics. Rather, it allowed a minority view to be held in a culture—journalism's own—where majority opinion is visibly strong.

Despite their self-image as cranky individualists, journalists are inclined to do as their peers do. The popular imagination records this fact in countless portraits of a hungry press pack, bounding up the courthouse steps to engulf the key witness, star attorney, or victorious defendant. In movie after Hollywood movie, variations on this scene appear. It is perhaps our most potent image of press power, linked through a vast relay of signs to our experience of modern celebrity, judicial trial, political renown, sudden fame. But to watch reporters and camera crews gang up, we don't need to visit the video store. An evening of television news will suffice, since this is a scene so common that its repeat appearance has been given several names.

The "feeding frenzy" is political scientist Larry Sabato's term for pack journalism. His book documents case after case in the national press. Less menacing is the phrase "the boys on the bus," after Timothy Crouse's classic work on campaign reporting. "Feeding the beast" is how the same phenomenon looks to a White House press secretary who must master the art or suffer the consequences.[19] It would not be possible to feed the beast, there would be no beast to be fed, if reporters and editors did not think and behave as one. Journalists go where they know their peers go. They ask what others in the corps would ask. The pressures of daily news work, which involve remaking the world every twenty-four hours (or more often), put a further premium on consensus behavior. The safe thing to do is follow the pack.

This is not to say there aren't many acts of dissent from herd judgment; there are. Still, the instinct suggests something significant about our press. It is not a monolith; rather, its members stay members by seeking a similar brand of news. By seeking it, they also produce a common culture for themselves, which curves back to exert its own influence on the tribe. If journalists compete hard to get the story first, get it right, and get it whole, they do not compete as vigorously on the terrain of civic priorities, over their choice of master narratives, or in the selection of a world view, a public philosophy, to guide their efforts.

World view? Public philosophy? We don't have one, we don't need one, said many in the mainstream press. It's our job to find out what's happening, not to decide what's good for the nation or the community. This attitude, which had its honorable and dubious sides, was a further expression of newsroom culture. Michael Janeway, former editor of the *Boston Globe* and later a journalism school dean, put it well:

> The press says as a matter of professional identity, and I myself have said as a journalist, that our business is facts, the public has a right to know them, freedom has a price, we let the chips fall where they may, we are not in the philosophy business. . . . It says, no one got into this business to be loved, weighty reflection about our role is for journalism schools and op-ed pages, not for the reporter and the editor under the gun or on the trail of the next Watergate.

In 1998, the next Watergate came to pass during the impeachment trauma. "The press presumed to understand what was important, and what was not, in a way that many Americans came to resent," according to one account in the *New York Times*. What is this but a problem of philosophy, a delicate exercise in moral authority? Tim Russert, Washington bureau chief for NBC, said that when he and his colleagues focus so relentlessly on a single story, as they did for more than a year, "we may find ourselves driving the story."[20] With this offhand admission, the foundations of American journalism begin slowly to crack. For there is little in the mind of the mainstream press, no usable language or reliable map, to instruct journalists in their intermittent role as event driver. It happens, but when it happens the people involved are at sea, intellectually. They cannot explain to themselves or us where they are driving things or why they have chosen a particular route. "Press Debates Where It Wants to Take the Current Scandal in Washington." That headline we are unlikely to see.

A culture that disavows weighty reflection will always find it hard to cope with such episodes, in which the story of what's happening and the happenings themselves merge to form a third category—the news-saturated event, a hybrid of politics, journalism, and, increasingly, the entertainment media.[21] If this hybrid exists, then so does a problem of philosophy among newspeople, who must decide what they want to contribute during these ordeals, knowing that they help create or sustain them.

Serious journalists take pride in their work as different from entertainment, although they are constantly noting how the distinction gets blurred. At the same time, they set themselves apart from politics and worry when the border between the two is breached. We are fortunate that they stake their identity on these separations, since the pressure to erase them is insidious and intense. We need newsrooms that will hold the line against crass commercialism and ideological temptation, but this only tells us what threatens public service, not what the service should accomplish.

Max Frankel, who spent his entire career at the *New York Times,* wrote with pride about how his newspaper "frames the intellectual and emotional agenda of serious Americans."[22] He may be overstating it, but not by much. If framing an agenda is something that responsible journalists can do, not only at the *Times* but elsewhere in the culture, then we might expect a healthy public discourse on the subject, and a lively debate among editors on how best to practice this intricate art. We might hope that journalism schools would teach courses on the skills required, that ethics codes would offer principled advice, that news organizations would tell us something— anything—about their thinking on such matters. But what do we find?

Critics who constantly accuse the press of "having an agenda," journalists who generally regard these complaints as obtuse, self-serving, or unfair.

Problems of identity (are we observers or players, chroniclers or agenda setters?) are closely related to problems of trust. If we know that the front page is not amusement or ideology, this helps us trust in the *Times,* and in every other news team that obeys the same scruple. But it's not clear where trust is supposed to reside when the act under review is frame fixing or agenda setting. "We frame it like it is"? Not very convincing, that. Even more troublesome are all the instances of the press becoming a factor in the events it portrays. "We may find ourselves driving the story." The typical pattern is subtler, of course. The press is organizing our attention, fitting it into narrative grooves and conversational templates. Or it is casting the lead characters—not telling them what to say, but knowing full well what they are likely to say. Journalists act when they pose urgent questions, though the answers are left to others. Whatever the answers are, the reporters' questions are the ones that get asked.

Knowing these things, we are wrong to assume that our investment in news is well protected when journalists hold to an image of themselves as detached. "No one elected the press," E. J. Dionne wrote, "yet the press is now an intimate part of everything having to do with elections. The press is not there to make political decisions, yet everything the press does shapes those decisions." Where a crowd of journalists gathers, there will be a happening made for such a crowd. Where the priorities of the news media are clear, others will shape their own priorities accordingly. And in this back and forth motion the culture of news imprints a certain pattern on public life, even as public life springs up to be reported as news. As sociologist Michael Schudson has observed, "The news media necessarily incorporate into their work a certain view of politics, and they will either do so intelligently and critically or unconsciously and routinely."[23]

Here is the point at which detachment fails the press. It depletes the imagination of people who are caught up in the world they're trying to portray. The discipline required to separate news from views, information from opinion, cannot do all the heavy lifting in journalism, although the work it does is honorable and necessary. There will always be times when the press is intimately involved in setting the terms of public debate, composing a narrative line, moving problems up and down the attention ladder, or casting about for heroes and villains. It is a truism to point out that such things require good judgment. Done one way, they can always be done

another. Schudson's point is that there's an alternative to conscious deliberation about the crafting of the present by journalism. The alternative is to say,
"that's not in our job description," which really means: we'll let our routines
decide for us.

But a routine cannot generate alternatives to itself. Until press people
ask themselves what sort of politics needs to thrive alongside the occasional
eruptions of history; until they inquire into the forms of reporting, analysis,
and commentary that will let a problem-solving ethic come consistently
alive; until they can claim some further responsibility for the quality of
deliberation and debate, which they do so much to affect, the conditions
that make for trouble will remain in place. And the power of the press to
remake itself will be displaced onto ingrained habits and peer pressure.

Granted, the serious press cannot control what happens at the intersection of media, politics, and public sentiment. But it has control enough to
steer itself in a recovered direction or two. Public journalism tried to suggest
one by heading for the places where civic engagement met the news, news
strengthened conversation, and conversation treated the problems of a democracy. There, it said, is the best chance to connect with a live public. And
there is where the press can find the right kind of agenda, in full recognition
of its role.

"Citizens want us to do a better job in helping them and their communities address tough problems," wrote Cole Campbell. "They turn to us as
one source, but not necessarily an exalted one, in piecing together their sense
of the world. And they can see in what we publish and broadcast, despite our
protestations that we only cover what's before us, that we have an underlying
philosophy directing us to cast our coverage nets in one direction and not
another." Which direction is needed? Campbell found his answer in another
question: "How can we—as familiar strangers, as a democratic culture, as a
political community—have better conversations?" Journalism serves well
when it actively creates that possibility, he said. "We cannot give up description of the present," Campbell added, "it is essential to directing attention,
testing reality and framing issues. But we should not let it dominate our
mindset and our type set and our studio sets. We should make equal room
for conceiving of alternative ways of living in a just world."[24]

In advancing strange propositions like these, public journalism did not
appeal to a majority in the press. With few exceptions, elite opinion was
wary or hostile. But by enduring as a minority sentiment, an approach that
seemed right to some, the movement demonstrated that divergence was

possible in the consensus-driven culture of the newsroom. This was an accomplishment. There were different ways to align the news with its natural constituency, an active public. There were different claims to make on the identity of public servant. There were different definitions of what mattered, tied to other ideas of the good. Not all of them were good ideas. But it was useful for the press to sift and judge among them, and to have on record a national experiment in journalism during a time of creeping doubt.

10 Conclusion

What Are Journalists For?

The title of this book is a question we need to ask for every age: what are journalists for? It can be read in at least two ways. First, why do we need journalists? What do they do for us and what could they be doing, if they wanted to do more? Second, what do they stand for? And what are they willing to stand up for, as public-spirited professionals?

Prevailing wisdom in the press has a reply to these questions. Journalists, in this view, give us timely information about matters of common importance; they entertain and enlighten us with compelling stories; they act as our surrogate or watchdog before the high and mighty, asking sharp questions and demanding straight answers; they expose wrongdoing and the abuse of public trust; and they put before us a range of views, through opinion forums marked as such. What do journalists stand for? They uphold the public's right to know, a spirit of openness and honesty in the conduct of public business, the free flow of information and ideas, along with truthfulness, accuracy, balance, and fair play in the news. Beyond that, standing up for things is best left to others. Journalists do not join the parade because their job is to report on the parade.

From the 1920s on, this philosophy helped create a strong institution—profitable, powerful, and, on the whole, dedicated to public service. The answer sketched above has served the press well. But if the press is not well now, if it has problems that imperil its future, can it continue to rely on that answer alone? Suppose, then, that the standard view is not wrong, but wrongly begun. To know what we need from journalists, we have to say something about the times in which we live.

A glance at press history shows how often the role of the press has changed. During America's break from Britain, journalists took sides as revolutionaries or loyalists, mounting arguments and sounding alarms. In the early history of the republic, they were creatures of political parties or servants of the merchant classes. Then, in the mid–nineteenth century, they began to address a rising middle class and working people, finding a mass audience for news and the advertising revenue that brought independence from political patrons.

In the twentieth century they have professionalized themselves, moving from mere independence to objectivity and evolving into a quasi-official adversary in the political sphere. They have learned to employ radio, television, and now the Internet as platforms for their work, enlarging its human dimension and adding new roles to an expanding repertoire. Before television there were no anchorpeople. But now the anchor as a cultural figure presides for us during wars, elections, and other moments of high drama. This is journalism evolving in order to remain contemporary, for if it is not contemporary, of the times, it cannot tell us about the times. And that is its job.

What, then, keeps the craft of journalism current, in tune with the society whose story it seeks to tell? The answer seems obvious. The press stays current by following current affairs. It keeps track of events simply by going about its task, which is to bring us the news. Newsrooms, in this way of thinking, are self-informing places. They educate their inhabitants to a shifting sense of the world by sending them out to report on it. But take a closer look at this logic. When a reporter leaves the office to attend a school board meeting, she leaves with an assignment: bring back a story, her editors say. She also departs with certain ideas in her head about where the story is found. A school board meeting is considered a good place to discover what's happening because that's where official business comes into public view. Voices are heard there, decisions get made, policy is set. Moreover, the people on the board are public representatives. What they do counts because their job is to know what counts for us—and to act accordingly.

So inside the report on last night's board meeting is an idea or two. And these ideas are what bring us the news, as much as the correspondent who bears them. A reporter who believes that what's happening in the schools begins with the classroom and ends with the board room, leaves the office with a different map for finding the education story. Thus, we cannot say much about the newsroom's ways of knowing unless we consider the ideas that lead reporters to want to know certain things. And here we come upon a weakness in the culture of the press. Its members want to believe that they are "not in the philosophy business," as Michael Janeway put it. But everything about their business suggests the opposite.[1]

Imagine, for a moment, that you are assigned to the health and medicine beat for a large metropolitan newspaper like the *Globe*. How can you do that job without a few ideas about health and medicine, an understanding that points to places where your subject takes reportable form? "Health," after all, is everywhere, in every home, but a reporter can't be everywhere, only those places where a story may be waiting. And if the story that's delivered doesn't hit home, if the issues it visits don't speak to the troubles that visit us, then the reason for this faulty connection may lie not in shoddy reporting but in the act of reasoning that sent a reporter out to find one sort of tale, rather than another. Without ideas that serve as daily viewfinders, journalists cannot see before them a reportable world. How good are these ideas? Only a press that consciously puts itself in the philosophy business can know.

From this perspective, journalism begins not with the search for information or story but with the models and metaphors that propel the search. As early as 1959, the press was being called the fourth branch of government, to take account of a new logic among Washington journalists: they were an addition to the Constitution's system of checks and balances, a permanent counterweight to government power. The idea of an adversarial press is just that: an idea about how the press should stand toward public officials and others in power. It borrows from the legal system and its adversarial ethic. It came alive in journalism after the McCarthy era, and it grew stronger in the aftermath of Vietnam and Watergate. Defended as an idea, there is much to say on behalf of an adversarial press. Where we would be without the aggressive questioning and other habits of scrutiny journalists developed as they put into practice this image of themselves? Further in the dark, no doubt. Doesn't official lying on the scale seen in postwar America deserve some response? I think it does. And when the press responded in the 1960s and 1970s, it demonstrated that different times call for different journalisms—different replies to the standing question, what are journalists for?[2]

The press cannot speak to the same country twice. Nor can it claim that its common paths to news are the only ones imaginable. Which is simply to say it's a big world out there, too big to be blanketed, even by an army of trained reporters. To cover the news is to judge what is newsworthy; such estimates of worth involve ideas about politics and power, images of democracy, views of culture and the individual, all of which are subject to change as common conditions remake themselves. In these ways and others, journalism requires imagination: some way of conjuring with the world so as to station yourself within it and draw news from it.[3]

In the end, it is not the United States Constitution but our own constitution, as a people, that tells us what we need from journalists. Not the eternal principles of journalism but the evolving puzzles of our time give the press its public standing, a secure place from which to operate, and beliefs about how to operate in the service of some good. Which good journalists will serve is not up to them alone, but to us and them, for there is no effective journalism without people on the other end who put it to some use.

With our television clickers we can vote for the news or against it; but this is only one way in which the country shapes the journalism it sees. When the Supreme Court says the press cannot be prevented from publishing the Pentagon Papers; when Congress declares that broadcasters must operate in the public interest; when universities agree to educate young journalists and give them a sense of calling; when advertisers shift their dollars about and permit one form of journalism to thrive while another withers; when donors ring their local public radio station and pledge money to keep it alive; when we cancel the metropolitan daily because a suburban paper reports better on the towns in which we live; when we drift in large numbers to the Internet, seeking there a new kind of connection—through these events and many more the nation makes and remakes the field of possibility for its press.

What kind of field are we sowing for serious journalism in turn-of-the-century America? And what should journalists be making from it, if they want their craft to thrive as a public service? As I have tried to show, the 1990s were years in which a number of prominent people in the mainstream press examined those questions. They took note of the troubles in their institution and began to call their colleagues to some sort of response. In earlier chapters, I highlighted the words of David Broder, who worried aloud about the public's gradual withdrawal from domestic politics amid election campaigns that were little more than media manipulation. The press should try to help reconnect politics and government and assert more strongly "the public's right to hear its concerns discussed." In the public climate he saw ahead, anything less, Broder said, is unacceptable.[4]

At a conference of journalists in 1995, Robert MacNeil, the longtime anchor of the *MacNeil-Lehrer News Hour* on PBS, gave an address that went well beyond the usual rhetoric about the press and its role in a free society. MacNeil drew the distinction between media (an industry rising) and journalism (a craft in trouble), and went on to ask how he and his colleagues could rescue some of their lost dignity in a hypercommercialized climate. It would take, he said, an enlargement of soul: "We have to remember, as journalists, that we may be observers but we are not totally disinterested observers. We are not social engineers, but each one of us has a stake in the health of this democracy. Democracy and the social contract that makes it work are held together by a delicate web of trust, and all of us in journalism hold edges of the web. We are not just amused bystanders, watching the idiots screw it up."[5]

Journalists not only tell us about the world, they are part of the structure that holds it up. For if their accounts prove trustworthy, the entire society can trust that its affairs are being brought into public view, made part of a consultable record. The history that is happening to us, and the history we are trying to make, become more intelligible when news is made well. But the news on its own cannot produce an informed public, a climate of trust, or an intelligible world. If people know about politics but trust no one in it, they are unlikely to take the news very seriously. The characters, after all, are known to be liars, cheats, or shameless self-servers, so why put any stock in what they're saying or doing? The story can be consumed instead for its entertainment value, as marketed on weeknights by Jay Leno and his accomplished gag writers at NBC's *Tonight Show*. Leno's late-evening monologue, the work of a comedian with perfect pitch, is political journalism, too—social commentary for an audience primed to treat politics as a joke.

In even the healthiest public climate, an honored space must be set aside for satirists like Leno. But can serious journalism have a place if the climate turns cynical, bewildered, and bored, if politics is regarded as a shadow play or fool's parade that runs on and on, but offers no hope of bettering our lives? Journalists held up the world, MacNeil asserted, because they were part of the social contract that made the country a democracy. The observer side of the journalist's self ended here, in the recognition that people in the press produce an important social good. They help make politics (and paying attention to it) worth our time and trouble.

They cannot just watch from the sidelines, jeering at what they see, for in the sound of that jeering is their job going to waste. MacNeil's warning, "We are not just amused bystanders, watching the idiots screw it up" means:

if they keep screwing up, and that's all we tell people, then we're the idiots, because Americans will quickly conclude that none of it matters. The house of politics cannot fall down and remain a compelling story. Only a doubled sense of professional self—the journalist as someone who holds up the world and also tells us about it—can show the way to "regaining dignity," the title of MacNeil's published remarks. "Let us take back the name of journalist," he said. "Let's try and rescue some young journalists before they run away with the media circus, or join the cult of infotainment and are beyond deprogramming. Names are important. We are what we call ourselves. And for 40 years I have been proud to call myself a journalist. I think media stinks!"[6]

"Media stinks." But it can stink and still succeed. Journalism, MacNeil noted, cannot. Two years later, Ted Koppel, a broadcaster with equally high standing among his peers, spoke out on a similar theme. Addressing an awards dinner sponsored by the Committee to Protect Journalists, Koppel took note of the extreme courage shown by reporters and photographers who document the horrors of the world in dangerous places such as war zones and under dictatorships. The dinner was held in honor of such people, who "antagonize those with money, political power and guns" and risk their lives on behalf of truth.

"We, on the other hand, tremble at nothing quite so much as the thought of boring our audiences," he said, referring to the majority of mainstream journalists. Antagonizing the rich and powerful did not involve "any great risk to our safety" in a free society where the adversarial role was well established. But journalism had other enemies in America: declining ad revenues, "diversification and the vertical integration of communications empires," as well as "the breezier, chattier styles" that mark the fading lines between news and entertainment.

> There is, after all, a haunting paradox in the notion that, even as we honor journalists abroad for [risking their lives], their own stories and the stories they cover are increasingly unlikely to lead any of our broadcasts or appear on any of our front pages. We celebrate their courage even as we exhibit little of our own. It is not death or torture or imprisonment that threaten us as American journalists; it is the trivialization of our industry. We are free to write and report whatever we believe is important. But if what is important does not appeal to the reading and viewing appetites of our consumers, we'll give them something that does.

Journalists had no one holding a gun to their heads when they allowed stories like the O. J. Simpson trial to balloon out of proportion. Giving people what they appear to want was thought to be sufficient excuse.
But it was a flimsy and shortsighted one. We have a responsibility to do
more, Koppel said. The press should "resist and reject the comfortable
illusion that Americans don't care about what's happening." If they seem not
to care, the likely reason is "they've been lulled into believing" that faraway
events "will have no real impact on their lives." And who was responsible
for that?

With more tools and better skills than any previous generation of journalists, "we're afraid of the competition, afraid of earning less money, afraid
of losing our audience," Koppel said. "We cannot allow that to continue to
be the case. Only if each of us accepts the challenge to reinvigorate what we
do, with a genuine sense of mission, can we sustain the hope that American
journalism will again become, as it many times has been, a shining example
to the rest of the world."[7]

Broder, MacNeil, and Koppel spoke as individuals. In 1997, a Committee of Concerned Journalists arose to articulate a shared sense of the troubles
in the press. The group was led by Bill Kovach, head of the Nieman Foundation at Harvard University, and Tom Rosenstiel, a former reporter at the *Los
Angeles Times* and *Newsweek* who had quit the profession to direct the Project
for Excellence in Journalism, funded by the Pew Charitable Trusts. In its
founding statement, the committee proposed to "summon journalists to a
period of national reflection" during a critical moment for the American
press. While in many respects the craft has never been better ("consider the
supply of information or the skill of reporters"), on the horizon were "revolutionary changes" in technology, the economics of news, and the connection to the public that "are pulling journalism from its traditional moor-
ings." The heart of the statement read:

> As audiences fragment and our companies diversify, there is growing
> debate within news organizations about our responsibilities as businesses
> versus our responsibilities as journalists. Many journalists feel a sense of lost
> purpose. There is even doubt about the meaning of news, doubt evident
> when serious journalistic organizations drift toward opinion, infotainment
> and sensation out of balance with news.
>
> Journalists share responsibility for the uncertainty. Our values and pro-
> fessional standards are often vaguely expressed and inconsistently honored.

We have been slow to change habits in the presentation of news that may have lost their relevance. Change is necessary.

Yet as we change we assert some core principles that are enduring. They are those that make journalism a public service central to self-government. They define our profession not as the act of communicating but as a set of responsibilities. Journalism can entertain, amuse and lift our spirits, but news organizations must also cover the matters vital to the well being of increasingly diverse communities to foster the debate upon which democracy depends. The First Amendment implies obligations as well as freedom.

For much of our history, we believed we could let our work enunciate these principles and our owners and managers articulate these responsibilities. Today, too often, the principles in our work are hard to discern or lost in the din, and our leaders feel constrained.

Now we believe journalists must speak for themselves. We call on our colleagues to join a community of professionals to clarify the purpose and principles that distinguish our profession from other forms of communication.[8]

Common to all these declarations—from Broder, MacNeil, Koppel, and the committee—was a sense of alarm as journalists confronted a dimming future. Particularly prominent was the rising threat to professional standards in a media universe that had scant respect for the notion of public service. All four statements called on journalists to be more than observers of a depressing scene. All sought to ground the work of the journalist in the needs of a healthy democracy. And the shared tone of urgency made another statement: We have to do better. We cannot continue on our present course. The stakes are larger now. We have to speak out. We have to act.

Such moments do not come around every year, or even every generation. They are rare intervals in the life of an institution. In my own haunt, the university, there were problems almost as deep as the ones facing journalists. During the 1990s, state legislatures were asking, "What are those professors doing with all their free time?" Government funding for basic research was drying up. The tenure system, which carried its own abuses, was gradually eroding as more and more positions were filled by part-time instructors. The academy's elite, accustomed to a guild mentality, commonly spoke to one another rather than to the society as a whole, leaving it ill prepared for controversies about "political correctness" and "multiculturalism" when they burst into public view. Meanwhile, economic pressures were mounting and an era of cutbacks had begun on many campuses. And while some were aware of the dangers and spoke out, no committee of concern arose to address such problems. No visible reform movement emerged to begin experimenting with another vision of the university, more attuned to the troubles of the day.[9]

The journalists I came to know agreed with David Broder that the time had come to reconnect citizens and politics. They tried to live the dual identity Robert MacNeil described: chroniclers of the public world, and also part of the structure that holds it up. Although they were often accused of giving the people what they want, their real goal was to start where citizens start and thereby restore a sense of relevance and urgency to the news. "No more journalism for journalists" was one way of putting it. Putting it into practice was taxing work. It took the kind of commitment Ted Koppel wanted to see—a genuine sense of mission. Like the committee of concern headed by Kovach and Rosenstiel, the people involved in public journalism saw large changes ahead, and they tried to respond with a return to first principles. The principles they put first involved democracy as something we do; citizens as the ones who do it; politics as making choices, facing problems, talking it out; and a press that would assist in such things.

Behind these principles lay another: Even in their role as observers, journalists made choices about where to stand. And these choices followed from the picture of the public world they held in mind as they went about their work. People with press passes could place themselves inside or outside the community, on the supporting rim of politics or in the viewing box with the rest of the gang. Recall Tony Wharton, the reporter at the *Virginian-Pilot,* who left his colleagues behind the scenes to reenter the rotunda through a public entrance and pay his respects to Barbara Jordan, a political figure he admired. He was rejoining his fellow citizens, deciding to have their experience instead of his profession's.

When Karen Weintraub, also of the *Pilot,* was confronted with a raucous public hearing between homeowners and city officials, she started listening to the intensity and conviction inside the two conversations going on in the room—rather than tuning in to the fight between two groups. By fixing her ear to a different frequency, Weintraub made herself into a different kind of reporter. Her job description changed. Telling the story now meant repairing the lines of communication between people who were talking past one another. For this and Weintraub's other attempts at the civic style, a different ethic emerged: "do no harm."

Listen to Teresa Hanafin, an editor of the *Boston Globe*, reflecting on her revised job description at a seminar on public journalism:

> I have increasingly seen my role as a journalist as finding common ground. I am extremely offended by the *Crossfire* mentality that exists in political life. . . . It is extremely unproductive; it is even destructive at times. It consists of angry sound bites that mean nothing and serve no purpose but to polarize. . . .
>
> So I have moved from the detached, objective person—just spewing out reams of information and hoping on good faith that people will take the information and act—to realizing that we have to be more of a player in helping people act on that information.[10]

"I have moved." Dennis Foley of the *Orange County Register* moved in his thinking when he saw that people were angry, not just apathetic. "But they were angry at us as much as they were at the political system." The press was part of the inside game, but it took scant responsibility for the game's corrosive effects. "This was intolerable and had to change," he said, adding in his remarks to colleagues that journalists "are responsible both for what they see and for what they do."

In each of these cases, a map of the public world is remade and the journalist is set down at a different spot: with citizens and their points of contact with the public world. By moving about in civic space—in their imaginations and in their work—public journalists refashioned their professional identity, adding the task of repair to the job description. The house of politics became a residence, rather than a disaster scene the correspondent visits, pencil in hand. "A successful community is one where people know what's going on and take responsibility for it," said Buzz Merritt. By picturing such a place, Merritt placed himself inside the political community, helping it succeed at its biggest challenge, which was seizing hold of public business and "jointly deciding about things."[11]

In asking what public journalism achieved, my own reply would begin with journalists like Merritt, Wharton, Weintraub, Hanafin, and Foley, who found another map of the public terrain and starting using it. They looked to places where politics and civic life were broken, in order to begin there a kind of repair work, which I have also called public work. By undertaking it, they changed the tenor of their reports and employed the power of the press to different ends: wider participation, a community that grapples a bit better with its problems, a discussion that's about something more than winning.

They also refashioned themselves as journalists—not by leaving traditional duties behind, but by enlarging the soul of a craft they loved. They kept up their membership in the profession, but they extended it to mean something further: membership in the polity as well as the fraternity. The journalist as a "fair-minded participant" in a democracy that works was Merritt's phrase for it.

The journalist as bystander, watching the fools commit their follies, was the identity of choice for a good many in the mainstream press. Some of them were the doubters and critics of civic journalism, who wanted to preserve the press by holding fast to custom and routine. They had reasons for sticking where they stood, since they recognized that Merritt's fair-minded participant was risking a lot. Dual membership in the polity and the profession was a confusing, unsettled place—at times, a dangerous spot from which to operate.

Bringing people together to talk could easily leave them more estranged from one another. Finding common ground could get in the way of spotting troubled ground, or the hard facts that spelled doom for civic action but had to be told. Inviting citizens to act made you responsible, in a way, for how they acted. Was this the job of a free press? The people who experimented with public journalism didn't know. But they knew this: they were alive in unknown territory. Cheryl Carpenter of the *Charlotte Observer* talked about it: "Then I got past the 'we do not know what we are doing' and I said to myself, 'This is scary. I don't like it. It is scary and it is testing me in ways that I have not been tested before. And it does not feel right.'"

Totaled up, these risks left little doubt: it was safer to watch from the sidelines and comment with open eyes on a sad, broken, or—if we get lucky—inspiring scene. But was it really possible to *be* on the sidelines in the media age? That was one thing public journalists asked. Was it right to see yourself this way, as a bystander? And if the risks in civic journalism were real, which in the end was riskier: standing by or shifting stance? Carpenter, frightened that she had gone too far with the paper's "Taking Back Our Neighborhoods" project, decided to keep moving: "Then it went from [fear] to, 'Something is happening.' It was 'something is happening in this room,' a room where I was talking to citizens, and then after the meeting, I thought: 'Well, something is happening to me, too.'"

Her words may sound melodramatic to some. For me and others present, Carpenter spoke of an internal struggle. She was no longer an outsider to the troubled neighborhoods where her newspaper would declare: "Here, something needs to be done, the work of repair, and we're going to call the citizens of Charlotte to it." But she and her colleagues still had a duty to watch and tell. Could they expect themselves to do both: repair and report? Settled wisdom said no. But seeing something alive in a church basement discussion, knowing that you had placed yourself there, with citizens, threw much of this wisdom—and Carpenter herself—into doubt. "Something is happening to me" means: I'm having to see myself another way, as both actor and observer. I'm becoming a different kind of knower in a community that needs to know and also act on what it knows.

Journalists like Carpenter went somewhere else to find the work of a free press. They brought to a halt the rhythms of daily practice, clearing room for deeper reflection on the nature of their craft and their identity within it. All of which was unusual, as thoughtful people in the press knew. "For all the accelerating pace of news and the growing demand for context and analysis, journalists remain largely communicators, not analysts," wrote Tom Rosenstiel. "Our skills are in gathering information and transmitting it to people's homes. We are masters of motion, not thought."[12]

Reporters and editors go to work knowing there is always news to report, events to cover, another scene to be sent home to people. But what if the masters of motion need to stop the drift of daily practice so that they can see that scene in a wider way? Posing this question means coming into conscious possession of the models and metaphors that make journalism what it is. In the revised model I have suggested, journalists are people who make things—in addition to finding things: the facts, the story, the truth. What does the press make? MacNeil's "delicate web of trust" is one answer. Rosenstiel offered another, which I have also used here: mapmaking. "Like a map of a city," he wrote, "journalism reduces events in size and accessibility while remaining faithful to the basic features of the original. The metaphor suggests that journalism has a responsibility to proportion and context. And it implies need. It helps citizens to make their way, in a democratic, participatory republic."[13]

If journalism was more like cartography—than, say, photography—then the cartographers could ask themselves: what kind of map do people need from us these days? As soon as they are seen as more than information providers or watchdogs, journalists emerge in a variety of interesting guises: as dramatists, model makers, timekeepers. They build public stages, fill them with actors, and frame the action in a certain way. They map public space and hand us the map. Public journalism was a philosophy for a press that could understand news and commentary in this fuller way, as an imaginative art, in which the artisans bring the public world alive for us—first, by building a scale model of it in their heads, then by using the model to do their work.[14]

Of course, citizens must do their work. "Democracy means paying attention," Robert Bellah and his colleagues write in *The Good Society*. Information—news and views of what's going on—will aid us in this act. But something else is required: our decision to see ourselves as having public as well as private lives. The informed citizen becomes informed not just by consuming the news but by producing an inner map on which personal experience meets public life, the local greets the national and global, the immediate joins with distant happenings to draw a wider picture. "You give us twenty-two minutes, we give you the world," boasts WINS, an all-news radio station in New York. But it was never so. Unless I seek it, the world in its wider dimension can never be mine.[15]

Democracy means paying attention to public business regarded as your own. Pat Richardson, the citizen in Norfolk who sat in on the *Virginian-Pilot*'s retreat, later wrote these words to her fellow residents: " 'Why bother getting involved in health care issues? It will be decided by the special interest groups.' 'Why should I talk to anybody on the City Council?' Everything gets decided behind the scenes anyway.' 'Why think I'm going to talk to the newspaper? They just try to dig up dirt so people will buy their papers.' " Richardson wanted to quarrel with these attitudes. But her plea went beyond the usual "get involved." She was asking people to include themselves in the political scene when they sketched it in their heads.

Will they? We can never know for sure. But to assume that this sort of act is out of reach for my fellow citizens is one of the most dangerous habits I can fall into as a citizen, a scholar, or a journalist. For if every adult in the country cannot make for themselves a reasonably good map of the present, then the country's affairs can never be public affairs in the truest sense. They will become the guarded possession of experts, or a playing field for professionals—lobbyists, pollsters, reporters, and officials, all of whom are authorized to "know" in place of a public that cannot ever know.

Thus the importance of public work, which, in the view of Harry Boyte and Nancy Kari, "begins where people are in their everyday environments" and ends in "building capacities for public life."[16] If we succeed in this work, then a scattered population can become a public, at home in the wider present because it has done what's required to find itself there. This was one part of John Dewey's message: build a better place for the public, and the public may one day find its place. Walter Lippmann, Dewey's contemporary, saw the matter differently. At best he took what could be termed a stoic stance. Such is the modern world, he argued: too big for us to know, too complicated for us to manage by fully democratic means. Let us see it with unclouded eyes and still find a place for the limited capacities of the average citizen.

American society has found a politics and a public culture that knows how to do what Lippmann advised: give citizens an up or down vote at election time (although fewer and fewer use it), watch them protest when angry (although just as many protest by dropping out), and delegate the remaining work to experts, officials, and professionals who command specialized knowledge (although the web of trust that connects them to the nation may be in slow collapse). The country also has an advanced system for packaging audiences and aiming messages at them, including the poll-tested appeals we hear from candidates and interest groups. A lively and often sophisticated popular culture, with astounding visuals that seem to enchant the world, is among our biggest and most profitable exports.

And now we greet the emergence of the World Wide Web, with its vast potential for linking and learning, trade and education. What it will do to the public screen—and our common experience—no one knows. But there's this to contemplate: on the Web, every reader is also a writer, every consumer a potential producer. Everyone there is in potential reach of everyone else who is there. These are new conditions for journalists, and they stand out even at high tide in the hype that often surrounds Web talk.[17]

Superintending all this is a powerful institution we Americans have largely created: the media, whether we still call it "mass" or not. The United States makes media well, so well we market it to the world. But can it still make journalism well? There is no longer any point in confusing the two. The media, we should realize, is the audience production business. People's time is the raw material, and as every programmer knows, time is a scarce resource. There are only twenty-four hours in a day, even as the sites that welcome a visit today expand exponentially. Attention is the media's finished product. When the media gets done doing what it does, your time, my time, and the time of our fellow citizens has been collected at an attention site where someone can be persuaded to pay. It can be MTV, a self-help book, an on-line service, a beauty magazine, or the multiplex at the local mall. The media doesn't care.

The point of having journalists around is not to produce attention, but to make our attention more productive. When journalists get done doing what they do, we should find it easier to meet public challenges and get our work done as citizens.[18] Journalism, then, is where the media gets democratic in principle—that's why it's important. It is not a business, although it may be housed within a business. Journalism is best understood as one of the arts of democracy; as MacNeil, Koppel, and the committee of concern all recognized, this art is more and more threatened by the media. Journalists are worried about this. Americans are, too. Just what are we making ourselves into when we make media so well—and go on to remake politics and culture in its image? Until that question comes on the table, we will grope around in our present state: fascinated and repelled, bored or disgusted by what the media sends across the public screen in its alternately jolting and soothing fashion.

In the confusing, exploding, and increasingly commercialized universe the media help make, we find a million or more entry points for our attention. The citizen cruising the Web will be able to stop and visit almost anywhere, or so it seems. We can see a vast increase in social space upon us, even if we cannot discern the civic character it will have. Perhaps a commercial society, wired like never before, can get along with a weakened public sphere, although it's just as likely that in our weakness and wiredness we will drift along, wherever technology, global rivalries, population flows, and the ever fluctuating market take us.

In the political realm, we can even have a kind of democracy without citizens, as Robert Entman phrased it, if we're willing to call whatever we get from politics a democracy, the best we can do. Though fewer of us may vote, the ones who do vote give self-government the leg of legitimacy it needs to stand. While trust in the system evaporates, we can still trust that the system will survive, that a people without illusions are better off when their institutions fail, as they inevitably will. And then there's the young. Tuned to the possibilities of newer media, they may yet show us how to "connect" and point to where the next common culture can be found. Toward our public follies, we can try to strike a stoic stance, even if we can't always tell when stoicism fades into cynicism. Journalists can become stoics themselves, as Maureen Dowd of the *New York Times* advised.[19]

Or they can try another course. And that's what public journalism was about, in my view. What it accomplished lay in the simple fact of response—but also, in the depth of that response. It is one thing to say, "We're in trouble." It's another to add, "We have to change the way we work." It is one thing to declare, "We cannot continue on our present path." It's another to head down a different path in a spirit of experiment. It is one thing to reaffirm your principles, another to find different principles for a different time. Changing your tune is part of it, changing your self the heart of it. Public journalism achieved that kind of change—for a minority in the American press.

To see why it was needed, just picture the following scene. Early in the primary season, the Democratic candidates for president meet face to face in a televised debate in New Hampshire. A surprisingly detailed and serious discussion unfolds—surprising, especially, to the journalists who have been covering the campaign. Residents of the state appear hungry for such talk; about 140,000 of them have tuned in. Democracy for once seems to be working: the candidates are debating the issues, the press is noticing, the public is paying attention. But as the evening wears on, journalists who must report on the debate are getting anxious. Where's the story line? Finally, one reporter, watching in his hotel room, shakes an impatient fist at the screen. "Less substance, damn it," he cries. "More fireworks!"

Regrettably, the scene is not a fantasy. It is described in Rosenstiel's book *Strange Bedfellows*, an examination of campaign coverage in 1992. The fist-shaking journalist was Robert Shogan, Rosenstiel's colleague at the *Los Angeles Times* and a veteran political writer. But it could have been any number of reporters or producers, cursing their misfortune to be present for a substantive discussion that was low on confrontational heat. To be fair to Shogan, it is doubtful that his heart's desire was for less substance in politics. He was simply noting, with some irony, the incompatibility between the needs of a democracy and the demands on a working journalist.[20]

But why should the incompatibility exist? And if it does, shouldn't something be done about it? The scene Rosenstiel sketched is disturbing, since it appears to suggest that when politics works well, journalism cannot. "Less substance, more fireworks" says that the craft's routines, or its assumptions about the audience, do not permit an honest reporter to emphasize what matters. A situation of this sort cannot endure for long. Either politics will become fireworks, or journalism will prove substanceless. Shogan was speaking for a profession that had worked itself into a difficult bind. The bind begins with a thin and often contradictory philosophy among those who tend to eschew philosophy and therefore lack fresh answers to the question, What are journalists for?

Public journalism meant trying to find a better answer. People took a hard look at the declining audience for news, the unraveling of community life, the spectacle that politics had become in a fragmenting nation, the growing disconnect between themselves and citizens. And they asked in straightforward fashion, what can we do? The answers they found put them in the philosophy business and suggested a variety of things journalists could be for.

Here, then, is how the movement answered the questions contained in the title of this book.

Why do we need journalists? To be timely and accurate in telling the story of events. But along with information, we need an invitation to join in those events—as people with public as well as private lives. Like the information it conveys, the invitation the news contains should be current, in the sense that it speaks to our daily lives and present troubles. And it should prove accurate, as fact, but accurate also as a map, guiding us toward the places where public challenges are found.

We need journalists to be balanced in their treatment of public affairs, no doubt. But there are other forms of "balance" beyond those in common use. Balancing skepticism with hope is as vital as balancing quote with quote. A better balance is reachable between news that tells of problems and news that talks of problem solving. Balance is needed between two ways of seeing people: on one hand as viewers or readers, consumers of a product; on the other as citizens, participants in their common affairs. When the right mix is found, commercial success joins public purpose.

As journalists grapple deeply with these problems of proportion, other questions rise to the surface: How to balance the imperatives of distance and detachment with another imperative, willing membership in the community that journalists address. For press people are citizens, too, and ill advised to forget this fact or wish it away. How to balance a view of politics as a grubby and manipulative business with another view—politics as the art of making choices and seizing possibilities. How to balance discomforting truths with inspirational ones. How to set mind and soul in balance for a craft that draws on both. Journalists stay useful, they keep their art contemporary, when they negotiate these tensions with intelligence and verve.

We need journalists to watch over things for us, since we do not go where they go or see what they see. But the things they can watch for go well beyond the corrupt official, the dissembling politician, the bungling bureaucracy. The press needs to watch for places where we lose touch with the public world by letting our attention lapse, our indifference grow. It should keep itself alert to the points of contact between our felt troubles and larger issues that rise on the public screen. Training their sights on public problems, journalists can watch carefully for the best points of entry, where people can raise their voices, lend their views, make use of their talents, get involved. Knowing that a fascination with the larger world lives in all of us, they can try to keep track of the human hunger to know, which never quite dies, amid all the other appetites to which our popular culture caters.

From these and other connecting points journalists can bring us the news and also why it matters. They can connect personal life and self-interest with public life and the common interest, for the story we need from them is a story like that. In general, the press can watch over the public square to prevent its slipping away from us. For if politics and public affairs become a distant scene with sordid characters unable to earn our respect, a closed loop where the usual suspects talk only to each other, an empty spectacle that sheds no light on what matters most, then the watchdog will have failed in its custodial duty—although our leaders and ourselves will share mightily in the blame.

Where do journalists stand? Inside the political community, not on another planet or up in the reviewer's box. Although they have a distinct role in reporting to the public about its affairs, they do not have a distinct identity that removes them from the public, as migrants who are not members, witnesses without standing in the world they tell us about. Standing with us, as fellow citizens, does not mean taking sides in favor of this policy or that party. But it does mean that journalism cannot succeed in the fullest sense if democracy falters for the many or gets highjacked by the few.

When a discussion that is needed does not materialize; when the missing voices outnumber the noisy ones in an important debate; when there are possibilities to be glimpsed but not many of us see them; when common opinion, thinly grounded, needs to mature into public judgment, on which stronger decisions can be made; when our public institutions fail to meet their task—when conditions like this appear, journalists who stand with citizens will not stand by in the belief that there is nothing to be done. They will see what they can do, within the limits of their power and role. And they will learn where those limits are, not by consulting some fixed code or standard script, but through experiment, invention, and reflection.

Admittedly, it is tricky business to stand with citizens, to lend them a hand, and still tell the truths they don't always want to hear. Only a journalism that is open to a variety of public stances can find the right one to hold at any given time. Fact finder for people or deep listener to them, a digger into problems or an aid to problem solvers, a platform for journalists and the knowledge they command or a forum for others to speak their minds and hearts, a weaver of stories or a civic connector—the press can stand in all these roles, and contribute something different with each. And it can realize: there are ways of facing even the darkest facts that leave us open to the task of remaking them.

What do journalists stand for? Freedom of information, an open flow of ideas, honesty and candor in public business, the people's right to know— certainly. But it is equally certain that none of these things matter unless we have not just the right but the means to know, unless we show a will to inform ourselves, unless we are given a decent chance to get into the game, put our ideas and experience to use. An engaged and informed public, alert to common troubles and prepared to play its part, may emerge at one moment and disappear the next. For this reason we need the press to be steadier in its vision than a busy society can ever be.

Journalists make it their business to be knowledgeable and alert. They come to work ready to play a part in a public drama, even as they fill a job in a private business. Through this steady work they stand for something: the argument that democracy and civic life are an everyday affair and everyone's business. That's why the dwindling audience for serious news is a civic ordeal, and not just a marketplace verdict. If "public affairs are for everyone" is one thing the press can uphold, there are others: Politics as public property, not the province of a knowledge class. Public discussion as a prelude to public decisions, which remain incomplete without it. Deliberation as an art within reach of average citizens, who have something to say if they are heard with patience and imagination. Democracy as a learning experience for everyone involved. When journalists stand for these values they uphold democracy seen a certain way: as something we do, rather than what is done to us by the system and its hired hands.

In the years ahead, there may be no people calling themselves public journalists. By 1997, I noticed that the name was already disappearing from use, even in the newsrooms where the idea had been most influential. People found they didn't need the title anymore, and they went back to calling their work "good journalism."

All those who want to do good through journalism feel the ground below them shifting at century's end. We are being brought together and split apart in a pattern vastly different than the one that held from 1945 on. Suburban living, technology's changing code, an exploding commercial culture, the drift of our politics and public talk, the kind of shared and civic experiences we seek, the education we give ourselves and offer our youth, the looming colossus called the media—the great social weave from which journalism rises is again shifting form.

This should not surprise us because it has happened before. But it can alert us that now is a good time to ask what journalists should be doing, in the pragmatic tradition for which Americans are well known. A good pragmatist takes a look at the present state of things before coming to working principles; and so it is for journalism. Its possibilities and problems are different than they were in, say, 1974, when Richard Nixon resigned and the press felt a surge of power, as a righteous institution performing well in an hour of need. Today, what we most need from journalists is their enlivened imaginations, as they try to picture a scene where democracy and citizenship are not in a slow fade. Should the American press give up the search for such a prospect, its own prospects are likely to dim in the years ahead.

Whatever happens, let it not be said that no one in journalism saw the danger whole, for I know some people who did. They put their heads together and tried to act. Without knowing the best course, they decided to experiment. Public journalism is just a name for their story, which is incomplete and marked by doubt. But the biggest stories are always unfinished. They are the tales we tell ourselves about ourselves.

Notes

Introduction: What We're Doing Isn't Working

1. Michael Schudson warns against the "dangers of seeing journalism as journalists themselves do." See his discussion in *The Power of News* (Cambridge: Harvard University Press, 1995): 12–13. Also helpful are Herbert J. Gans, *Deciding What's News* (New York: Pantheon, 1979), and Paul H. Weaver, *News and the Culture of Lying* (New York: Free Press, 1994).

2. On the origins of the Project on Public Life and the Press, see Jay Rosen, "Making Things More Public: On the Political Responsibility of the Media Intellectual," *Critical Studies in Mass Communication* 11:4 (1994): 373–74.

3. I have been influenced in this view by James W. Carey. See his *Communication as Culture* (Boston: Unwin Hyman, 1989): 20–21. See also my interpretation of Carey in Jay Rosen, "We'll Have That Conversation," in Eve Stryker Munson and Catherine A. Warren, eds., *James Carey: A Critical Reader* (Minneapolis: University of Minnesota Press, 1997): 196–202. On journalism as imaginative work see also G. Stuart Adam, *Notes Toward a Definition of Journalism* (St. Petersburg, Fla.: Poynter Institute for Media Studies, 1993): 11–20.

4. For a good overview of the movement, the people involved, and their critics, see "Civic Journalism: Can Press Reforms Revitalize Democracy?" *CQ Researcher* 6:35 (Sept. 20, 1996): 817–40. For a range of views among scholars, see Jay Black, ed., *Mixed News: The Public/Civic/Communitarian Journalism Debate* (Mahwah, N.J.: Lawrence Erlbaum, 1997), and Theodore L. Glasser, ed., *The Idea of Public Journalism* (New York: Guilford, 1999). For a first-person account from a journalist who helped give shape to public journalism, see Davis Merritt, *Public Journalism and Public Life* (Mahwah, N.J.: Lawrence Erlbaum, 1995). For a sympathetic view from a Washington journalist, see James

Fallows, *Breaking the News* (New York: Pantheon, 1996): chapter 6. For a highly skeptical treatment from a member of the national press corps, see Michael Kelly, "Media Culpa," *New Yorker* (Nov. 4, 1996): 45–46, 48–49. A textbook that tries to explain public journalism for students and educators is Arthur Charity, *Doing Public Journalism* (New York: Guilford, 1995).

For examples of trade journal and press review treatment, see Tony Case, "Public Journalism Denounced," *Editor and Publisher* (Nov. 12, 1994): 14–15; Mike Hoyt, "Are You Now, or Will You Ever Be a Civic Journalist?" *Columbia Journalism Review* (Sept.–Oct. 1995): 27–33; Alicia C. Shepard, "The Gospel of Public Journalism," *American Journalism Review* (Sept. 1994): 28–34.

5. See, for example, "Interview: Jay Rosen," *Dallas Morning News* (Aug. 27, 1995): 1J, 10J.

6. Among the places I stopped, sometimes more than once: the *Akron Beacon Journal,* the *Austin American Statesman,* the *Boston Globe,* the *Charlotte Observer,* the *Colorado Springs Gazette,* the Columbia *State,* the *Dayton Daily News,* the *Des Moines Register,* the *Detroit Free Press,* the *Indianapolis Star,* the *Lexington Herald-Leader,* the *Miami Herald,* the Minneapolis *Star-Tribune,* National Public Radio in Washington, the Norfolk *Virginian-Pilot,* the *Orange County Register,* the *Orlando Sun-Sentinel,* the *Philadelphia Inquirer,* the *Pittsburgh Post-Gazette,* the Portland *Oregonian,* the *St. Louis Post-Dispatch,* the *St. Paul Pioneer Press,* the *San Francisco Chronicle,* the *San Jose Mercury News,* the Spokane *Spokesman-Review,* the *Tampa Tribune,* the Washington bureau of Knight-Ridder, the *Wichita Eagle,* and the *Wisconsin State Journal.* I also addressed such organizations as the National Conference of Editorial Writers, the Associated Press Managing Editors, the National Association of Opinion Page Editors, the Newspaper Association of America, editors and publishers of the Gannett, McClatchy, Ottaway, and Knight-Ridder chains, the New York Associated Press, the New England AP, several seminars at the Nieman Foundation at Harvard, and the Freedom Forum Media Studies Center in New York. I spoke to the journalism fellows at the University of Michigan, the Knight Fellows at Stanford University, students and faculty at Berkeley's School of Journalism, Columbia University, Indiana University, Northwestern University, the University of Texas at Austin, and the University of South Carolina, among others.

7. See "Rethinking Journalism and Rebuilding Civic Life," *National Civic Review* 85 (1996), published by the National Civic League; "Rebuilding Communities," *National Voter* 45 (1995), publication of the League of Women Voters; Christopher Conte, "Angels in the Newsroom," *Governing* (August 1996): 20–24. In 1995, the Association for Education in Journalism and Mass Communication, the leading professional organization for academics studying journalism, founded a civic journalism interest group.

8. Merritt, *Public Journalism and Public Life,* 5.

9. On the confusion, consternation, and crisis of purpose in the American press during the 1990s, see these treatments by journalists: E. J. Dionne, *They Only Look Dead* (New York: Simon and Schuster, 1996): 231–62; James Fallows, *Breaking the News* (New York: Pantheon, 1996); William Greider, *Who Will Tell the People?* (New York: Simon and Schuster, 1992): 287–306; Howard Kurtz, *Media Circus* (New York: Times Books, 1993); Tom Rosenstiel, *The Beat Goes On* (New York: Twentieth Century Fund, 1994);

James D. Squires, *Read All About It!* (New York: Times Books, 1993); Paul Taylor, *See How They Run* (New York: Knopf, 1990). For my own analysis of the troubles in the press, see Jay Rosen, *Getting the Connections Right* (New York: Twentieth Century Fund, 1996): 8–11, 18–33. An interesting think tank document is *A Call to Leadership* (St. Petersburg, Fla.: Poynter Institute of Media Studies, 1992).

10. For background on the scholarly issues addressed by the National Issues Convention, see two books by the event's designer, James S. Fishkin, *Democracy and Deliberation* (New Haven: Yale University Press, 1991), and *The Voice of the People* (New Haven: Yale University Press, 1995). For an exchange among political scientists and pollsters on the theory and practice of the NIC, see "The 'Deliberative Opinion Poll' Comes to Texas— And to Campaign '96," *Public Perspective* 7:1 (1996): 1–20, and "The NIC Revisited," *Public Perspective* 7:3 (1996): 16–50. For a preview of the event in a journalism review, see Maggie Balough, "Changing Techniques," *Quill* (Jan.–Feb. 1996): 20–22. See also the assessment afterward in Terri Burke, "People Spoke: Who Listened?" *Quill* (March 1996): 33–34.

　　For examples of news coverage of the NIC, see Sam Attlessy and Wayne Slater, "Absent Candidates Catch Flak, Others Spar at Austin Forum," *Dallas Morning News* (Jan. 21, 1996): 1A, 25A; Dana Milbank, "Meeting Convened on National Issues Finds Isolationists," *Wall Street Journal* (Jan. 22, 1996): B3; Dick Polman, "In Austin, 'Average' Americans Step Back From Conservative GOP," *Philadelphia Inquirer* (Jan. 22, 1996): 1A; R. G. Ratcliffe, "Convention Delegates Give Mixed Reviews of Issues Conference," *Houston Chronicle* (Jan. 22, 1996): 9A, 11A; Michael Tacket, "Conference Elicits Anxiety Over Economy," *Chicago Tribune* (Jan. 21, 1996): 1, 12; Ernest Tollerson, "Gathering Tries Out a New Political Prism," *New York Times* (Jan. 22, 1996): A10; John E. Yang, " 'Real People' Face Issues, Candidates in Experiment on Citizenship," *Washington Post* (Jan. 22, 1996): A6. For my own commentary on the event, see Jay Rosen, "Take Back the Campaign," *Nation* (Feb. 19, 1996): 10.

11. See the discussion guide prepared for the event, *Issues '96: A Guide to Public Deliberation* (New York: Public Agenda Foundation, 1996).

12. These were scenes I and others witnessed. As one reporter in attendance wrote: "The convention ended with . . . a round of hugs and picture-taking and emotional farewells among people who were strangers just 72 hours before. And as they left, many who came to Austin feeling cynical, detached or simply overwhelmed said they were leaving with a new sense of their own power to participate in the governance of their community and the nation." Daniel M. Weintraub, "Issues Convention Changes Outlook of O.C. Woman," *Orange County Register* (Jan. 22, 1996): 3.

13. Project on Public Life and the Press, transcript of seminar proceedings, Jan. 22, 1996, Austin, Texas (Dayton: Kettering Foundation, 1996): 7, 1. On the delegates' search for the gray areas, see also Jim Morrill, "Average Folks Take a Fresh Look at the Issues," *Charlotte Observer* (Jan. 22, 1996): 1A.

14. Jim Morrill, telephone interview with author, Jan. 26, 1996. See also Jim Morrill, "It's Politics on a Scale for People," *Charlotte Observer* (Jan. 20, 1996): 1A, 14A.

15. Project on Public Life and the Press transcript, 4. See also Daniel M. Weintraub, "America in One Room," *Orange County Register* (Jan. 21, 1996): A16.

16. See, for example, Jim Morrill, "Average Folks Take a Fresh Look at the Issues," *Charlotte Observer* (Jan. 22, 1996): 1A.

17. Project on Public Life and the Press transcript, 8. Flaherty described the citizens' eagerness to engage one another and one of the tearful scenes that ensued in his report after the convention. Mike Flaherty, "Issue Convention Changes Minds," *Wisconsin State Journal* (Jan. 28, 1996): 5B.

18. Steve Berg, telephone interview with the author, Jan. 26, 1996.

19. Project on Public Life and the Press transcript, 10. For a similar observation about Americans' reluctance to fit themselves into ideologically convenient categories, see E. J. Dionne, "The Liberal Revival," *Washington Post* (Feb. 4, 1996): C1.

20. Project on Public Life and the Press transcript, 3.

21. Ibid., 19–20.

22. For observations on the gap between citizens and candidates at the convention, see Pete Weitzel and Tony Wharton, "Questions Reveal Frustration with Leadership," Norfolk *Virginian-Pilot* (Feb. 4, 1996): J1, J13.

23. Project on Public Life and the Press transcript, 4–6.

24. Ibid., 17–18; see also Nena Baker, "What If They Held a National Forum and . . . ," Portland *Oregonian* (Jan. 22, 1996): 1A; Holly Heyser, telephone interview with author, Jan. 26, 1996.

25. Tony Wharton, telephone interview with author, Jan. 27, 1996.

Chapter 1: As Democracy Goes, So Goes the Press

1. Jay Rosen, "The Impossible Press: American Journalism and the Decline of Public Life" (Ph.D. diss., New York University, 1986). On the problem of the public, see John Dewey, *The Public and Its Problems* (New York: Henry Holt, 1927); Walter Lippmann, *Public Opinion* (1922; reprint, New York: Free Press, 1965). For thoughtful interpretations with applications to journalism, see Christopher Lasch, *The Revolt of the Elites and the Betrayal of Democracy* (New York: Norton, 1995): chapter 9; James W. Carey, "The Press and the Public Discourse," *Center Magazine* (March–April 1987): 6–7, and "The Press, Public Opinion, and Public Discourse," in Theodore L. Glasser and Charles T. Salmon, eds., *Public Opinion and the Communication of Consent* (New York: Guilford, 1995): 389–92.

2. Jay Rosen, "Newspapers' Future Depends on Shaping Trends in How People Live," *Bulletin of the American Society of Newspaper Editors* (December 1989): 18 (italics in original).

3. See Jürgen Habermas, *The Structural Transformation of the Public Sphere*, trans. Thomas Burger with Frederick Lawrence (Cambridge: MIT Press, 1989). See also Craig Calhoun, ed., *Habermas and the Public Sphere* (Cambridge: MIT Press, 1992); Bruce Robbins, ed., *The Phantom Public Sphere* (Minneapolis: University of Minnesota Press, 1993); and John Durham Peters, "Distrust of Representation: Habermas on the Public Sphere," *Media, Culture, and Society* 15:4 (1993): 541–71, for a view from a communication scholar.

4. To take one measure of the decline in readership: In a March 1995 national survey, only 45 percent of Americans said they had read a daily newspaper the previous day, down from 58 percent in February 1994 and from 71 percent in a comparable study in 1965. Report from Times Mirror Center for the People and the Press, Washington, D.C. (April 6, 1995): 9, 29. On lost readership and the efforts to combat it, see Susan Miller, "America's Dailies and the Drive to Capture Lost Readers," *Gannett Center Journal* 1:1 (spring 1987): 56–68; Leo Bogart, *Preserving the Press: How Daily Newspapers Mobilized to Keep Readers* (New York: Columbia University Press, 1991); Richard O'Mara, "The Flight from Newspapers," *Quill* (March 1990): 34–37; Howard Kurtz, "Yesterday's News: Why Newspapers Are Losing Their Franchise," in Frank Denton and Howard Kurtz, *Reinventing the Newspaper* (New York: Twentieth Century Fund, 1993); Howard Kurtz, *Media Circus: The Trouble with America's Newspapers* (New York: Times Books, 1993): 311–37. See also my discussion of the economic crisis in daily journalism in Jay Rosen, *Getting the Connections Right* (New York: Twentieth Century Fund, 1996): 19–20.

5. Jack Fuller, *News Values: Ideas for an Information Age* (Chicago: University of Chicago Press, 1996): 199.

6. James K. Batten, "America's Newspapers: What Are Our Prospects?" Press-Enterprise Lecture Series (Riverside, Calif.: Press-Enterprise, 1989): 2, 3, 7–8.

7. Ibid., 8, 10, 11, 6.

8. Ibid., 11–13.

9. James K. Batten, William Allen White Lecture (Lawrence: University of Kansas, 1990): 11–12, 15.

10. *USA Today,* writes Howard Kurtz of the *Washington Post,* "made its name spoon-feeding McNuggets of news to the video generation." Kurtz, *Media Circus,* 6; on the same theme, see also 344–47. Also see Doug Underwood, *When MBAs Rule the Newsroom* (New York: Columbia University Press, 1993): xiii, 96–97.

11. James K. Batten, commencement address, Coker College, Hartsville, S.C. (May 12, 1990): 10.

12. Robert D. Putnam, "Bowling Alone: America's Declining Social Capital," *Journal of Democracy* 6:1 (1995): 66.

13. Ibid., 69, 77. For Putnam's other work on social capital and civic participation, see Robert D. Putnam, *Making Democracy Work* (Princeton: Princeton University Press, 1993), "The Prosperous Community: Social Capital and Public Life," *American Prospect* 13 (spring 1993): 35–42, and "The Strange Disappearance of Civic America," *American Prospect* 24 (winter 1996): 34–48.

14. For example, Anthony Flint, "Has Democracy Gone Awry?" *Boston Globe Magazine* (Oct. 20, 1996): 16, 43–47; Everett C. Ladd, "The Data Just Don't Show Erosion of America's 'Social Capital,'" *Public Perspective* 7:4 (June–July 1996): 1, 5–6; Nicolas Lemann, "Kicking in Groups," *Atlantic Monthly* (April 1996): 22, 24–26; Katha Pollitt, "For Whom the Ball Rolls," *Nation* (April 15, 1996): 9.

15. Nancy Fraser uses the term "late capitalist" throughout her essay "Rethinking the Public Sphere: A Contribution to the Critique of Actually Existing Democracy," in Calhoun, ed., *Habermas and the Public Sphere,* 109–42. For examples of criticism of media com-

panies from the left, see J. Herbert Altschull, *Agents of Power* (New York: Longman, 1984); Benjamin Bagdikian, *The Media Monopoly,* 4th ed. (Boston: Beacon, 1992); Edward S. Herman and Noam Chomsky, *Manufacturing Consent* (New York: Pantheon, 1988); Michael Parenti, *The Politics of the News Media* (New York: St. Martin's, 1993).

16. A typical observation from the political left is, "The existing media market of ideas is . . . like the larger economic market of which it is a part: oligopolistic and accessible mostly to those who possess vast amounts of capital, or who hold views that are pleasing to the possessors of capital." Parenti, *Politics of the News Media,* 30.

    For representative examples of criticism from the right, see Edith Efron, *The News Twisters* (New York: Manor Books, 1972); S. Robert Lichter, Stanley Rothman, and Linda Lichter, *The Media Elite* (Bethesda, Md.: Adler and Adler, 1986); William A. Rusher, *The Coming Battle for the Media* (New York: William Morrow, 1988). For commentary from journalists observing the liberal bias of their colleagues, see John Corry, *My Times* (New York: Putnam, 1993), and Paul H. Weaver, *News and the Culture of Lying* (New York: Free Press, 1994). A useful analysis of both the left's and the right's complaints is Michael Schudson, *The Power of News* (Cambridge: Harvard University Press, 1995): 4–9.

17. Daniel C. Hallin takes a view similar to this, although he underlines the antipolitical tendencies that are "deeply rooted in the structure and ideology of the American news media." Daniel C. Hallin, "The American News Media: A Critical Theory Perspective," in John Forester, ed., *Critical Theory and Public Life* (Cambridge: MIT Press, 1995): 143.

18. This account is drawn from my earlier discussions of the Columbus case. See Jay Rosen, "Making Journalism More Public," *Communication* 12:4 (1991): 270–76; Jay Rosen, "Politics, Vision, and the Press," in Jay Rosen and Paul Taylor, *The New News vs. the Old News* (New York: Twentieth Century Fund, 1992): 11–15; and Jay Rosen, "Community Action: Sin or Salvation?" *Quill* (March 1992): 30–33. It also draws on two accounts from journalists in Columbus: Jack Swift, address to South Dakota Newspaper Association annual convention, May 5, 1990; Billy Winn, "Public Journalism: An Early Attempt," *Nieman Reports* (winter 1993): 54–56. See also Alicia C. Shepard, "Death of a Pioneer," *American Journalism Review* (Sept. 1994): 35. For a scholarly interpretation from a communitarian perspective, see Clifford G. Christians, John P. Ferré, and P. Mark Fackler, *Good News* (New York: Oxford University Press, 1993): 87–91. Also see James W. Carey, "A Republic, If You Can Keep It," in Eve Stryker Munson and Catherine A. Warren, eds., *James Carey: A Critical Reader* (Minneapolis: University of Minnesota Press, 1997): 223–25.

19. Winn, "Public Journalism," 55.

20. Dewey, *The Public and Its Problems,* 219.

21. Billy Watson, interview with author, June 14, 1991.

22. Jim Houston, interview with author, June 14, 1991.

23. "Building Community Connections," transcript of panel discussion at the American Society of Newspaper Editors annual convention, Washington, D.C., April 8, 1992: 46.

24. Jack Swift, address to South Dakota Newspaper Association annual convention, May 5, 1990: 3.

25. Two books by journalism historian Thomas C. Leonard are helpful on the theme of advocacy in newspapers. See his discussion of nineteenth-century newspapers urging readers to join a cause in *News for All* (New York: Oxford University Press, 1995): 57–61. Also see his discussion of muckraking and reform journalism in *The Power of the Press* (New York: Oxford University Press, 1986): 166–221.

26. For example, Jay Rosen, "To Be or Not to Be: Newspapers May Be Our Last Best Hope for Recreating 'Public Life' in Local Communities," *American Society of Newspaper Editors Bulletin* (Oct. 1991): 16–19; Rosen, "Community Action," 30–33.

27. Batten, William Allen White Lecture, 21–22.

28. For an early treatment of this theme by a journalist, see Douglas Cater, *The Fourth Branch of Government* (Boston: Houghton Mifflin, 1959).

29. On the rise of an adversarial culture in journalism during the 1960s, see Michael Schudson, *Discovering the News* (New York: Basic, 1978): 176–83. On the mythology of Watergate in American journalism, see Michael Schudson, *Watergate and American Memory* (New York: Basic, 1992): 103–26. For a view from a journalist on the "post-Watergate syndrome" in the press, see Davis Merritt, *Public Journalism and Public Life* (Mahwah, N.J.: Lawrence Erlbaum, 1995): 56–62. For a view from a political scientist on the same development, see Larry J. Sabato, *Feeding Frenzy* (New York: Free Press, 1991): 61–64.

30. According to James D. Squires, a former reporter for the *Nashville Tennessean* and former editor of the *Chicago Tribune*, "it was dramatic press accounts of oppression in the South that produced desegregation across the land, as well as a public rebuke of the war in Vietnam." James D. Squires, *Read All About It!* (New York: Times Books, 1993): 223. Jonathan Cohn, an editor at the *American Prospect* and later the *New Republic*, echoed this view when he wrote: "Historically, journalism's greatest contributions to politics have come in the form of iconoclasm—editors and writers who took stands contrary to conventional wisdom, stretched the boundaries of debate with provocative reporting, and forced readers to think more broadly." Jonathan Cohn, "Should Journalists Do Community Service?" *American Prospect* 22 (summer 1995): 16.

    Margaret Leonard, a former editor at the *Tallahassee Democrat*, observed: "I grew up in the South. . . . Most of the people I knew didn't want to hear about civil rights, but it was in the newspaper so they had to read it—and it changed the country." Quoted in Cohn, "Should Journalists Do Community Service?" 17.

    In his classic study of newsrooms at work, sociologist Herbert J. Gans took note of the journalist's latent fear of the audience. Herbert J. Gans, *Deciding What's News* (New York: Vintage, 1979): 234–35. On readers' demands degrading the editorial product, see Underwood, *When MBAs Rule the Newsroom*.

31. Squires, *Read All About It!* 8.

32. A sharp analysis of what I have called the cult of toughness is Adam Gopnik, "Read All About It," *New Yorker* (Dec. 12, 1994): 84, 86–90, 92–94, 96, 98–102.

33. Michael J. O'Neill, "A Problem for the Republic—A Challenge for Editors," address to the American Society of Newspaper Editors, May 5, 1982, reprinted in *The Adversarial Press* (St. Petersburg, Fla.: Modern Media Institute, 1983): 2, 3, 7.

34. Ibid., 6–7, 12, 3–4.
35. Ibid., 12, 14–15.
36. Ibid., 23–24.
37. See, for example, the dour assessments of *Washington Post* political writer E. J. Dionne in *Why Americans Hate Politics* (New York: Simon and Schuster, 1991): 316–17; and Sidney Blumenthal, *Pledging Allegiance* (New York: HarperCollins, 1990).
38. Quoted in Paul Taylor, *See How They Run* (New York: Knopf, 1990): 20.
39. See, for example, Kiku Adatto, *Picture Perfect* (New York: Basic, 1993); Kathleen Hall Jamieson, *Dirty Politics* (New York: Oxford University Press, 1992); Thomas E. Patterson, *Out of Order* (New York: Knopf, 1993); Sabato, *Feeding Frenzy*. For an analysis from a journalist who covered presidential campaigns, see Taylor, *See How They Run*.
40. Joan Didion, "Insider Baseball," *New York Review of Books* (Oct. 19, 1988): 19.
41. Todd Gitlin, "Blips, Bites, and Savvy Talk," *Dissent* (winter 1990): 19. Italics in original.
42. Quoted in Blumenthal, *Pledging Allegiance,* 301. On the "Snoopy" image, see Roger Simon, *Road Show* (New York: Farrar, Straus & Giroux, 1990): 8.
43. Quoted in Kiku Adatto, "Sound Bite Democracy: Network Evening News Presidential Campaign Coverage, 1968 and 1988," Research Paper R-2 (Cambridge, Mass.: Joan Shorenstein Barone Center on Press, Politics, and Public Policy, Harvard University: 1990): 13, 7. Gitlin, "Blips, Bites, and Savvy Talk," 19. See also Jamieson, *Dirty Politics,* 3–4, 174.
44. Jamieson, *Dirty Politics,* 10–11.
45. Tom Rosenstiel, *Strange Bedfellows* (New York: Hyperion, 1993): 33. Borger is quoted in Patterson, *Out of Order,* 72. See also Timothy J. Russert, "For '92, the Networks Have to Do Better," *New York Times* (April 4, 1990): E23. On reporters quitting the political beat, see Rosenstiel, *Strange Bedfellows,* 33; also the remarks of David Broder in *The James K. Batten Symposium on Civic Journalism* (Washington, D.C.: Pew Center for Civic Journalism, 1995): 3.
46. David S. Broder, "Democracy and the Press," *Washington Post* (Jan. 3, 1990): A15.
47. *James K. Batten Symposium on Civic Journalism,* 2–3. A good introduction to the Kettering Foundation's work is *Framing Issues: Building a Structure for Public Discussions* (Dayton: Kettering Foundation, 1995). On the National Issues Forums, see David Mathews, *Politics for People* (Urbana: University of Illinois Press, 1994): 108–9, 180–87; and James S. Fishkin, *The Voice of the People* (New Haven: Yale University Press, 1995): 164–65.
48. Harwood Group, *Citizens and Politics: A View from Main Street America* (Dayton: Kettering Foundation, 1991).
    Leonard Downie, executive editor of the *Post,* noted Broder's longtime use of the technique of conversing with citizens at a panel discussion in 1994. See "Public Journalism: New Wave or New Threat?" transcript of the Associated Press Managing Editors annual convention, Oct. 12, 1994: 10. Broder also describes his living-room discussions with voters in David Broder, "A New Assignment for the Press," Press-Enterprise Lecture Series (Riverside, Calif.: Press-Enterprise, 1991).
49. Harwood Group, *Citizens and Politics,* 3–4. For other examples of Harwood's work, see the Harwood Group, *Meaningful Chaos: How People Form Relationships with Public Concerns* (Dayton: Kettering Foundation, 1993); *Timeless Values: Staying True to Jour-*

nalistic Principles in the Age of New Media (Reston, Va.: American Society of Newspaper Editors, 1995); *Tapping Civic Life: How to Report First, and Best, What's Happening in Your Community* (Washington, D.C.: Pew Center for Civic Journalism, 1996); Richard C. Harwood, *America's Struggle Within* (Washington, D.C.: Pew Center for Civic Journalism, 1995).

50. Harwood Group, *Citizens and Politics,* 5–7.
51. Broder, "New Assignment for the Press," 1–3.
52. Ibid., 4–5.
53. Ibid., 8–9, 12–13.
54. Katharine Q. Seelye, "Wouldn't Mother Have Been Proud?" *New York Times* (June 18, 1995): sec. 4, p. 5.
55. Davis Merritt, telephone interview with author, Dec. 10, 1996.
56. Davis Merritt, "Up Front, Here's Our Election Bias," *Wichita Eagle* (Sept. 9, 1990): 13A.
57. For an example of such analysis, see William Safire, "The Double Wedge," *New York Times* (Feb. 23, 1995): A23.
58. The description that follows is adapted from Steve Smith, "Your Vote Counts: The Wichita Eagle's Election Project," *National Civic Review* (summer 1991): 24–30, and Merritt, *Public Journalism and Public Life,* chapter 7. See also Michael Hoyt, "The Wichita Experiment," *Columbia Journalism Review* (July–Aug. 1992): 43–47; and John Bare, "Case Study—Wichita and Charlotte: The Leap of a Passive Press to Activism," *Media Studies Journal* 6:4 (1992): 149–60.
59. *Wichita Eagle* (Oct. 7, 1990): 1D, 2D.
60. Merritt, *Public Journalism and Public Life,* 82. On the adversarial pose, see the analysis of journalism's "culture of aggression" in Gopnik, "Read All About It," 84, 86–90, 92–94, 96, 98–102. On the limitations of balance, see Merritt, *Public Journalism and Public Life,* 19–20.
61. The description that follows is adapted from the *Wichita Eagle*'s special reprint, *Solving It Ourselves: The People Project* (Wichita: Wichita Eagle and Beacon Publishing Company, 1992), Merritt, *Public Journalism and Public Life,* 84–86, and from various internal planning memos provided by Merritt.
62. Alexis de Tocqueville, *Democracy in America,* 2 vols., trans. George Lawrence (New York: Harper and Row: 1966): 513–25
63. Dionne, *Why Americans Hate Politics,* 354.
64. Merritt, *Public Journalism and Public Life,* 86.
65. Ibid., 83.
66. The description that follows is developed from Edward D. Miller, *The Charlotte Project* (St. Petersburg, Fla.: Poynter Institute for Media Studies, 1994). See also Bare, "Case Study—Wichita and Charlotte," 149–60.
67. Rich Oppel, "We'll Help You Regain Control of the Issues," *Charlotte Observer* (Jan. 12, 1992): A1. See also Broder, "Democracy and the Press," A15; Broder, "New Assignment for the Press," 12.
68. Miller, *The Charlotte Project,* 16. The reorientation required an extraordinary effort. Virtually the entire staff from business reporters to feature writers contributed something to the revamped coverage. Space was also increased. Coverage of the presidential

race almost doubled over the previous campaign—some 18,000 square inches, compared with 10,500 in 1988. According to Poynter, issue coverage went from 1,890 square inches in 1988 (18 percent of total) to 5,716 square inches in 1992 (32 percent). Coverage of campaign strategy fell from 21 percent of the total in 1988 to 11 percent in 1992; horse-race polls declined from 6.1 percent to 1.4 percent. News of what the candidates did and said was consistent in percentage terms with 1988. Miller, *The Charlotte Project*, 65–67.

69. Project on Public Life and the Press, transcript of seminar at American Press Institute, Reston, Va., Nov. 10–12, 1993 (Dayton: Kettering Foundation, 1993): 117.

70. Seelye, "Wouldn't Mother Have Been Proud?"

Chapter 2: In Search of a Different Story

1. Thomas Bender, *Intellect and Public Life* (Baltimore: Johns Hopkins University Press, 1993): 6, 130–32.

2. Ibid., 10, 135.

3. See Alicia C. Shepard, "Death of a Pioneer," *American Journalism Review* (Sept. 1994): 35.

4. Merritt's reflections on his career appear in Davis Merritt, *Public Journalism and Public Life* (Mahwah, N.J.: Lawrence Erlbaum, 1995): 29–87.

5. This and the previous quotation are from the transcript of a roundtable discussion sponsored by the Kettering Foundation and the S. I. Newhouse School of Public Communication, Sept. 25, 1991, New York City (Dayton: Kettering Foundation, 1991).

6. David Mathews, *Politics for People* (Urbana: University of Illinois Press, 1994): 2–3.

7. Knight Foundation, *1993 Annual Report* (Miami: John S. and James L. Knight Foundation, 1993): 86, 92.

8. I discuss the origins of the Project on Public Life and the Press in Jay Rosen, "Making Things More Public: On the Political Responsibility of the Media Intellectual," *Critical Studies in Mass Communication* 11:4 (1994): 373–74.

9. Jürgen Habermas, *The Structural Transformation of the Public Sphere*, trans. Thomas Burger with Frederick Lawrence (Cambridge: MIT Press, 1989): 22–23, 35–37, 54–56, 127–29, 162–66, 176–78, 182–85, 194–95, 209–10.

10. Ibid., 247. For a range of views in the debate over the public sphere, see Craig Calhoun, ed., *Habermas and the Public Sphere* (Cambridge: MIT Press, 1992), and Bruce Robbins, ed., *The Phantom Public Sphere* (Minneapolis: University of Minnesota Press, 1993). Two useful historical interpretations are Joan Landes, *Women and the Public Sphere in the Age of the French Revolution* (Ithaca, N.Y.: Cornell University Press, 1988), and Michael Warner, *Letters of the Republic* (Cambridge: Harvard University Press, 1990). See John Durham Peters, "Distrust of Representation: Habermas on the Public Sphere," *Media, Culture, and Society* 15:4 (1993): 541–71, for a view from a communication scholar. Also see John Durham Peters and Kenneth Cmiel, "Media Ethics and the Public Sphere," *Communication* 12:3 (1991): 197–215, for applications to the press.

11. Walter Lippmann, *Public Opinion* (1922; reprint, New York: Free Press, 1965): 8–19, 53–60, 158, 173, 201–9, 215–30.

12. Walter Lippmann, *The Phantom Public* (New York: Harcourt, Brace, 1925): 69–70, 126, 149–50.

13. Lippmann, *Public Opinion,* 234–35, 239–49; Lippmann, *The Phantom Public,* 155.

14. John Dewey, "Public Opinion," *New Republic* (May 3, 1922): 286. For an interpretation of Dewey along these lines, see Robert B. Westbrook, *John Dewey and American Democracy* (Ithaca, N.Y.: Cornell University Press, 1991): xiv–xvi, 40–42, 165–66, 248–49, 292–93.

15. John Dewey, *The Public and Its Problems* (New York: Henry Holt, 1927): 125–28, 131–32, 137–42, 168–69, 177–81.

16. Ibid., 182–84.

17. Ibid., 166, 203–8, 213, 151–52, 216–19. For other summaries and interpretations of the Lippmann-Dewey exchange, see Stanley Aronowitz, "Is a Democracy Possible? The Decline of the Public in the American Debate," in Robbins, ed., *The Phantom Public Sphere,* 75–92; James W. Carey, *Culture as Communication* (Boston: Unwin Hyman, 1989): 75–82; Daniel Czitrom, *Media and the American Mind: From Morse to McLuhan* (Chapel Hill: University of North Carolina Press): 91–124; Christopher Lasch, *The Revolt of the Elites and the Betrayal of Democracy* (New York: Norton, 1995): chapter 9; John Durham Peters, "Democracy and American Mass Communication Theory: Dewey, Lippmann, and Lazarsfeld," *Communication* 11:3 (1989): 199–220; John Durham Peters, "Revising the Eighteenth-Century Script," *Gannett Center Journal* 3 (spring 1989): 152–67; Alan Ryan, *John Dewey and the High Tide of American Liberalism* (New York: Norton, 1995): 201–18; Michael Schudson, *Discovering the News: A Social History of American Newspapers* (New York: Basic, 1978): 122–34; Ronald Steel, *Walter Lippmann and the American Century* (New York: Vintage, 1981): 180–85; Westbrook, *John Dewey and American Democracy,* 294–319.

18. On this criticism of Lippmann and the "realist" outlook on democracy see Westbrook, *John Dewey and American Democracy,* xv–xvi; 299–300; James W. Carey, "The Press and the Public Discourse," *Center Magazine* (March–April 1987): 6–7, and "The Press, Public Opinion, and Public Discourse," in Theodore L. Glasser and Charles T. Salmon, eds., *Public Opinion and the Communication of Consent* (New York: Guilford, 1995): 389–92.

19. Dewey explicitly wrote that his study was "an intellectual or hypothetical one," with "no attempt to state how the required conditions might come into existence," in *The Public and Its Problems,* 157.

20. For an interesting treatment of this theme, see Daniel T. Rodgers, *Contested Truths* (New York: Basic, 1987): chapter 6, 176–78, 203–11.

21. Carey, "The Press and the Public Discourse," 5–6.

22. See Jane J. Mansbridge, "The Rise and Fall of Self-Interest in the Explanation of Political Life," in Jane J. Mansbridge, ed., *Beyond Self-Interest* (Chicago: University of Chicago Press, 1990): 9. The phrase "who gets what, when, how" comes from an influential book by Harold D. Lasswell, *Politics: Who Gets What, When, How* (New York: McGraw-Hill, 1936). Perhaps the key work in what has been called the realist school of democratic thinking is Joseph A. Schumpeter, *Capitalism, Socialism, and Democracy* (1942; reprint, New York: Harper and Row, 1962). Mansbridge offers a concise summary of Schumpeter's perspective in *Beyond Self-Interest,* 8. Also essential in understanding the rise of the realist school and interest-group thinking is Robert A.

Dahl, *A Preface to Democratic Theory* (Chicago: University of Chicago Press, 1956). For a critical overview of these developments, see Edward Purcell, *The Crisis in Democratic Theory* (Lexington: University of Kentucky Press, 1973). On the theme of citizen participation in classical and contemporary thought about democracy, see Carole Pateman, *Participation and Democratic Theory* (London: Cambridge University Press, 1970). For a good summary of the entire problem of how to conceive of modern democracy, see Robert A. Dahl, *Democracy and Its Critics* (New Haven: Yale University Press, 1989).

23. See, for example, Benjamin Barber, *Strong Democracy* (Berkeley: University of California Press, 1984); Michael J. Sandel, *Liberalism and the Politics of Justice* (Cambridge: Cambridge University Press, 1982); and *Democracy's Discontent* (Cambridge: Harvard University Press, 1996).

24. On the founding of the American Society of Newspaper Editors and the Associated Press Managing Editors, see Michael Emery and Edwin Emery, *The Press and America*, 6th ed. (Englewood Cliffs, N.J.: Prentice-Hall, 1988): 578, 431.

25. Benjamin Ginsberg, *The Captive Public* (New York: Basic, 1987): 60. On the professionalization of American journalism based on some of Lippmann's ideals, see Schudson, *Discovering the News*, 151–59. On the rise of objectivity and its difficult passage into the 1960s, ibid., 145–86. On the influence of the professional ideal in journalism, see also James W. Carey, "The Communications Revolution and the Professional Communicator," in Eve Stryker Munson and Catherine A. Warren, eds., *James Carey: A Critical Reader* (Minneapolis: University of Minnesota Press, 1997): 136–41. A provocative treatment of the journalist's claims to professionalism is Paul H. Weaver, *News and the Culture of Lying* (New York: Free Press, 1994): 57–58, 125–28, 195–96. See also Herbert J. Gans, *Deciding What's News* (New York: Knopf, 1979); Gans calls his book a study of "the values and the ideology of a profession which deems itself objective and non-ideological" (xiv).

   The literature on opinion polling is vast. A useful historical survey is Susan Herbst, *Numbered Voices* (Chicago: University of Chicago Press, 1993). Also important is Ginsberg, *The Captive Public*. An early work praising the science of polling as an instrument of democracy is George Gallup and Saul Rae, *The Pulse of Democracy* (New York: Simon and Schuster, 1940). For contemporary accounts on the press and polling, see Albert H. Cantril, *The Opinion Connection* (Washington, D.C.: Congressional Quarterly Press, 1991); Thomas E. Mann and Gary R. Orren, eds., *Media Polls and American Politics* (Washington, D.C.: Brookings Institution, 1992); Charles T. Salmon and Theodore L. Glasser, "The Politics of Polling and the Limits of Consent," in Glasser and Salmon, eds., *Public Opinion and the Communication of Consent*, 437–58.

26. Daniel Hallin remarks on the "decline of a politically committed journalism and its replacement by a professional journalism that claimed to stand above politics." Professionalization, he notes, "narrows [political] discussion to questions of technique that can be approached with a detached realism." Daniel C. Hallin, "The American News Media: A Critical Theory Perspective," in John Forester, ed., *Critical Theory and Public Life* (Cambridge: MIT Press, 1995): 140.

   One noteworthy attempt to address fundamental questions about democracy and journalism was the work of the Commission on Freedom of the Press, published in 1947.

Chaired by Robert Hutchins, president of the University of Chicago, and funded by Henry Luce, the founder of *Time* magazine, the commission produced a report that has continued to hold deep interest for scholars and critics, although its influence on mainstream journalism was negligible. Commission on Freedom of the Press, *A Free and Responsible Press* (Chicago: University of Chicago Press, 1947). On the report's lasting significance despite "its neglect by the contemporary world," see Lee C. Bollinger, *Images of a Free Press* (Chicago: University of Chicago Press, 1991): 28–34. For a discussion connecting the work of the Hutchins Commission to public journalism, see James W. Carey, "In Defense of Public Journalism," in Theodore Glasser, ed., *The Idea of Public Journalism* (New York: Guilford, 1999).

27. On this point see Rosen, "Making Things More Public," 369–74.

28. Quoted in *Speaking of Public Journalism: Talks from the Project on Public Life and the Press* (Dayton: Kettering Foundation, 1997): 4, 9–10, 4. See also Carey's remarks on the adversarial press in "The Culture in Question," in Munson and Warren, eds., *James Carey: A Critical Reader*, 336–37.

29. William James, *Pragmatism and the Meaning of Truth* (Cambridge: Harvard University Press, 1975): 31–32, 34; see also 169–70. For my understanding of pragmatism in Dewey's thought I have relied on Ryan, *John Dewey and the High Tide of American Liberalism*, and Westbrook, *John Dewey and American Democracy*. A useful critique is John Patrick Diggins, *The Promise of Pragmatism* (Chicago: University of Chicago Press, 1994).

30. On the founding of the Pew Center for Civic Journalism, see G. Bruce Knecht, "Why a Big Foundation Gives Newspapers Cash to Change Their Ways," *Wall Street Journal* (Oct. 17, 1996): A1; "Civic Journalism: Can Press Reforms Revitalize Democracy?" *CQ Researcher* 35:6 (Sept. 1996): 831–32. For an example of how Fouhy and Schaffer began spreading the word, see Ed Fouhy and Jan Schaffer, "Civic Journalism: Growing and Evolving," *Nieman Reports* (spring 1995): 16–18.

31. See Edward D. Miller, *The Charlotte Project* (St. Petersburg, Fla.: Poynter Institute for Media Studies, 1994). The Poynter Institute had cooperated with the *Charlotte Observer* in its 1992 experiment with election coverage and sponsored some early discussions on public life and the press, similar to the Kettering Foundation's work in the same period. Later, Poynter collaborated with Fouhy and the Pew Center in designing seminars for journalists.

32. Knecht, "Why a Big Foundation Gives Newspapers Cash"; Ed Fouhy, "Foundations: Nurturing Journalistic Values or Threatening Independence?" *Civic Catalyst* (Jan. 1997): 2, 12.

33. Gil Thelen, "The Newspaper Can Help Our Community Set Its Course," Columbia *State* (Nov. 21, 1993): B2.

34. Chris Peck, "A Step Back, A Step Ahead," Spokane *Spokesman-Review* (Feb. 6, 1994): B2.

35. Carey, "The Press and the Public Discourse," 14.

Chapter 3: Applying Practice to Theory

1. Davis Merritt, *Public Journalism and Public Life* (Mahwah, N.J.: Lawrence Erlbaum, 1995): 83.

2. Howard Kurtz, *Media Circus: The Trouble with America's Newspapers* (New York: Times Books, 1993), 6–7. On the same general themes see also Mark Jurkowitz, "Reforming the Media," *Boston Globe Magazine* (July 9, 1995): 18, 20, 22–25, 30–31.

3. Quoted in Doug Underwood, *When MBAs Rule the Newsroom* (New York: Columbia University Press, 1993): 14.

4. Max Jennings, unpublished manuscript for *presstime* (1995): 1, 3–8.

5. *Dayton Daily News*, south edition (Oct. 25, 1995): sec. Z4, p. 1

6. Jennings, unpublished manuscript for *presstime*, 9.

7. Max Jennings, address to Pulliam Fellows, Phoenix, Ariz. (July 20, 1995): 2–4.

8. Ibid., 6–7, 9.

9. See Isabel Wilkerson, "Riots in Los Angeles, Around the Nation," *New York Times* (May 1, 1992): A23; Laurie Goodstein, Don Phillips, "New Yorkers Sent Home Early, Unrest Subsides Across the Country," *Washington Post* (May 2, 1992): A13.

10. Ron Kirksey, "Blacks, Whites Live in Parallel Realities," *Akron Beacon Journal* (March 1, 1993): A5.

11. Ron Kirksey, Michael Holley, and Bob Paynter, "Black, White Chasm Deepens," *Akron Beacon Journal* (March 1, 1993): A1, A4.

12. Carl Chancellor and Bob Dyer, "A Separate, but Equal, Focus on Our Differences," *Akron Beacon Journal* (Feb. 28, 1993): A1, A6, A7.

13. Reprint of the *Akron Beacon Journal* series "A Question of Color" (Akron: Akron Beacon Journal, 1994): 1.

14. See the report on the Akron initiative in Lisa Austin, *Public Life and the Press: A Progress Report* (Dayton, Ohio: Kettering Foundation, 1995): 1–3.

15. "A Question of Color," 1; Coming Together Project, 1996 annual report. A sampling from the list shows the range of groups involved: Akron Bar Association, Akron Black Nurses Association, American Friends Service Committee, Broadman Baptist Church, Catholic Commission, Central Presbyterian Church, East High School, Habitat for Humanity, Junior League of Akron, Kappa Alpha Psi Fraternity, League of Women Voters (Akron Area), Magical Theater Company, NAACP (Akron Branch), National Council of Jewish Women, Portage Country Club, the Salvation Army, Telxon Corporation, Unitarian Universalist Church, United Way of Summit County, University of Akron Black Cultural Center, Vietnam Vet Rap Group, Walsh Jesuit High School, West Side Neighbors, Inc., YMCA of Summit County, and on and on through the civic landscape of the Akron area.

16. Coming Together Project, 1996 annual report.

17. Jonathan Cohn, "Should Journalists Do Community Service?" *American Prospect* 22 (summer 1995): 16. In December 1997, President Bill Clinton came to Akron as part of his attempt to build a national dialogue on race. He chose the city in part because of the record established by the Coming Together Project. James Bennet, "Clinton, at Meeting on Race, Struggles to Sharpen Dialogue," *New York Times* (Dec. 4, 1997): A1, A26; Steven A. Holmes, "In Akron, Dialogue but Few Changes," *New York Times* (Dec. 4, 1997): A26.

18. See Daniel Yankelovich, *Coming to Public Judgment* (Syracuse: Syracuse University Press, 1991): 63–65, 116–20, 134–36, 166–70. Elder described the development of his

thinking at the Project on Public Life and the Press, transcript of seminar proceedings, August 14, 1995, American Press Institute (Dayton: Kettering Foundation, 1995): 60–64.

19. San Jose Mercury News, *Discussion Guide: Affirmative Action and Equal Opportunity* (San Jose: San Jose Mercury News, 1995).

20. Rob Elder, "Affirmative Reaction," *San Jose Mercury News* (Oct. 22, 1995): 7F.

21. Ibid.

22. I have borrowed the observation about TV as a flow experience from Raymond Williams, *Television: Technology and Cultural Form* (New York: Schocken, 1975): 86–118.

23. Quoted in James Bennet, "Nightline Pulls the Plug on Convention Coverage," *New York Times* (Aug. 15, 1996): A19.

24. Elizabeth Kolbert, "Of the TV, by the TV, for the TV," *New York Times* (Aug. 18, 1996): sec. 4, p. 5.

25. On the historic broadcasts from Israel and South Africa, see Ted Koppel and Kyle Gibson, *Nightline* (New York: Times Books, 1996): 65–117.

26. Dennis Foley, presentation to the Project on Public Life and the Press seminar, Feb. 7, 1997, American Press Institute (Dayton: Kettering Foundation, 1997): 3.

27. Ibid., 1.

28. Ibid., 3.

29. Jonathan Schell, *History in Sherman Park* (New York: Knopf, 1987): 3–5.

30. Joan Didion, "Insider Baseball," *New York Review of Books* (Oct. 19, 1988): 20. I have adapted this discussion of Schell and Didion from Jay Rosen, "Making Journalism More Public," *Communication* 12:4 (1991): 280–82.

31. Daniel M. Weintraub, "Issues: Bob Dole Would Demand More Parental Control and Responsibility in Schools," *Orange County Register* (Aug. 13, 1996): N6.

32. James W. Carey, "The Press and the Public Discourse," *Center Magazine* (March–April 1987): 14.

33. Wendy Lawton, "Bruce Takes on District 11," *Colorado Springs Gazette* (Oct. 22, 1996): A1, A3.

34. Paul Taylor, *See How They Run* (New York: Knopf, 1990): 27.

35. For some useful scholarly works on framing in journalism, see Robert M. Entman, "Framing: Toward Clarification of a Fractured Paradigm," *Journal of Communication* 43:4 (1993): 51–58; Shanto Iyengar, *Is Anyone Responsible?* (Chicago: University of Chicago Press, 1991); W. Russell Neuman, Marion R. Just, and Ann N. Crigler, *Common Knowledge* (Chicago: University of Chicago Press, 1992). See also the discussion of schemas in Thomas E. Patterson, *Out of Order* (New York: Knopf, 1993): 53–93. On framing as a conceptual tool in public journalism, see Jay Rosen, "Public Journalism as a Democratic Art" in Jay Rosen, Davis Merritt, and Lisa Austin, *Public Journalism, Theory and Practice: Lessons From Experience* (Dayton: Kettering Foundation, 1997): 3–24.

36. I am guided in this approach by James W. Carey, *Communication as Culture* (Boston: Unwin Hyman, 1989): 19–21; and an earlier classic, Murray Edelman, *The Symbolic Uses of Politics* (Urbana: University of Illinois Press, 1964).

37. Steve Smith, "Framing from the Center of the Community," in *Change: Living It, Embracing It, Measuring It* (Reston, Va.: American Society of Newspaper Editors, 1997): 4–5.

38. Ibid., 6–7.
39. Michael J. Sandel, *Democracy's Discontent* (Cambridge: Harvard University Press, 1996): 3. For some key texts in communitarian thought, see Robert N. Bellah, Richard Madsen, William M. Sullivan, Ann Swidler, Steven M. Tipton, *Habits of the Heart* (Berkeley: University of California Press, 1985), and a sequel by the same authors, *The Good Society* (New York: Knopf, 1991); Amitai Etzioni, *The Spirit of Community* (New York: Crown, 1993); Michael J. Sandel, *Liberalism and the Politics of Justice* (Cambridge: Cambridge University Press, 1982).
40. Sandel, *Democracy's Discontent,* 4, 5.

Chapter 4: Does It Help the Citizen Decide?

1. All quotations in this section are from an unpublished transcript of a candidates' meeting at the Norfolk *Virginian-Pilot,* Sept. 18, 1995.
2. See Barbara Ballard and Susan Goranson, "Public Journalism: Does the Paper Measure Up?" (Norfolk: League of Women Voters of South Hampton Roads, 1995).
3. Cole C. Campbell, "League Takes Us at Our Word, Studies Our Effort to Serve Citizens Better," Norfolk *Virginian-Pilot* (June 18, 1995): A2.
4. For an instance of the job-candidate metaphor at work, see "Voter's Guide: Decision 96," special section of the Norfolk *Virginian-Pilot* (Oct. 27, 1996), sec. 5.
5. Cole C. Campbell, "We Must Discuss Issues to Ensure a Stronger and Less Divisive Society," Norfolk *Virginian-Pilot* (April 9, 1995): A2.
6. Unless otherwise noted, this account relies on Tony Wharton, research memo for the Project on Public Life and the Press (Dayton: Kettering Foundation): 4–5.
7. Harwood Group, "Meaningful Chaos: How People Form Relationships to Public Concerns" (Dayton: Kettering Foundation, 1993): 2–3.
8. On the paper's use of community conversations see Norfolk *Virginian-Pilot,* "Reporting on Public Life," report prepared for the Project on Public Life and the Press seminar, Nov. 10–12, 1994, American Press Institute (Dayton: Kettering Foundation, 1994).
9. See the "Special Virginia Report" prepared for Virginia newspapers by the Virginia Associated Press, *Daily Press, Richmond Times-Dispatch, Roanoake Times & World News,* Norfolk *Virginian-Pilot,* Sept. 11–15, 1994.
10. Tony Wharton, "Crowd Echoes Allen's Cry Against Parole," Norfolk *Virginian-Pilot* (Aug. 27, 1994): B3.
11. See *The James K. Batten Symposium on Civic Journalism and Award for Excellence in Civic Journalism,* an edited transcript (Washington, D.C.: Pew Center for Civic Journalism, 1995): 22.
12. This account relies on "The Public Journalism Journey of the Virginian-Pilot," presentation to the Project on Public Life and the Press seminar, Aug. 14, 1995, American Press Institute (Dayton: Kettering Foundation, 1995).
13. The key readings included James W. Carey, "The Press and the Public Discourse," *Center Magazine* (March–April 1987): 4–32; Harwood Group, *Citizens and Politics*

(Dayton: Kettering Foundation, 1991); Daniel Yankelovich, *Coming to Public Judgment* (Syracuse: Syracuse University Press, 1991); Jay Rosen, "Public Journalism as a Democratic Art," in Jay Rosen, Davis Merritt, and Lisa Austin, *Public Journalism, Theory and Practice: Lessons From Experience* (Dayton: Kettering Foundation, 1997): 3–24; David Mathews, *Politics for People* (Urbana: University of Illinois Press, 1994); Francis Fukuyama, *Trust: The Social Virtues and the Creation of Prosperity* (New York: Free Press, 1995).

14. For example, "Create coherence by describing the big picture surrounding an issue, reminding people of the issue's history and what's at stake for the community." Dennis Hartig, "Changing the Personality of Local News Pages," *Civic Catalyst* (fall 1997): 8.

15. Bill Burke, "To Our Readers: This Page Will Explore Trends, Their Causes," Norfolk *Virginian-Pilot* (March 4, 1997): B3.

16. For scholarly readings of the First Amendment's freedom of the press clause that support Knepler's, see Lee C. Bollinger, *Images of a Free Press* (Chicago: University of Chicago Press, 1991); James W. Carey, "A Republic, If You Can Keep It," in Eve Stryker Munson and Catherine A. Warren, eds., *James Carey: A Critical Reader* (Minneapolis: University of Minnesota Press, 1997): 207–27; Cass R. Sunstein, *Democracy and the Problem of Free Speech* (New York: Free Press, 1993).

Chapter 5: Doing Less Harm

1. Davis Merritt, *Public Journalism and Public Life* (Mahwah, N.J.: Lawrence Erlbaum, 1995): 124.
2. Ibid., 58–59, 62.
3. Project on Public Life and the Press, transcript of seminar proceedings, Nov. 12, 1993, American Press Institute (Dayton: Kettering Foundation, 1993): 27.
4. Ibid., Nov. 11, 1994, 42.
5. Ibid., 5–6.
6. Ibid., 9.
7. Ibid., June 13, 1994, 44–45.
8. Ibid., March 25, 1995, 43–44.
9. Ibid., Nov. 11, 1994, 17–18.
10. Ibid., March 25, 1995, 14.
11. Ibid., Nov. 11, 1993, 74–75.
12. Ibid., June 13, 1994, 19–21.
13. Ibid., 7–9
14. Ibid., Nov. 11, 1993, 63.
15. *Civic Catalyst* is the newsletter of the Pew Center for Civic Journalism in Washington, D.C.
16. Davis Merritt, "Public Journalism and Public Life," *National Civic Review* (summer–fall 1995): 265–66.
17. In order to render it more readable, I have edited Carpenter's account and omitted the ellipses.

Chapter 6: Journalism Is What It Is

1. David Remnick, "Scoop," *New Yorker* (Jan. 29, 1996): 42. In 1998, Remnick was named editor of the magazine.
2. *Reporting on Public Life,* presentation by editors of the Norfolk *Virginian-Pilot* to the Project on Public Life and the Press seminar, American Press Institute, Nov. 10–12, 1994.
3. Remnick, "Scoop," 42.
4. *Reporting on Public Life.*
5. These were the most common objections from journalists. Scholars of the press had other complaints. Public journalism was accused of misreading the exchange between Lippmann and Dewey; failing to pose a significant challenge to corporate control of the news media; adopting a sentimental or thinly reasoned view of democracy; promoting a hazy conception of itself that muddles important problems of definition; skirting important questions of power, justice, and inequality; relying too much on foundation support; neglecting to consider historical precedents in its eagerness to be seen as "new"; overburdening the press with responsibilities it cannot meet; declining to offer a potent challege to journalistic authority; and offering an illusion of empowerment and participation rather than the real thing. These and other criticisms are found throughout Theodore L. Glasser, ed., *The Idea of Public Journalism* (New York: Guilford, 1999). They are also present in Jay Black, ed., *Mixed News: The Public/Civic/Communitarian Journalism Debate* (Mahwah, N.J.: Lawrence Erlbaum, 1997). A particularly heated critique is Thomas Frank, "Triangulation Nation," *Baffler* 11 (winter 1998): 3–12, 75–93.
6. Paul Greenberg, "Public Journalism: Media's Latest Fad, Plague," *Dayton Daily News* (Nov. 14, 1996): 19A.
7. Michael Gartner, "Give Me Old-Time Journalism," *Quill* (Nov.–Dec. 1995): 68–69. See also Michael Gartner, "Public Journalism—Seeing Through the Gimmicks," *Media Studies Journal* 11:1 (winter 1997): 69–75.
8. John Dewey, "America and the World," *Nation* (March 14, 1918), reprinted in John Dewey, *Characters and Events,* 2 vols. (New York: Henry Holt, 1929): vol. 2, 644; John Dewey, "Pragmatic America," *New Republic* (April 12, 1922), reprinted in Dewey, *Characters and Events,* vol. 2, 545–46.
9. The best overview of this history is Michael Schudson, *Discovering the News* (New York: Basic, 1978). The standard journalism history text is Michael Emery, Edwin Emery, and Nancy L. Roberts, *The Press and America,* 8th ed. (New York: Allyn & Bacon, 1996). See also Mitchell Stephens, *A History of News* (New York: Viking, 1988): 183–288; Thomas C. Leonard, *News for All* (New York: Oxford University Press, 1995); and James W. Carey's brief sketch in "The Press and the Public Discourse," *Center Magazine* (March–April, 1987): 8–16.
10. James W. Carey, "A Republic—If You Can Keep It," in Eve Stryker Munson and Catherine A. Warren, eds., *James Carey: A Critical Reader* (Minneapolis: University of Minnesota Press, 1997): 218.
11. Ibid., 217, 218, 220.
12. Quoted in Eric Black, "Journalism Tests New Definition of Involvement," Minneapolis *Star-Tribune* (April 8, 1996): A8.

13. Michael Gartner, "Give Me Old-Time Journalism," 68–69. Gartner, in the Joe Creason Lecture, University of Kentucky, Lexington (April 14, 1997), also said: "Jay Rosen, the professor who sort of invented the movement, writes in tongues, and I can never figure out what he is saying."

14. As the historian Richard Hofstadter wrote, "To an extraordinary degree the work of the Progressive movement rested upon its journalism. The fundamental cultural achievement of American Progressivism was the business of exposure, and journalism was the chief occupational source of its creative writers." The Progressive movement's "characteristic contribution was that of the socially responsible reporter-reformer." Richard Hofstadter, The Age of Reform (New York: Knopf, 1955): 185. For evidence of this view see Lincoln Steffens, The Shame of the Cities (1904; reprint, New York: Hill & Wang, 1957): 1–18. See also Theodore L. Glasser and James S. Ettema, "Investigative Journalism and the Moral Order," Critical Studies in Mass Communication 6:1 (March 1989): 4–6; Thomas C. Leonard, The Power of the Press (New York: Oxford University Press, 1986): 193–223; Arthur Weinberg and Lila Weinberg, eds., The Muckrakers (New York: Putnam, 1964): xviii–xxii.

On the press as an addition to the three branches of government set down in the Constitution, see Lee C. Bollinger, Images of a Free Press (Chicago: University of Chicago Press, 1991): 52–61, 177; Douglass Cater, The Fourth Branch of Government (Boston: Houghton Mifflin, 1959); Lucas A. Powe, Jr., The Fourth Estate and the Constitution (Berkeley: University of California Press, 1991). For a view of journalism history that regards the American press as a creation of politics and government policy, see Timothy E. Cook, Governing with the News (Chicago: University of Chicago Press, 1998).

15. Michael Gartner was not the only one to spot a connection between public journalism and the publication of the Unabomber's manifesto. See William Serrin, "Publishing the Unabomber: Responsible or Reckless?" Washington Post (Sept. 24, 1995): C3.

16. Mike Hoyt, "Are You Now, or Will You Ever Be a Civic Journalist?" Columbia Journalism Review (Sept.–Oct. 1995): 29–30.

17. Brian MacQuarrie, "Press Critic Decries 'Civic Journalism,' Media Mergers," Boston Globe (Nov. 15, 1996): A9.

18. Quoted in Marilyn Kalfus, "Public Journalism: Can News Media Play Advocate?" Orange County Register (Jan. 20, 1996): A17.

19. William Glaberson, "Press," New York Times (Feb. 27, 1995): D7.

20. Christopher Conte, "Angels in the Newsroom," Governing (Aug. 1996): 22.

21. Alicia C. Shepard, "Death of a Pioneer," American Journalism Review (Sep. 1994): 35.

22. Bill Babcock, a former journalist who moved on to an academic post at the University of Minnesota, captured the essence of the anti-experimental attitude in labeling public journalism the "flavor of the month" in 1996. "I get worried when journalists put themselves in the role of advocates for anything, even something as harmless-sounding as civic connectedness," Babcock said. "Journalism's job is to give the public a full array of information which they may choose to use or not use to become more connected." Eric Black, "Journalism Tests New Definition of Involvement," Minneapolis Star-Tribune (April 8, 1996): A8.

23. Alicia C. Shepard, "The Gospel of Public Journalism," *American Journalism Review* (Sept. 1994): 31.

24. Quoted in Hoyt, "Are You Now, or Will You Ever Be a Civic Journalist?" 30.

25. Hiley Ward, review of *Doing Public Journalism* by Arthur Charity, *Editor and Publisher* (Feb. 17, 1996): 23.

26. Lynne Enders Glaser, " 'New' Concept in Journalism Urges Advocacy," *Fresno Bee* (Oct. 23, 1994): B9; and Lynne Enders Glaser, "Media Advocacy to Push Causes Steps Over the Line," *Fresno Bee* (Oct. 30, 1994): B9. A similarly provocative headline is Kalfus, "Public Journalism: Can News Media Play Advocate?" A16.

27. William F. Woo, "As Old Gods Falter: Public Journalism and the Tradition of Detachment," Press-Enterprise Lecture Series (Riverside, Calif.: Press-Enterprise, 1995): 11–12.

28. Greenberg, "Public Journalism," 19A.

29. Arthur Charity, *Doing Public Journalism* (New York: Guilford, 1995): 144–45. Italics in original.

30. Jean Bethke Elshtain, *Democracy on Trial* (New York: Basic, 1995): 81.

31. Quoted in Hoyt, "Are You Now, or Will You Ever Be a Civic Journalist?" 29.

32. Phyllis Kaniss, *The Media and the Mayor's Race* (Bloomington: Indiana University Press): 21. I have adapted this section from Jay Rosen, *Getting the Connections Right* (New York: Twentieth Century Fund, 1996): 67–70.

33. Kaniss, *Media and the Mayor's Race*, 23.

34. Quoted in Alicia C. Shepard, "The Real Public Journalism," *American Journalism Review* (Jan.–Feb. 1995): 25.

35. *The James K. Batten Symposium and Award for Excellence in Civic Journalism* (Washington, D.C.: Pew Center for Civic Journalism, 1995): 25.

36. Shepard, "The Real Public Journalism," 25.

37. *James K. Batten Symposium*, 25.

Chapter 7: *The* New York Times *and the* Washington Post *on Public Journalism*

1. Michael Kelly, "David Gergen, Master of the Game," *New York Times Magazine* (Oct. 31, 1993): 64, 80, 94, 97.

2. "Our national politics has become a competition for images or between images, rather than between ideals," Boorstin wrote. Daniel Boorstin, *The Image* (1961; reprint, New York: Atheneum, 1978): 249. Jonathan Schell, *The Time of Illusion* (New York: Random House, 1975); see especially Schell's remarks on the "doctrine of credibility" during the Vietnam era, 9–11, 91–95, 133–34, 380–83, 341–87. The testimony of journalists who covered Reagan is scattered throughout Mark Hertsgaard, *On Bended Knee* (New York: Farrar, Straus & Giroux, 1988).

3. Václav Havel, "The Power of the Powerless," in John Keane, ed., *The Power of the Powerless* (Armonk, N.Y.: M. E. Sharpe, 1990): 23–95.

4. Kelly, "David Gergen," 97, 103.

5. "News About the Magazine," *New York Times Magazine* (Oct. 31, 1993): 9.

6. Quoted in Maureen Dowd, "Raffish and Rowdy," *New York Times* (March 31, 1996): sec. 4, p. 15.

7. A. M. Rosenthal, "Protest from a Member," *New York Times* (Jan. 10, 1997): A33.

8. William Glaberson, "A New Press Role: Solving Problems," *New York Times* (Oct. 3, 1994): D6.

9. Jay Rosen, "Beyond Objectivity," *Nieman Reports* (winter 1993): 53.

10. The ellipses in this interview are in the original.

11. William Glaberson, "Press," *New York Times* (Feb. 27, 1995): D7.

12. Davis Merritt, telephone interview with author, Dec. 12, 1997.

13. Max Frankel, "Fix-It Journalism," *New York Times Magazine* (May 21, 1995): 28, 30.

14. Paul Taylor, *See How They Run* (New York: Knopf, 1990): 23. On the origins of the adversarial attitude in the press, see Michael Schudson, *Discovering the News* (New York: Basic, 1978): 176–83. On Trilling's concept of an adversarial culture, see Lionel Trilling, *Beyond Culture* (New York: Viking, 1965): xii–xiii.

15. See, for example, James W. Carey, "The Press, Public Opinion, and Public Discourse" in Eve Stryker Munson and Catherine A. Warren, eds., *James Carey: A Critical Reader* (Minneapolis: University of Minnesota Press, 1997): 242–44; Herbert J. Gans, *Deciding What's News* (New York: Random House, 1979): 68–69, 203–6; Theodore L. Glasser and James S. Ettema, "Investigative Journalism and the Moral Order," *Critical Studies in Mass Communication* 6:1 (March 1989): 4–6; Michael Schudson, *The Power of News* (Cambridge: Harvard University Press, 1995): 66, 70.

16. James Fallows, *Breaking the News: How the News Media Undermine American Democracy* (New York: Pantheon, 1996): 3–5, 7–8, 6.

17. Fallows reflected on this experience in James Fallows, "The Puff Adder's Nest of Modern Journalism," keynote address, *The James K. Batten Symposium and Award For Excellence in Civic Journalism* (Washington, D.C.: Pew Center for Civic Journalism, 1996): 11–14. See also Fallows, *Breaking the News*, 4, 247.

18. Ibid., 240–43, 267, 247. Italics are in the original in the phrase "will rise or fall with the political system."

19. Fallows, "The Puff Adder's Nest," 14.

20. Fallows, *Breaking the News*, 7, 9.

21. Howell Raines, "The Fallows Fallacy," *New York Times* (Feb. 25, 1996): sec. 4, p. 14.

22. Richard Harwood, "The Legitimacy of 'Civic Journalism,'" *Washington Post* (March 8, 1996): A21. Richard Harwood, "Civic Journalism 101," *Washington Post* (Jan. 17, 1995): A19. This Richard Harwood is a different person from the researcher with the same name whose work was discussed in Chapters 1 and 4.

23. Frank Rich, "The Capital Gang," *New York Times* (Jan. 13, 1996): A23.

24. Max Frankel, "Get Thee to Mental Gym," *New York Times Magazine* (May 19, 1996): 28. Italics are in the original.

25. Quoted in Alicia C. Shepard, "The Pew Connection," *American Journalism Review* (April, 1996): 28.

26. Christopher Lehmann-Haupt, "Depicting News Coverage as a Performing Art," review of *Breaking the News* by James Fallows, *New York Times* (Jan. 22, 1996): B2. In the *New York Times Book Review*, political analyst Kevin Phillips wrote a lukewarm review that avoided public journalism and the whole subject of reform. He noted that all the juicy material was in the first half of the book. "The last hundred pages slump into John

Dewey, Walter Lippmann and a turgid dissection of coverage of President Clinton's health care proposal." Kevin Phillips, "Bad News," review of *Breaking the News* by James Fallows, *New York Times Book Review* (Jan. 28, 1996): 8.

27. Dowd, "Raffish and Rowdy"; Maureen Dowd, "Bottomless and Topless," *New York Times* (June 9, 1996): sec. 4, p. 15.

28. Iver Peterson, "Civic-Minded Pursuits Gain Ground at Newspapers," *New York Times* (March 4, 1996): D7; Francis X. Clines, "Cynics Repent," *New York Times* (May 4, 1997): sec. 4, p. 5; "The Color of Mendacity," *New York Times* (July 19, 1996): A26.

29. Gene Roberts, *Corporatism vs. Journalism*, Press-Enterprise Lecture Series (Riverside, Calif.: Press-Enterprise, 1996): 19, 12. I have treated the argument about disinvestment as the cause of journalism's troubles in Jay Rosen, *Getting the Connections Right* (New York: Twentieth Century Fund, 1996): 31–33

30. Katharine Q. Seelye, "Wouldn't Mother Have Been Proud?" *New York Times* (June 18, 1995): sec. 4, p. 5.

31. Jonathan Yardley, "Government by All Those People," review of *The Voice of the People* by James S. Fishkin, *Washington Post* (Dec. 27, 1995): F2.

32. Taylor, *See How They Run*, 5, 15–16, 248, 257

33. Paul Taylor, "Political Coverage in the 1990s," in Jay Rosen and Paul Taylor, *The New News vs. the Old News* (New York: Twentieth Century Fund, 1992): 46, 48–49.

34. Taylor, *See How They Run*, 266; Taylor, "Political Coverage in the 1990s," 58–60.

35. Quoted in Francis X. Clines, "Behind the Drive for Free TV Time for Candidates," *New York Times* (April 20, 1996): 10. Taylor also discussed his proposal in "Political Coverage in the 1990s," 61–67, and Paul Taylor and Walter Cronkite, "Politics in Prime Time," *Washington Post* (Feb. 2, 1996): A17.

36. David Broder, keynote address to *The James K. Batten Symposium on Civic Journalism* (Washington, D.C.: Pew Center for Civic Journalism, 1995): 2–4. Broder later put some distance between himself and public journalism. In a speech at Stanford University in 1996, he said he doubted that the press could take on the task of engaging people in democratic politics. According to scholar Theodore Glasser, this meant that Broder could no longer be described as a "champion of public journalism." Theodore L. Glasser, ed., *The Idea of Public Journalism* (New York: Guilford, 1999): 2–4.

37. E. J. Dionne, remarks to *The James K. Batten Symposium on Civic Journalism* (Washington, D.C.: Pew Center for Civic Journalism, 1995): 5.

38. E. J. Dionne, *They Only Look Dead* (New York: Simon and Schuster, 1996): 251, 253–54, 262, 261; italics in original. See also 243–46 on the growing trend toward analysis in political journalism and its need to show an "edge."

39. Quoted in Marilyn Kalfus, "Public Journalism: Can the News Media Play Advocate?" *Orange County Register* (Jan. 20, 1996): 16. For other accounts featuring Downie as a critic of public journalism, see Fallows, *Breaking the News*, 260–67; Howard Kurtz, "When News Media Go to Grass Roots, Candidates Often Don't Follow," *Washington Post* (June 4, 1996): A6; Alicia C. Shepard, "The Gospel of Public Journalism," *American Journalism Review* (Sept. 1994): 30, 33.

40. Leonard Downie, Jr., "News and Opinion at the Post," *Washington Post* (Oct. 18, 1992): C7.

41. Downie's comments came at a panel on "What Responsibilities Does Press Freedom Entail?" at the Association for Education in Journalism and Mass Communication annual convention, Washington, D.C., Aug. 11, 1989. I wrote about Downie's surrender of his vote in Jay Rosen, *Getting the Connections Right* (New York: Twentieth Century Fund, 1996): 79–80, and Jay Rosen, "In the Booth With the Press," *Nation* (April 1, 1996): 10.

42. This exchange is from "Public Journalism: New Wave or New Threat?" panel discussion at the Associated Press Managing Editors annual convention, Philadelphia, Oct. 12, 1994.

43. Rem Rieder, "Public Journalism: Stop the Shooting," *American Journalism Review* (Nov.–Dec. 1995): 6.

44. Downie quoted in Fallows, *Breaking the News*, 263. Taylor, "Political Coverage in the 1990s," 59.

45. David S. Broder, *A New Assignment for the Press*, Press-Enterprise Lecture Series (Riverside, Calif.: Press-Enterprise, 1991): 5; David S. Broder, "Democracy and the Press," *Washington Post* (Jan. 3, 1990): A15.

46. Competing views of citizenship and how they have figured in public life is given historical treatment in Michael Schudson, *The Good Citizen* (New York: Free Press, 1998).

47. Joann Byrd, "Conversations with the Community," *Washington Post* (Feb. 5, 1995): C6.

48. Joann Byrd, "Journalism: Add an 'S' and a 'C,'" *Washington Post* (March 21, 1993): C6. See also Joann Byrd, "Get Me Rewrite: Conflict Isn't the Whole Story," address to Carol Burnett Fund for Responsible Journalism annual conference, University of Hawaii at Manoa, March 11, 1993.

49. Byrd made her remarks at "The Idea of Public Journalism," symposium at Stanford University, April 26, 1996.

50. Geneva Overholser, "Learning from 'Civic Journalism,'" *Washington Post* (Sept. 17, 1995): C6.

51. On this point see my 1994 speech, "Public Journalism as a Democratic Art," reprinted in Jay Rosen, Davis Merritt, and Lisa Austin, *Public Journalism—Theory and Practice: Lessons from Experience* (Dayton: Kettering Foundation, 1997): 8. "If public journalism one day loses its name, becoming 'just good journalism,' it will have succeeded."

Chapter 8: Design Flaw or Driver Error

1. Carey's remarks appear in *Speaking of Public Journalism* (Dayton: Kettering Foundation, 1997): 8–9. See also my essay on Carey, Jay Rosen, "'We'll Have That Conversation,'" in Eve Stryker Munson and Catherine A. Warren, eds., *James Carey: A Critical Reader* (Minneapolis: University of Minnesota Press, 1997): 191–206.

2. See John H. McManus, *Market-Driven Journalism* (Thousand Oaks, Calif.: Sage, 1994) for analysis and reporting on this trend. See also Phyllis Kaniss, *Making Local News* (Chicago: University of Chicago Press, 1991).

3. Philip Meyer, "An Ethic for the Information Age," in L. Hodges, ed., *Social Responsibility: Business, Journalism, Law, Medicine* (Lexington, Va.: Washington and Lee University, 1990): 15.

4. Phyllis Kaniss, *The Media and the Mayor's Race* (Bloomington: Indiana University Press, 1995): 89–90, 156–57.

5. Mike Hoyt, "Are You Now, or Will You Ever Be a Civic Journalist?" *Columbia Journalism Review* (Sept.–Oct. 1995): 27–28.

6. I did, in this case, criticize the project in print and later discussed my complaints with the *Mercury News* editors during a 1996 visit to the newspaper. See Jay Rosen, *Getting the Connections Right* (New York: Twentieth Century Fund, 1996): 51–52.

7. Cover of *Editor and Publisher*, March 13, 1995.

8. The phrase comes from McManus, *Market-Driven Journalism*. On Gannett's marketing orientation, see Doug Underwood, *When MBAs Rule the Newsroom* (New York: Columbia University Press, 1993): xii–xvii, 28–31, 91–105, 111–12, 149–52.

9. Gannett also had a long record of dishonest business dealings that included attempts at price fixing, anticompetitive practices aimed at weeklies that competed for advertising, and other sly or crude tricks that drew the interest of prosecutors at the U.S. Justice Department, who started an investigation in 1981. (It was later dropped when the Reagan administration settled in with a more pro-business philosophy toward such matters.) In the 1970s, Gannett was successfully sued in a civil action charging it with inflating circulation figures in the sale of a newspaper in Hartford. These and other hardball tactics—some clearly illegal—are well documented by journalist Richard McCord in his exposé *The Chain Gang* (Columbia: University of Missouri Press, 1996).

10. Ibid., 188. See also Ben H. Bagdikian, *The Media Monopoly*, 4th ed. (Boston: Beacon, 1992): 68.

11. I should note that I was paid one thousand dollars by Gannett for my appearance.

Chapter 9: What Was Public Journalism?

1. Leslie Fiedler, *What Was Literature* (New York: Simon and Schuster, 1982).

2. I have borrowed this description from Jay Rosen, "The Action of the Idea," in Theodore L. Glasser, ed., *The Idea of Public Journalism* (New York: Guilford, 1999).

3. Campbell's remarks appear in *The James K. Batten Symposium and Award for Excellence in Civic Journalism* (Washington, D.C.: Pew Center for Civic Journalism, 1995): 20.

4. Mark Jurkowitz, "Talking Back," *Boston Globe Magazine* (Feb. 25, 1996): 24; Geneva Overholser, "Learning from 'Civic Journalism,'" *Washington Post* (Sept. 17, 1995): C6.

5. Thelen made his remarks at the Project on Public Life and the Press seminar, American Press Institute, Reston, Va., June 28, 1997.

6. Hamburger quoted in Jay Rosen, *Getting the Connections Right* (New York: Twentieth Century Fund, 1996): 76. See also Steve Smith, "Your Vote Counts: The Wichita Eagle's Election Project," *National Civic Review* (summer 1991): 24–30.

7. Matthew V. Storin, "Civic Journalism: Part of the Solution," in *James K. Batten Symposium*, 6–7. For a perceptive treatment of the differences between "cosmopolitan" and "provincial" journalism, see Howard M. Ziff, "Practicing Responsible Journalism," in Deni Elliot, ed., *Responsible Journalism* (Beverly Hills, Calif.: Sage, 1986): 151–66.

8. On communitarian thought, see Amitai Etzioni, "Liberals and Communitarians," *Par-

tisan Review 57:2 (spring 1990): 215–27; Amitai Etzioni, *The Spirit of Community* (New York: Crown, 1993); Robert N. Bellah, Richard Madsen, William M. Sullivan, Ann Swidler, and Steven M. Tipton, *Habits of the Heart: Individualism and Commitment in American Life* (Berkeley: University of California Press, 1985), and the sequel by the same authors, *The Good Society* (New York: Knopf, 1991). Also see Michael J. Sandel, ed., *Liberalism and Its Critics* (Oxford: Basil Blackwell, 1984). On the implications of communitarian thought for the idea of public journalism, see the essays in Jay Black, ed., *Mixed News* (Mahwah, N.J.: Lawrence Erlbaum, 1997).

9. David Mathews, *Politics for People* (Urbana: University of Illinois Press, 1994). On civil investing, see Mary Ann Zehr, "Getting Involved in Civic Life," *Foundation News and Commentary* (May–June 1996): 21–27; Bruce Sievers, "Can Philanthropy Solve the Problem of Civil Society?" *Kettering Review* (Dec. 1997): 62–70. On the work of the National Civic League see two handbooks, *The Civic Index: A New Approach to Improving Community Life* (Denver: National Civic League, 1993); and *The Civic Index: Profiles in Community Building* (Denver: National Civic League, 1994). See also various issues of the organization's journal, *National Civic Review*. Founded in 1994 at the initiative of the National Civic League, the Alliance for National Renewal describes itself on its World Wide Web site (http://www.ncl.org/anr) as a network of "190 community building organizations working to address the serious issues facing America and its communities." They include "institutions, communities and individuals from the public, private and nonprofit sectors who realize it is time to set aside turf battles and work together toward a shared vision of improving communities."

10. Millennium Communications Group, *Communications as Engagement* (New York: Rockefeller Foundation, 1994). The sections quoted here are taken from the report's World Wide Web site (http://cdinet.com/Millennium/Report/report.html).

11. On this theme see Jay Rosen, "Making Things More Public," *Critical Studies in Mass Communication* 11:4 (Dec. 1994): 363–88; Jay Rosen, "Public Journalism, A Case for Public Scholarship," *Change* (May–June 1995): 34–38; Davis Merritt and Jay Rosen, *Imagining Public Journalism,* Roy H. Howard Public Lecture (Bloomington: University of Indiana School of Journalism, April 1995). See also Alan Wolfe's critical assessment in "The Promise and Flaws of Public Scholarship," *Chronicle of Higher Education* (Jan. 10, 1997): B4–B5, and my reply, Jay Rosen, "Public Scholars, In Search of a Usable Present—A Reply to Alan Wolfe," *Higher Education Exchange* (Dayton: Kettering Foundation, 1997): 44–49.

12. Harry C. Boyte and Nancy N. Kari, *Building America* (Philadelphia: Temple University Press, 1996): 165–73; James S. Fishkin, *The Voice of the People* (New Haven: Yale University Press, 1995): 156–60.

13. James Fallows, *Breaking the News* (New York: Pantheon, 1996): 236–44; Davis Merritt, "Democracy from the Bottom Up," *Wichita Eagle* (Oct. 27, 1996): 23; Cole Campbell, remarks in *James K. Batten Symposium,* 22. I reflect on the Dewey-Lippmann exchange and its movement into journalism in Rosen, "The Action of the Idea."

14. John Dewey, *The Public and Its Problems* (New York: Henry Holt, 1927): 180–81.

15. "Civic Lessons" (Philadelphia: Pew Charitable Trusts, 1997). The principal researchers

were Lewis Friedland of the University of Wisconsin at Madison, Esther Thorson of the University of Missouri, and Steven Chaffee of Stanford University.

16. Philip Meyer and Deborah Potter, *Effects of Citizen-Based Journalism in the 1996 National Elections* (St. Petersburg, Fla.: Poynter Institute for Media Studies, 1996).

17. David Blomquist and Cliff Zukin, *Does Public Journalism Work?* (Washington, D.C.: Pew Center for Civic Journalism, 1997). For other reports and evaluations, see Frank Denton and Esther Thorson, *Civic Journalism, Does It Work?* (Washington, D.C.: Pew Center for Civic Journalism, 1995); Edmund B. Lambeth, Philip Meyer, and Esther Thorson, *Assessing Public Journalism* (Columbia: University of Missouri Press, 1998).

18. A useful account of the difficulties in changing the occupational culture of journalism is Alicia C. Shepard, "The Change Agents," *American Journalism Review* (May 1998): 42–49. For contemporaneous commentary on the press and the Clinton scandals, see Jonathan Alter, "The New Powers That Be," *Newsweek* (Jan. 18, 1999): 23–25; Steven Brill, "Pressgate," *Brill's Content* 1:1 (July–Aug. 1998): 122–51; Todd Gitlin, "The Clinton-Lewinsky Obsession," *Washington Monthly* 30:12 (Dec. 1998): 13–19; Sherri Ricchiardi, "Double Vision," *American Journalism Review* (April 1998): 31–35; Jules Witcover, "Where We Went Wrong," *Columbia Journalism Review* (March–April 1998): 18–25. On the theme of a disconnect see Geneva Overholser, "Media Mistrust," *Washington Post* (Nov. 12, 1998): A21; Robert J. Samuelson, "Washington Disconnected," *Washington Post* (Jan. 6, 1999): A25; Janny Scott, "In Scandal Coverage, Risky Era for the News Business," *New York Times* (Dec. 24, 1998): A16.

19. Larry J. Sabato, *Feeding Frenzy* (New York: Free Press, 1991); Timothy Crouse, *The Boys on the Bus* (New York: Random House, 1972). Descriptions of how the White House press is "fed" news can be found throughout Mark Hertsgaard, *On Bended Knee* (New York: Farrar, Straus & Giroux, 1988), and Howard Kurtz, *Spin Cycle* (New York: Simon and Schuster, 1998).

20. Michael Janeway, "The Press and Privacy: Rights and Rules," in W. Lawson Taitte, ed., *The Morality of Mass Media* (Dallas: University of Texas, 1994): 129–30; Scott, "In Scandal Coverage, Risky Era." Russert is quoted in David Broder and Dan Balz, "Scandal's Damage Wide, if Not Deep," *Washington Post* (Feb. 11, 1999): A1.

21. An excellent treatment of this theme and its consequences for American politics is Hugh Heclo, "Hyperdemocracy," *Wilson Quarterly* (winter 1999): 62–71.

22. The fuller passage reads: "Most of us lifers at the *Times* think of the paper as the only worthy medium of communication. It reaches the most influential, interesting, and powerful people on earth. It is the 'house organ' of the smartest, most talented, and most influential Americans at the height of American power. And while its editorial opinions or the views of individual columnists and critics can be despised or dismissed, the paper's daily package of news cannot. It frames the intellectual and emotional agenda of serious Americans." Max Frankel, *The Times of My Life and My Life with the Times* (New York: Random House, 1999): 414–15.

23. E. J. Dionne, *They Only Look Dead* (New York: Simon and Schuster, 1996): 254; Michael Schudson, *The Power of News* (Cambridge: Harvard University Press, 1995): 222.

24. Cole Campbell, "Journalism as a Democratic Art," in Theodore L. Glasser, ed., *The Idea of Public Journalism* (New York: Guilford, 1999): x–xi, xxxii–xxxiii.

Chapter 10: What Are Journalists For?

1. Michael Janeway, "The Press and Privacy: Rights and Rules," in W. Lawson Taitte, ed., *The Morality of the Mass Media,* (Dallas: University of Texas at Dallas, 1993): 129–30. For a collection of essays by authors who uncover ideas behind the routines of mainstream journalism, see Robert Karl Manoff and Michael Schudson, eds., *Reading the News* (New York: Pantheon, 1986). A neglected essay on journalism as a "habit of mind" is "The Journalist," in Joseph Bensman and Robert Lilienfield, *Craft and Consciousness* (New York: John Wiley, 1973): 207–32. On the ideas that bring us the news, see also the discussion of objectivity, values, and ideology in Herbert J. Gans, *Deciding What's News* (New York: Random House, 1979): 182–213; and Douglas Birkhead, "An Ethics of Vision for Journalism," in Robert K. Avery and David Eason, *Critical Perspectives on Media and Society* (New York: Guilford, 1991): 226–39.

2. Douglass Cater, *The Fourth Branch of Government* (Boston: Houghton Mifflin, 1959). On the adversarial attitude in the press, see Michael Schudson, *Discovering the News* (New York: Basic, 1978): 176–83. See also the analysis by political scientist Samuel P. Huntington in *American Politics: The Politics of Disharmony* (Cambridge: Harvard University Press, 1981): 188–96. For two skeptical treatments of the adversarial mentality, see Paul H. Weaver, *News and the Culture of Lying* (New York: Free Press, 1994), especially 168–71; and Edward S. Herman and Noam Chomsky, *Manufacturing Consent* (New York: Pantheon, 1988), especially 171, 185, 212–13, 301. Weaver's perspective comes more from the political right; Herman and Chomsky are firmly on the left.

3. Two fine but very different treatments of this theme are James W. Carey, "The Press, Public Opinion, and Public Discourse" in Theodore L. Glasser and Charles T. Salmon, eds., *Public Opinion and the Communication of Consent* (New York: Guilford, 1995): 389–92.; and G. Stuart Adam, *Notes Toward a Definition of Journalism* (St. Petersburg, Fla.: Poynter Institute for Media Studies, 1993), especially 11–20. See also the thoughtful work of David L. Eason, "The New Journalism and the Image-World," *Critical Studies in Mass Communication* 1:1 (March 1984): 51–64, and "On Journalistic Authority," *Critical Studies in Mass Communication* 3:4 (Dec. 1986): 429–47.

4. David S. Broder, "Democracy and the Press, *Washington Post* (Jan. 3, 1990): A15. See also David S. Broder, *A New Assignment for the Press,* Press-Enterprise Lecture Series (Riverside, Calif.: Press-Enterprise, 1991).

5. Robert MacNeil, "Regaining Dignity," *Media Studies Journal* 9:3 (summer 1995): 110–11; see also 103–4 on media as distinguished from journalism.

6. Ibid., 111.

7. Ted Koppel, "Journalism Under Fire," *Nation* (Nov. 24, 1997): 23–24.

8. *A Statement of Concern* (Washington, D.C.: Committee of Concerned Journalists, 1997). Among the original signers were several people whose ideas have figured in this book. In addition to Bill Kovach and Tom Rosenstiel, they included James Carey, Richard Harwood, Max King, Robert MacNeil, Geneva Overhosler, John Seigenthaler, and Matt Storin.

9. A good treatment of some of these themes is R. Eugene Rice, *Making a Place for the New American Scholar* (Washington, D.C.: American Association for Higher Education, 1996). See also Ernest T. Boyer, *Scholarship Reconsidered* (Princeton, N.J.: Carnegie

Foundation for the Advancement of Teaching, 1990). In my own interpretation of the civic challenge facing the academy, I have benefited from Thomas Bender, *Intellect and Public Life* (Baltimore: Johns Hopkins University Press, 1993): 127–39; James W. Carey, "Political Correctness and Cultural Studies," in Eve Stryker Munson and Catherine A. Warren, eds., *James Carey: A Critical Reader* (Minneapolis: University of Minnesota Press, 1997): 270–91; Richard Rorty, "Intellectuals in Politics," *Dissent* (fall 1991): 483–90; Alan Wolfe, "The Feudal Culture of the Postmodern University," *Wilson Quarterly* (winter 1996): 54–66. Russell Jacoby's *The Last Intellectuals* (New York: Farrar, Straus & Giroux) overstates its case, but is provocative nonetheless, as is his treatment of the so-called culture wars in academia, in *Dogmatic Wisdom* (New York: Doubleday, 1994). For an array of perspectives on improving the university's contribution to civic life, see *Change* magazine's January–February 1997 issue.

10. Hanafin made her remarks at the Project on Public Life and the Press seminar, American Press Institute, Reston, Va., March 23–25, 1995 (Dayton, Ohio: Kettering Foundation, 1995): 285.

11. Davis Merritt, "Public Journalism: What It Means, How It Works," in Jay Rosen and Davis Merritt, *Public Journalism, Theory and Practice* (Dayton: Kettering Foundation, 1994): 22.

12. Tom Rosenstiel, *The Beat Goes On* (New York: Twentieth Century Fund, 1994): 46.

13. Ibid., 37.

14. I elaborate on this theme in Jay Rosen, " 'We'll Have That Conversation,' " in Munson and Warren, eds., *James Carey: A Critical Reader,* 191–206.

15. Robert N. Bellah, Richard Madsen, William M. Sullivan, Ann Swidler, and Steven M. Tipton, *The Good Society* (New York: Knopf, 1991): 254.

16. Harry C. Boyte and Nancy N. Kari, *Building America* (Philadelphia: Temple University Press, 1996): 9.

17. For a generally optimistic view of what the world of new media will bring, especially for the young, see Jon Katz, *Virtuous Reality* (New York: Random House, 1997). For a more skeptical view see David Shenk, *Data Smog* (New York: HarperCollins, 1997). See also Howard Rheingold, *The Virtual Community* (New York: Addison-Wesley, 1993), on the civic potential of what has been called cyberspace, and Sherry Turkle, *Life on the Screen* (New York: Touchstone, 1997), for an inquiry into personal identity and the Internet. On the implications for journalism, see two special sections in *Nieman Reports,* "Can Journalism Shape the New Technologies?" 68:2 (summer 1994), and "Running Scared into the On-Line Era," 69:2 (summer 1995). See also Katherine Fulton, "A Tour of Our Uncertain Future," *Columbia Journalism Review* (March–April 1996): 19–26; Todd Oppenheimer, "A Virtual Reality Check," *Columbia Journalism Review* (March–April 1996): 27–29; J. D. Lasica, "Net Gain," *American Journalism Review* (Nov. 1996): 20–33; and the special section "The Future of On Line Journalism," *Columbia Journalism Review* (July–Aug. 1997): 30–37.

18. I discuss this theme in Jay Rosen, "The Media Is the Mess," *Nation* (Feb. 5, 1996): 25–28.

19. Robert Entman, *Democracy Without Citizens* (New York: Oxford University Press, 1989); Maureen Dowd, "Bottomless and Topless," *New York Times* (June 9, 1996): sec. 4, p. 15.

20. Tom Rosenstiel, *Strange Bedfellows* (New York: Hyperion, 1993): 55.

Index

CPSIA information can be obtained at www.ICGtesting.com
Printed in the USA
LVOW12s1259200814

399937LV00007B/351/P